D1137915

Contents

First published in 2003 by Philip's a division of Octopus Publishing Group Ltd 2–4 Heron Quays London E14 4JP

www.philips-maps.co.uk

Second edition 2004
First impression 2004

Cartography by Philip's
Copyright © 2004 Philip's

Ordnance Survey®

This product includes mapping data licensed from Ordnance Survey®, with the permission of the Controller of Her Majesty's Stationery Office. © Crown copyright 2004. All rights reserved. Licence number 100011710

Information for Tourist Attractions in England supplied by the British Tourist Authority / English Tourist Board.

Information for National Parks, Areas of Outstanding Natural Beauty, National Trails and Country Parks in Wales supplied by the Countryside Council for Wales. Information for National Parks, Areas of Outstanding Natural Beauty, National Trails and Country Parks in England supplied by the Countryside Agency. Data for Regional Parks, Long Distance Footpaths and Country Parks in Scotland provided by Scottish Natural Heritage.

Gaelic name forms used in the Western Isles provided by Comhairle nan Eilean.

Data for the National Nature Reserves in England provided by English Nature. Data for the National Nature Reserves in Wales provided by Countryside Council for Wales. Darparwyd data'n ymwneud â Gwarchodfeydd Natur Cenedlaethol Cymru gan Gyngor Cefn Gwlad Cymru.

Information on the location of National Nature Reserves in Scotland was provided by Scottish Natural Heritage.

Data for National Scenic Areas in Scotland provided by the Scottish Executive Office. Crown copyright material is reproduced with the permission of the Controller of HMSO and the Queen's Printer for Scotland. Licence number C02W0003960.

Printed in Great Britain by Scotprint

000186615

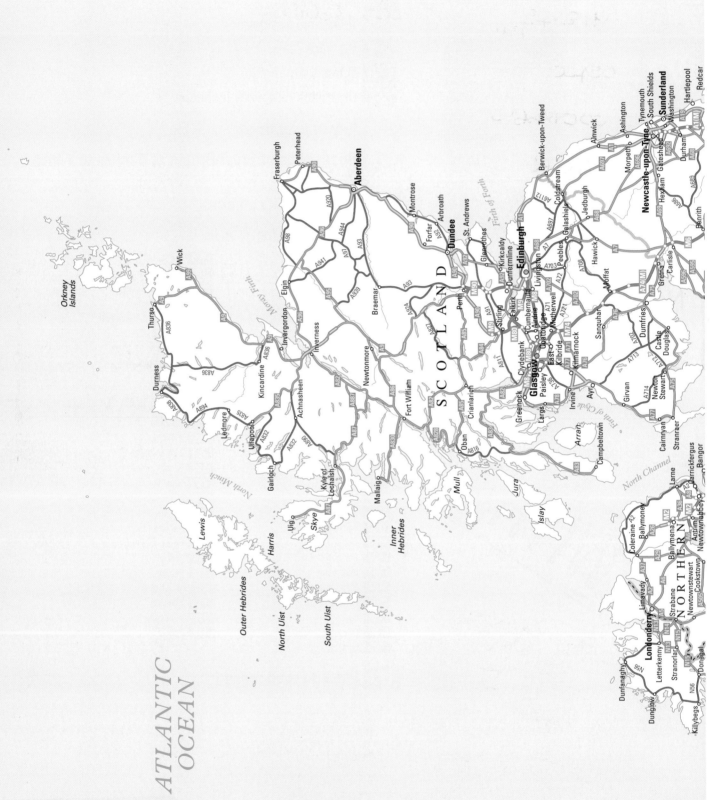

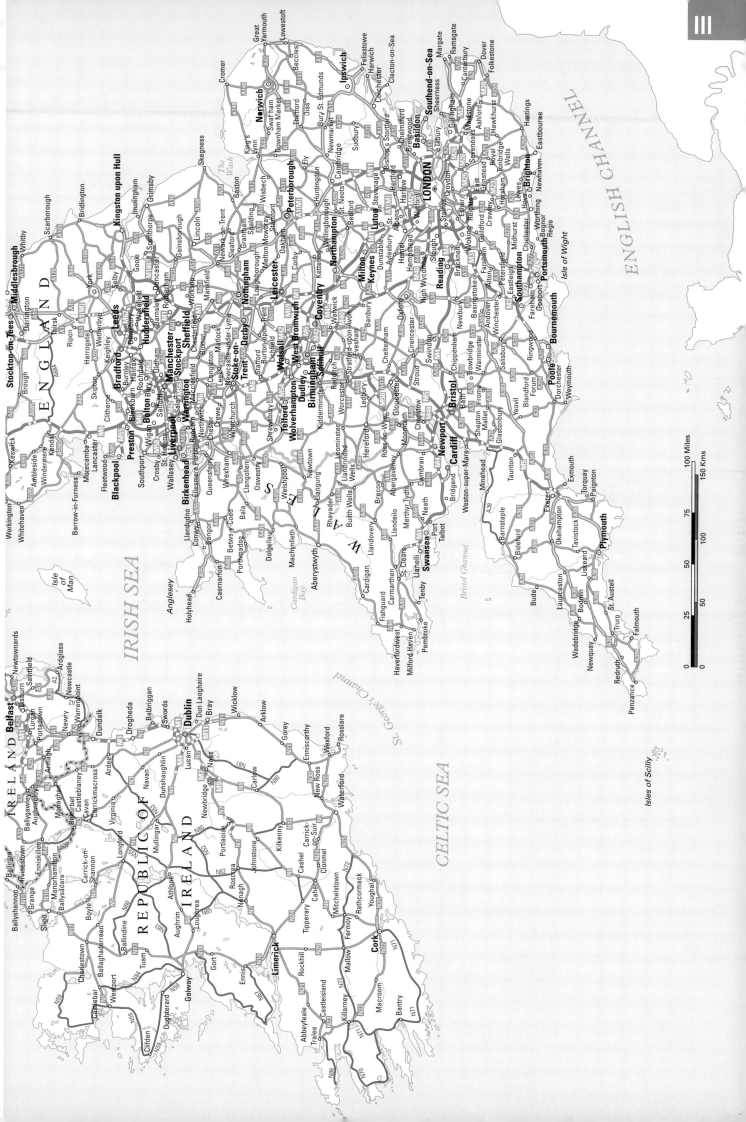

Road map symbols

M6	Motorway, toll motorway
4 5	Motorway junction – full, restricted access
S S	Motorway service area – full, restricted access
	Motorway under construction
A453	Primary route – dual, single carriageway
S 5	Service area, roundabout, multi-level junction
4 5	Numbered primary route junction – access, restricted access
	Primary route under construction
	Narrow primary route
Derby	Primary destination
A34	A road – dual, single carriageway
	A road under construction
	Narrow A road
B2135	B road – dual, single carriageway
	B road under construction
	Narrow B road
	Minor road – over 4 metres wide, under 4 metres wide
	Minor road with restricted access
2	Distance in miles
	Tunnel
TOLL	Toll, steep gradient – arrow points downhill
	National trail – England and Wales
	Long distance footpath – Scotland
	Railway with station
	Level crossing, tunnel
	Preserved railway with station
	National boundary
	County / unitary authority boundary
	Car ferry, catamaran
	Passenger ferry, catamaran
	Hovercraft, freight ferry
CALAIS 1:15 Ferry	Ferry destination, journey time – hrs : mins
	Car ferry – river crossing
	Principal airport, other airport
	National park
	Area of Outstanding Natural Beauty – England and Wales National Scenic Area – Scotland / forest park / regional park / national forest
	Woodland
	Beach
	Linear antiquity
	Roman road
1066	Hillfort, battlefield – with date
795	Viewpoint, national nature reserve, spot height – in metres
	Golf course, youth hostel, national sporting venue
	Camp site, caravan site, camping and caravan site
P&R	Shopping village, park and ride
29	Adjoining page number – road maps

Tourist information

† Abbey / cathedral / priory	⊕ Historic ship	ℤ Tourist information centre – open all year
🏛 Ancient monument	🏠 House	ℤ Tourist information centre – open seasonally
⌂ Aquarium	⌂ House and garden	
🏛 Art gallery	▓ Motor racing circuit	🐘 Zoo
🦅 Bird collection / aviary	🏛 Museum	✦ Other place of interest
🏰 Castle	Ⓟ Picnic area	
🏛 Church	Preserved railway	**Relief**
🏛 Country park – England and Wales	Race course	
🏛 Country park – Scotland	Roman antiquity	
🐑 Farm park	Safari park	
❀ Garden	Theme park	

Feet	metres
3000	914
2600	792
2200	671
1800	549
1400	427
1000	305
0	0

Road map scale: 1: 265 320, 4·2 miles to 1inch

0 1 2 3 4 5 6 7 8 9 miles

0 1 2 3 4 5 6 7 8 9 10 11 12 13 14 15km

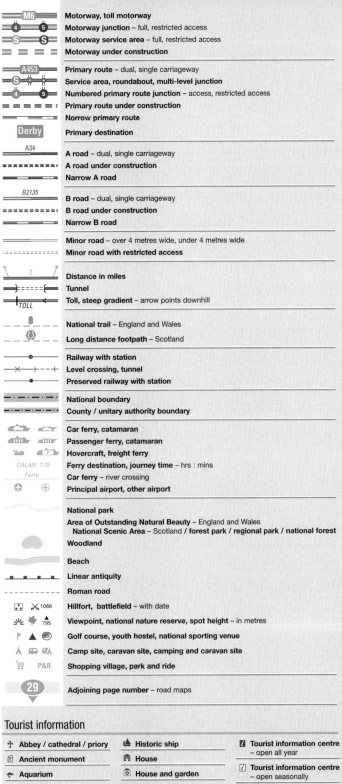

Distance table

How to use this table

Bristol
169 / 272 Cambridge
45 / 72, 190 / 306 Cardiff
277 / 446, 264 / 425, 289 / 465 Carlisle
175 / 282, 116 / 187, 209 / 336, 142 / 229 Doncaster
202 / 325, 125 / 201, 238 / 383, 389 / 626, 242 / 390 Dover
430 / 692, 406 / 654, 441 / 710, 152 / 245, 275 / 443, 523 / 842 Dundee
373 / 600, (345 / 555), 385 / 620, 96 / 154, 219 / 352, 462 / 744, 56 / 90 Edinburgh
76 / 122, 249 / 401, 121 / 195, 353 / 568, 251 / 404, 248 / 399, 518 / 834, 450 / 724 Exeter

Distances are shown in miles and, in *italics*, kilometres. For example, the distance between Cambridge and Edinburgh is 345 miles or 555 kilometres.

London distance table

(Each cell: miles on top, kilometres in *italics* below.)

Aberdeen: 517 / *832*

Aberystwyth: 211 445 / *340 716*

Ayr: 394 183 317 / *634 295 510*

Berwick-upon-Tweed: 352 182 311 134 / *567 293 501 216*

Birmingham: 117 420 114 289 274 / *188 676 183 465 441*

Blackpool: 226 308 153 180 181 123 / *364 496 246 290 291 198*

Bournemouth: 107 564 207 436 412 147 270 / *172 908 333 702 663 237 435*

Braemar: 482 59 143 148 385 281 524 / *776 95 652 230 238 620 452 843*

Brighton: 52 573 253 446 409 163 286 92 534 / *84 922 407 718 658 262 460 148 859*

Bristol: 122 493 253 370 362 81 204 82 477 147 / *196 793 201 595 583 130 328 132 768 237*

Cambridge: 54 471 214 357 306 100 208 154 438 116 169 / *87 758 344 575 493 161 335 248 705 187 272*

Cardiff: 157 505 105 382 368 103 209 117 483 182 45 190 / *253 813 169 615 592 166 336 188 778 293 72 306*

Carlisle: 301 221 224 93 87 196 87 343 196 370 277 264 289 / *484 356 360 150 140 315 140 552 316 596 446 425 465*

Doncaster: 171 344 176 235 184 94 94 235 310 236 175 116 209 142 / *275 554 283 378 296 151 151 378 499 380 282 187 336 229*

Dover: 71 588 297 478 424 194 312 174 553 82 202 125 238 389 242 / *114 947 478 769 683 312 502 280 890 132 325 201 383 626 390*

Dundee: 448 67 376 117 113 349 183 495 52 517 430 406 441 152 275 523 / *721 108 605 188 182 562 385 797 84 832 692 654 710 245 443 842*

Edinburgh: 390 125 320 73 57 292 183 439 91 456 373 345 385 96 219 462 56 / *628 201 515 117 92 470 295 707 146 734 600 555 620 154 352 744 90*

Exeter: 181 569 201 446 428 157 282 82 550 184 75 282 121 353 251 248 518 450 / *291 916 323 718 689 253 454 132 885 296 122 401 195 568 404 399 834 724*

Fishguard: 260 504 56 373 371 170 209 222 493 291 154 270 112 297 247 331 460 399 230 / *418 811 90 600 597 274 336 357 794 468 248 435 180 478 398 533 740 642 370*

Fort William: 510 149 430 133 190 392 296 539 125 575 486 479 485 206 357 596 127 144 560 486 / *821 240 692 214 306 631 476 867 201 926 782 771 781 332 575 959 204 232 901 782*

Glasgow: 397 145 320 33 101 292 183 439 110 468 373 372 385 96 249 488 83 44 449 376 101 / *639 233 515 53 163 470 295 707 177 753 600 599 620 154 401 786 134 71 723 605 163*

Gloucester: 109 468 102 330 318 56 174 90 443 159 35 125 50 247 150 191 410 349 111 153 454 346 / *175 753 164 531 512 90 280 159 713 256 56 198 90 398 241 307 660 562 179 246 731 557*

Great Yarmouth: 128 517 294 402 345 180 252 240 477 180 275 82 284 320 167 185 484 386 335 366 527 419 225 / *206 832 473 647 555 290 406 386 768 290 443 132 457 515 269 298 779 621 539 589 848 674 362*

Harwich: 76 535 281 425 372 167 275 187 504 128 217 67 246 336 194 125 469 413 279 337 543 432 196 82 / *122 861 452 684 599 269 443 301 811 206 349 108 396 541 312 201 755 665 449 542 874 695 316 132*

Holyhead: 269 439 111 305 311 148 141 288 426 334 206 270 216 231 181 360 394 333 282 167 438 330 191 334 349 / *433 707 179 491 501 238 227 463 686 538 332 435 348 372 291 580 634 536 454 269 705 531 307 538 562*

Inverness: 550 105 486 199 215 458 348 597 75 617 530 505 549 262 383 622 132 158 618 542 66 166 500 504 569 474 / *885 169 782 320 346 737 560 961 121 993 867 813 884 422 617 1001 212 254 995 872 106 267 811 890 916 763*

John o' Groats: 663 232 601 328 342 574 478 724 202 741 668 630 680 391 507 746 259 285 744 671 195 295 628 677 693 603 129 / *1067 373 967 550 924 769 1165 325 1193 1075 1014 1094 629 816 1201 417 459 1197 1080 314 475 1011 1090 1116 970 208*

Kingston upon Hull: 184 364 223 251 185 134 127 264 327 245 233 139 244 158 47 256 207 196 231 254 209 260 65 196 234 309 372 634 / *296 586 359 404 298 216 204 425 526 394 375 224 393 254 76 412 475 377 497 451 594 409 272 333 316 372 634 834*

Kyle of Lochalsh: 586 189 499 212 263 471 372 618 159 651 552 555 564 275 432 671 186 216 628 567 79 179 528 602 611 514 84 189 445 / *943 304 803 341 423 758 599 1048 256 893 908 443 695 1080 299 348 1011 913 127 288 850 969 983 827 135 304 716*

Land's End: 297 692 313 570 552 281 405 205 665 308 200 374 245 477 374 390 405 741 763 421 / *478 1114 504 917 888 452 652 330 1070 496 322 602 394 768 602 613 1033 924 198 568 1104 922 378 718 628 652 1193 1397 678 1228*

Leeds: 189 327 169 221 156 113 72 255 293 260 194 145 232 119 29 260 258 202 270 237 329 215 174 196 223 176 360 487 55 394 405 / *304 526 272 341 251 182 116 410 472 419 313 233 373 192 47 418 415 325 435 381 530 346 280 315 359 283 579 784 89 634 652*

Leicester: 97 414 153 299 252 39 140 158 389 166 120 68 137 185 349 296 196 209 422 311 349 336 57 114 358 166 110 329 187 159 168 132 / *156 666 246 481 406 63 225 254 626 267 193 109 248 332 119 298 562 476 315 336 679 505 137 225 237 306 742 947 164 805 515 153*

Lincoln: 131 383 199 274 224 90 128 209 357 197 183 85 208 191 92 202 314 247 272 399 291 159 135 216 427 554 44 476 371 68 51 / *211 616 320 441 360 145 206 336 575 317 295 137 335 307 63 325 505 397 437 642 468 256 206 249 348 687 892 71 766 597 109 82*

Liverpool: 202 341 104 213 219 93 49 234 318 272 161 194 169 120 86 299 286 216 237 160 329 248 120 265 348 386 427 164 615 822 209 655 581 75 130 129 / *325 549 167 343 352 150 79 377 512 438 259 312 272 193 138 481 460 348 381 257 530 348 226 325 386 427 164 615 822 209 655 581 121 209 208*

Manchester: 185 340 129 211 196 80 48 227 318 257 161 165 183 119 61 276 265 215 236 197 329 215 124 373 500 95 606 805 153 654 581 64 148 135 56 / *298 547 208 341 315 129 77 365 512 414 259 266 295 192 98 444 426 346 380 317 530 346 200 600 805 153 654 581 64 148 135 56*

Newcastle upon Tyne: 286 235 257 149 64 207 149 347 201 352 299 241 352 57 144 358 166 110 364 329 253 168 406 428 452 496 438 431 636 212 512 802 148 301 256 270 212 / *460 378 414 240 103 333 208 558 323 567 481 388 523 92 183 576 267 177 586 529 407 238 628 628 452 496 438 431 636 212 512 802 148 301 256 270 212*

Norwich: 114 496 276 382 166 232 214 457 175 252 62 262 289 147 174 422 308 343 504 385 20 73 311 529 654 149 582 421 176 119 105 185 264 / *183 798 444 615 528 267 373 344 735 282 406 100 422 465 237 280 679 589 496 552 811 620 328 32 117 501 852 1053 240 937 678 283 192 169 354 298 425*

Nottingham: 122 393 164 274 221 50 111 183 353 193 145 82 205 328 262 221 153 150 150 298 692 896 145 771 555 113 40 56 73 157 130 / *196 633 264 441 356 80 179 295 568 311 233 134 277 312 69 330 528 422 356 354 646 472 177 240 155 298 692 896 145 771 555 113 40 56 158 118 253 209*

Oban: 499 178 412 94 180 384 285 530 141 565 465 468 407 188 346 585 117 123 549 481 49 92 441 515 523 427 117 244 346 128 665 307 419 387 308 307 233 492 390 / *803 286 663 151 290 618 459 853 227 910 748 753 768 303 557 942 188 198 884 774 79 148 710 829 843 687 188 393 557 206 1070 494 674 623 496 494 375 792 628*

Oxford: 57 483 154 353 324 64 187 90 465 108 260 165 465 372 156 201 372 328 64 78 108 174 119 134 174 418 233 227 697 599 251 330 760 573 84 322 233 383 187 159 168 132 / *92 777 248 568 521 103 301 145 749 174 119 ... 856 1056 309 885 441 270 117 221 277 232 418 233 175 744*

Plymouth: 218 615 237 492 474 203 328 128 587 224 122 293 167 399 297 300 552 496 46 264 305 157 365 316 242 293 283 283 410 343 587 199 / *351 990 382 792 763 327 528 206 945 361 196 472 269 642 478 483 888 798 74 425 958 797 253 588 497 528 1069 1271 571 1085 143 509 389 472 455 455 660 552 430 945 320*

Portsmouth: 70 560 222 430 401 141 264 52 547 49 175 242 162 201 234 348 234 473 453 195 234 142 162 348 354 161 25 547 162 201 76 / *113 901 357 692 645 227 425 84 881 78 156 142 229 234 377 620 377 761 192 356 267 501 987 1186 433 1019 417 414 261 323 409 380 542 333 307 877 124 283*

Sheffield: 159 360 159 245 190 76 86 216 320 194 120 194 152 18 245 291 237 215 248 126 167 168 520 65 427 361 33 62 46 72 38 135 37 339 135 283 230 / *256 579 256 394 306 122 138 348 515 364 193 312 245 30 394 468 378 346 396 203 267 301 837 105 687 581 53 100 74 116 61 201 235 60 546 217 455 370*

Shrewsbury: 160 399 77 269 265 45 98 185 371 226 103 191 176 109 159 111 176 155 216 92 451 303 89 187 451 303 89 187 130 82 / *258 642 124 433 426 72 158 298 597 364 166 256 179 283 175 404 531 441 288 233 615 438 143 362 386 182 705 912 272 726 488 175 135 214 93 111 323 150 586 171 362 333 132*

Southampton: 77 547 201 417 388 128 251 31 532 61 76 148 121 324 209 143 500 438 93 541 433 51 164 293 598 723 618 228 137 204 221 206 176 530 64 151 21 199 185 / *124 880 323 671 624 206 404 50 856 98 122 238 195 521 336 230 805 705 169 373 871 697 169 353 264 472 963 1164 412 947 698 228 185 356 356 521 232 283 853 103 243 34 320 298*

Stranraer: 402 228 325 51 170 297 188 444 194 457 378 379 390 101 257 496 167 112 450 392 96 135 552 686 660 544 422 610 417 237 942 354 531 480 356 254 649 467 238 610 805 742 423 446 716 / *647 367 523 82 274 478 303 715 312 765 608 610 628 163 414 798 269 200 731 631 154 135 552 686 660 544 422 610 417 237 942 354 531 480 356 254 649 467 238 610 805 742 423 446 716*

Swansea: 194 507 73 379 383 170 216 167 505 222 85 227 41 309 232 274 473 412 161 61 404 89 329 267 184 572 696 264 594 285 248 177 233 195 187 347 301 192 506 141 206 182 217 118 161 417 / *312 816 117 610 616 192 348 269 813 357 137 365 66 497 373 441 761 663 259 108 798 658 143 530 296 921 1120 425 956 459 399 285 314 301 559 485 309 815 227 332 293 349 190 259 671*

York: 207 198 195 214 148 130 96 269 285 272 165 244 121 34 322 250 194 287 261 330 217 189 201 328 204 362 771 37 407 411 24 108 99 84 181 73 307 181 333 278 52 133 258 222 272 / *333 513 314 344 238 209 154 433 459 443 357 266 393 195 56 454 402 312 462 420 531 349 320 528 771 60 655 621 39 174 159 135 291 124 494 509 385 214 415 357 438*

London *streets*

Restricted motorway junctions

M1	Northbound	Southbound
2	No exit	No access
4	No exit	No access
6a	No exit	No access
	Access from M25 only	Exit to M25 only
7	No exit	No access
	Access from M10 only	Exit to M10 only
17	No access	No exit
	Exit to M45 only	Access from M45 only
19	No exit to A14	No access from A14
21a	No access	No exit
23a	Exit to A42 only	
24a	No exit	No access
35a	No access	No exit
43	No exit to M621 northbound	
48	No exit to A1 southbound	

M2	Eastbound	Westbound
1	Access from A2 eastbound only	Exit to A2 westbound only

M3	Eastbound	Westbound
8	No exit	No access
10	No access	No exit
13	No access to M27 eastbound	
14	No exit	No access

M4	Eastbound	Westbound
1	Exit to A4 eastbound only	Access from A4 westbound only
2	Access to A4 eastbound only	Access to A4 westbound only
21	No exit	No access
23	No access	No exit
25	No exit	No access
25a	No exit	No access
29	No exit	No access
38		No access
39	No exit or access	No exit
41	No access	No exit
41a	No exit	No access
42		Exit to A483 only

M5	Northbound	Southbound
10	No exit	No access
11a	No access from A417 eastbound	No exit to A417 westbound

M6	Northbound	Southbound
4a	No exit	No access
	Access from M42 southbnd only	Exit to M42 only
5	No access	No exit
10a	No access	No exit
	Exit to M54 only	Access from M54 only
11a	No exit / access	No access / exit
	No access M6 Toll	
20	No exit to M56 eastbound	No access from M56 westbound
22	No access	No exit
24	No exit	No access
25	No access	No exit
30	No exit	No access
	Access from M61 northbound only	Exit to M61 southbound
31a	No access	No exit

M6 Toll	Northbound	Southbound
T1		No exit
T2	No exit / access	No access
T5	No exit	No access
T7	No access	No exit
T8	No access	No exit

M8	Eastbound	Westbound
8	No exit to M73 northbound	No access from M73 southbound
9	No access	No exit
13	No exit southbound	No access
14	No access	No exit
16	No exit	No access
17	No access	No exit
18		No exit
19	No exit to A814 eastbound	No access from A814 westbound
20	No access	No exit
21	No access	No exit
22	No exit	No access
	Access from M77 only	Exit to M77 only
23	No exit	No access
25	Exit to A739 northbound only	Exit to A739 northbound only
	Access from A739 southbound only	Access from A739 southbound only
25a	No exit	No access
28	No exit	No access
28a	No exit	No access

M9	Eastbound	Westbound
1a	No exit	No access
2	No access	No exit
3	No exit	No access
6	No access	No exit
8	No exit	No access

M11	Northbound	Southbound
4	No exit	No access

5	No access	No exit
9	No access	No exit
13	No access	No exit
14	No exit to A428 westbound	No exit
		Access from A14 west bound only

M20	Eastbound	Westbound
2	No access	No exit
3	No exit	No access
	Access from M26 eastbound only	Exit to M26 westbound only
11a	No access	No exit

M23	Northbound	Southbound
7	No exit to A23 southbound	No access from A23 northbound
10a	No exit	No access

M25	Clockwise	Anticlockwise
5	No exit to M26 eastbound	No access from M26 westbound
19	No access	No exit
21	No exit to M1 southbound	No exit to M1 south bound
	Access from M1 southbound only	Access from M1 southbound only
31	No exit	No access

M27	Eastbound	Westbound
10	No exit	No access
12	No access	No exit

M40	Eastbound	Westbound
3	No exit	No access
7	No exit	No access
7a	No exit	No access
13	No exit	No access
14	No access	No exit
16	No access	No exit

M42	Northbound	Southbound
1	No exit	No access
7	No access	No exit
	Exit to M6 northbound only	Access from M6 northbound only
7a	No access	No exit
	Exit to M6 only	Access from M6 northbound only
8	No exit	Exit to M6 northbound
	Access from M6 southbound only	Access from M6 southbound only

M45	Eastbound	Westbound
M1 junc 17	Access to M1 southbound only	No access from M1 southbound
With A45 (Dunchurch)	No access	No exit

M49	Southbound
18a	No exit to M5 northbound

M53	Northbound	Southbound
11	Exit to M56 eastbound only	Exit to M56 eastbound only
	Access from M56 westbound only	Access from M56 westbound only

M56	Eastbound	Westbound
2	No exit	No access
4	No exit	No access
7		No access
8	No exit or access	No exit
9	No access from M6 northbound	No access to M6 southbound
15	No exit to M53	No access from M53 northbound

M57	Northbound	Southbound
3	No exit	No access
5	No exit	No access

M58	Eastbound	Westbound
1	No exit	No access

M60	Clockwise	Anticlockwise
2	No exit	No access
3	No exit to A34 northbound	No exit to A34 north bound
4	No access to M56	No exit to M56
5	No exit to A5103 southbound	No exit to A5103 north bound
7	No access	No exit (Exit from J8 only)
14	No exit to A580	No access from A580
16	No exit	No access
25	No access	
26		No exit or access
27	No exit	No access

M61	Northbound	Southbound
2	No access from A580 eastbound	No exit from A580 westbound
3	No access from A580 eastbound	No exit from A580 westbound
M6 junc 30	No exit to M6 southbound	No access from M6 northbound

M62	Eastbound	Westbound
23	No access	No exit

M65	Eastbound	Westbound
9	No access	No exit
11	No exit	No access

M67	Eastbound	Westnd
1a	No access	No exit
2	No exit	No access

M69	Northbound	Southbound
2	No exit	No access

M73	Northbound	Southbound
2	No access from M8 or A89 eastbound	No exit to M8 or A89 westbound
	No exit to A89	No access from A89
3	Exit to A80 northbound only	Access from A80 southbound only

M74	Northbound	Southbound
2	No access	No exit
3	No exit	No access
7	No exit	No access
9	No exit or access	No access
10		No access
11	No exit	No access
12	No access	No exit

M77	Northbound	Southbound
4	No exit	No access
M8 junc 22	Exit to M8 eastbound only	Access from M8 westbound only

M80	Northbound	Southbound
3	No access	No exit
5	No access from M876	No exit to M876

M90	Northbound	Southbound
2a	No access	No exit
7	No exit	No access
8	No access	No exit
10	No access from A912	No exit to A912

M180	Northbound	Southbound
1	No access	No exit

M621	Eastbound	Westbound
4	No exit or access	
5	No exit	No access
6	No access	No exit

M876	Northbound	Southbound
2	No access	No exit

A1(M)	Northbound	Southbound
2	No access	No exit
3		No access
5	No exit	No access
44	No exit, access from M1 only	Exit to M1 only
57	No access	No exit
65	No access	No exit

A3(M)	Northbound	Southbound
1		No access
4	No access	No exit

A38(M)	Northbound	Southbound
With Victoria Road (Park Circus) Birmingham	No exit	No access

A48(M)	Northbound	Southbound
M4 Junc 29	Exit to M4 eastbound only	Access from M4 westbound only
29a	Access from A48 eastbound only	Exit to A48 westbound only

A57(M)	Eastbound	Westbound
With A5103	No access	No exit
With A34	No access	No exit

A58(M)	Southbound
With Park Lane and Westgate, Leeds	No access

A64(M)	Eastbound	Westbound
With A58 Clay Pit Lane, Leeds	No access	No exit
With Regent Street, Leeds	No access	No access

A74(M)	Northbound	Southbound
18	No access	No exit
22	No access	No exit

A167(M)	Northbound	Southbound
With Camden St, Newcastle	No exit	No exit or access

A194(M)	Northbound	Southbound
A1(M) junc 65 Gateshead Western Bypass	Access from A1(M) northbound only	Exit to A1(M) southbound only

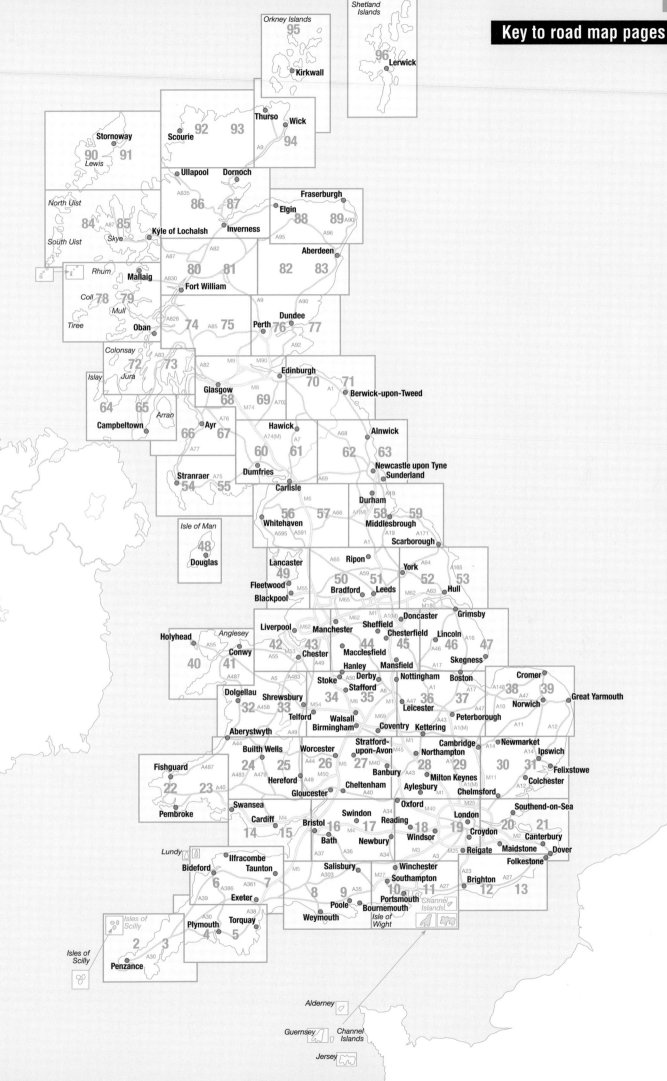

Isles of Scilly

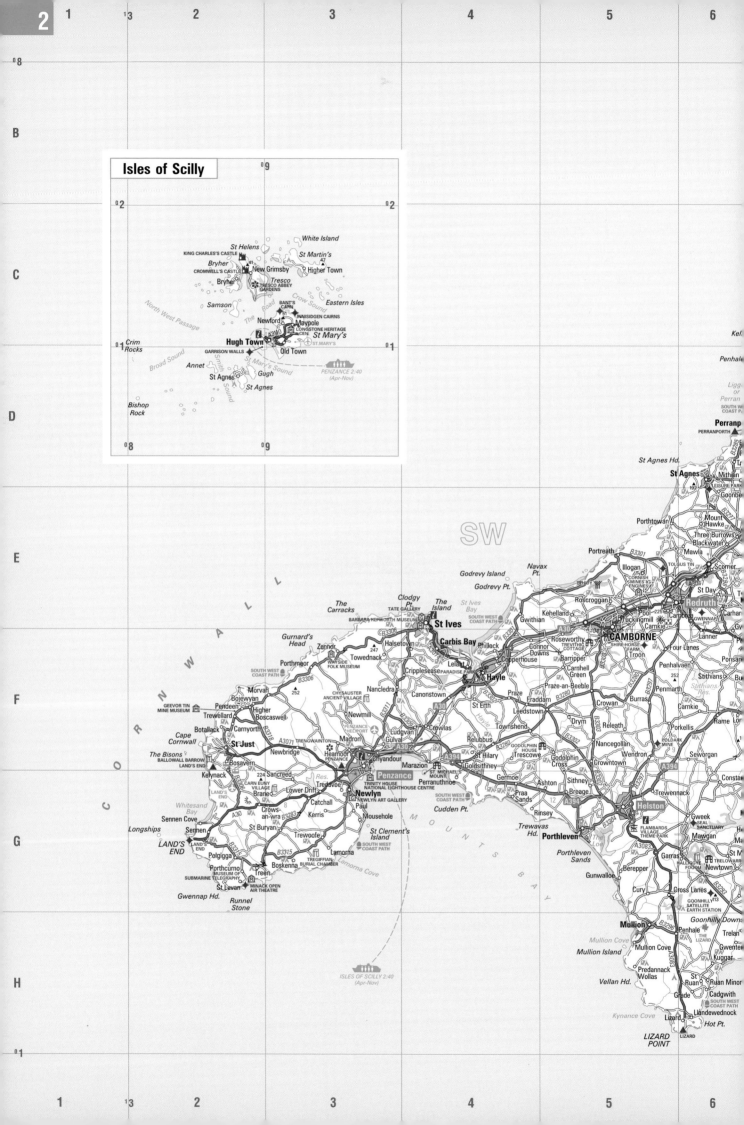

St Helens
White Island
KING CHARLES'S CASTLE
St Martin's
Bryher
CROMWELL'S CASTLE
New Grimsby
Higher Town
Bryher
Tresco
TRESCO ABBEY GARDENS
Samson
Eastern Isles
BANT'S CAIRN
INNISIDGEN CAIRNS
Newford
Maypole
LONGSTONE HERITAGE CEN
St Mary's
Hugh Town
ST.MARY'S
Old Town
GARRISON WALLS
Crim Rocks
Annet
Gugh
St Agnes
St Agnes
Bishop Rock

North West Passage
The Road
Crow Sound
Broad Sound
St Mary's Sound
Smith Sound

PENZANCE 2:40 (Apr-Nov)

Perranp
PERRANPORTH
St Agnes Hd.
St Agnes
Mithian
LEISURE PARK
Goonbe
Porthtowan
Mount Hawke
Three Burrows
Blackwater
Mawla
Portreath
Illogan
TOLGUS TIN
Scorrier
Roscroggan
St Day
Redruth
Pool
Carharr
Tuckingmill
Carnkie
GWENNAP
Gy
CORNISH MINES & ENGINES
Godrevy Island
Navax Pt.
CAMBORNE
SHIRE HORSE FARM
Four Lanes
Lanner
Godrevy Pt.
St Ives Bay
SOUTH WEST COAST PATH
Gwithian
Kehelland
Roseworthy
TREVITHE COTTAGE
Barripper
Penhalvaen
The Carracks
Clodgy Pt.
The Island
Connor Downs
Carnhell Green
Praze-an-Beeble
Stithians
Penmarth
Carnkie
Rame Lor
TATE GALLERY
St Ives
Copperhouse
Praze
Fraddam
Burras
BARBARA HEPWORTH MUSEUM
Carbis Bay
Rhillack
Leedstown
Crowan
Releath
Stithians Res.
252
Nancegollan
Porkellis
Gurnard's Head
Zennor
Halsetown
Hayle
St Erth
Townshend
Drym
Wendron
Sewo
WAYSIDE FOLK MUSEUM
Towednack
CRIPPLESEASE
PARADISE PARK
Praze
POLDARK MINE
SOUTH WEST COAST PATH
Porthmeor
Nancledra
Canonstown
Relubbus
GODOLPHIN HOUSE
Godolphin Cross
Crowntown
Morvah
Bojewyan
Newmill
CHYSAUSTER ANCIENT VILLAGE
A30
Ludgvan
Crowlas
Germoe
Ashton
Sithney
GEEVOR TIN MINE MUSEUM
Pendeen
Higher Boscaswell
PENZANCE HELIPORT
Madron
Gulval
ST. MICHAEL'S MOUNT
Goldsithney
Breage
A394
Helston
Trewellard
Carnyorth
TRENGWAINTON
Heamoor
Chyandour
Marazion
Perranuthnoe
Germoe
GWEEK SEAL SANCTUARY
Botallack
The Bisons
Newbridge
Penzance
TRINITY HOUSE NATIONAL LIGHTHOUSE CENTRE
Praa Sands
FLAMBARDS VILLAGE THEME PARK
Mawgan
St Just
Tredavoe
Cudden Pt.
Rinsey
BALLOWALL BARROW
LAND'S END
Bosavern
Sancreed
Newlyn
Paul
SOUTH WEST COAST PATH
Trewavas Hd.
Garras
St M
TRELOWARR
Kelynack
CARN EUNY ANCIENT VILLAGE
NEWLYN ART GALLERY
Porthleven
The Loe
HALLIGYE FOGOU
Newtown
Brane
Lower Drift
Mousehole
Porthleven Sands
Berepper
Whitesand Bay
Crows-an-wra
Kerris
St Clement's Island
Gunwalloe
Cross Lanes
Sennen Cove
Catchall
GOONHILLY SATELLITE EARTH STATION
Sennen
St Buryan
Trewoofe
Lamorna
SOUTH WEST COAST PATH
Cury
Goonhilly Downs
LAND'S END
Polgigga
Boskenna
TREGIFFIAN BURIAL CHAMBER
Lamorna Cove
Mullion
Penhale
THE LIZARD
Trelan
Gwenter
MUSEUM OF SUBMARINE TELEGRAPHY
Porthcurno
Treen
Mullion Cove
Kuggar
St Levan
MINACK OPEN AIR THEATRE
Mullion Island
Predannack Wollas
Gwennap Hd.
Runnel Stone
Vellan Hd.
St Ruan
Ruan Minor
Grade
Cadgwith
Kynance Cove
SOUTH WEST COAST PATH
Llandewednock
Lizard
Hot Pt.
LIZARD POINT
Lizard

SW

CORNWALL

MOUNT'S BAY

ISLES OF SCILLY 2:40 (Apr-Nov)

Longships

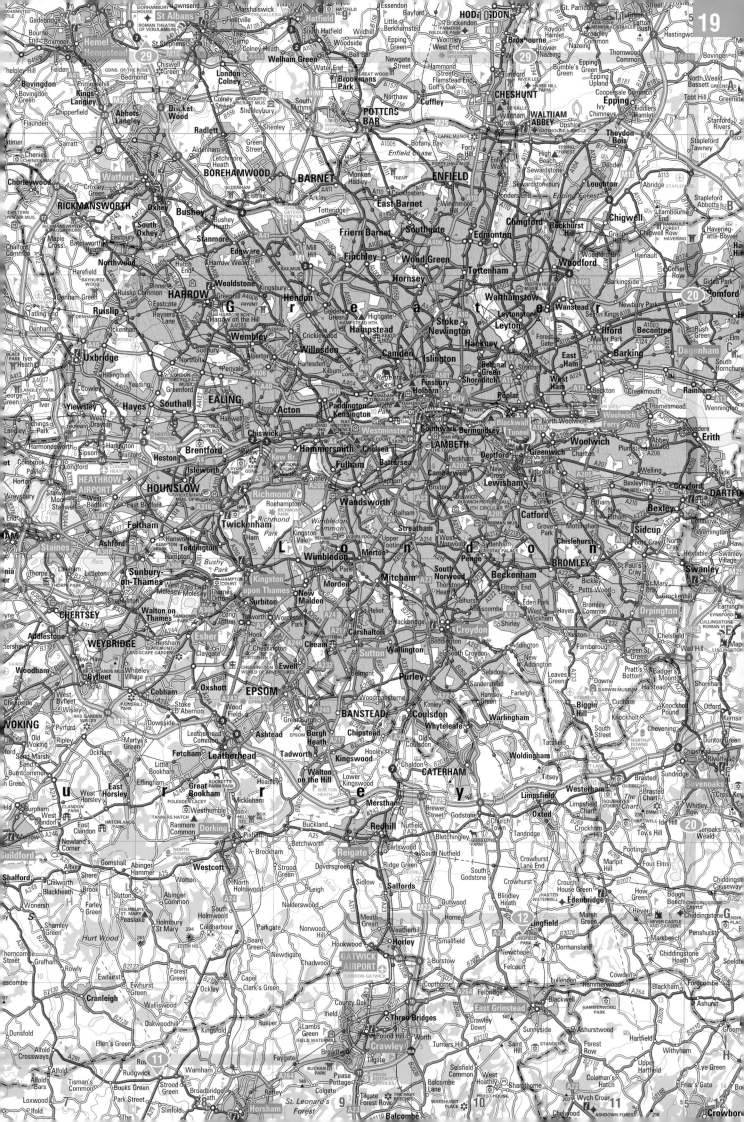

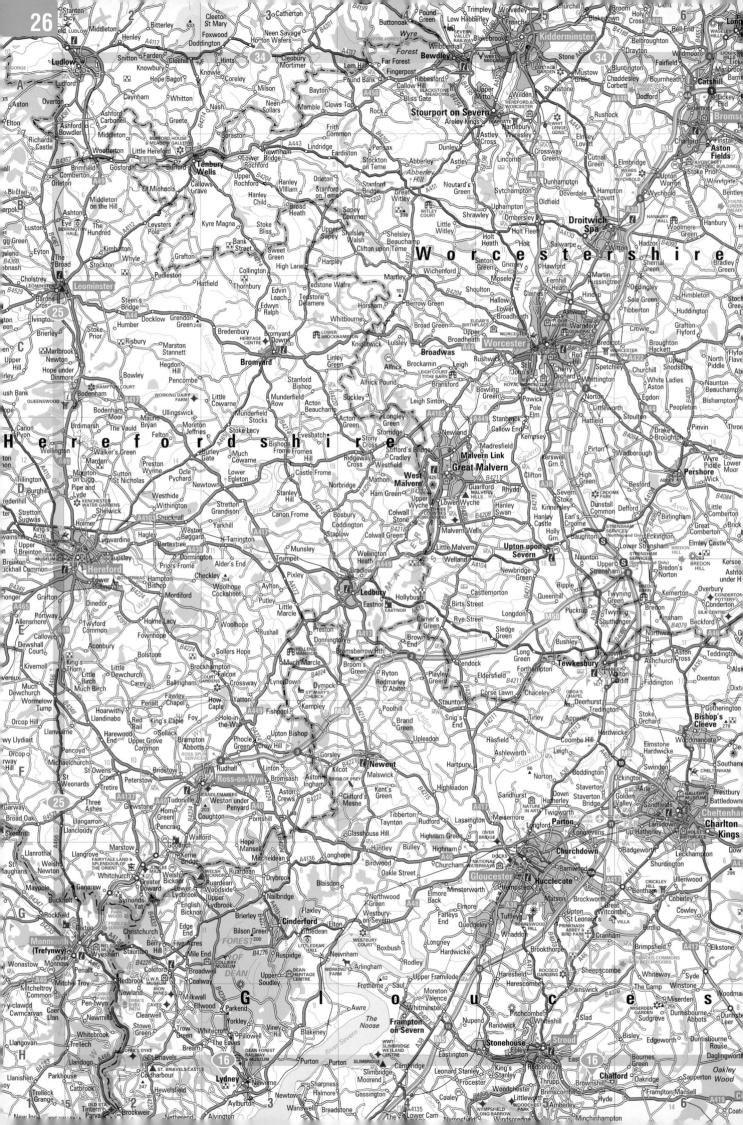

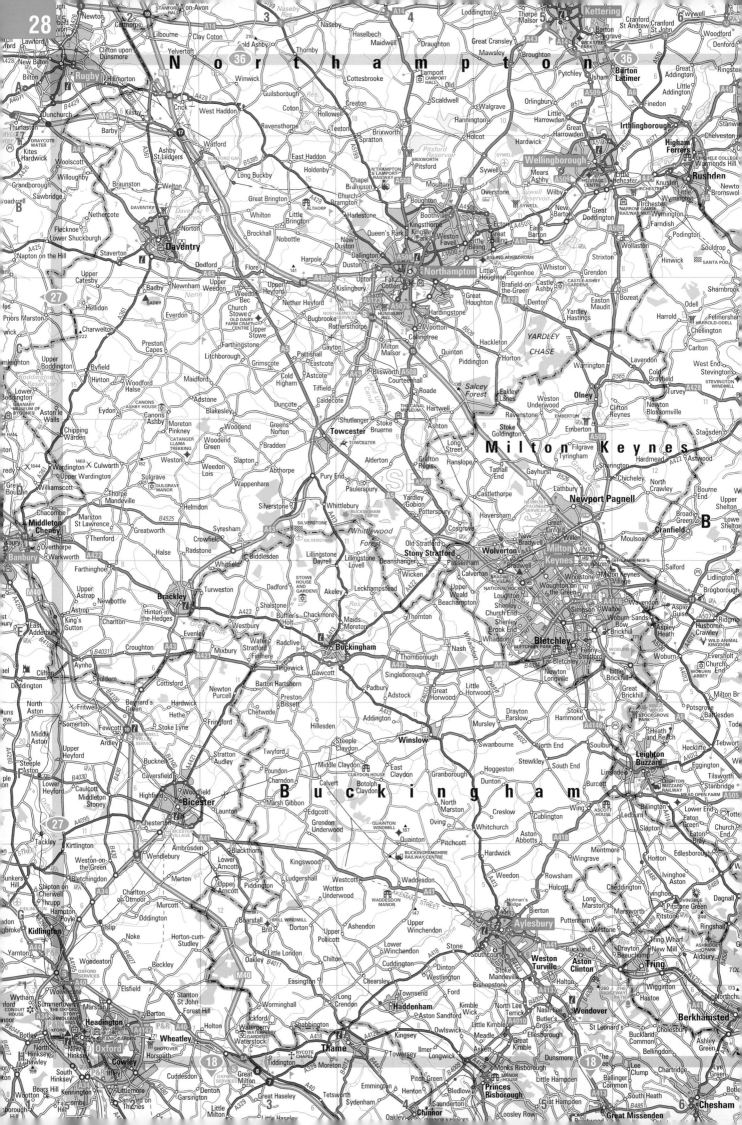

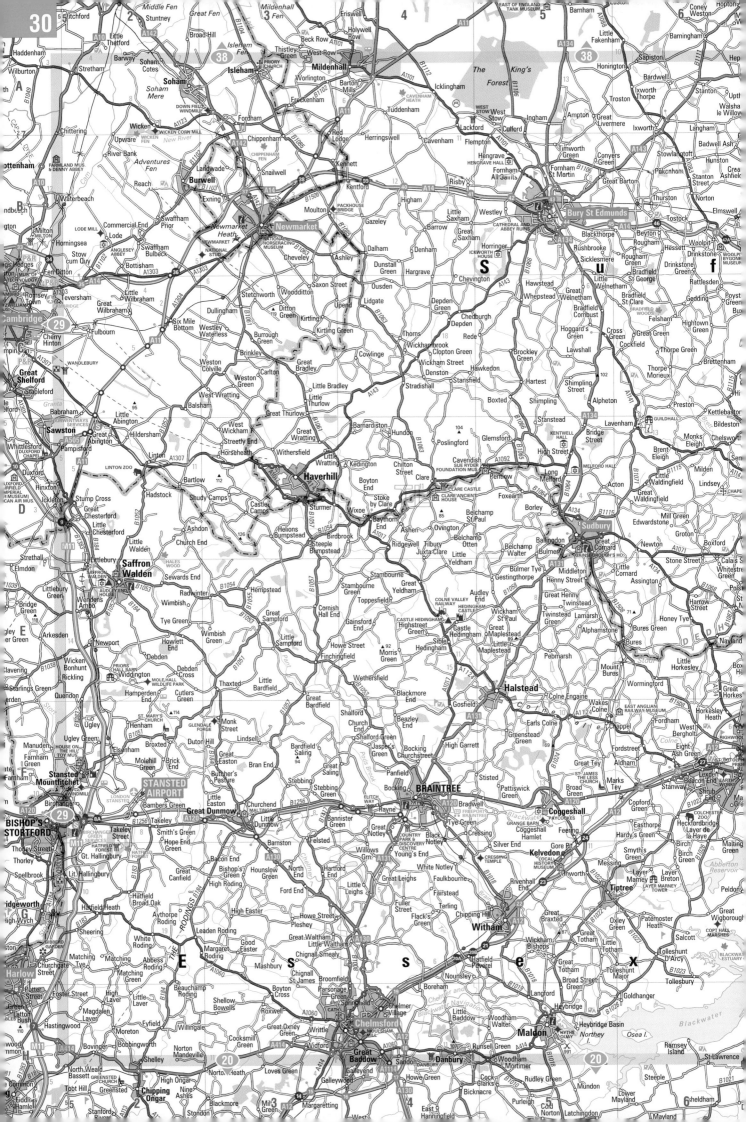

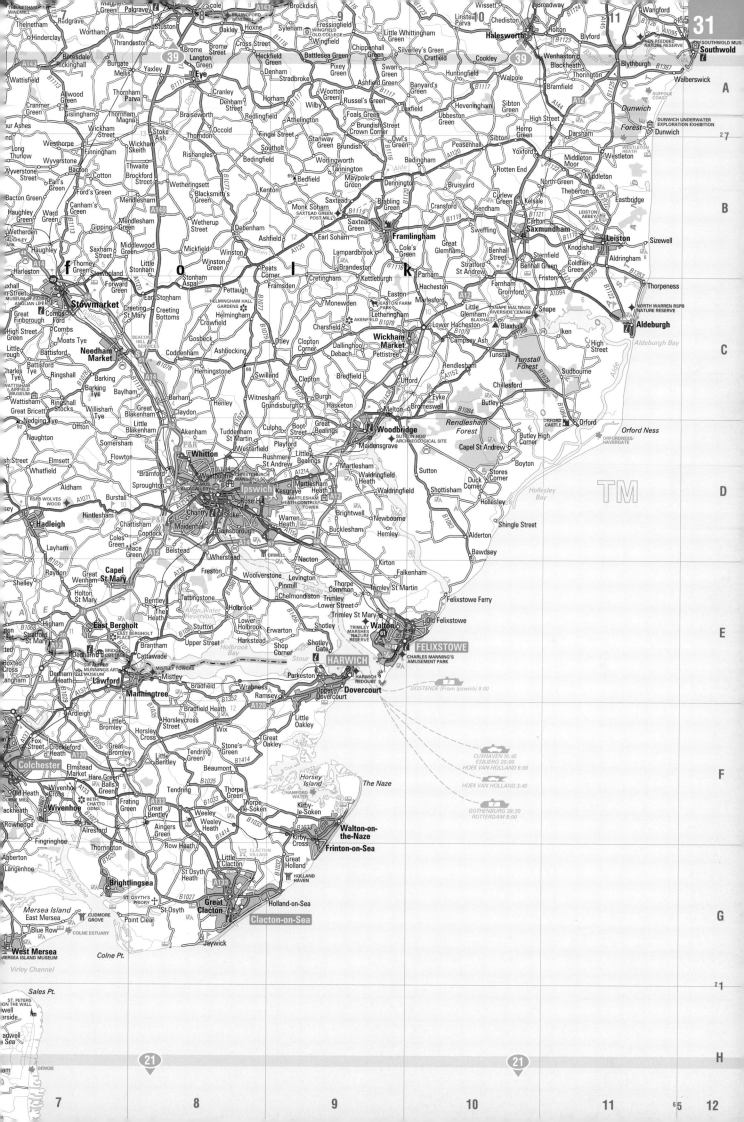

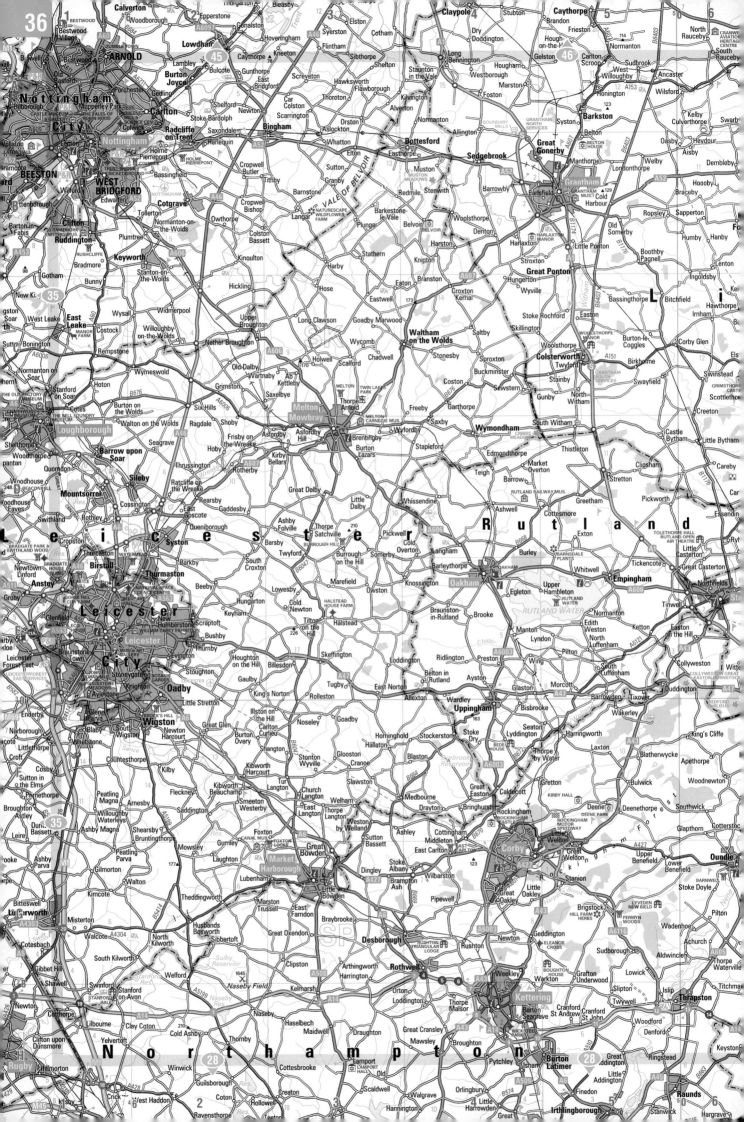

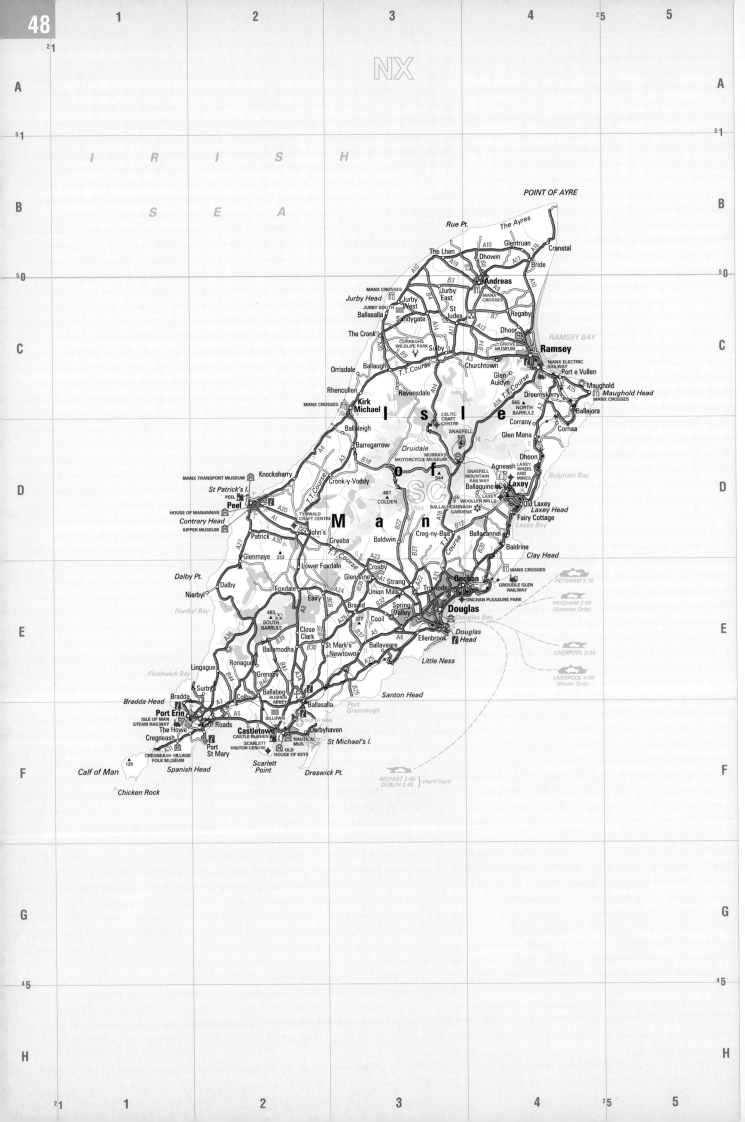

NX

I R I S H

S E A

POINT OF AYRE

Rue Pt.   The Ayres

The Lhen   Glentruan   Cranstal
          Dhowin   A16
          A10   Bride
                    A17
Manx Crosses   A19   B2   B6
Jurby Head   A10   B3   Andreas
          Jurby West   Jurby East   A9
JURBY SOUTH   St   Manx   A10
Ballasalla   Judes   Crosses
          Sandygate   B7   Regaby
The Cronk   Dhoor   *RAMSEY BAY*
          CURRAGHS   Churchtown   GROVE   Ramsey
          WILDLIFE PARK   Sulby   A3   MUSEUM   MANX ELECTRIC
Orrisdale   Ballaugh   9   B14   RAILWAY   Port e Vullen
                    T.T. Course   Glen   Maughold
Rhencullen   Ravensdale   Auldyn   T.T. Course   Maughold Head
                              A18   Dreemskerry   A15   MANX CROSSES
MANX CROSSES   Kirk   CELTIC   565   Corrany   Ballajora
          Michael   CRAFT   NORTH
          Ballaleigh   CENTRE   SNAEFELL   BARRULE   Cornaa
                    621   14   Glen Mona
          Barregarrow   *Druidale*   Dhoon
                    MURRAYS   SNAEFELL   Agneash   LAXEY
                    MOTORCYCLE MUSEUM   MOUNTAIN   WHEEL
MANX TRANSPORT MUSEUM   Knocksharry   Res.   RAILWAY   AND MINES   *Bulgham Bay*
          544   Ballaquine   Laxey
St Patrick's I.   Cronk-y-Voddy   Ballaheannagh   LAXEY   Old Laxey
PEEL   *I   s   l   e*   487   GARDENS   WOOLLEN MILLS   Laxey Head
Peel   TYNWALD   COLDEN   A18   Fairy Cottage
HOUSE OF MANANNAN   CRAFT CENTRE   *o   f*   B22   Creg-ny-Baa   Ballacannell   *Laxey Bay*
Contrary Head   St John's   *M   a   n*   B12   Baldrine
KIPPER MUSEUM   Patrick   A30   Greeba   SC   A21   Onchan   *Clay Head*
          A1   Baldwin   A22   MANX CROSSES
          Glenmaye   333   Lower Foxdale   A23   Crosby   Tromode   GROUDLE GLEN
Dalby Pt.   Glen Vine   A1   Strang   ONCHAN PLEASURE PARK   RAILWAY   *HEYSHAM 3:30*
          Dalby   Foxdale   Union Mills   Douglas
Niarbyl   Eairy   B36   Braaid   Spring   *Douglas Bay*   *HEYSHAM 2:00*
Niarbyl Bay   483   A24   Valley   Cooil   *(Summer Only)*
          SOUTH   A3   Ballaveare   A6   Ellenbrook   *Douglas Head*
          BARRULE   222   St Mark's   A25   *LIVERPOOL 2:30*
Lingague   Close   Ballamodha   B30   Newtown   *Little Ness*
          Clark   B41   *LIVERPOOL 4:00*
Surby   Ronague   Grenaby   A3   B25   *Santon Head*   *(Winter Only)*
Bradda Head   Bradda   Colby   Ballabeg   RUSHEN   *Port*
Port Erin   Ballasalla   *Greenaugh*
ISLE OF MAN   A5   5   BILLOWN
STEAM RAILWAY   Four Roads   Derbyhaven
The Howe   Castletown
Cregneash   CASTLE RUSHEN   NAUTICAL
          SCARLETT   MUS.   *St Michael's I.*
CREGNEASH VILLAGE   128   Port   VISITOR CENTRE   OLD
FOLK MUSEUM   St Mary   HOUSE OF KEYS
Calf of Man   *Spanish Head*   Scarlett   *BELFAST 2:45*
          Point   *Dreswick Pt.*   *DUBLIN 2:45* *(April-Sept)*
Chicken Rock

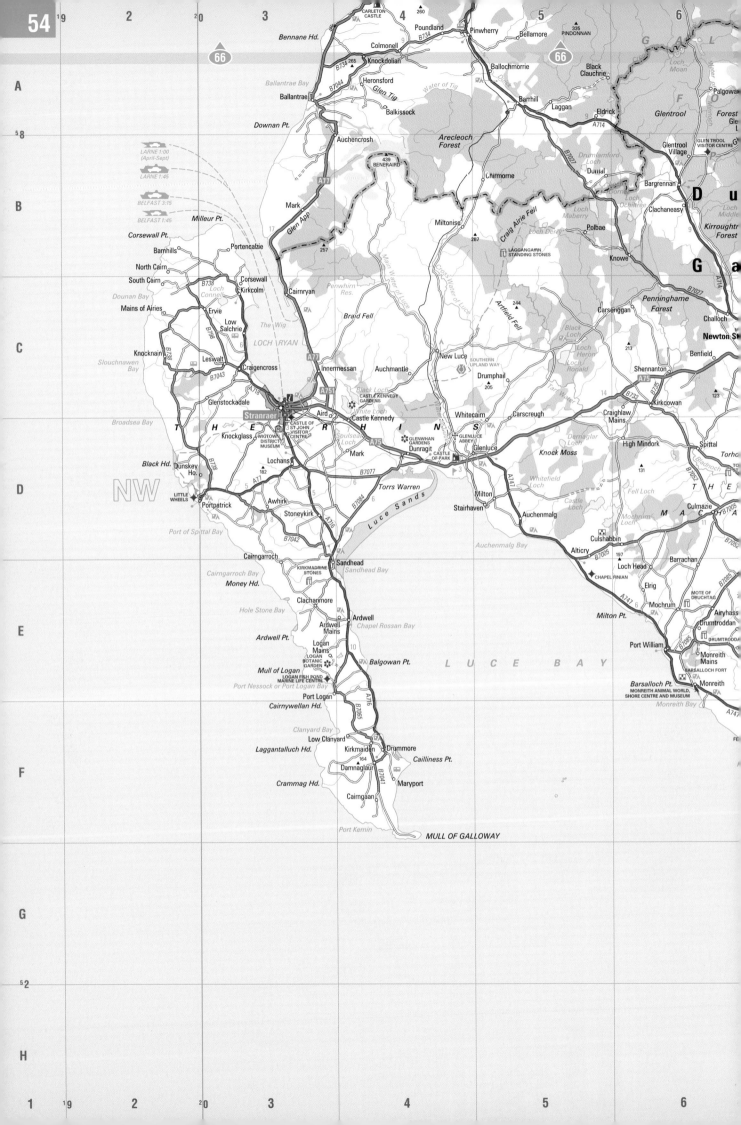

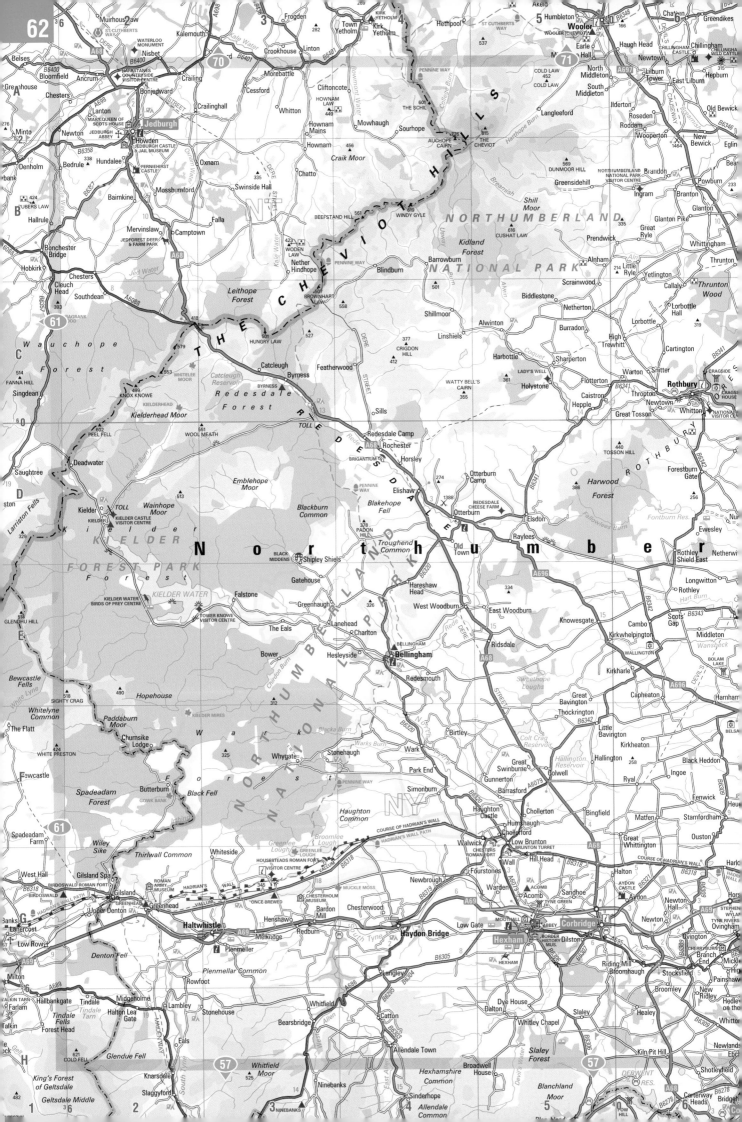

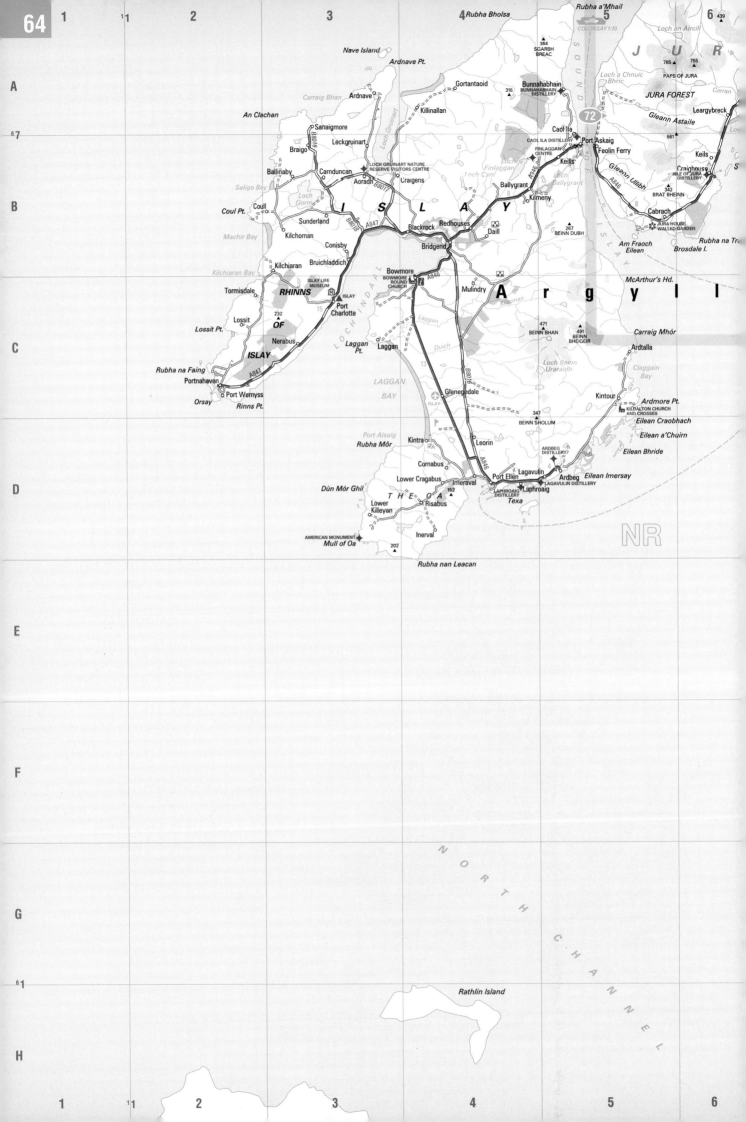

J U R

COLONSAY 1:10

Loch an Aircill

Loch a Chnuic
Bhric

785 ▲   755 ▲
PAPS OF JURA

364
**SGARBH
BREAC**

JURA FOREST

Corran

A

Nave Island

Ardnave Pt.

Gortantaoid

Bunnahabhain
**BUNNAHABHAIN
DISTILLERY**

316

Leargybreck

Gleann Astaile

67

Carraig Bhan

Ardnave

Killinallan

561 ▲

An Clachan

Caol Ila

72

Sanaigmore

Leckgruinart

CAOL ILA DISTILLERY
**FINLAGGAN
CENTRE**

Port Askaig

Keils

Braigo

B8017

Loch
Finlaggan

Feolin Ferry

Craighouse
**ISLE OF JURA
DISTILLERY**

Ballinaby

Carnduncan

**LOCH GRUINART NATURE
RESERVE VISITORS CENTRE**

Craigens

Keills

Loch
Cam

Gleann Ullibh

Aoradh   B8017

Ballygrant

Loch
Ballygrant

A846

BRAT BHEINN

342

B

Saligo Bay

Loch
Gorm

Coull

Ballygrant

Kilmeny

Cabrach

Coul Pt.

Sunderland

B8018

A847

Blackrock

Redhouses

Daill

267
BEINN DUBH

**JURA HOUSE
WALLED GARDEN**

Machir Bay

Kilchoman

Bridgend

Am Fraoch
Eilean

Brosdale I.

Rubha na Tra

Conisby

Bruichladdich

Bowmore
**BOWMORE
ROUND
CHURCH**

Mulindry

Kilchiaran Bay

Kilchiaran

**ISLAY LIFE
MUSEUM**

A846

McArthur's Hd.

C

Tormisdale

RHINNS

Islay

Port
Charlotte

Kilnaughton

471
BEINN BHAN

491
**BEINN
BHEIGEIR**

Carraig Mhór

Ardtalla

Lossit

232

Loch Beinn
Uraraidh

Claggain
Bay

Lossit Pt.

OF

Nerabus

Loch
Indaal

Laggan
Pt.

Laggan

B8016

Kintour

Ardmore Pt.

ISLAY

15

Duich

347
BEINN SHOLUM

**KILDALTON CHURCH
AND CROSSES**

Eilean Craobhach

Rubha na Faing

A847

13

Glenegedale

Eilean a'Chuirn

Portnahaven

Port Wemyss

**LAGGAN
BAY**

ISLAY

Eilean Bhride

Orsay

Rinns Pt.

Port Alsaig

Rubha Mór

Kintra

Leorin

Ardbeg
**ARDBEG
DISTILLERY**

D

Dùn Mór Ghil

THE OA

Cornabus

352

A846

Lagavulin

Eilean Imersay

Lower Cragabus

Imeraval

Port Ellen

LAGAVULIN DISTILLERY

Ardbeg

Lower
Killeyan

Risabus

**LAPHROAIG
DISTILLERY**

Laphroaig

Inerval

Texa

AMERICAN MONUMENT

Mull of Oa

202

NR

Rubha nan Leacan

E

F

N
O
R
T
H

C
H
A
N
N
E
L

G

61

Rathlin Island

H

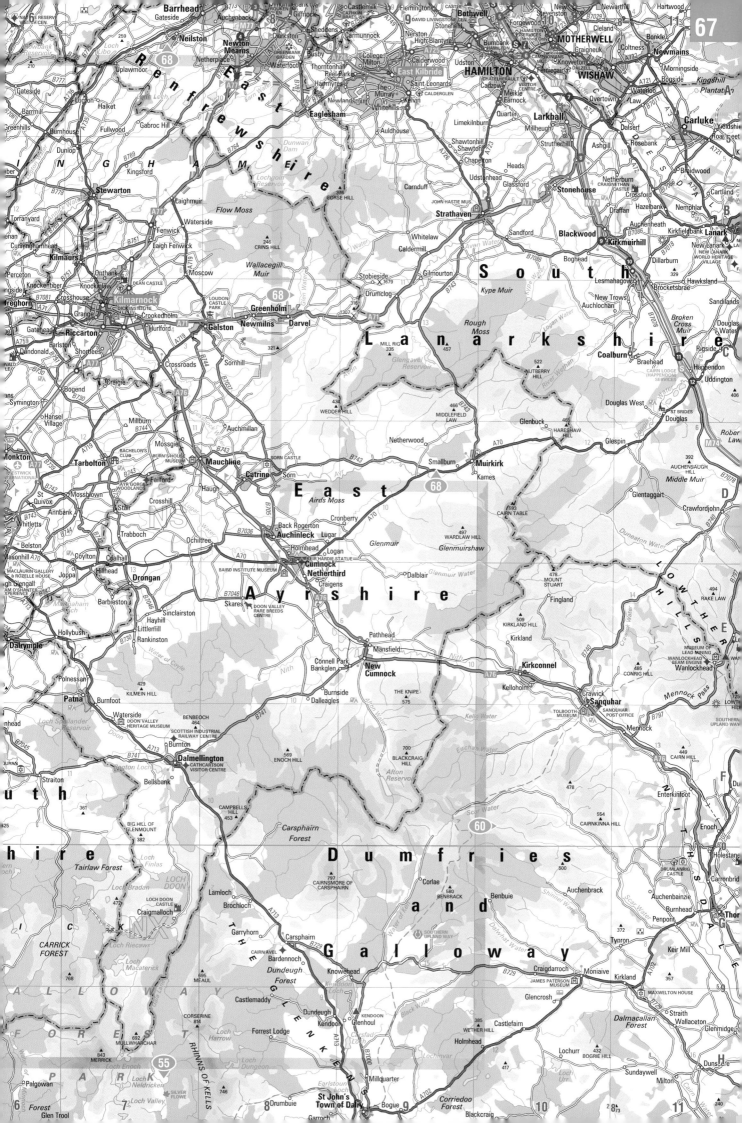

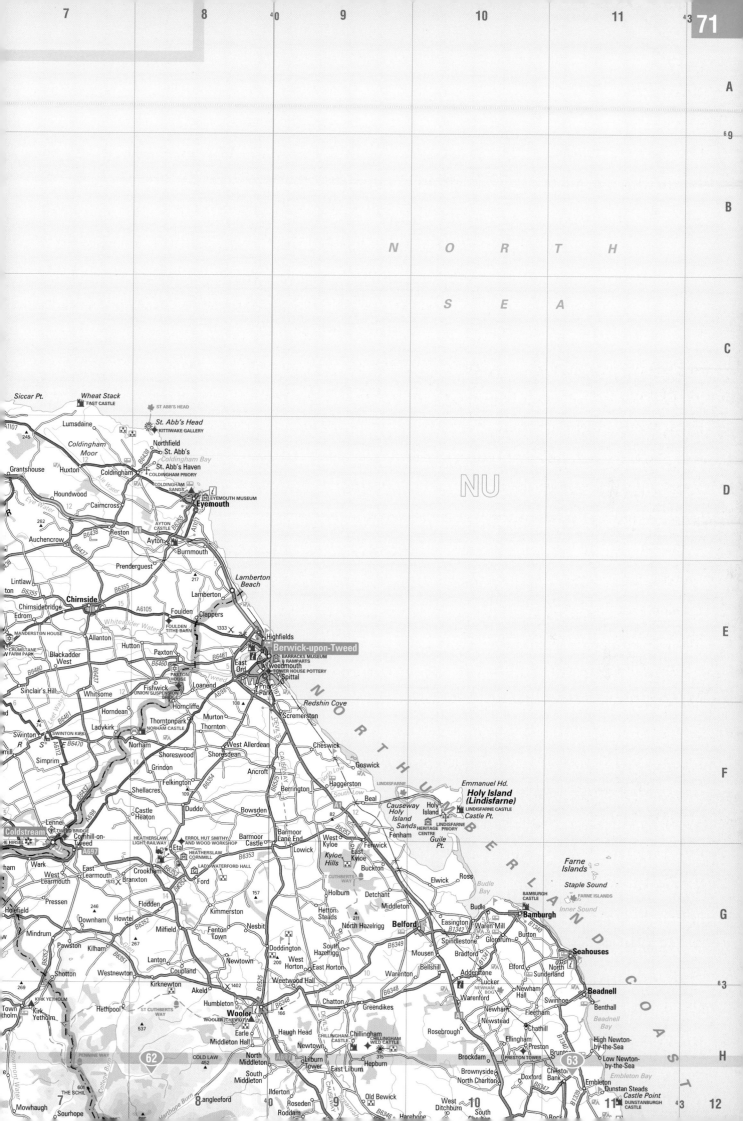

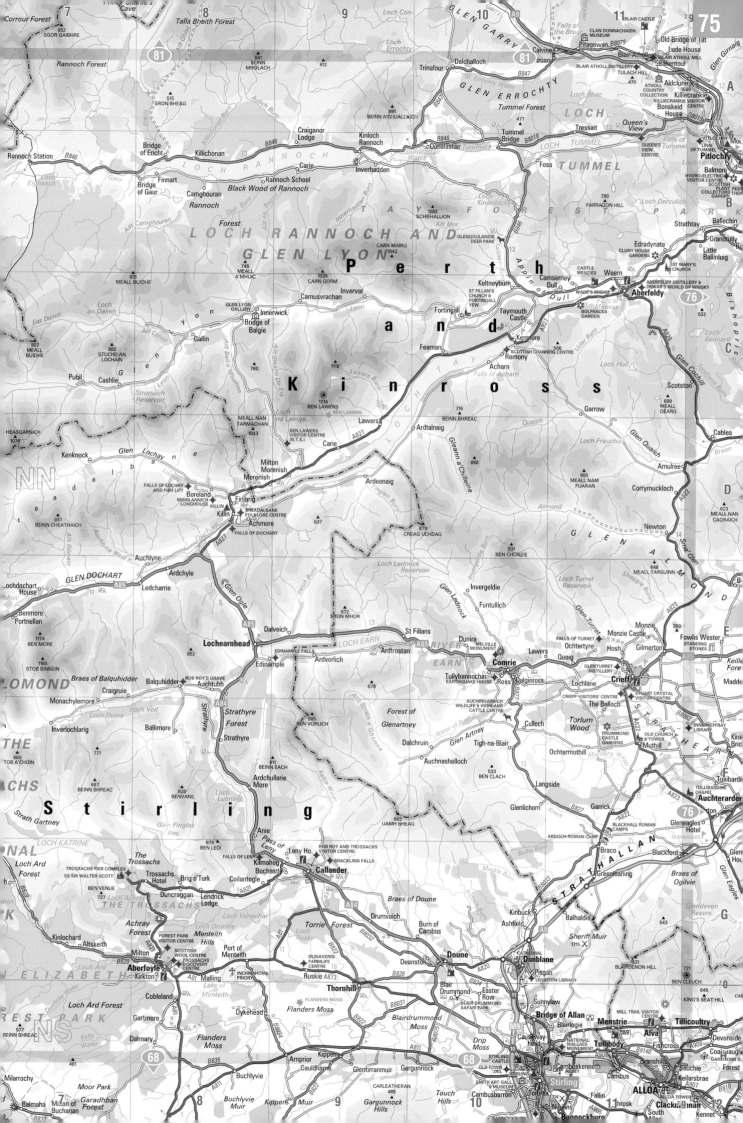

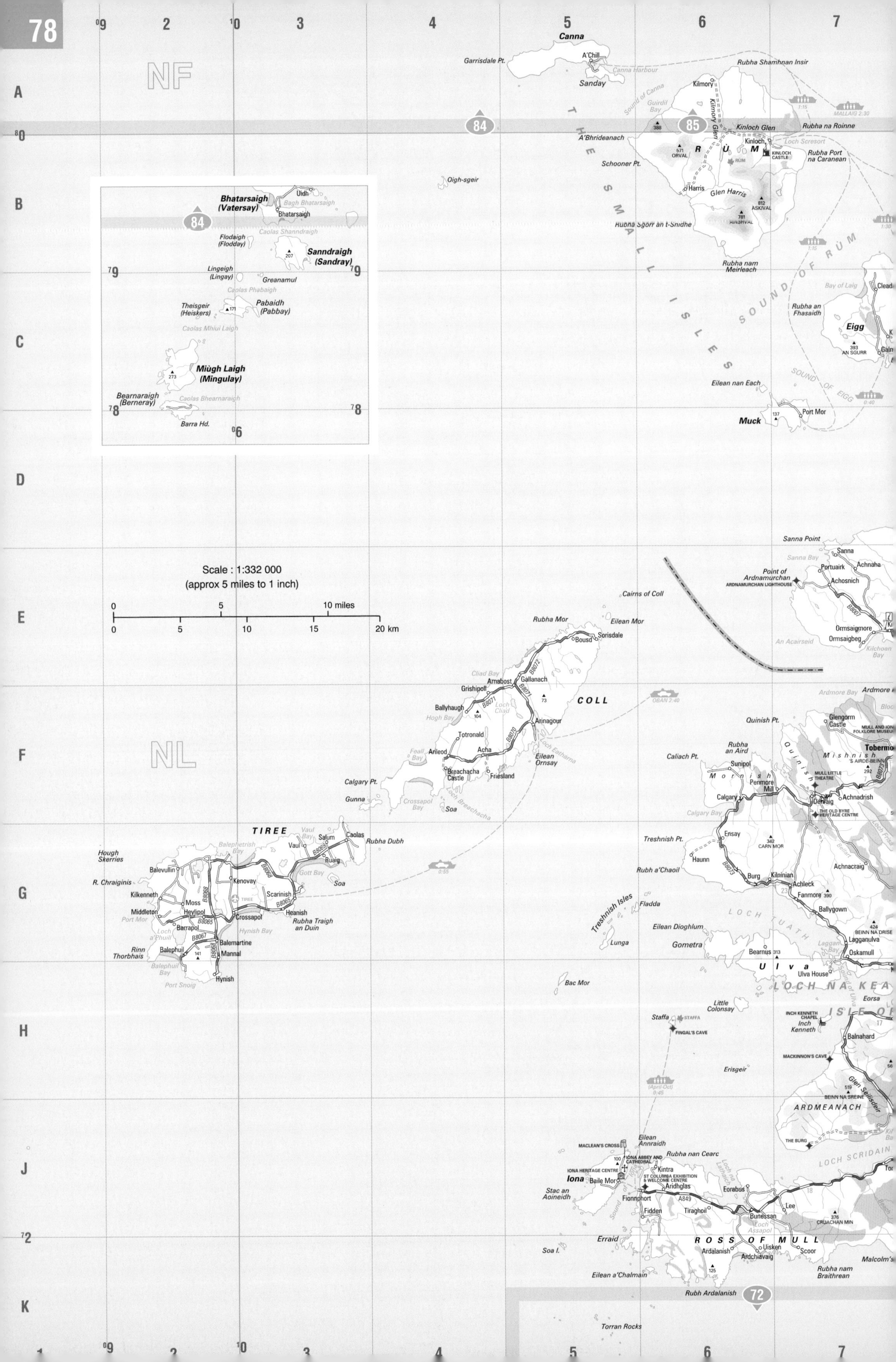

NF

Canna

Garrisdale Pt.
A'Chill
Sanday
Canna Harbour

Sound of Canna
Rubha Shamhnan Insir

Kilmory
Kilmory Glen
Kinloch Glen
Rubha na Roinne

84

85
388
Loch Scresort

A'Bhrideanach
Kinloch
KINLOCH CASTLE
Rubha Port na Carannean

Oigh-sgeir
Schooner Pt.
571 ORVAL
R Ù M
BÉINN

Harris
Glen Harris
812 ASKIVAL

781 AINSHVAL

Rubha Sgòrr an t-Snidhe

Rubha nam Meirleach

Bay of Laig
Clead

Rubha an Fhasaidh

Eigg
393 AN SGURR
Galr

Eilean nan Each

Sanna Point

Sanna Sanna Bay
Portuairk Achnaha

Point of Ardnamurchan
ARDNAMURCHAN LIGHTHOUSE
Achosnich

Eilean nan Each

Eilean Mor
An Acairseid
Ormsaigmore
Ormsaigbeg
Kilchoan

Muck
137
Port Mor

Inset box:

Uidh
**Bhatarsaigh
(Vatersay)**
Bhatarsaigh
Bagh Bhatarsaigh

84

Caolas Shanndraigh

Flodaigh
(Flodday)
207
**Sanndraigh
(Sandray)**

Lingeigh
(Lingay)
Greanamul

Theisgeir
(Heiskers)
171
Pabaidh
(Pabbay)

Caolas Phabaigh

Caolas Mhiul Laigh

273
**Miùgh Laigh
(Mingulay)**

Bearnaraigh
(Berneray)
Caolas Bhearnaraigh

Barra Hd.

Scale

Scale : 1:332 000
(approx 5 miles to 1 inch)

0 ... 5 ... 10 miles
0 ... 5 ... 10 ... 15 ... 20 km

NL

Rubha Mor
Cairns of Coll
Eilean Mor
Bousd Sorisdale

Cliad Bay
Arnabost
Gallanach
Grishipoll
Ballyhaugh
104
73
COLL
Loch Cliad
Arinagour
OBAN 2:40

Hogh Bay
Totronald
Arileod
Acha
Eilean Ornsay

Feall Bay
Breachacha Castle
Friesland
Loch Breachacha

Calgary Pt.
Gunna
Crossapol Bay
Soa

T I R E E
Vaul Bay
Vaul
Salum
Caolas
Rubha Dubh

Hough Skerries
Balephetrish Bay
Ruaig
Soa
Gott Bay

R. Chraiginis
Kenovay
Scarinish
Heanish
Rubha Traigh an Duin

Kilkenneth
Moss
Heylipol
Crossapol

Middleton
Barrapol
Balemartine
Mannal
141
Balephuil

Rinn Thorbhais
Port Mor
Loch a'Phuill
Balephuil Bay
Hynish
Port Snoig

Treshnish Pt.
Caliach Pt.
Rubha an Aird
Sunipol

Quinish Pt.
Glengorm Castle
MULL AND IONA FOLKLORE MUSEUM

Tobermory
S AIRDE-BÉINN
292
M i s h n i s h

Mornish
Penmore Mill
Calgary
Dervaig
MULL LITTLE THEATRE
THE OLD BYRE HERITAGE CENTRE
Achnadrish

Ensay
342 CARN MOR
Achnacraig

Haunn
Burg
Kilninian
Achleck
23
Fanmore
390

Treshnish Isles
Rubh a'Chaoil
Fladda
Ballygown
Lunga
Eilean Dioghlum
454 BEINN NA DRISE
Lagganulva

Gometa
Bearnus 313
Oskamull

Bac Mor
U l v a
Ulva House
Eorsa
LOCH NA KEA

Little Colonsay
INCH KENNETH CHAPEL
Inch Kenneth
Balnahard

Staffa
STAFFA
FINGAL'S CAVE
MACKINNON'S CAVE

Erisgeir
THE BURG
Glen Seilisdeir
519
BEINN NA SREINE
A R D M E A N A C H
LOCH SCRIDAIN

MACLEAN'S CROSS
Eilean Annraidh
Rubha nan Cearc

IONA ABBEY AND CATHEDRAL
IONA HERITAGE CENTRE
ST COLUMBA EXHIBITION & WELCOME CENTRE
100
Kintra
Iona
Baile Mor
Aridhglas
Eorabus
Lee
18

Stac an Aoineidh
Fionnphort
A849
Bunessan
376 CRUACHAN MIN

Fidden
Tiraghoil
R O S S   O F   M U L L

Errald
Ardalanish
Uisken
Scoor

Soa I.
24 125
Ardchiavaig
Rubha nam Braithrean

Eilean a'Chalmain

Rubh Ardalanish
72

Torran Rocks

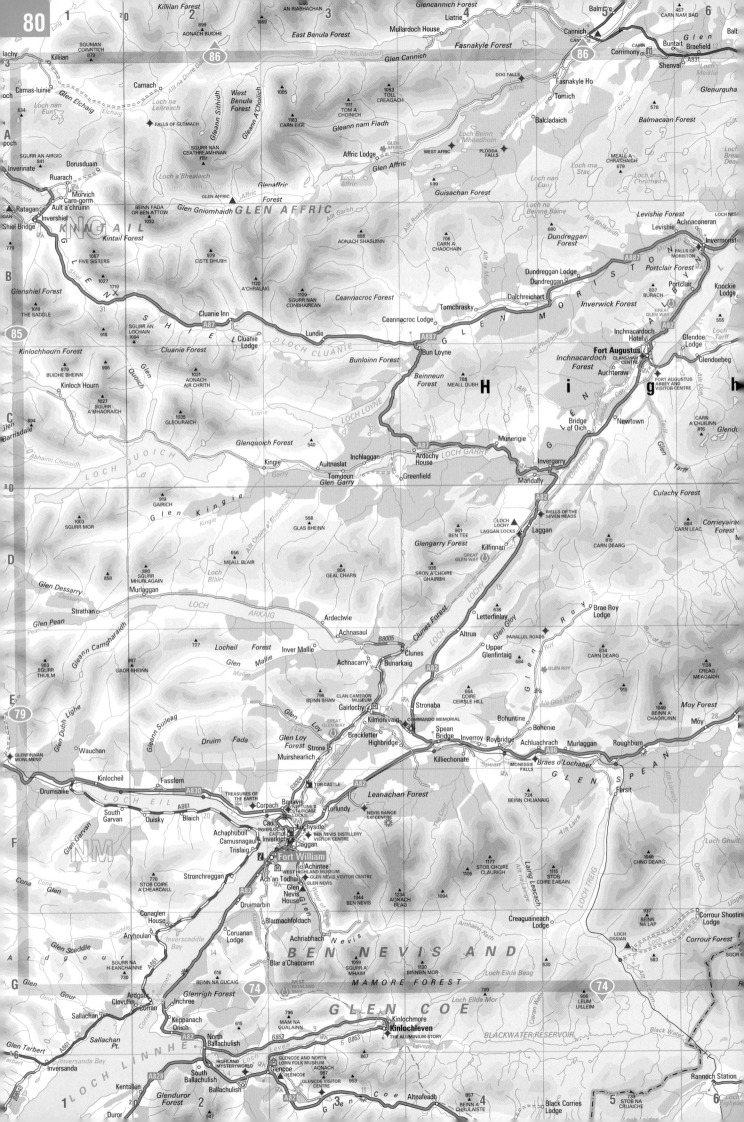

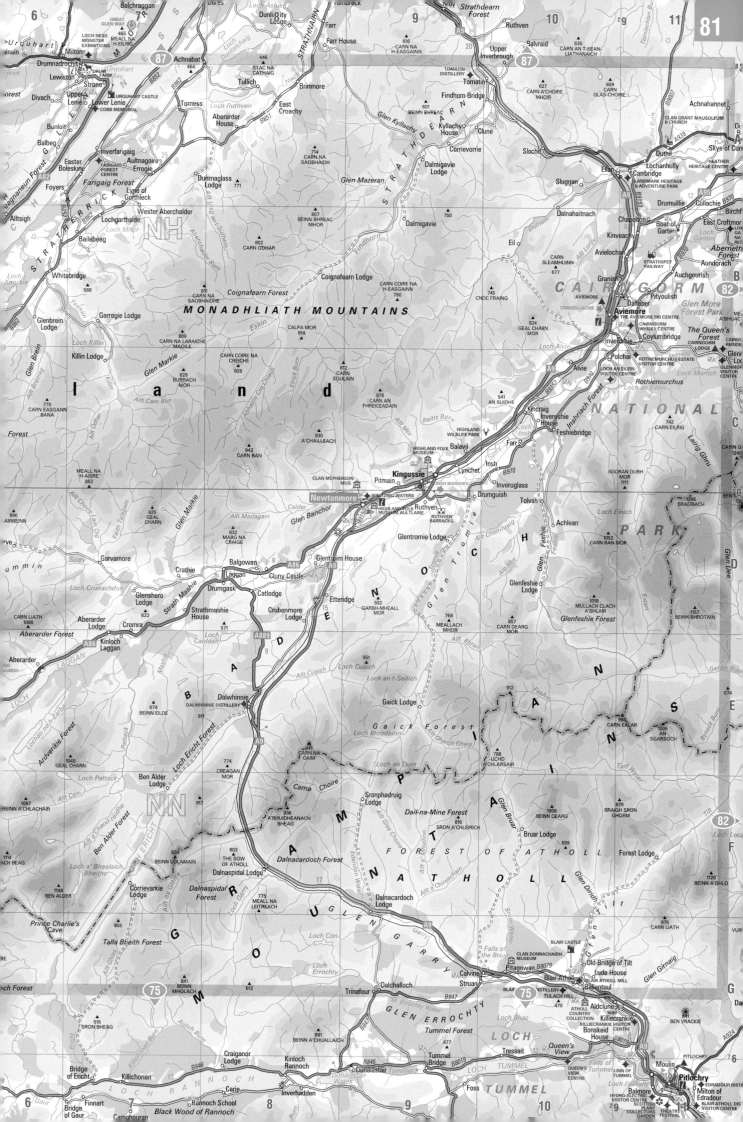

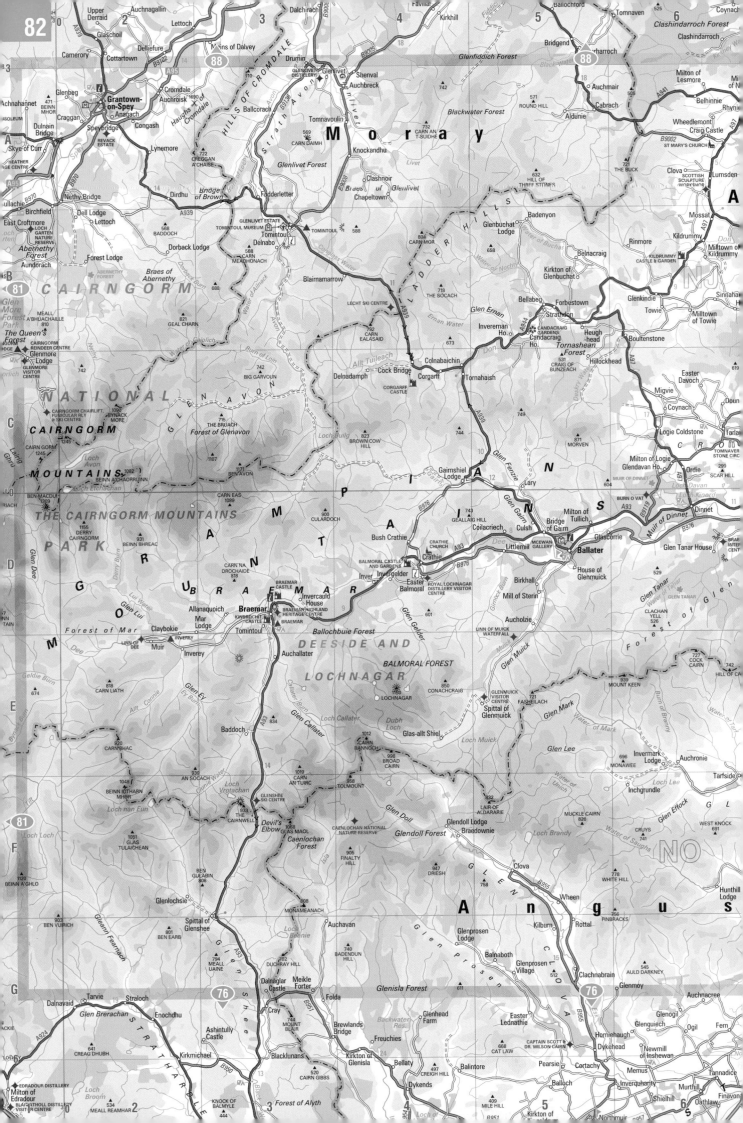

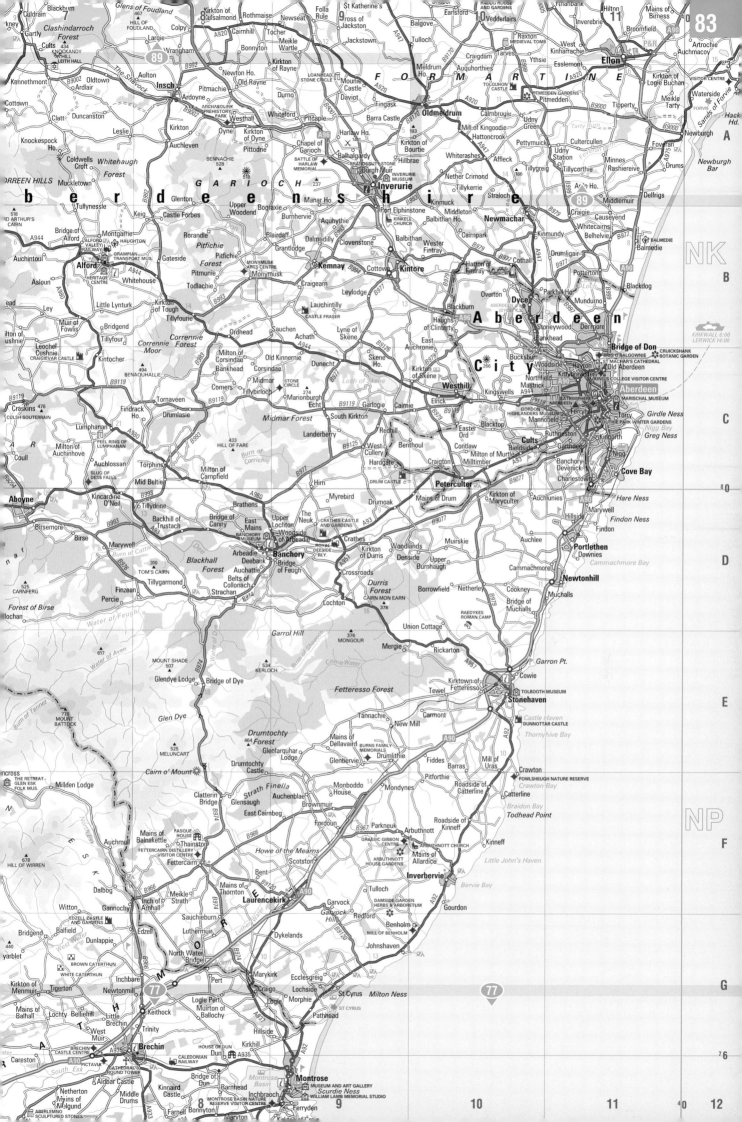

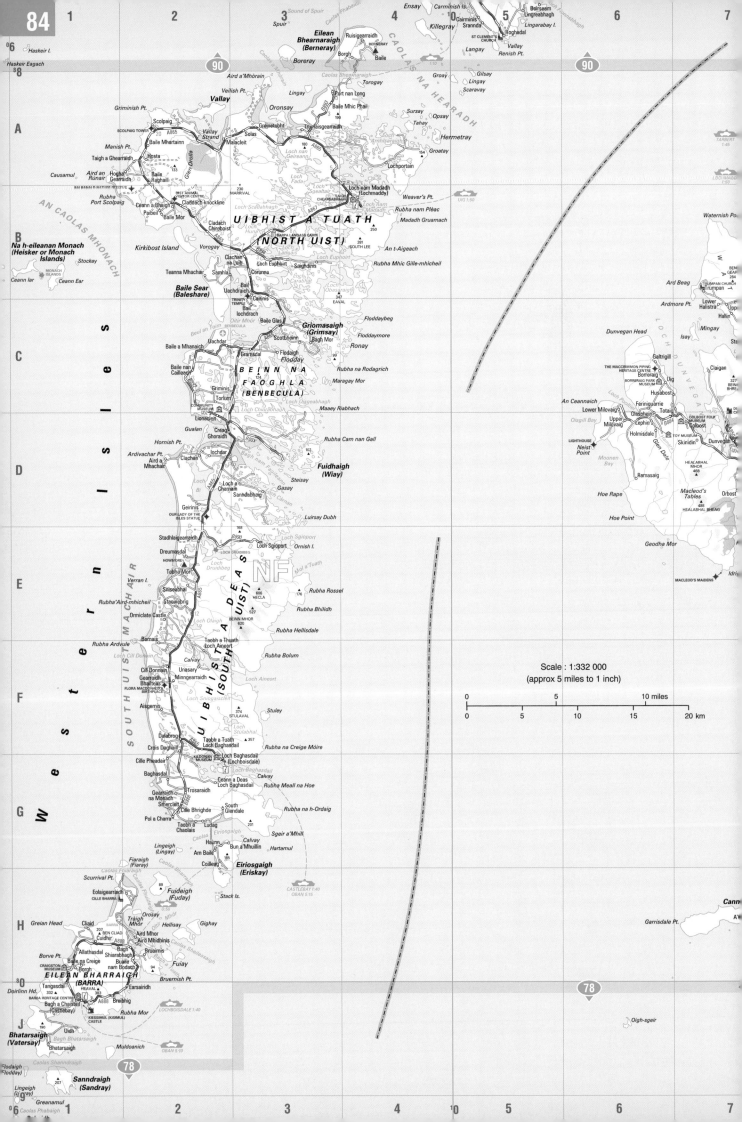

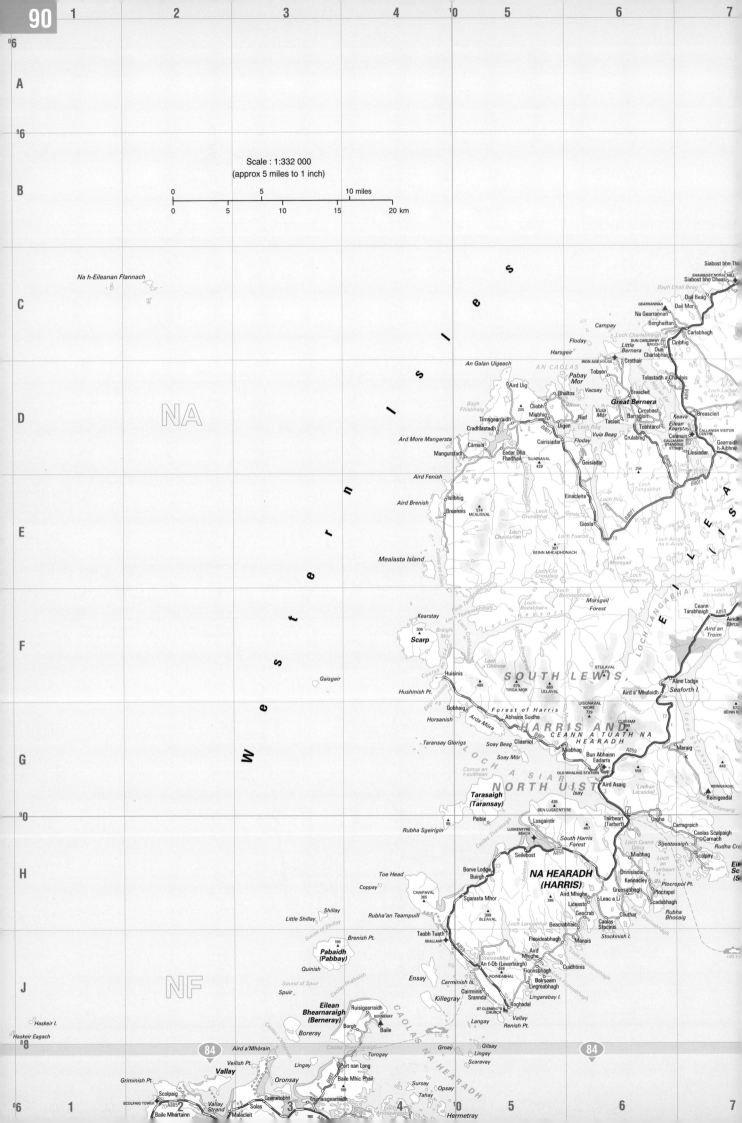

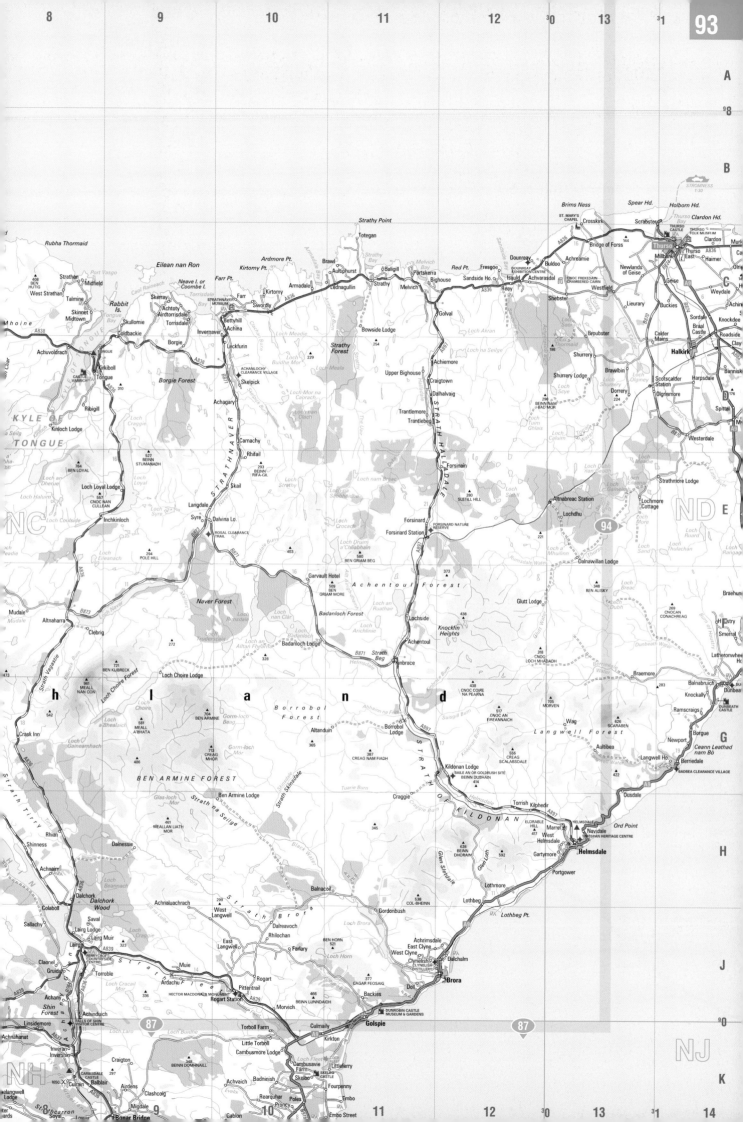

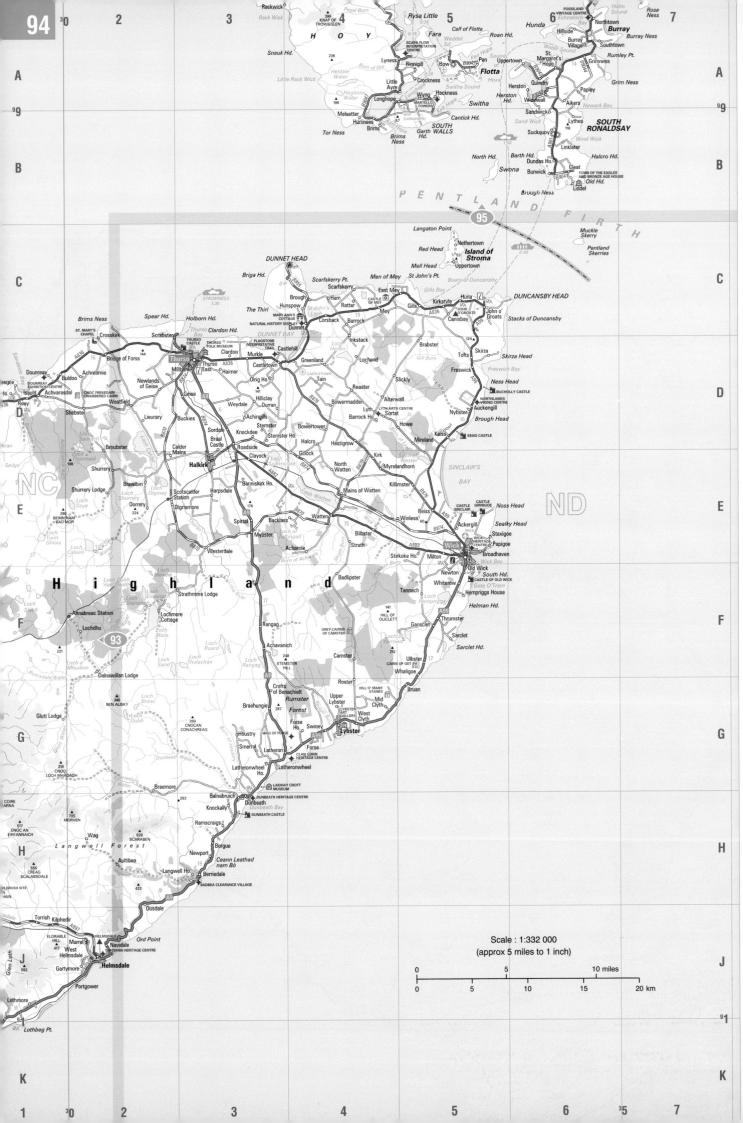

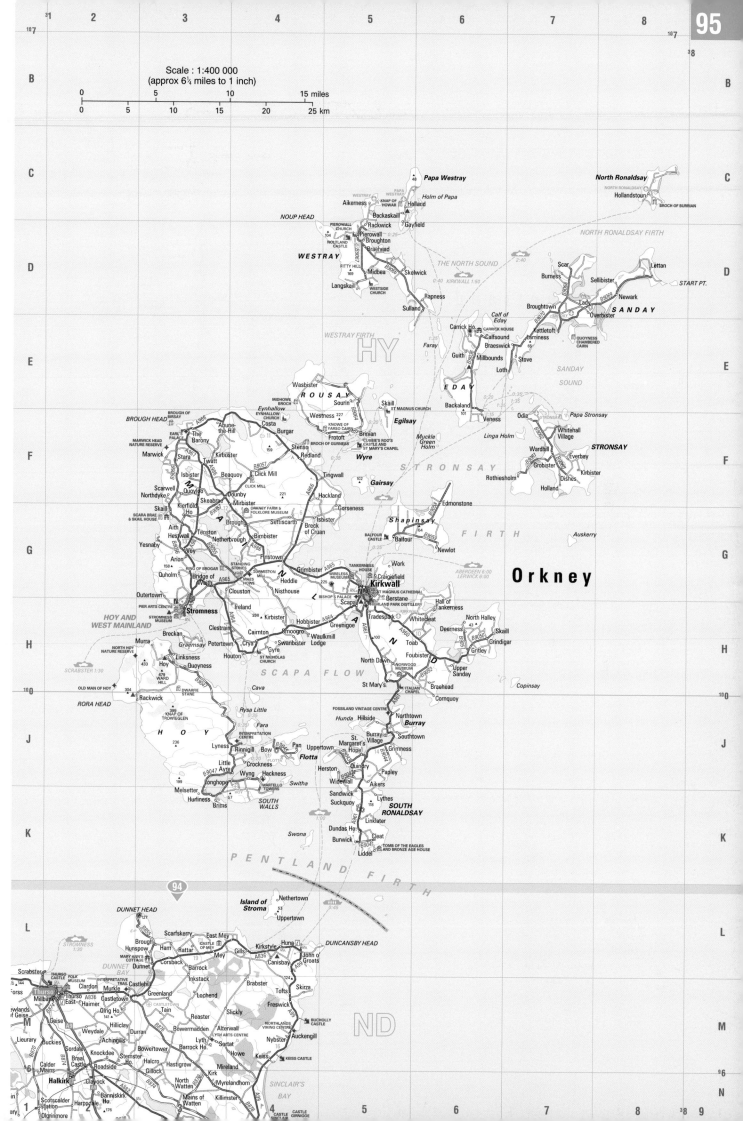

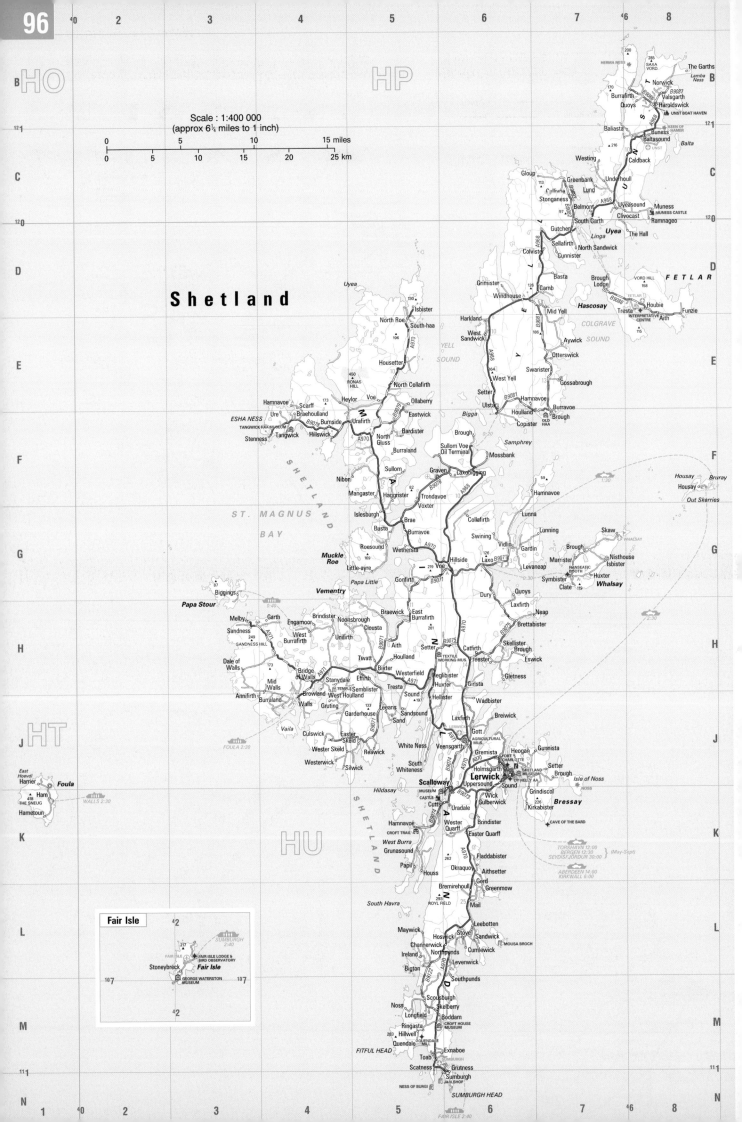

Key to Town Plan Symbols

Motorway	Shopping Streets
Primary Route Dual/Single	Railway
Main Road Dual/Single	Tramway with Station
Secondary Road Dual/Single	Railway/ Bus Station
Minor Through Road/ One Way Street	Shopping Precinct/ Retail Park
Pedestrian Roads	Park

✝	Abbey/Cathedral	⌖	Railway Station
	Ancient Monument		Roman Antiquity
	Aquarium		Safari Park
	Art Gallery		Shopmobility
	Bird Garden		Theatre
	Building of Public Interest	i	Tourist Information Centre (open all year)
	Castle	i	Tourist Information Centre (open summer only)
	Church of interest		Zoo
	Cinema		Other Place of Interest
	Garden		Underground/ Metro Station
	Historic Ship	H	Hospital
	House	P	Parking
	House & Garden		Police
	Museum	PO	Post Office
	Preserved Railway	▲	Youth Hostel

Aberdeen

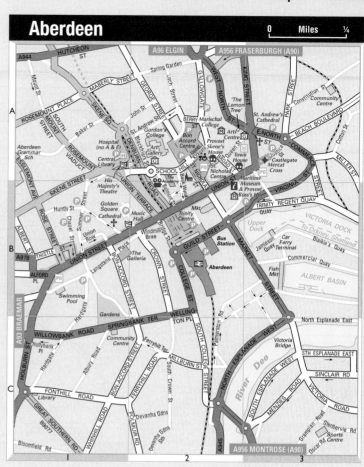

Bath

Blackpool

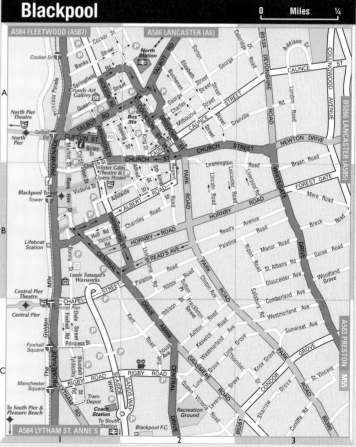
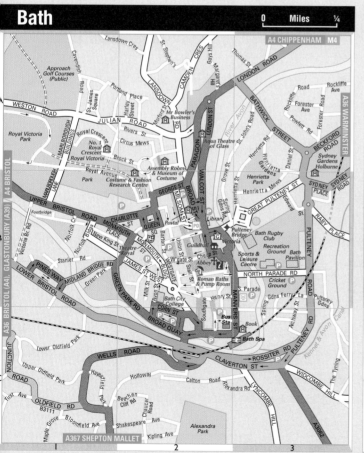

Birmingham

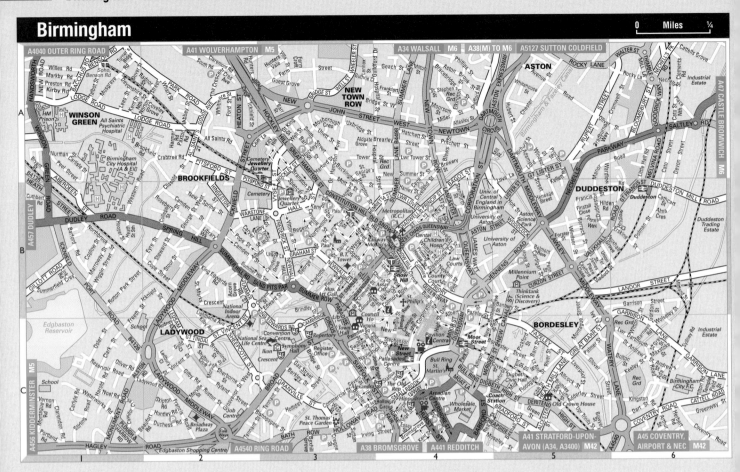

Bournemouth

Bradford

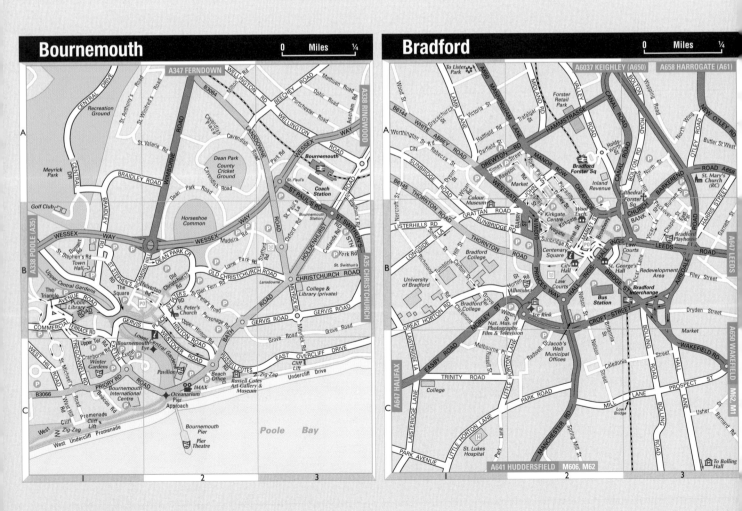

Bristol

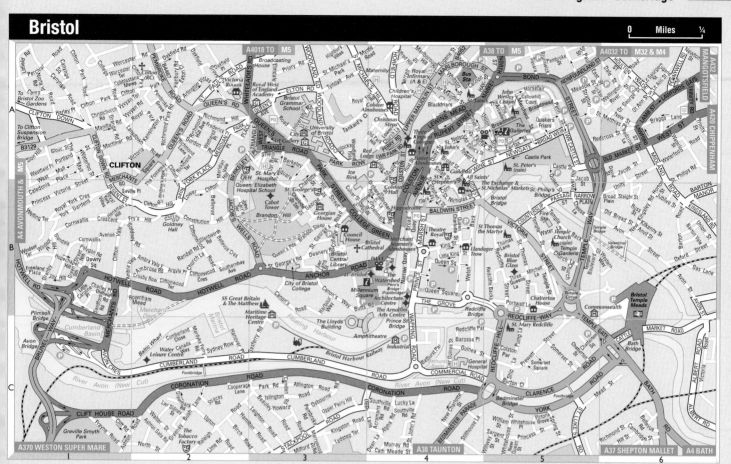

Brighton

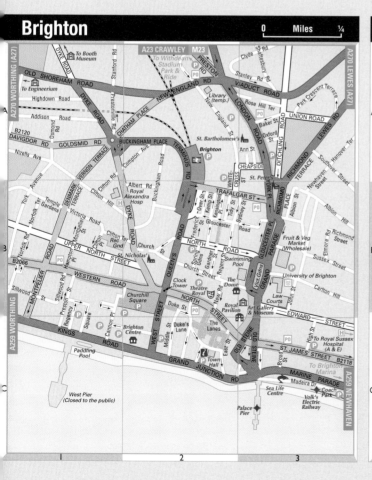

Cambridge

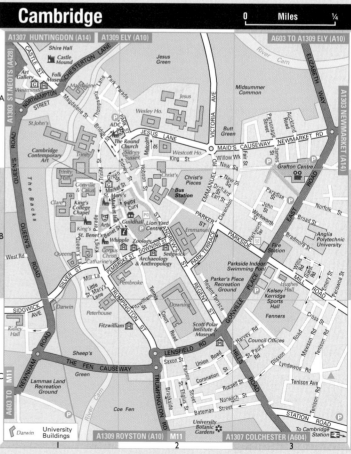

Cardiff / Caerdydd

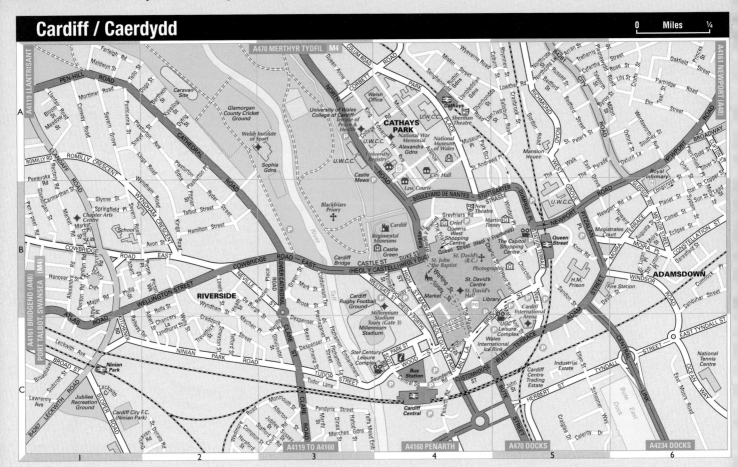

Canterbury

Cheltenham

Chester

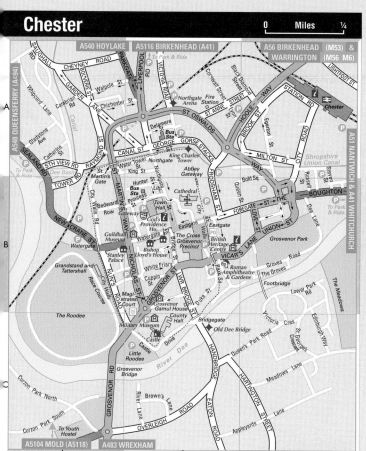

Colchester

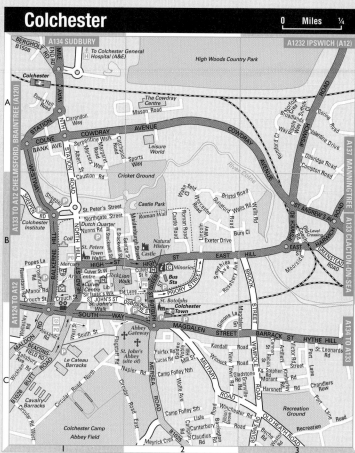

Coventry

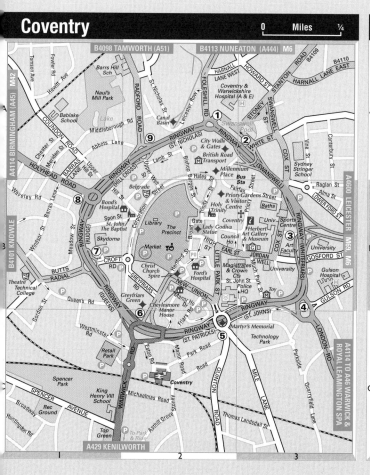

Croydon

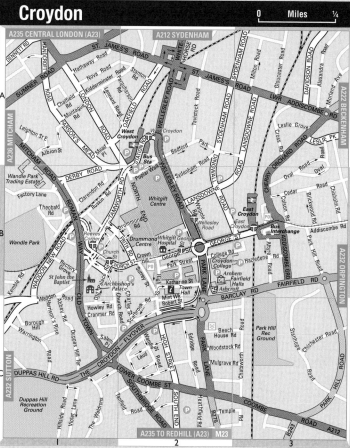

Derby

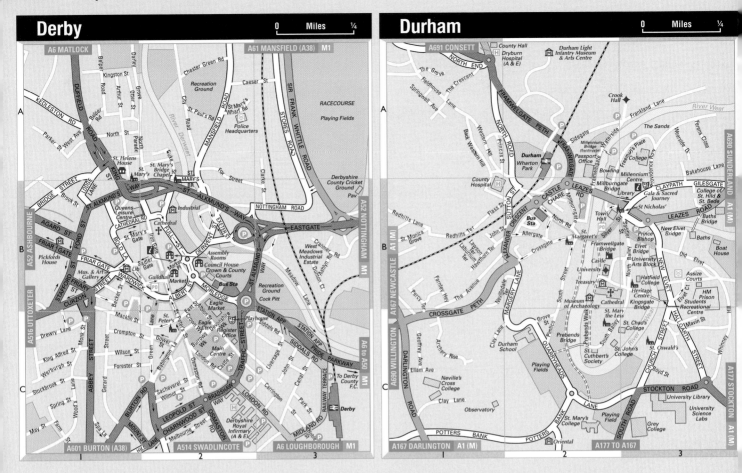

Durham

Edinburgh

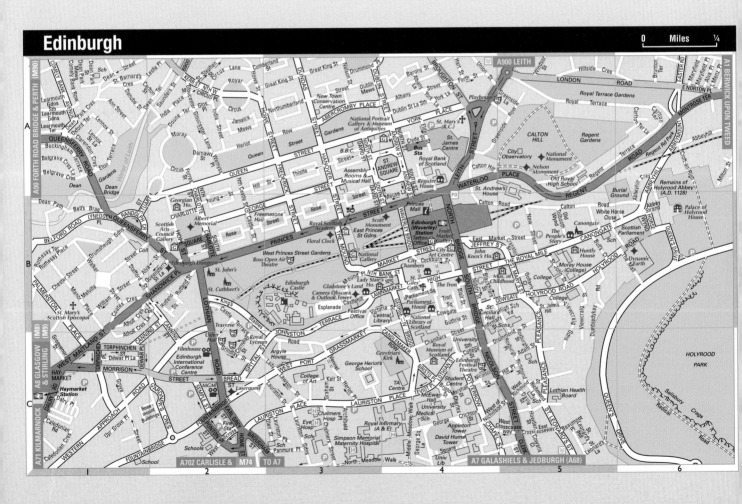

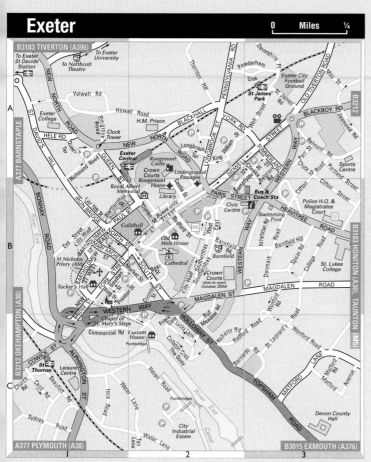

Exeter

0 Miles ¼

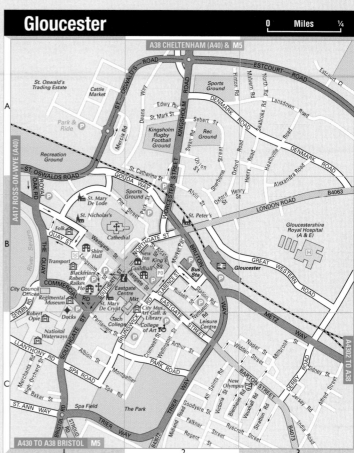

Gloucester

0 Miles ¼

Glasgow

0 Miles ¼

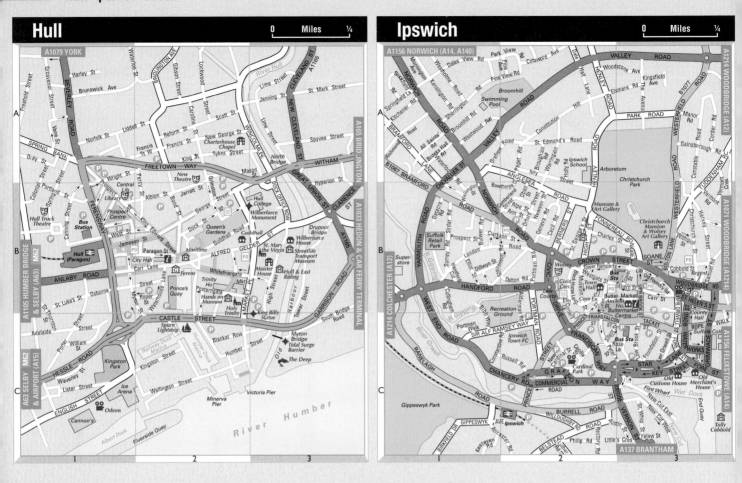

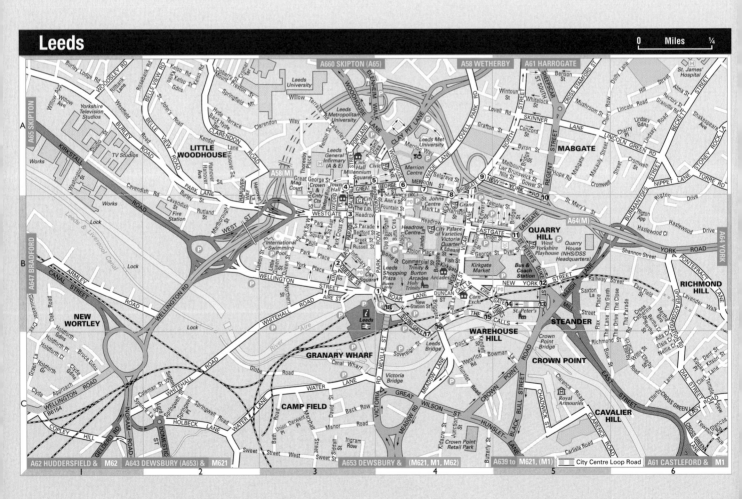

Leicester

0 Miles ¼

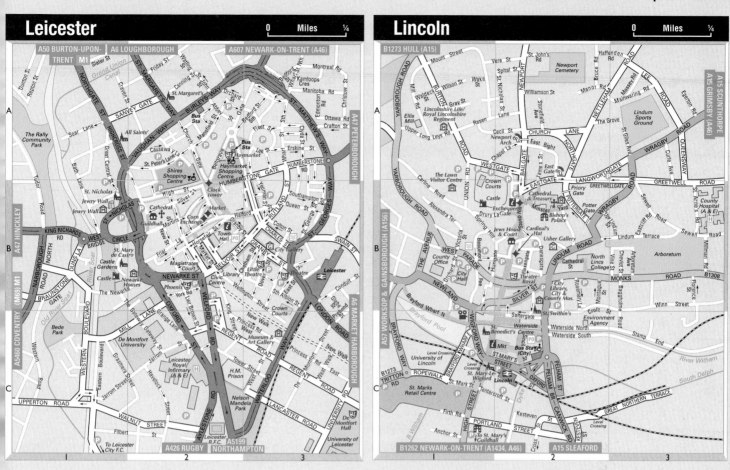

Lincoln

0 Miles ¼

Liverpool

0 Miles ¼

Manchester

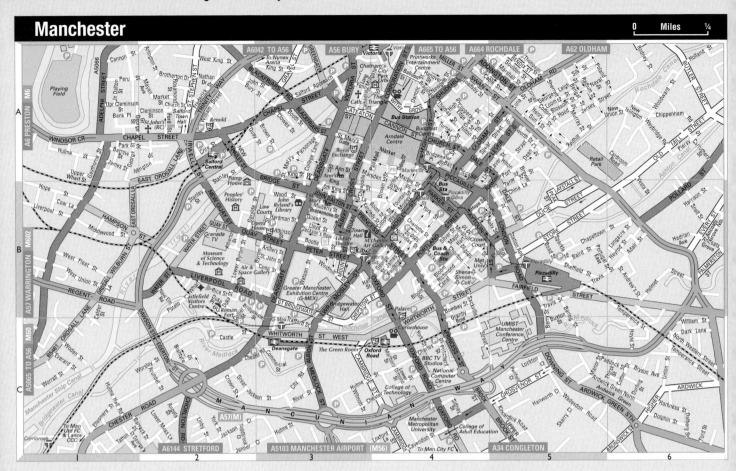

Middlesbrough

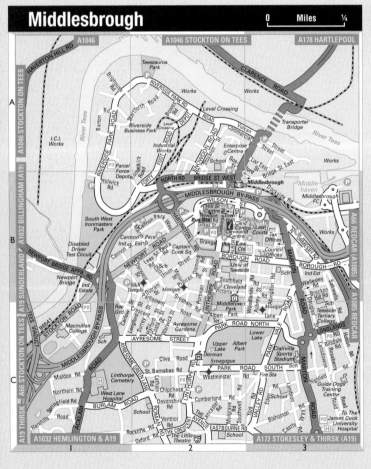

Milton Keynes

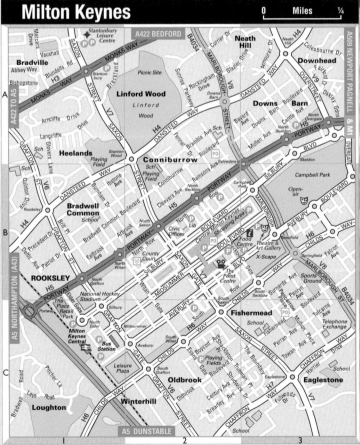

Newcastle-upon-Tyne

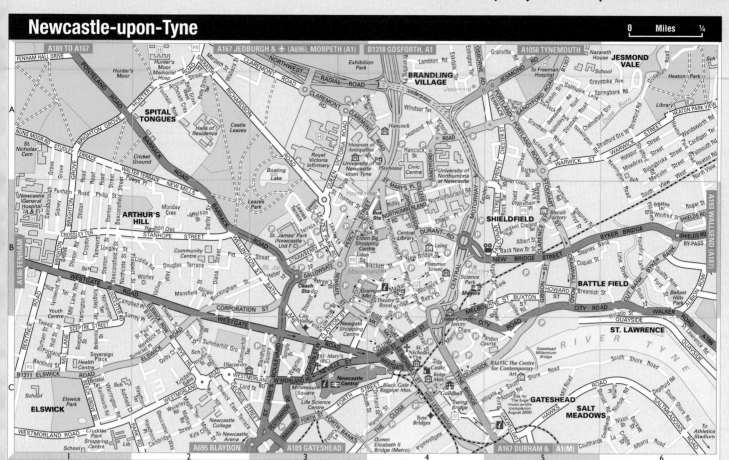

Northampton

Norwich

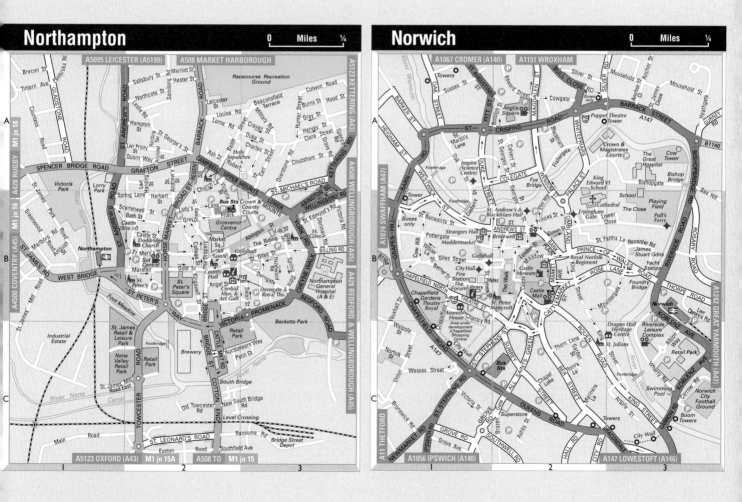

Nottingham

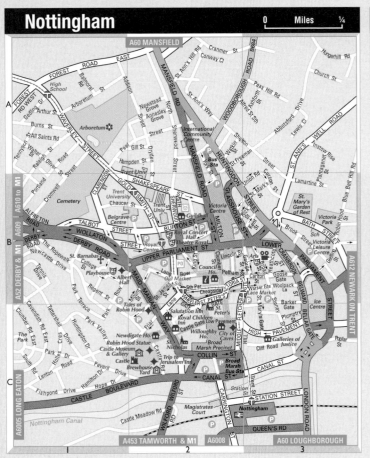

Oxford

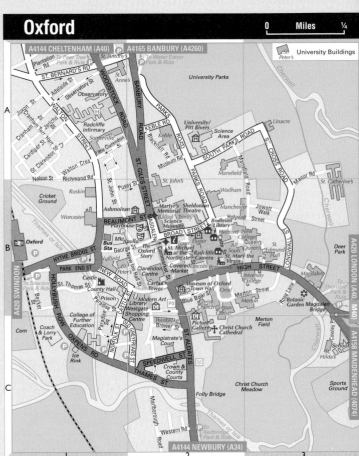

Plymouth

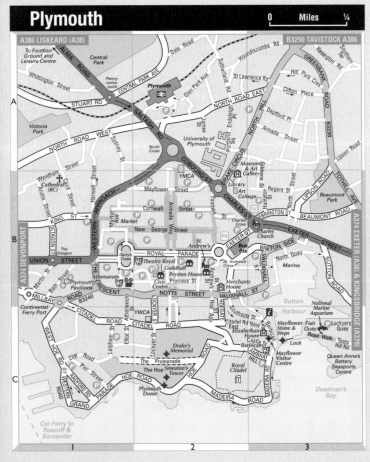

Portsmouth

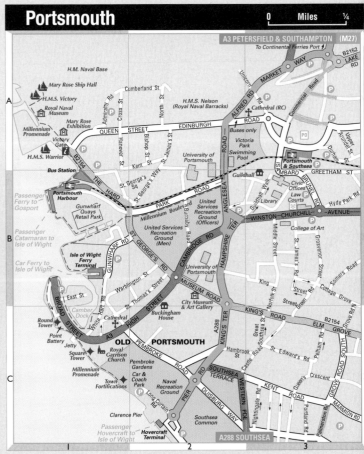

Reading

0 Miles ¼

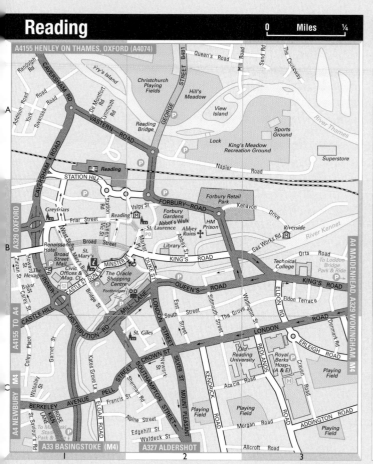

Salisbury

0 Miles ¼

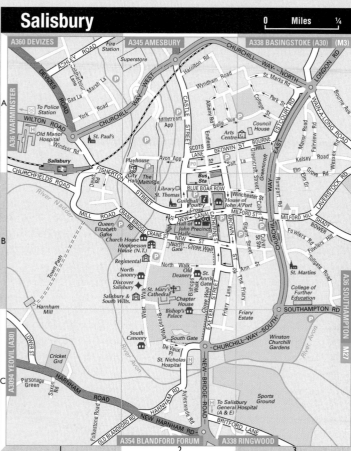

Scarborough

0 Miles ¼

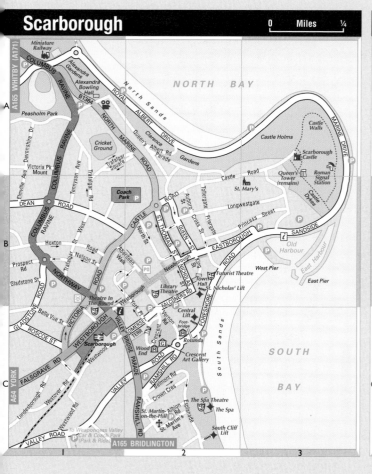

Southampton

0 Miles ¼

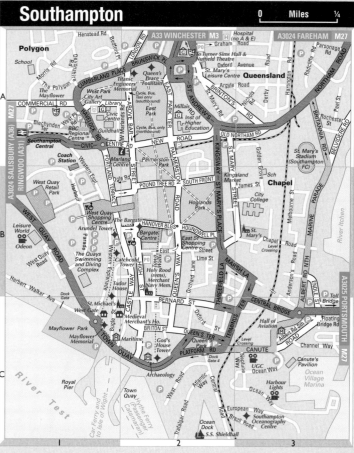

Sheffield

0 — Miles — ¼

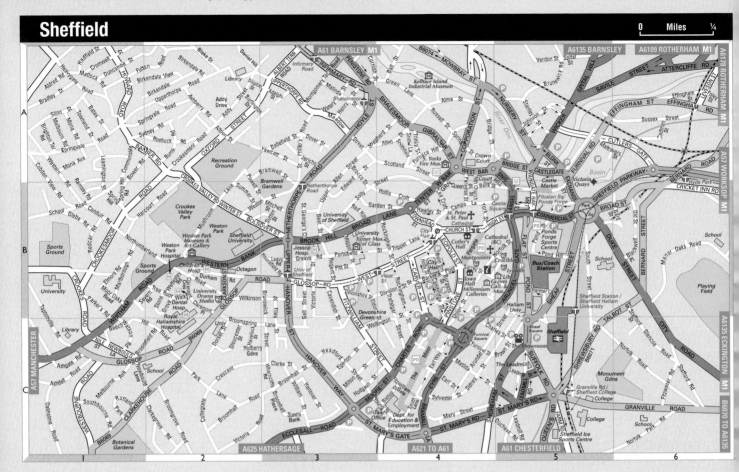

A61 BARNSLEY M1 · B6074 · A6135 Barnsley · A6109 ROTHERHAM M1 · A6178 ROTHERHAM M1 · A57 WORKSOP M1

ATTERCLIFFE RD · CRICKET INN RD · A6135 ECKINGTON M1 · B6070 A6135

A625 HATHERSAGE · A621 TO A61 · A61 CHESTERFIELD

A57 MANCHESTER

Stoke-on-Trent (Hanley)

0 — Miles — ¼

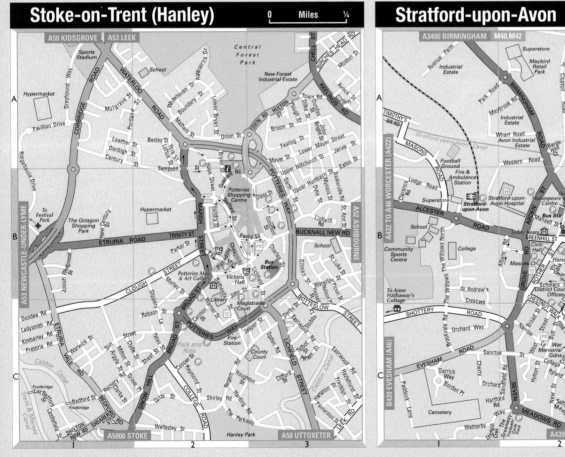

A50 KIDSGROVE · A53 LEEK · A52 ASHBOURNE

A53 NEWCASTLE-UNDER-LYME

A5006 STOKE · A50 UTTOXETER

Stratford-upon-Avon

0 — Miles — ¼

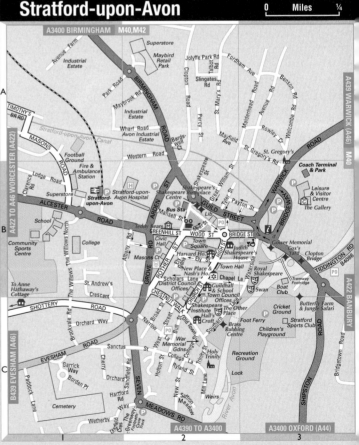

A3400 BIRMINGHAM M40, M42 · A439 WARWICK (A46) M40 · A422 BANBURY

A422 TO A46 WORCESTER (A442)

B439 EVESHAM (A46) · A4390 TO A3400 · A3400 OXFORD (A44)

Sunderland

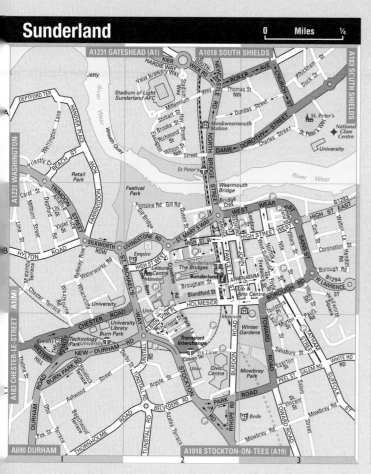

Swansea / Abertawe

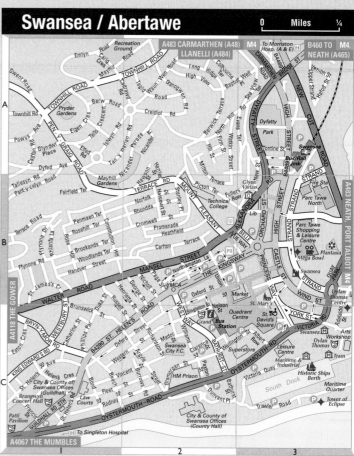

Telford

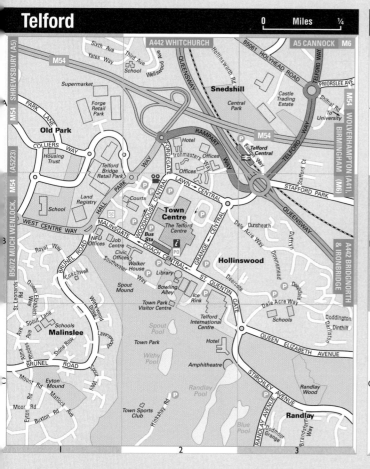

Torquay

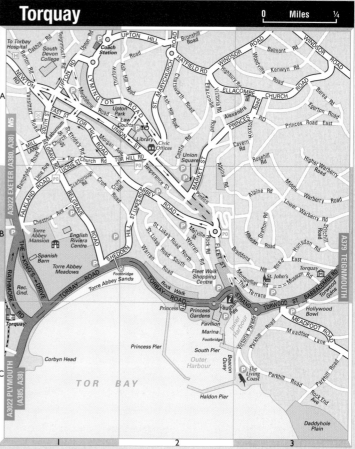

Winchester

0   Miles   ¼

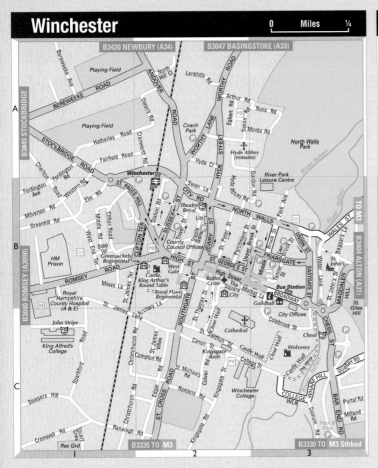

Windsor

0   Miles   ¼

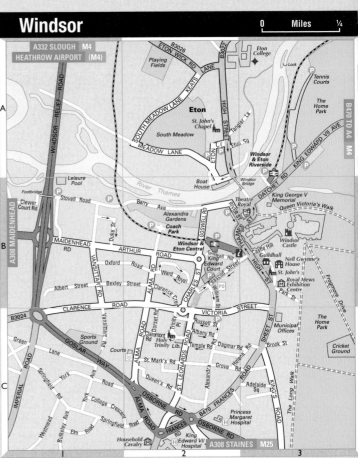

Worcester

0   Miles   ¼

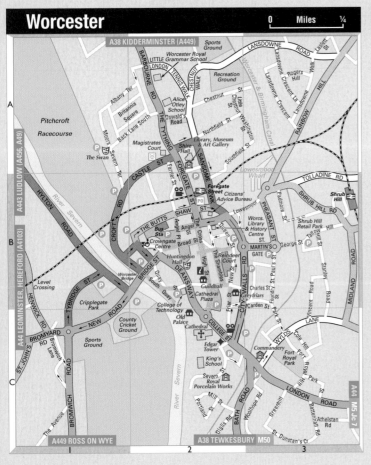

York

0   Miles   ¼

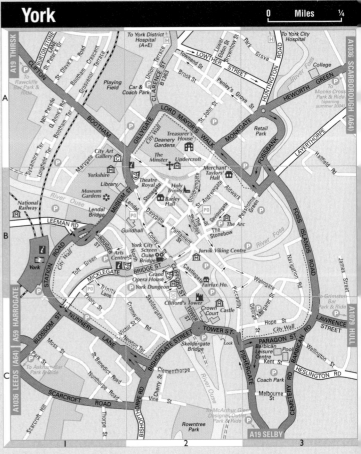

How to use the index

Example: Westcott *Devon* 7 F9
— grid square
— page number
— county or unitary authority

Abbreviations

Aberd C	Aberdeen City	Brighton/Hove	City of Brighton and Hove
Aberds	Aberdeenshire	Bristol	City and County of Bristol
Angl	Isle of Anglesey	Bucks	Buckinghamshire
Arg/Bute	Argyll & Bute	C/Edinb	City of Edinburgh
Bath/NE Som'set	Bath & North East Somerset	C/Glasg	Glasgow City
Beds	Bedfordshire	C/York	City of York
Bl Gwent	Blaenau Gwent	Caerph	Caerphilly
Blackb'n	Blackburn with Darwen	Cambs	Cambridgeshire
Blackp'l	Blackpool	Card	Cardiff
Bournem'th	Bournemouth	Carms	Carmarthenshire
Brackn'l	Bracknell Forest	Ceredig'n	Ceredigion
Bridg	Bridgend	Ches	Cheshire

Clack	Clackmannanshire	Herts	Hertfordshire	Newp	City and County of Newport	Southend	Southend-on-Sea
Cornw'l	Cornwall	I/Man	Isle of Man	Northants	Northamptonshire	Staffs	Staffordshire
Cumb	Cumbria	I/Scilly	Isles of Scilly	Northum	Northumberland	Stirl	Stirling
D'lington	Darlington	I/Wight	Isle of Wight	Nott'ham	City of Nottingham	Stockton	Stockton on Tees
Denbs	Denbighshire	Invercl	Inverclyde	Notts	Nottinghamshire	Stoke	Stoke-on-Trent
Derby	Derbyshire	Kingston/Hull	Kingston upon Hull	Oxon	Oxfordshire	Swan	Swansea
Derby C	Derby City	Lancs	Lancashire	Perth/Kinr	Perth and Kinross	Telford	Telford and Wrekin
Dumf/Gal	Dumfries & Galloway	Leics	Leicestershire	Peterbro	Peterborough	Thur'k	Thurrock
Dundee C	Dundee City	Leics C	Leicester City	Plym'th	Plymouth	Torf	Torfaen
E Ayrs	East Ayrshire	Lincs	Lincolnshire	Portsm'th	Portsmouth	Tyne/Wear	Tyne and Wear
E Dunb	East Dunbartonshire	London	Greater London	Redcar/Clevel'd	Redcar and Cleveland	V/Glam	Vale of Glamorgan
E Loth	East Lothian	M/Keynes	Milton Keynes	Renf	Renfrewshire	W Berks	West Berkshire
E Renf	East Renfrewshire	Mersey	Merseyside	Rh Cyn Taff	Rhondda Cynon Taff	W Dunb	West Dunbartonshire
ER Yorks	East Riding of Yorkshire	Merth Tyd	Merthyr Tydfil	Rutl'd	Rutland	W Isles	Western Isles
E Sussex	East Sussex	Middlesbro	Middlesbrough	S'thampton	Southampton	W Loth	West Lothian
Falk	Falkirk	Midloth	Midlothian	S Ayrs	South Ayrshire	W Midlands	West Midlands
Flints	Flintshire	Monmouths	Monmouthshire	S Gloucs	South Gloucestershire	W Sussex	West Sussex
Glos	Gloucestershire	N Ayrs	North Ayrshire	S Lanark	South Lanarkshire	W Yorks	West Yorkshire
Gtr Man	Greater Manchester	N Lincs	North Lincolnshire	S Yorks	South Yorkshire	Warwick	Warwickshire
Gwyn	Gwynedd	N Som'set	North Somerset	Scot Borders	Scottish Borders	Wilts	Wiltshire
H'land	Highland	N Yorks	North Yorkshire	Shetl'd	Shetland	Windsor	Windsor and Maidenhead
Hants	Hampshire	Neath P Talb	Neath Port Talbot	Shrops	Shropshire	Worcs	Worcestershire
Hartlep'l	Hartlepool					Wrex	Wrexham
Heref'd	Herefordshire						

Asgarby Lincs 47 F7
Ash Kent 20 E2
Ash Kent 21 F9
Ash Som'set 8 B3
Ash Surrey 18 F5
Ash Bullayne Devon 7 F6
Ash Green Warwick 35 G9
Ash Magna Shrops 34 B1
Ash Mill Devon 7 D6
Ash Priors Som'set 7 D10
Ash Street Suffolk 31 D7
Ash Thomas Devon 7 E9
Ash Vale Surrey 18 F5
Ashampstead W Berks 18 D2
Ashbocking Suffolk 31 C8
Ashbourne Derby 44 H5
Ashbrittle Som'set 7 D9
Ashburton Devon 5 E8
Ashbury Devon 6 G4
Ashbury Oxon 17 C9
Ashby N Lincs 46 B3
Ashby by Partney Lincs 47 F8
Ashby cum Fenby NE Lincs 46 B6
Ashby de la Launde Lincs 46 G4
Ashby-de-la-Zouch Leics 35 D9
Ashby Folville Leics 36 D3
Ashby Magna Leics 36 F1
Ashby Parva Leics 35 G11
Ashby Puerorum Lincs 47 E7
Ashby St Ledgers Northants 28 B2
Ashby St Mary Norfolk 39 E9
Ashchurch Glos 26 E6
Ashcombe Devon 5 D10
Ashcott Som'set 15 H10
Ashdon Essex 30 D2
Ashe Hants 18 G2
Asheldham Essex 20 A6
Ashen Essex 30 D4
Ashendon Bucks 28 G4
Ashfield Carms 24 F3
Ashfield Stirl 75 G10
Ashfield Suffolk 31 B9
Ashfield Green Suffolk 31 A9
Ashfold Crossways W Sussex 11 B11
Ashford Devon 6 C4
Ashford Hants 9 C10
Ashford Kent 13 B9
Ashford Surrey 19 D7
Ashford Bowdler Shrops 26 A2
Ashford Carbonell Shrops 26 A2
Ashford Hill Hants 18 E2
Ashford in the Water Derby 44 F5
Ashgill S Lanarks 68 F6
Ashill Devon 7 E9
Ashill Norfolk 38 E4
Ashill Som'set 8 C2
Ashingdon Essex 20 B5
Ashington Northum 63 E8
Ashington Som'set 8 B4
Ashington W Sussex 11 C10
Ashintully Castle Perth/Kinr 76 A4
Ashkirk Scot Borders 61 A10
Ashlett Hants 10 D3
Ashleworth Glos 26 F5
Ashley Cambs 30 B3
Ashley Ches 43 D10
Ashley Devon 6 E5
Ashley Dorset 9 D10
Ashley Glos 16 B6
Ashley Hants 10 E1
Ashley Hants 10 A2
Ashley Northants 36 F3
Ashley Staffs 34 B3
Ashley Green Bucks 28 H6
Ashley Heath Dorset 9 D10
Ashley Heath Staffs 34 B3
Ashmanhaugh Norfolk 39 C9
Ashmansworth Hants 17 F11
Ashmansworthy Devon 6 E2
Ashmore Dorset 9 C8
Ashorne Warwick 27 C10
Ashover Derby 45 F7
Ashow Warwick 27 A10
Ashprington Devon 5 F9
Ashreigney Devon 6 E5
Ashtead Surrey 19 F8
Ashton Ches 43 F8
Ashton Cornw'l 2 G5
Ashton Hants 10 C4
Ashton Heref'd 26 B2
Ashton Inverd 73 F11
Ashton Northants 28 D4
Ashton Northants 37 G6
Ashton Common Wilts 16 F5
Ashton-In-Makerfield Gtr Man 43 C8
Ashton Keynes Wilts 17 B7
Ashton under Hill Worcs 26 E6
Ashton-under-Lyne Gtr Man 44 C3
Ashton upon Mersey Gtr Man 43 C10
Ashurst Hants 10 C2
Ashurst Kent 12 C4
Ashurst W Sussex 11 C10
Ashurstwood W Sussex 12 C3
Ashwater Devon 6 G2
Ashwell Herts 29 E9
Ashwell Rutl'd 36 D4
Ashwell Som'set 8 C2
Ashwellthorpe Norfolk 39 F7
Ashwick Som'set 16 G3
Ashwicken Norfolk 38 D3
Ashybank Scot Borders 61 B11
Askam in Furness Cumb 49 B2
Askern S Yorks 45 A9
Askerswell Dorset 8 E4
Askett Bucks 28 H5
Askham Cumb 57 D7
Askham Notts 45 E11
Askham Bryan C/York 52 E1
Askham Richard C/York 51 E11
Asknish Arg/Bute 73 D8
Askrigg N Yorks 57 G11
Askwith N Yorks 51 E7
Aslackby Lincs 37 B6
Aslacton Norfolk 39 F7
Aslockton Notts 36 B3
Asloun Aberds 83 B7
Aspatria Cumb 56 B3
Aspenden Herts 29 F10
Asperton Lincs 37 B8
Aspley Guise Beds 28 E6
Aspley Heath Beds 28 E6
Aspull Gtr Man 43 B9
Asselby ER Yorks 52 G3
Asserby Lincs 47 E8
Assington Suffolk 30 E6
Assynt Ho. H'land 87 E8
Astbury Ches 44 F2
Astcote Northants 28 C3
Asterley Shrops 33 E9
Asterton Shrops 33 F9
Asthall Oxon 27 G9
Asthall Leigh Oxon 27 G10
Astley Shrops 33 D11
Astley Warwick 35 G9
Astley Worcs 26 B4
Astley Abbotts Shrops 34 F3
Astley Bridge Gtr Man 43 A10
Astley Cross Worcs 26 B5
Astley Green Gtr Man 43 C10
Aston Ches 43 H9
Aston Ches 43 E8
Aston Derby 44 D5
Aston Heref'd 25 A11
Aston Herts 29 F9
Aston Oxon 17 A10
Aston Shrops 33 C11
Aston Staffs 34 A3
Aston S Yorks 45 D8
Aston Telford 34 E2
Aston W Midlands 35 G6
Aston Wokingham 18 C4
Aston Abbotts Bucks 28 F5
Aston Botterell Shrops 34 G2
Aston-by-Stone Staffs 34 B5
Aston Cantlow Warwick 27 C8
Aston Clinton Bucks 28 G5
Aston Crews Heref'd 26 F3
Aston Cross Glos 26 E6
Aston End Herts 29 F9
Aston Eyre Shrops 34 F2
Aston Fields Worcs 26 B6
Aston Ingham Heref'd 26 F3
Aston juxta Mondrum Ches 43 G9
Aston le Walls Northants 27 C11
Aston Magna Glos 27 E8
Aston Munslow Shrops 33 G11
Aston on Clun Shrops 33 G9
Aston-on-Trent Derby 35 C10
Aston Rogers Shrops 33 E9
Aston Rowant Oxon 18 B4
Aston Sandford Bucks 28 H4
Aston Somerville Worcs 27 E7
Aston Subedge Glos 27 D8
Aston Tirrold Oxon 18 C2
Aston Upthorpe Oxon 18 C2
Astrop Northants 28 E2
Astwick Beds 29 E9
Astwood M/Keynes 28 D6
Astwood Worcs 26 C5
Astwood Bank Worcs 27 B7
Aswarby Lincs 37 B6
Aswardby Lincs 47 E7
Atch Lench Worcs 27 C7
Atcham Shrops 33 E11
Athelhampton Dorset 9 E6
Athelington Suffolk 31 A9
Athelney Som'set 8 B2
Athelstaneford E Loth 70 C4
Atherington Devon 6 D4
Atherstone Warwick 35 F9
Atherstone on Stour Warwick 27 C9
Atherton Gtr Man 43 B9
Atley Hill N Yorks 58 F3
Atlow Derby 44 H6
Attadale H'land 86 H2
Attadale Ho. H'land 86 H2
Attenborough Notts 35 B11
Atterby Lincs 46 C3
Attercliffe S Yorks 45 D7
Attleborough Norfolk 38 F6
Attleborough Warwick 35 F9
Attlebridge Norfolk 39 D7
Atwick ER Yorks 53 D7
Atworth Wilts 16 E5
Aubourn Lincs 46 F3
Auchagallon N Ayrs 66 C1
Auchallater Aberds 82 E3
Aucharnie Aberds 89 D6
Auchattie Aberds 83 D8
Auchavan Angus 82 G3
Auchbreck Moray 82 A4
Auchenback E Renf 68 E4
Auchenbainzie Dumf/Gal 60 D4
Auchenblae Aberds 83 F9
Auchenbrack Dumf/Gal 60 D3
Auchenbreck Arg/Bute 73 E9
Auchencairn Dumf/Gal 55 D10
Auchencairn Dumf/Gal 60 E5
Auchencairn N Ayrs 66 D3
Auchencrosh S Ayrs 54 B4
Auchencrow Scot Borders 71 D7
Auchendinny Midloth 69 D11
Auchengray S Lanarks 69 E8
Auchenhalrig Moray 88 B3
Auchenheath S Lanarks 69 F7
Auchenlochan Arg/Bute 73 F8
Auchenmalg Dumf/Gal 54 D5
Auchensoul S Ayrs 66 G5
Auchentiber N Ayrs 67 B6
Auchertyre H'land 85 F13
Auchgourish H'land 81 B11
Auchincarroch W Dunb 68 B3
Auchindrain Arg/Bute 73 C9
Auchindrean H'land 86 C4
Auchininna Aberds 89 D6
Auchinleck E Ayrs 67 D8
Auchinloch N Lanarks 68 C5
Auchinroath Moray 88 C2
Auchintoul Aberds 83 B7
Auchiries Aberds 89 E10
Auchlee Aberds 83 D10
Auchleven Aberds 83 A8
Auchlochan S Lanarks 69 G7
Auchlossan Aberds 83 C7
Auchlunies Aberds 83 D10
Auchlyne Stirl 75 E8
Auchmacoy Aberds 89 E9
Auchmair Moray 82 A5
Auchmantle Dumf/Gal 54 C4
Auchmillan E Ayrs 67 D8
Auchmithie Angus 77 C9
Auchmuirbridge Fife 76 G5
Auchmull Angus 83 F7
Auchnacree Angus 77 A7
Auchnagallin H'land 87 H13
Auchnagatt Aberds 89 D9
Auchnaha Arg/Bute 73 E8
Auchnashelloch Perth/Kinr 75 F10
Aucholzie Aberds 82 D5
Auchrannie Angus 76 B5
Auchroisk H'land 82 A2
Auchronie Angus 82 E6
Auchterarder Perth/Kinr 76 F2
Auchteraw H'land 80 C5
Auchterderran Fife 76 H5
Auchterhouse Angus 76 D6
Auchtermuchty Fife 76 F5
Auchterneed H'land 87 E8
Auchtertool Fife 69 A11
Auchtertyre Moray 88 C1
Auchtubh Stirl 75 E8
Auckengill H'land 94 D5
Auckley S Yorks 45 B10
Audenshaw Gtr Man 44 C3
Audlem Ches 34 A2
Audley Staffs 43 G10
Audley End Essex 30 E5
Auds Aberds 89 B6
Aughton ER Yorks 52 F3
Aughton Lancs 43 B6
Aughton Lancs 50 C1
Aughton S Yorks 45 D8
Aughton Wilts 17 F9
Aughton Park Lancs 43 B7
Auldearn H'land 87 F12
Aulden Heref'd 25 C11
Auldgirth Dumf/Gal 60 E5
Auldhame E Loth 70 B4
Auldhouse S Lanarks 68 E5
Ault a'chruinn H'land 80 A1
Aultanrynie H'land 92 F6
Aultbea H'land 91 J13
Aultdearg H'land 86 E5
Aultgrishan H'land 91 J12
Aultguish Inn H'land 86 D6
Aultibea H'land 93 G13
Aultiphurst H'land 93 C11
Aultmore Moray 88 C4
Aultnagoire H'land 81 A7
Aultnamain Inn H'land 87 C9
Aultnaslat H'land 80 C3
Aulton Aberds 83 A8
Aundorach H'land 82 B1
Aunsby Lincs 36 B6
Auquhorthies Aberds 89 F8
Aust S Glos 16 C2
Austendike Lincs 37 C8
Austerfield S Yorks 45 C10
Austrey Warwick 35 E8
Austwick N Yorks 50 C3
Authorpe Lincs 47 D8
Authorpe Row Lincs 47 E9
Avebury Wilts 17 E8
Aveley Thurr'k 20 C2
Avening Glos 16 B5
Averham Notts 45 G11
Aveton Gifford Devon 5 G7
Avielochan H'land 81 B11
Aviemore H'land 81 B10
Avington Hants 10 A4
Avington W Berks 17 E10
Avoch H'land 87 F10
Avon Hants 9 E10
Avon Dassett Warwick 27 D11
Avonbridge Falk 69 C8
Avonmouth Bristol 15 D11
Avonwick Devon 5 F8
Awbridge Hants 10 B2
Awhirk Dumf/Gal 54 D3
Awkley S Glos 16 C2
Awliscombe Devon 7 F10
Awre Glos 26 H4
Awsworth Notts 35 A10
Axbridge Som'set 15 F10
Axford Hants 18 G3
Axford Wilts 17 D9
Axminster Devon 8 E1
Axmouth Devon 8 E1
Axton Flints 42 D4
Aycliff Kent 21 G10
Aycliffe Durham 58 D3
Aydon Northum 62 G6
Aylburton Glos 16 A3
Ayle Northum 57 B9
Aylesbeare Devon 7 G9
Aylesbury Bucks 28 G5
Aylesby NE Lincs 46 B6
Aylesford Kent 20 F4
Aylesham Kent 21 F9
Aylestone Leics C 36 E1
Aylmerton Norfolk 39 B7
Aylsham Norfolk 39 C7
Aylton Heref'd 26 E3
Aymestrey Heref'd 25 B11
Aynho Northants 28 E2
Ayot St Lawrence Herts 29 G8
Ayot St Peter Herts 29 G9
Ayr S Ayrs 66 D6
Aysgarth N Yorks 58 H1
Ayside Cumb 49 A3
Ayston Rutl'd 36 E4
Aythorpe Roding Essex 30 G2
Ayton Scot Borders 71 D8
Aywick Shetl'd 96 E7
Azerley N Yorks 51 B8

B

Babbacombe Torbay 5 E10
Babbinswood Shrops 33 B9
Babcary Som'set 8 B4
Babel Carms 24 E5
Babell Flints 42 E4
Babraham Cambs 30 C2
Babworth Notts 45 D10
Bac W Isles 91 C9
Bachau Angl 40 B6
Back of Keppoch H'land 79 C9
Back Rogerton E Ayrs 67 D8
Backaland Orkney 95 E6
Backaskaill Orkney 95 C5
Backbarrow Cumb 49 A3
Backe Carms 23 E7
Backfolds Aberds 89 C10
Backford Ches 43 E7
Backford Cross Ches 43 E6
Backhill Aberds 89 E7
Backhill Aberds 89 E10
Backhill of Clackriach Aberds 89 D9
Backhill of Fortree Aberds 89 D9
Backhill of Trustach Aberds 83 D8
Backies H'land 93 J11
Backlass H'land 94 E4
Backwell N Som'set 15 E10
Backworth Tyne/Wear 63 F9
Bacon End Essex 30 G3
Baconsthorpe Norfolk 39 B7
Bacton Heref'd 25 E10
Bacton Norfolk 39 B9
Bacton Suffolk 31 B7
Bacton Green Suffolk 31 B7
Bacup Lancs 50 G4
Badachro H'land 85 A12
Badanloch Lodge H'land 93 F10
Badavanich H'land 86 F4
Badbury Swindon 17 C8
Badby Northants 28 C2
Badcall H'land 92 D5
Badcaul H'land 86 B3
Baddeley Green Stoke 44 G3
Baddesley Clinton Warwick 27 A9
Baddesley Ensor Warwick 35 F8
Baddidarach H'land 92 G3
Baddoch Aberds 82 E3
Baddock H'land 87 F10
Badenscoth Aberds 89 E7
Badenyon Aberds 82 B5
Badger Shrops 34 F3
Badger's Mount Kent 19 E11
Badgeworth Glos 26 G6
Badgworth Som'set 15 F9
Badicaul H'land 85 F12
Badingham Suffolk 31 B10
Badlesmere Kent 21 F7
Badlipster H'land 94 F4
Badluarach H'land 86 B2
Badminton S Glos 16 C5
Badnaban H'land 92 G3
Badninish H'land 87 B10
Badrallach H'land 86 B3
Badsey Worcs 27 D7
Badshot Lea Surrey 18 G5
Badsworth W Yorks 45 A8
Badwell Ash Suffolk 30 B6
Bae Colwyn = Colwyn Bay Conwy 41 C10
Bag Enderby Lincs 47 E7
Bagby N Yorks 51 A10
Bagendon Glos 27 H7
Bagh a Chaisteil = Castlebay W Isles 84 J1
Bagh Mor W Isles 84 C3
Bagh Shiarabhagh W Isles 84 H2
Baghasdal W Isles 84 G2
Bagillt Flints 42 E5
Baginton Warwick 27 A10
Baglan Neath P Talb 14 B3
Bagley Shrops 33 C10
Bagnall Staffs 44 G3
Bagnor W Berks 17 E11
Bagshot Surrey 18 E6
Bagshot Wilts 17 E10
Bagthorpe Norfolk 38 B3
Bagthorpe Notts 45 G8
Bagworth Leics 35 E10
Bagwy Llydiart Heref'd 25 F11
Bail Ard Bhuirgh W Isles 91 B9
Bail Uachdraich W Isles 84 B3
Baildon W Yorks 51 F7
Baile W Isles 90 J4
Baile a Mhanaich W Isles 84 C2
Baile Ailein W Isles 91 E7
Baile an Truiseil W Isles 91 B8
Baile Boidheach Arg/Bute 72 F6
Baile Glas W Isles 84 C3
Baile Mhartainn W Isles 84 A2
Baile Mhic Phail W Isles 84 A3
Baile Mor Arg/Bute 78 J5
Baile Mor W Isles 84 B2
Baile na Creige W Isles 84 H1
Baile nan Cailleach W Isles 84 C2
Baile Raghaill W Isles 84 A2
Bailebeag H'land 81 B7
Baileyhead Cumb 61 F11
Bailiesward Aberds 88 E4
Baillieston C/Glasg 68 D5
Baill'lochdrach W Isles 84 C3
Baill'Ur Tholastaidh W Isles 91 C10
Bainbridge N Yorks 57 G11
Bainsford Falk 69 B7
Bainshole Aberds 88 E6
Bainton ER Yorks 52 D5
Bainton Peterbro 37 E6
Bairnkine Scot Borders 62 B2
Baker Street Thurr'k 20 C3
Baker's End Herts 29 G10
Bakewell Derby 44 F6
Bala = Y Bala Gwyn 32 B5
Balachuirn H'land 85 D10
Balavil H'land 81 C9
Balbeg H'land 86 H7
Balbeggie Perth/Kinr 76 E4
Balbithan Aberds 83 B9
Balbithan Ho. Aberds 83 B10
Balblair H'land 87 E10
Balblair H'land 87 B8
Balby S Yorks 45 B9
Balchladich H'land 92 F3
Balchraggan H'land 87 H8
Balchraggan H'land 87 G8
Balchrick H'land 92 D4
Balchrystie Fife 77 G7
Balcladaich H'land 80 A4
Balcombe W Sussex 12 C2
Balcombe Lane W Sussex 12 C2
Balcomie Fife 77 F9
Balcurvie Fife 76 G6
Baldersby N Yorks 51 B9
Baldersby St James N Yorks 51 B9
Balderstone Lancs 50 F2
Balderton Ches 42 F6
Balderton Notts 46 G2
Baldhu Cornw'l 3 E6
Baldinnie Fife 77 F7
Baldock Herts 29 E9
Baldovie Dundee C 77 D7
Baldrine I/Man 48 D4
Baldslow E Sussex 13 E6
Baldwin I/Man 48 D3
Baldwinholme Cumb 56 A5
Baldwin's Gate Staffs 34 A3
Bale Norfolk 38 B6
Balearn Aberds 89 C10
Balemartine Arg/Bute 78 G2
Balephuil Arg/Bute 78 G2
Balerno C/Edinb 69 D10
Balevullin Arg/Bute 78 G2
Balfield Angus 83 G7
Balfour Orkney 95 G5
Balfron Stirl 68 B4
Balfron Station Stirl 68 B4
Balgaveny Aberds 89 D6
Balgavies Angus 77 B8
Balgonar Fife 69 A9
Balgove Aberds 89 E8
Balgowan H'land 81 D8
Balgown H'land 85 B8
Balgrochan E Dunb 68 C5
Balgy H'land 85 C13
Balhaldie Stirl 75 G11
Balhalgardy Aberds 83 A9
Balham London 19 D9
Balhary Perth/Kinr 76 C5
Baliasta Shetl'd 96 C8
Baligill H'land 93 C11
Balintore Angus 76 B5
Balintore H'land 87 D11
Balintraid H'land 87 D10
Balk N Yorks 51 A10
Balkeerie Angus 76 C6
Balkemback Angus 76 D6
Balkholme ER Yorks 52 G3
Balkissock S Ayrs 54 A4
Ball Shrops 33 C9
Ball Haye Green Staffs 44 G3
Ball Hill Hants 17 E11
Ballabeg I/Man 48 E2
Ballacannel I/Man 48 D4
Ballachulish H'land 74 B3
Ballajora I/Man 48 C4
Ballaleigh I/Man 48 D3
Ballamodha I/Man 48 E2
Ballantrae S Ayrs 54 A3
Ballaquine I/Man 48 D4
Ballards Gore Essex 20 B6
Ballasalla I/Man 48 C3
Ballasalla I/Man 48 E2
Ballater Aberds 82 D5
Ballaugh I/Man 48 C3
Ballaveare I/Man 48 E3
Ballcorach Moray 82 A3
Ballechin Perth/Kinr 76 B2
Balleigh H'land 87 C10
Ballencrieff E Loth 70 C3
Ballentoul Perth/Kinr 81 G10
Ballidon Derby 44 G6
Balliemore Arg/Bute 73 E9
Balliemore Arg/Bute 79 J11
Ballikinrain Stirl 68 B4
Ballimeanoch Arg/Bute 73 B9
Ballimore Arg/Bute 73 E8
Ballimore Stirl 75 F8
Ballinaby Arg/Bute 64 B3
Ballindean Perth/Kinr 76 E5
Ballingdon Suffolk 30 D5
Ballinger Common Bucks 18 A6
Ballingham Heref'd 26 E2
Ballingry Fife 76 H4
Ballinlick Perth/Kinr 76 C2
Ballinluig Perth/Kinr 76 B2
Ballintuim Perth/Kinr 76 B4
Balloch Angus 76 B6
Balloch H'land 87 G10
Balloch N Lanarks 68 C6
Balloch W Dunb 68 B2
Ballochan Aberds 83 D7
Ballochford Moray 88 E3
Ballochmorrie S Ayrs 54 A5
Balls Cross W Sussex 11 B8
Balls Green Essex 31 F7
Ballygown Arg/Bute 78 G7
Ballygrant Arg/Bute 64 B4
Ballyhaugh Arg/Bute 78 F4
Balmacara H'land 85 F13
Balmacara Square H'land 85 F13
Balmaclellan Dumf/Gal 55 B9
Balmacneil Perth/Kinr 76 B2
Balmacqueen H'land 85 A9
Balmae Dumf/Gal 55 E9
Balmaha Stirl 68 A3
Balmalcolm Fife 76 G6
Balmeanach H'land 85 D10
Balmedie Aberds 83 B11
Balmer Heath Shrops 33 B10
Balmerino Fife 76 E6
Balmerlawn Hants 10 D2
Balmichael N Ayrs 66 C2
Balmirmer Angus 77 D8
Balmore H'land 85 D7
Balmore H'land 86 H6
Balmore H'land 87 G11
Balmore Perth/Kinr 76 B2
Balmule Fife 69 B11
Balmullo Fife 77 E7
Balmungie H'land 87 F10
Balnaboth Angus 82 G5
Balnabruaich H'land 87 E10
Balnabruich H'land 94 H3
Balnacoil H'land 93 H11
Balnacra H'land 86 G2
Balnafoich H'land 87 H9
Balnagall H'land 87 C11
Balnaguard Perth/Kinr 76 B2
Balnahard Arg/Bute 72 D3
Balnahard Arg/Bute 78 H7
Balnain H'land 86 H7
Balnakeil H'land 92 C6
Balnaknock H'land 85 B9
Balnapaling H'land 87 E10
Balne N Yorks 52 H1
Balochroy Arg/Bute 65 C8
Balone Fife 77 F7
Balornock C/Glasg 68 D5
Balquharn Perth/Kinr 76 D3
Balquhidder Stirl 75 E8
Balsall W Midlands 35 H8
Balsall Common W Midlands 35 H8
Balsall Heath W Midlands 35 G6
Balscott Oxon 27 D10
Balsham Cambs 30 C2
Baltasound Shetl'd 96 C8
Balterley Staffs 43 G10
Baltersan Dumf/Gal 55 C7
Balthangie Aberds 89 C8
Baltonsborough Som'set 8 A4
Balvaird H'land 87 F8
Balvicar Arg/Bute 72 B6
Balvraid H'land 85 G13
Balvraid H'land 87 H11
Bamber Bridge Lancs 50 G1
Bambers Green Essex 30 F2
Bamburgh Northum 71 G10
Bamff Perth/Kinr 76 B5
Bamford Derby 44 D6
Bamford Gtr Man 44 A2
Bampton Cumb 57 E7
Bampton Devon 7 D8
Bampton Oxon 17 A10
Bampton Grange Cumb 57 E7
Banavie H'land 80 F3
Banbury Oxon 27 D11
Bancffosfelen Carms 23 E9
Banchory Aberds 83 D8
Banchory-Devenick Aberds 83 C11
Bancycapel Carms 23 E9
Bancyfelin Carms 23 E8
Bancyffordd Carms 23 C9
Bandirran Perth/Kinr 76 D5
Banff Aberds 89 B6
Bangor Gwyn 41 C7
Bangor-is-y-coed Wrex 43 H6
Banham Norfolk 39 G6
Bank Hants 10 D1
Bank Newton N Yorks 50 D5
Bank Street Worcs 26 B3
Bankend Dumf/Gal 60 G6
Bankfoot Perth/Kinr 76 D3
Bankglen E Ayrs 67 E9
Bankhead Aberd C 83 B10
Bankhead Aberds 83 C8
Banknock Falk 68 C6
Banks Cumb 61 G11
Banks Lancs 49 G3
Bankshill Dumf/Gal 61 E7
Banningham Norfolk 39 C8
Banniskirk Ho. H'land 94 E3
Bannister Green Essex 30 F3
Bannockburn Stirl 69 A7
Banstead Surrey 19 F9
Bantham Devon 5 G7
Banton N Lanarks 68 C6
Banwell N Som'set 15 F9
Banyard's Green Suffolk 31 A9
Bapchild Kent 20 E6
Bar Hill Cambs 29 B10
Barabhas W Isles 91 C8
Barabhas Iarach W Isles 91 C8
Barabhas Uarach W Isles 91 B8
Barachandroman Arg/Bute 79 J9
Barassie S Ayrs 66 C6
Baravullin Arg/Bute 79 H11
Barbaraville H'land 87 D10
Barber Booth Derby 44 D5
Barbieston S Ayrs 67 E7
Barbon Cumb 50 A2
Barbridge Ches 43 G9
Barbrook Devon 6 B6
Barby Northants 28 A2
Barcaldine Arg/Bute 74 C2
Barcheston Warwick 27 E9
Barcombe E Sussex 12 E3
Barcombe Cross E Sussex 12 E3
Barden N Yorks 58 G2
Barden Scale N Yorks 51 D6
Bardennoch Dumf/Gal 67 G8
Bardfield Saling Essex 30 F3
Bardister Shetl'd 96 F5
Bardney Lincs 46 F5
Bardon Leics 35 D10
Bardon Mill Northum 62 G3
Bardowie E Dunb 68 C4
Bardrainney Inverd 68 C2
Bardsea Cumb 49 B3
Bardsey W Yorks 51 E9
Bardwell Suffolk 30 A6
Bare Lancs 49 C4
Barfad Arg/Bute 73 G7
Barford Norfolk 39 E7
Barford Warwick 27 B9
Barford St John Oxon 27 E11
Barford St Martin Wilts 9 A9
Barford St Michael Oxon 27 E11
Barfrestone Kent 21 F9
Bargod = Bargoed Caerph 15 B7
Bargoed = Bargod Caerph 15 B7
Bargrennan Dumf/Gal 54 B6
Barham Cambs 37 H7
Barham Kent 21 F9
Barham Suffolk 31 C8
Barharrow Dumf/Gal 55 D9
Barhill Dumf/Gal 55 C11
Barholm Lincs 37 E6
Barkby Leics 36 E2
Barkestone-le-Vale Leics 36 B3
Barkham Wokingham 18 E4
Barking London 19 C11
Barking Suffolk 31 C7
Barking Tye Suffolk 31 C7
Barkingside London 19 C11
Barkisland W Yorks 51 H6
Barkston Lincs 36 A5
Barkston N Yorks 51 F10
Barkway Herts 29 E10
Barlaston Staffs 34 B4
Barlavington W Sussex 11 C8
Barlborough Derby 45 E8
Barlby N Yorks 52 F2
Barlestone Leics 35 E10
Barley Herts 29 E10
Barley Lancs 50 E4
Barley Mow Tyne/Wear 58 A3
Barleythorpe Rutl'd 36 E4
Barling Essex 20 C6
Barlow Derby 45 E7
Barlow N Yorks 52 G2
Barlow Tyne/Wear 63 G7
Barmby Moor ER Yorks 52 E3
Barmby on the Marsh ER Yorks 52 G2
Barmer Norfolk 38 B4
Barmoor Castle Northum 71 G8
Barmoor Lane End Northum 71 G9
Barmouth = Abermaw Gwyn 32 D2
Barmpton D'lington 58 E4
Barmston ER Yorks 53 D7
Barnack Peterbro 37 E6
Barnacle Warwick 35 G9
Barnard Castle Durham 58 E1
Barnard Gate Oxon 27 G11
Barnardiston Suffolk 30 D4
Barnbarroch Dumf/Gal 55 D11
Barnburgh S Yorks 45 B8
Barnby Suffolk 39 G10
Barnby Dun S Yorks 45 B10
Barnby in the Willows Notts 46 G2
Barnby Moor Notts 45 D10
Barnes Street Kent 20 G3
Barnet London 19 B9
Barnetby le Wold N Lincs 46 B4
Barney Norfolk 38 B5
Barnham Suffolk 38 H4
Barnham W Sussex 11 D8
Barnham Broom Norfolk 39 E6
Barnhead Angus 77 B9
Barnhill Ches 43 G7
Barnhill Dundee C 77 D7
Barnhill Moray 88 C1
Barnhills Dumf/Gal 54 B2
Barningham Durham 58 E1
Barningham Suffolk 38 H5
Barnoldby le Beck NE Lincs 46 B6
Barnoldswick Lancs 50 E4
Barns Green W Sussex 11 B10
Barnsley Glos 27 H7
Barnsley S Yorks 45 B7
Barnstaple Devon 6 C4
Barnston Essex 30 G3
Barnston Mersey 42 D5
Barnstone Notts 36 B3
Barnt Green Worcs 27 A7
Barnton Ches 43 E9
Barnton C/Edinb 69 C10
Barnwell All Saints Northants 36 G6
Barnwell St Andrew Northants 36 G6
Barnwood Glos 26 G5
Barochreal Arg/Bute 79 J11
Barons Cross Heref'd 25 C11
Barr S Ayrs 66 G5
Barra Castle Aberds 83 A9
Barrachan Dumf/Gal 54 E6
Barrack Aberds 89 D8
Barraglom W Isles 90 D6
Barrahormid Arg/Bute 72 E6
Barran Arg/Bute 79 J11
Barrapol Arg/Bute 78 G2
Barras Aberds 83 E10
Barras Cumb 57 E10
Barrasford Northum 62 F5
Barravullin Arg/Bute 73 C7
Barregarrow I/Man 48 D3
Barrhead E Renf 68 E3
Barrhill S Ayrs 54 A5
Barrington Cambs 29 D10
Barrington Som'set 8 C2
Barripper Cornw'l 2 F5
Barrmill N Ayrs 67 A6
Barrock H'land 94 C4
Barrock Ho. H'land 94 D4
Barrow Lancs 50 F3
Barrow Rutl'd 36 D4
Barrow Suffolk 30 B4
Barrow Green Kent 20 E6
Barrow Gurney N Som'set 15 E11
Barrow Haven N Lincs 53 G6
Barrow-in-Furness Cumb 49 C2
Barrow Island Cumb 49 C1
Barrow Nook Lancs 43 B7
Barrow Street Wilts 9 A7
Barrow upon Humber N Lincs 53 G6
Barrow upon Soar Leics 36 D1
Barrow upon Trent Derby 35 C9
Barroway Drove Norfolk 38 E1
Barrowburn Northum 62 B4
Barrowby Lincs 36 B4
Barrowcliff N Yorks 59 H11
Barrowden Rutl'd 36 E5
Barrowford Lancs 50 F4
Barrows Green Ches 43 G9
Barrows Green Cumb 57 H7
Barrow's Green Mersey 43 D8
Barry Angus 77 D8
Barry = Y Barri V/Glam 15 E7
Barry Island V/Glam 15 E7
Barsby Leics 36 D2
Barsham Suffolk 39 G9
Barston W Midlands 35 H8
Bartestree Heref'd 26 D2
Barthol Chapel Aberds 89 E8
Barthomley Ches 43 G10
Bartley Hants 10 C2
Bartley Green W Midlands 34 G6
Bartlow Cambs 30 D2
Barton Cambs 29 C11
Barton Ches 43 G7
Barton Glos 27 F8
Barton Lancs 42 B6
Barton Lancs 49 F5
Barton N Yorks 58 F3
Barton Oxon 28 H2
Barton Torbay 5 E10
Barton Warwick 27 C8
Barton Bendish Norfolk 38 E3
Barton Hartshorn Bucks 28 E3
Barton in Fabis Notts 35 B11
Barton in the Beans Leics 35 E9
Barton-le-Clay Beds 29 E7
Barton-le-Street N Yorks 52 B3
Barton-le-Willows N Yorks 52 C3
Barton Mills Suffolk 30 A4
Barton on Sea Hants 9 E11
Barton on the Heath Warwick 27 E9
Barton St David Som'set 8 A4
Barton Seagrave Northants 36 H4
Barton Stacey Hants 17 G11
Barton Turf Norfolk 39 C9
Barton-under-Needwood Staffs 35 D7
Barton-upon-Humber N Lincs 52 G6
Barton Waterside N Lincs 52 G6
Barugh S Yorks 45 B7
Barway Cambs 37 H11
Barwell Leics 35 F10
Barwick Herts 29 G10
Barwick Som'set 8 C4
Barwick in Elmet W Yorks 51 F9
Baschurch Shrops 33 C10
Bascote Warwick 27 B11
Basford Green Staffs 44 G3
Bashall Eaves Lancs 50 E2
Bashley Hants 9 E11
Basildon Essex 20 C4
Basingstoke Hants 18 F3
Baslow Derby 44 E6
Bason Bridge Som'set 15 G9
Bassaleg Newp 15 C8
Bassenthwaite Cumb 56 C4
Bassett S'thampton 10 C3
Bassingbourn Cambs 29 D10
Bassingfield Notts 36 B2
Bassingham Lincs 46 F3
Bassingthorpe Lincs 36 C5
Basta Shetl'd 96 D7
Baston Lincs 37 D7
Bastwick Norfolk 39 D10
Baswick Steer ER Yorks 53 E6
Batchworth Heath Herts 19 B7
Batcombe Dorset 8 D5
Batcombe Som'set 16 H3
Bate Heath Ches 43 E9
Batford Herts 29 G8
Bath Bath/NE Som'set 16 E4
Bathampton Bath/NE Som'set 16 E4
Bathealton Som'set 7 D9
Batheaston Bath/NE Som'set 16 E4
Bathford Bath/NE Som'set 16 E4
Bathgate W Loth 69 D8
Bathley Notts 45 G11
Bathpool Cornw'l 4 D3
Bathpool Som'set 8 B1
Bathville W Loth 69 D8
Batley W Yorks 51 G8
Batsford Glos 27 E8
Battersby N Yorks 59 F6
Battersea London 19 D9
Battisborough Cross Devon 5 G6
Battisford Suffolk 31 C7
Battisford Tye Suffolk 31 C7
Battle E Sussex 12 E6
Battle Powys 25 E7
Battledown Glos 26 F6
Battlefield Shrops 33 D11
Battlesbridge Essex 20 B4
Battlesden Beds 28 F6
Battlesea Green Suffolk 39 H8
Battleton Som'set 7 D8
Battram Leics 35 E10
Battramsley Hants 10 E2
Baughton Worcs 26 D5
Baughurst Hants 18 F2
Baulking Oxon 17 B10
Baumber Lincs 46 E6
Baunton Glos 17 A7
Baverstock Wilts 9 A9
Bawburgh Norfolk 39 E7
Bawdeswell Norfolk 38 C6
Bawdrip Som'set 15 H9
Bawdsey Suffolk 31 D10
Bawtry S Yorks 45 C10
Baxenden Lancs 50 G3
Baxterley Warwick 35 F8
Baybridge Hants 10 B4
Baycliff Cumb 49 B2
Baydon Wilts 17 D9
Bayford Herts 29 H10
Bayford Som'set 8 B6
Bayles Cumb 57 B9
Baylham Suffolk 31 C8
Baynard's Green Oxon 28 F2
Bayston Hill Shrops 33 E10
Baythorn End Essex 30 D4
Bayton Worcs 26 A3
Beach H'land 79 F10
Beachampton Bucks 28 E4
Beachamwell Norfolk 38 E3
Beachans Moray 87 G13
Beacharr Arg/Bute 65 D7
Beachborough Kent 21 H8
Beachley Glos 16 B2
Beacon Devon 7 F10
Beacon End Essex 30 F6
Beacon Hill Surrey 18 H5
Beacon's Bottom Bucks 18 B4
Beaconsfield Bucks 18 C6
Beacrabhaic W Isles 90 H6
Beadlam N Yorks 52 A2
Beadlow Beds 29 E8
Beadnell Northum 71 H11
Beaford Devon 6 E4
Beal Northum 71 F9
Beal N Yorks 51 G11
Beamhurst Staffs 35 B6
Beaminster Dorset 8 D3
Beamish Durham 58 A3
Beamsley N Yorks 51 D6
Bean Kent 20 D2
Beanacre Wilts 16 E6
Beanley Northum 62 B6
Beaquoy Orkney 95 F4
Bear Cross Bournem'th 9 E9
Beardwood Blackb'n 50 G2
Beare Green Surrey 19 G8
Bearley Warwick 27 B8
Bearnus Arg/Bute 78 G6
Bearpark Durham 58 B3
Bearsbridge Northum 62 H3
Bearsden E Dunb 68 C4
Bearsted Kent 20 F4
Bearstone Shrops 34 B3
Bearwood Heref'd 25 C10
Bearwood Poole 9 E9
Bearwood W Midlands 34 G6
Beattock Dumf/Gal 60 C6
Beauchamp Roding Essex 30 G2
Beauchief S Yorks 45 D7
Beaufort Bl Gwent 25 G8
Beaufort Castle H'land 87 G8
Beaulieu Hants 10 D2
Beauly H'land 87 G8
Beaumaris Angl 41 C8
Beaumont Cumb 61 H9
Beaumont Essex 31 F8
Beaumont Hill D'lington 58 E3
Beausale Warwick 27 A9
Beauworth Hants 10 B4
Beaworthy Devon 6 G3
Beazley End Essex 30 F4
Bebington Mersey 42 D6
Bebside Northum 63 E8
Beccles Suffolk 39 F10
Becconsall Lancs 49 G4
Beck Foot Cumb 57 G8
Beck Hole N Yorks 59 F9
Beck Row Suffolk 38 H2
Beck Side Cumb 49 A2
Beckbury Shrops 34 E3
Beckenham London 19 E10
Beckermet Cumb 56 F2
Beckfoot Cumb 56 F3
Beckfoot Cumb 56 B2
Beckford Worcs 26 E6
Beckhampton Wilts 17 E7
Beckingham Lincs 46 G2
Beckingham Notts 45 D11
Beckington Som'set 16 F5
Beckley E Sussex 13 D7
Beckley Hants 9 E11
Beckley Oxon 28 G2
Beckton London 19 C11
Beckwithshaw N Yorks 51 D8
Becontree London 19 C11
Bed-y-coedwr Gwyn 32 C3
Bedale N Yorks 58 H3
Bedburn Durham 58 C2
Bedchester Dorset 9 C7
Beddau Rh Cyn Taff 14 C6
Beddgelert Gwyn 41 F7
Beddingham E Sussex 12 F3
Beddington London 19 E10
Bedfield Suffolk 31 B9
Bedford Beds 29 C7
Bedham W Sussex 11 B9
Bedhampton Hants 10 D6
Bedingfield Suffolk 31 B8
Bedlam N Yorks 51 C8
Bedlington Northum 63 E8
Bedlington Station Northum 63 E8
Bedlinog Merth Tyd 14 A6
Bedminster Bristol 16 D2
Bedmond Herts 19 A7
Bednall Staffs 34 D5
Bedrule Scot Borders 62 B2
Bedstone Shrops 33 H9
Bedwas Caerph 15 C7
Bedworth Warwick 35 G9
Bedworth Little Heath Warwick 35 G9
Beeby Leics 36 E2
Beech Hants 18 H3
Beech Staffs 34 B4
Beech Hill Gtr Man 43 B8
Beech Hill W Berks 18 E3
Beechingstoke Wilts 17 F7
Beedon W Berks 17 D11
Beeford ER Yorks 53 D7
Beeley Derby 44 F6
Beelsby NE Lincs 46 B6
Beenham W Berks 18 E2
Beeny Cornw'l 4 B2
Beer Devon 7 H11
Beer Hackett Dorset 8 C4
Beercrocombe Som'set 8 B2
Beesands Devon 5 G9
Beesby Lincs 47 D8
Beeson Devon 5 G9
Beeston Beds 29 D8
Beeston Ches 43 G8
Beeston Norfolk 38 D5
Beeston Notts 35 B11
Beeston W Yorks 51 F8
Beeston Regis Norfolk 39 A7
Beeswing Dumf/Gal 55 C11
Beetham Cumb 49 B4
Beetley Norfolk 38 D5
Begbroke Oxon 27 G11
Begelly Pembs 22 F6
Beggar's Bush Powys 25 B9
Beguildy Powys 33 H7
Beighton Norfolk 39 E9
Beighton S Yorks 45 D8
Beighton Hill Derby 44 G6
Beith N Ayrs 66 A6
Bekesbourne Kent 21 F8
Belaugh Norfolk 39 D8
Belbroughton Worcs 34 H5
Belchamp Otten Essex 30 D5
Belchamp St Paul Essex 30 D4
Belchamp Walter Essex 30 D5
Belchford Lincs 46 E6
Belford Northum 71 G10
Belhaven E Loth 70 C5
Belhelvie Aberds 83 B11
Belhinnie Aberds 82 A6
Bell Bar Herts 29 H9
Bell Busk N Yorks 50 D5
Bell End Worcs 34 H5
Bell o' th'Hill Ches 43 H8
Bellabeg Aberds 82 B5
Bellamore S Ayrs 66 H5
Bellanoch Arg/Bute 72 D6
Bellaty Angus 76 B5
Belleau Lincs 47 E8
Bellehiglash Moray 88 E1
Bellerby N Yorks 58 G2
Bellever Devon 5 D7
Belliehill Angus 77 A8
Bellingdon Bucks 28 H6
Bellingham Northum 62 E4
Belloch Arg/Bute 65 E7
Bellochantuy Arg/Bute 65 E7
Bells Yew Green E Sussex 12 C5
Bellsbank E Ayrs 67 F7
Bellshill N Lanarks 68 D6
Bellshill Northum 71 G10
Bellspool Scot Borders 69 G10
Bellsquarry W Loth 69 D9
Belmaduthy H'land 87 F9
Belmesthorpe Rutl'd 36 E6
Belmont Blackb'n 50 H2
Belmont London 19 E9
Belmont S Ayrs 66 D6
Belmont Shetl'd 96 C7
Belnacraig Aberds 82 B5
Belowda Cornw'l 3 C8
Belper Derby 45 H7
Belper Lane End Derby 45 H7
Belsay Northum 63 F7

Caldwell *Derby* 35 D8
Caldwell *N Yorks* 58 E2
Caldy *Mersey* 42 D5
Caledrhydiau *Ceredig'n* 23 A9
Calfsound *Orkney* 95 E6
Calgary *Arg/Bute* 78 F6
Califer *Moray* 87 F13
California *Falk* 69 C8
California *Norfolk* 39 D11
Calke *Derby* 35 C9
Callakille *H'land* 85 C11
Callaly *Northum* 62 C6
Callander *Stirl* 75 G9
Callaughton *Shrops* 34 F2
Callestick *Cornw'l* 3 D6
Calligarry *H'land* 85 H11
Callington *Cornw'l* 4 E4
Callow *Heref'd* 25 E11
Callow End *Worcs* 26 D5
Callow Hill *Wilts* 17 C7
Callow Hill *Worcs* 26 A4
Callows Grave *Worcs* 26 B2
Calmore *Hants* 10 C2
Calmsden *Glos* 27 H7
Calne *Wilts* 17 D7
Calow *Derby* 45 E8
Calshot *Hants* 10 D3
Calstock *Cornw'l* 4 E5
Calstone Wellington *Wilts* 17 E7
Calthorpe *Norfolk* 39 B7
Calthwaite *Cumb* 56 B6
Calton *N Yorks* 50 D5
Calton *Staffs* 44 G5
Calveley *Ches* 43 G8
Calver *Derby* 44 E6
Calver Hill *Heref'd* 25 D10
Calverhall *Shrops* 34 B2
Calverleigh *Devon* 7 E8
Calverley *W Yorks* 51 F8
Calvert *Bucks* 28 F3
Calverton *M/Keynes* 28 E4
Calverton *Notts* 45 H10
Calvine *Perth/Kinr* 81 G10
Calvo *Cumb* 56 A3
Cam *Glos* 16 B4
Camas-luinie *H'land* 80 A1
Camasnacroise *H'land* 79 F11
Camastianavaig *H'land* 85 E10
Camasunary *H'land* 85 G10
Camault Muir *H'land* 87 G8
Camb *Shetl'd* 96 D7
Camber *E Sussex* 13 E8
Camberley *Surrey* 18 E5
Camberwell *London* 19 D10
Camblesforth *N Yorks* 52 G2
Cambo *Northum* 62 E6
Cambois *Northum* 63 E9
Camborne *Cornw'l* 2 E5
Cambourne *Cambs* 29 C10
Cambridge *Cambs* 29 C11
Cambridge *Glos* 16 A4
Cambridge Town *Southend* 20 C6
Cambus *Clack* 69 A7
Cambusavie Farm *H'land* 87 B10
Cambusbarron *Stirl* 68 A6
Cambuskenneth *Stirl* 69 A7
Cambuslang *S Lanarks* 68 D5
Cambusmore Lodge *H'land* 87 B10
Camden *London* 19 C9
Camelford *Cornw'l* 4 C2
Camelsdale *W Sussex* 11 A7
Camerory *H'land* 87 H13
Camer's Green *Worcs* 26 E4
Camerton *Bath/NE Som'set* 16 F3
Camerton *Cumb* 56 C2
Camerton *ER Yorks* 53 G8
Camghouran *Perth/Kinr* 75 B8
Cammachmore *Aberds* 83 D11
Cammeringham *Lincs* 46 D3
Camore *H'land* 87 B10
Camp Hill *Warwick* 35 F9
Campbeltown *Arg/Bute* 65 F8
Camperdown *Tyne/Wear* 63 F8
Campmuir *Perth/Kinr* 76 D5
Campsall *S Yorks* 45 A9
Campsey Ash *Suffolk* 31 C10
Campton *Beds* 29 E8
Camptown *Scot Borders* 62 B2
Camrose *Pembs* 22 D4
Camserney *Perth/Kinr* 75 C11
Camster *H'land* 94 F4
Camuschoirk *H'land* 79 E10
Camuscross *H'land* 85 G11
Camusnagaul *H'land* 80 F2
Camusnagaul *H'land* 86 C3
Camusrory *H'land* 79 B11
Camusteel *H'land* 85 D12
Camusterrach *H'land* 85 D12
Camusvrachan *Perth/Kinr* 75 C9
Canada *Hants* 10 C1
Canadia *E Sussex* 12 E6
Canal Side *S Yorks* 45 A10
Candacraig Ho. *Aberds* 82 B5
Candlesby *Lincs* 47 F8
Candy Mill *S Lanarks* 69 F9
Cane End *Oxon* 18 D3
Canewdon *Essex* 20 B5
Canford Bottom *Dorset* 9 D9
Canford Cliffs *Poole* 9 F9
Canford Magna *Poole* 9 E9
Canham's Green *Suffolk* 31 B7
Canholes *Derby* 44 E4
Canisbay *H'land* 94 C5
Cann *Dorset* 9 B7
Cann Common *Dorset* 9 B7
Cannard's Grave *Som'set* 16 G3
Cannich *H'land* 86 H6
Cannington *Som'set* 15 H8
Cannock *Staffs* 34 E5
Cannock Wood *Staffs* 34 D6
Canon Bridge *Heref'd* 25 D11
Canon Frome *Heref'd* 26 D3
Canon Pyon *Heref'd* 25 D11
Canonbie *Dumf/Gal* 61 F9
Canons Ashby *Northants* 28 C2
Canonstown *Cornw'l* 2 F4
Canterbury *Kent* 21 F8
Cantley *Norfolk* 39 E9
Cantley *S Yorks* 45 B10
Cantlop *Shrops* 33 E11
Canton *Card* 15 D7
Cantraybruich *H'land* 87 G10
Cantraydoune *H'land* 87 G10
Cantraywood *H'land* 87 G10
Cantsfield *Lancs* 50 B2
Canvey Island *Essex* 20 C4
Canwick *Lincs* 46 F3
Canworthy Water *Cornw'l* 4 B3
Caol *H'land* 80 F3
Caol Ila *Arg/Bute* 64 A5
Caolas *Arg/Bute* 78 G3
Caolas Scalpaigh *W Isles* 90 H7
Caolas Stocinis *W Isles* 90 H6
Capel *Surrey* 19 G8
Capel Bangor *Ceredig'n* 32 G2
Capel Betws Lleucu *Ceredig'n* 24 C3
Capel Carmel *Gwyn* 40 H3
Capel Coch *Angl* 40 B6
Capel Curig *Conwy* 41 E9
Capel Cynon *Ceredig'n* 23 B8
Capel Dewi *Ceredig'n* 23 B9
Capel Dewi *Ceredig'n* 32 G2
Capel Dewi *Carms* 23 D9
Capel Garmon *Conwy* 41 E10
Capel-gwyn *Angl* 40 C5
Capel Gwyn *Carms* 23 D9
Capel Gwynfe *Carms* 24 F4
Capel Hendre *Carms* 23 E10
Capel Hermon *Gwyn* 32 C3
Capel Isaac *Carms* 23 D10
Capel Iwan *Carms* 23 C7
Capel le Ferne *Kent* 21 H9
Capel Llanilltern *Card* 14 C6
Capel Mawr *Angl* 40 C6
Capel St Andrew *Suffolk* 31 D10
Capel St Mary *Suffolk* 31 E7
Capel Seion *Ceredig'n* 32 H2
Capel Tygwydd *Ceredig'n* 23 B7
Capel Uchaf *Gwyn* 40 F6
Capel-y-graig *Gwyn* 41 D7
Capelulo *Conwy* 41 C9
Capenhurst *Ches* 42 E6
Capernwray *Lancs* 49 B5
Capheaton *Northum* 62 E6
Cappercleuch *Scot Borders* 61 A8
Capplegill *Dumf/Gal* 61 C7
Capton *Devon* 5 F9
Caputh *Perth/Kinr* 76 D3
Car Colston *Notts* 36 A3
Carbis Bay *Cornw'l* 2 F4
Carbost *H'land* 85 E8
Carbost *H'land* 85 D9
Carbrook *S Yorks* 45 D7
Carbrooke *Norfolk* 38 E5
Carburton *Notts* 45 E10
Carcant *Scot Borders* 70 E2
Carcary *Angus* 77 B9
Carclaze *Cornw'l* 3 D9
Carcroft *S Yorks* 45 A9
Cardenden *Fife* 69 A11
Cardeston *Shrops* 33 D9
Cardiff = Caerdydd *Card* 15 D7
Cardigan = Aberteifi *Ceredig'n* 22 B6
Cardington *Beds* 29 D7
Cardington *Shrops* 33 F11
Cardinham *Cornw'l* 4 E2
Cardonald *C/Glasg* 68 D4
Cardow *Moray* 88 D1
Cardrona *Scot Borders* 70 G2
Cardross *Arg/Bute* 68 C2
Cardurnock *Cumb* 61 H7
Careby *Lincs* 36 D6
Careston *Angus* 77 B8
Carew *Pembs* 22 F5
Carew Cheriton *Pembs* 22 F5
Carew Newton *Pembs* 22 F5
Carey *Heref'd* 26 E2
Carfrae *E Loth* 70 D4
Cargenbridge *Dumf/Gal* 60 F5
Cargill *Perth/Kinr* 76 D4
Cargo *Cumb* 61 H9
Cargreen *Cornw'l* 4 E5
Carham *Northum* 71 G7
Carhampton *Som'set* 7 B9
Carharrack *Cornw'l* 2 E6
Carie *Perth/Kinr* 75 D9
Carie *Perth/Kinr* 75 B9
Carines *Cornw'l* 3 D6
Carisbrooke *I/Wight* 10 F3
Cark *Cumb* 49 B3
Carlabhagh *W Isles* 90 C7
Carland Cross *Cornw'l* 3 D7
Carlby *Lincs* 37 D6
Carlecotes *S Yorks* 44 B5
Carlesmoor *N Yorks* 51 B7
Carleton *Cumb* 57 D7
Carleton *Cumb* 56 A6
Carleton *Lancs* 49 F3
Carleton *N Yorks* 50 E5
Carleton Forehoe *Norfolk* 39 E6
Carleton Rode *Norfolk* 39 F7
Carlin How *Redcar/Clevel'd* 59 E8
Carlingcott *Bath/NE Som'set* 16 F3
Carlisle *Cumb* 61 H10
Carlops *Scot Borders* 69 E10
Carlton *Beds* 28 C6
Carlton *Cambs* 30 C3
Carlton *Leics* 35 E9
Carlton *Notts* 36 A2
Carlton *N Yorks* 59 H7
Carlton *N Yorks* 52 G2
Carlton *N Yorks* 51 A6
Carlton *N Yorks* 58 E2
Carlton *Stockton* 58 D4
Carlton *Suffolk* 31 B10
Carlton *S Yorks* 45 A7
Carlton *W Yorks* 51 G9
Carlton Colville *Suffolk* 39 G11
Carlton Curlieu *Leics* 36 F2
Carlton Husthwaite *N Yorks* 51 B10
Carlton in Cleveland *N Yorks* 58 F6
Carlton in Lindrick *Notts* 45 D9
Carlton le Moorland *Lincs* 46 G3
Carlton Miniott *N Yorks* 51 A9
Carlton on Trent *Notts* 45 F11
Carlton Scroop *Lincs* 36 A5
Carluke *S Lanarks* 69 E7
Carmarthen = Caerfyrddin *Carms* 23 D9
Carmel *Angl* 40 B5
Carmel *Carms* 23 E10
Carmel *Flints* 42 E4
Carmel *Guernsey* 11
Carmel *Gwyn* 40 E6
Carmont *Aberds* 83 E10
Carmunnock *C/Glasg* 68 E5
Carmyle *C/Glasg* 68 D5
Carmyllie *Angus* 77 C8
Carn-gorm *H'land* 80 A1
Carnaby *ER Yorks* 53 C7
Carnach *H'land* 86 B3
Carnach *H'land* 80 A2
Carnach *W Isles* 90 H7
Carnachy *H'land* 93 D10
Càrnais *W Isles* 90 D5
Carnbee *Fife* 77 G8
Carnbo *Perth/Kinr* 76 G3
Carnbrea *Cornw'l* 2 E5
Carnduff *S Lanarks* 68 F5
Carnduncan *Arg/Bute* 64 B3
Carne *Cornw'l* 3 F8
Carnforth *Lancs* 49 B4
Carnhedryn *Pembs* 22 D3
Carnhell Green *Cornw'l* 2 F5
Carnkie *Cornw'l* 2 F6
Carnkie *Cornw'l* 2 F5
Carno *Powys* 32 F5
Carnoch *H'land* 86 H6
Carnoch *H'land* 86 F5
Carnock *Fife* 69 B9
Carnon Downs *Cornw'l* 3 E6
Carnousie *Aberds* 89 C6
Carnoustie *Angus* 77 D8
Carnwath *S Lanarks* 69 F8
Carnyorth *Cornw'l* 2 F2
Carperby *N Yorks* 58 H1
Carpley Green *N Yorks* 57 H11
Carr *S Yorks* 45 C9
Carr Hill *Tyne/Wear* 63 G8
Carradale *Arg/Bute* 65 E9
Carragraich *W Isles* 90 H6
Carrbridge *H'land* 81 A11
Carrefour Selous *Jersey* 11
Carreg-wen *Pembs* 23 B7
Carreglefn *Angl* 40 B5
Carrick *Arg/Bute* 73 E8
Carrick *Fife* 77 E7
Carrick Castle *Arg/Bute* 73 D10
Carrick Ho. *Orkney* 95 E6
Carriden *Falk* 69 B9
Carrington *Gtr Man* 43 C10
Carrington *Lincs* 47 G7
Carrington *Midloth* 70 D2
Carrog *Conwy* 41 F9
Carrog *Denbs* 33 A7
Carron *Falk* 69 B7
Carron *Moray* 88 D2
Carron Bridge *N Lanarks* 68 B6
Carronbridge *Dumf/Gal* 60 D4
Carrshield *Northum* 57 B10
Carrutherstown *Dumf/Gal* 61 F7
Carrville *Durham* 58 B4
Carsaig *Arg/Bute* 79 J8
Carsaig *Arg/Bute* 72 E6
Carscreugh *Dumf/Gal* 54 D5
Carse Gray *Angus* 77 B7
Carse Ho. *Arg/Bute* 72 G6
Carsegowan *Dumf/Gal* 55 D7
Carseriggan *Dumf/Gal* 54 C6
Carsethorn *Dumf/Gal* 60 H5
Carshalton *London* 19 E9
Carsington *Derby* 44 G6
Carskiey *Arg/Bute* 65 H7
Carsluith *Dumf/Gal* 55 D7
Carsphairn *Dumf/Gal* 67 G8
Carstairs *S Lanarks* 69 F8
Carstairs Junction *S Lanarks* 69 F8
Carswell Marsh *Oxon* 17 B10
Carter's Clay *Hants* 10 B2
Carterton *Oxon* 27 H9
Carterway Heads *Northum* 58 A1
Carthew *Cornw'l* 3 D9
Carthorpe *N Yorks* 51 A9
Cartington *Northum* 62 C6
Cartland *S Lanarks* 69 F7
Cartmel *Cumb* 49 B3
Cartmel Fell *Cumb* 56 H6
Carway *Carms* 23 F9
Cary Fitzpaine *Som'set* 8 B4
Cas-gwent = Chepstow *Monmouths* 15 B11
Cascob *Powys* 25 D9
Cashlie *Perth/Kinr* 75 C7
Cashmoor *Dorset* 9 C8
Casnewydd = Newport *Newp* 15 C9
Cassey Compton *Glos* 27 G7
Cassington *Oxon* 27 G11
Cassop *Durham* 58 C4
Castell *Denbs* 42 F4
Castell-Howell *Ceredig'n* 23 B9
Castell-Nedd = Neath *Neath P Talb* 14 B3
Castell Newydd Emlyn = Newcastle Emlyn *Carms* 23 B8
Castell-y-bwch *Torf* 15 B8
Castellau *Rh Cyn Taff* 14 C6
Casterton *Cumb* 50 B2
Castle Acre *Norfolk* 38 D4
Castle Ashby *Northants* 28 C5
Castle Bolton *N Yorks* 58 G1
Castle Bromwich *W Midlands* 35 G7
Castle Bytham *Lincs* 36 D5
Castle Caereinion *Powys* 33 E7
Castle Camps *Cambs* 30 D3
Castle Carrock *Cumb* 61 H11
Castle Cary *Som'set* 8 A5
Castle Combe *Wilts* 16 D5
Castle Donington *Leics* 35 C10
Castle Douglas *Dumf/Gal* 55 C10
Castle Eaton *Swindon* 17 B8
Castle Eden *Durham* 58 C5
Castle Forbes *Aberds* 83 B8
Castle Frome *Heref'd* 26 D3
Castle Green *Surrey* 18 E6
Castle Gresley *Derby* 35 D8
Castle Heaton *Northum* 71 F8
Castle Hedingham *Essex* 30 E4
Castle Hill *Kent* 12 B5
Castle Huntly *Perth/Kinr* 76 E6
Castle Kennedy *Dumf/Gal* 54 D4
Castle O'er *Dumf/Gal* 61 D8
Castle Pulverbatch *Shrops* 33 E10
Castle Rising *Norfolk* 38 C2
Castle Stuart *H'land* 87 G10
Castlebay = Bagh a Chaisteil *W Isles* 84 J1
Castlebythe *Pembs* 22 D5
Castlecary *N Lanarks* 68 C6
Castlecraig *H'land* 87 E11
Castlefairn *Dumf/Gal* 60 E3
Castleford *W Yorks* 51 G10
Castlehill *Scot Borders* 69 G11
Castlehill *H'land* 94 D3
Castlehill *W Dunb* 68 C2
Castlemaddy *Dumf/Gal* 67 H8
Castlemartin *Pembs* 22 G4
Castlemilk *Dumf/Gal* 61 F7
Castlemilk *C/Glasg* 68 E5
Castlemorris *Pembs* 22 C4
Castlemorton *Worcs* 26 E4
Castleside *Durham* 58 B1
Castlethorpe *M/Keynes* 28 D5
Castleton *Angus* 76 C6
Castleton *Arg/Bute* 73 E7
Castleton *Derby* 44 D5
Castleton *Gtr Man* 44 A2
Castleton *Newp* 15 C8
Castleton *N Yorks* 59 F7
Castletown *Ches* 43 G7
Castletown *H'land* 94 D3
Castletown *H'land* 87 G10
Castletown *I/Man* 48 F2
Castletown *Tyne/Wear* 63 H9
Castleweary *Scot Borders* 61 C10
Castley *N Yorks* 51 E8
Caston *Norfolk* 38 F5
Castor *Peterbro* 37 F7
Catacol *N Ayrs* 66 B2
Catbrain *S Gloucs* 16 C2
Catbrook *Monmouths* 15 A11
Catchall *Cornw'l* 2 G3
Catchems Corner *W Midlands* 35 H8
Catchgate *Durham* 58 A2
Catcleugh *Northum* 62 C3
Catcliffe *S Yorks* 45 D8
Catcott *Som'set* 15 H9
Caterham *Surrey* 19 F10
Catfield *Norfolk* 39 C9
Catfirth *Shetl'd* 96 H6
Catford *London* 19 D10
Catforth *Lancs* 49 F4
Cathays *Card* 15 D7
Cathcart *C/Glasg* 68 D4
Cathedine *Powys* 25 F8
Catherington *Hants* 10 C5
Catherton *Shrops* 34 H2
Catlodge *H'land* 81 D8
Catlowdy *Cumb* 61 F10
Catmore *W Berks* 17 C11
Caton *Lancs* 49 C5
Caton Green *Lancs* 49 C5
Catrine *E Ayrs* 67 D8
Cat's Ash *Newp* 15 B9
Catsfield *E Sussex* 12 E6
Catshill *Worcs* 26 A6
Cattal *N Yorks* 51 D10
Cattawade *Suffolk* 31 E8
Catterall *Lancs* 49 E4
Catterick *N Yorks* 58 G3
Catterick Bridge *N Yorks* 58 G3
Catterick Garrison *N Yorks* 58 G2
Catterlen *Cumb* 57 C6
Catterline *Aberds* 83 F10
Catterton *N Yorks* 51 E11
Catthorpe *Leics* 36 H1
Cattistock *Dorset* 8 E4
Catton *Northum* 62 H4
Catton *N Yorks* 51 B9
Catwick *ER Yorks* 53 E7
Catworth *Cambs* 29 A7
Caudlesprings *Norfolk* 38 E5
Caulcott *Oxon* 28 F2
Cauldcots *Angus* 77 C9
Cauldhame *Stirl* 68 A5
Cauldmill *Scot Borders* 61 B11
Cauldon *Staffs* 44 H4
Caulkerbush *Dumf/Gal* 60 H5
Caulside *Dumf/Gal* 61 E10
Caunsall *Worcs* 34 G4
Caunton *Notts* 45 G11
Causeway End *Dumf/Gal* 55 C7
Causeway Foot *W Yorks* 51 F6
Causeway-head *Stirl* 75 H10
Causewayend *S Lanarks* 69 G9
Causewayhead *Cumb* 56 A3
Causey Park Bridge *Northum* 63 D7
Causeyend *Aberds* 83 B11
Cautley *Cumb* 57 G8
Cavendish *Suffolk* 30 D5
Cavendish Bridge *Leics* 35 C10
Cavenham *Suffolk* 30 B4
Caversfield *Oxon* 28 F2
Caversham *Reading* 18 D4
Caverswall *Staffs* 34 A5
Cavil *ER Yorks* 52 F3
Cawdor *H'land* 87 F11
Cawkwell *Lincs* 46 E6
Cawood *N Yorks* 52 F1
Cawsand *Cornw'l* 4 F5
Cawston *Norfolk* 39 C7
Cawthorne *S Yorks* 44 B6
Cawthorpe *Lincs* 37 C6
Cawton *N Yorks* 52 B2
Caxton *Cambs* 29 C10
Caynham *Shrops* 26 A2
Caythorpe *Lincs* 46 H3
Caythorpe *Notts* 45 H10
Cayton *N Yorks* 53 A6
Ceann a Bhaigh *W Isles* 84 B2
Ceann a Deas Loch Baghasdail *W Isles* 84 G2
Ceann Shiphoirt *W Isles* 91 F7
Ceann Tarabhaigh *W Isles* 90 F7
Ceannacroc Lodge *H'land* 80 B4
Cearsiadair *W Isles* 91 E8
Cefn Berain *Conwy* 42 F2
Cefn-brith *Conwy* 42 G2
Cefn Canol *Powys* 33 B8
Cefn-coch *Conwy* 41 D10
Cefn Coch *Powys* 33 C7
Cefn-coed-y-cymmer *Merth Tyd* 25 H7
Cefn Cribbwr *Bridg* 14 C4
Cefn Cross *Bridg* 14 C4
Cefn-ddwysarn *Gwyn* 32 B5
Cefn Einion *Shrops* 33 G8
Cefn-gorwydd *Powys* 24 D6
Cefn-mawr *Wrex* 33 A8
Cefn-y-bedd *Flints* 42 G6
Cefn-y-pant *Carms* 22 D6
Cefneithin *Carms* 23 E10
Cei-bach *Ceredig'n* 23 A9
Ceinewydd = New Quay *Ceredig'n* 23 A8
Ceint *Angl* 40 C6
Cellan *Ceredig'n* 24 D3
Cellarhead *Staffs* 44 H3
Cemaes *Angl* 40 A5
Cemmaes *Powys* 32 E4
Cemmaes Road *Powys* 32 E4
Cenarth *Carms* 23 B7
Cenin *Gwyn* 40 F6
Central *Invercl* 73 F11
Ceos *W Isles* 91 E8
Ceres *Fife* 77 F7
Cerne Abbas *Dorset* 8 D5
Cerney Wick *Glos* 17 B7
Cerrigceinwen *Angl* 40 C6
Cerrigydrudion *Conwy* 42 H2
Cessford *Scot Borders* 62 A3
Ceunant *Gwyn* 41 D7
Chaceley *Glos* 26 E5
Chacewater *Cornw'l* 3 E6
Chackmore *Bucks* 28 E3
Chacombe *Northants* 27 D11
Chad Valley *W Midlands* 34 G6
Chadderton *Gtr Man* 44 B3
Chadderton Fold *Gtr Man* 44 B2
Chaddesden *Derby C* 35 B9
Chaddesley Corbett *Worcs* 26 A5
Chaddleworth *W Berks* 17 D11
Chadlington *Oxon* 27 F10
Chadshunt *Warwick* 27 C10
Chadwell *Leics* 36 C3
Chadwell St Mary *Thurr'k* 20 D3
Chadwick End *W Midlands* 27 A9
Chadwick Green *Mersey* 43 C8
Chaffcombe *Som'set* 8 C2
Chagford *Devon* 5 C8
Chailey *E Sussex* 12 E2
Chain Bridge *Lincs* 37 A9
Chainbridge *Cambs* 37 E10
Chainhurst *Kent* 20 G4
Chalbury *Dorset* 9 D9
Chalbury Common *Dorset* 9 D9
Chaldon *Surrey* 19 F10
Chaldon Herring or *Dorset* 9 F6
Chale *I/Wight* 10 G3
Chale Green *I/Wight* 10 G3
Chalfont Common *Bucks* 19 B7
Chalfont St Giles *Bucks* 18 B6
Chalfont St Peter *Bucks* 19 B7
Chalford *Glos* 16 A5
Chalgrove *Oxon* 18 B3
Chalk *Kent* 20 D3
Challacombe *Devon* 6 B5
Challoch *Dumf/Gal* 54 C6
Challock *Kent* 21 F7
Chalton *Beds* 29 F7
Chalton *Hants* 10 C6
Chalvington *E Sussex* 12 F4
Chancery *Ceredig'n* 32 H1
Chandler's Ford *Hants* 10 B3
Channel Tunnel *Kent* 21 H8
Channerwick *Shetl'd* 96 L6
Chantry *Som'set* 16 G4
Chantry *Suffolk* 31 D8
Chapel *Fife* 69 A11
Chapel Allerton *Som'set* 15 F10
Chapel Allerton *W Yorks* 51 F9
Chapel Amble *Cornw'l* 3 B8
Chapel Brampton *Northants* 28 B4
Chapel Chorlton *Staffs* 34 B4
Chapel-en-le-Frith *Derby* 44 D4
Chapel End *Warwick* 35 F9
Chapel Green *Warwick* 35 G8
Chapel Green *Warwick* 27 B11
Chapel Haddlesey *N Yorks* 52 G1
Chapel Head *Cambs* 37 G9
Chapel Hill *Aberds* 89 E10
Chapel Hill *Lincs* 46 G6
Chapel Hill *Monmouths* 15 B11
Chapel Hill *N Yorks* 51 E9
Chapel Lawn *Shrops* 33 H9
Chapel-le-Dale *N Yorks* 50 B3
Chapel Milton *Derby* 44 D4
Chapel of Garioch *Aberds* 83 A9
Chapel Row *W Berks* 18 E2
Chapel St Leonards *Lincs* 47 E9
Chapel Stile *Cumb* 56 F5
Chapelgate *Lincs* 37 C10
Chapelhall *N Lanarks* 68 D6
Chapelhill *Dumf/Gal* 60 D6
Chapelhill *H'land* 87 D11
Chapelhill *N Ayrs* 66 B5
Chapelhill *Perth/Kinr* 76 E5
Chapelhill *Perth/Kinr* 76 D3
Chapelknowe *Dumf/Gal* 61 F9
Chapelton *Angus* 77 C9
Chapelton *Devon* 6 D4
Chapelton *H'land* 81 B11
Chapelton *S Lanarks* 68 F5
Chapeltown *Blackb'n* 50 H3
Chapeltown *Moray* 82 A4
Chapeltown *S Yorks* 45 C7
Chapmans Well *Devon* 6 G2
Chapmanslade *Wilts* 16 G5
Chapmore End *Herts* 29 G10
Chappel *Essex* 30 F5
Chard *Som'set* 8 D2
Chardstock *Devon* 8 D2
Charfield *S Gloucs* 16 B4
Charford *Worcs* 26 B6
Charing *Kent* 20 G6
Charing Cross *Dorset* 9 C10
Charing Heath *Kent* 20 G6
Charingworth *Glos* 27 E9
Charlbury *Oxon* 27 G10
Charlcombe *Bath/NE Som'set* 16 E4
Charlecote *Warwick* 27 C9
Charles *Devon* 6 C5
Charles Tye *Suffolk* 31 C7
Charlesfield *Dumf/Gal* 61 G7
Charleston *Angus* 76 C6
Charleston *Renf* 68 D3
Charlestown *Aberd C* 83 C11
Charlestown *Cornw'l* 3 D9
Charlestown *Derby* 44 C4
Charlestown *Dorset* 8 G5
Charlestown *Fife* 69 B9
Charlestown *Gtr Man* 44 B2
Charlestown *H'land* 87 G9
Charlestown *H'land* 85 A13
Charlestown *W Yorks* 50 G5
Charlestown of Aberlour *Moray* 88 D2
Charlesworth *Derby* 44 C4
Charleton *Devon* 5 G8
Charlton *London* 19 D11
Charlton *Hants* 17 G10
Charlton *Herts* 29 F8
Charlton *Northants* 28 E2
Charlton *Northum* 62 E4
Charlton *Som'set* 16 F3
Charlton *Telford* 34 D1
Charlton *Wilts* 9 B8
Charlton *Wilts* 17 F8
Charlton *Wilts* 16 C6
Charlton *Worcs* 27 D7
Charlton *W Sussex* 11 C7
Charlton Abbots *Glos* 27 F7
Charlton Adam *Som'set* 8 B4
Charlton-All-Saints *Wilts* 9 B10
Charlton Horethorne *Som'set* 8 B5
Charlton Kings *Glos* 26 F6
Charlton Mackerell *Som'set* 8 B4
Charlton Marshall *Dorset* 9 D7
Charlton Musgrove *Som'set* 8 B6
Charlton on Otmoor *Oxon* 28 G2
Charltons *Redcar/Clevel'd* 59 E7
Charlwood *Surrey* 19 G9
Charlynch *Som'set* 7 C11
Charminster *Dorset* 8 E5
Charmouth *Dorset* 8 E2
Charndon *Bucks* 28 F3
Charney Bassett *Oxon* 17 B10
Charnock Richard *Lancs* 50 H1
Charsfield *Suffolk* 31 C9
Chart Corner *Kent* 20 F4
Chart Sutton *Kent* 20 G5
Charter Alley *Hants* 18 F2
Charterhouse *Som'set* 15 F10
Charterville Allotments *Oxon* 27 G10
Chartham *Kent* 21 F8
Chartham Hatch *Kent* 21 F8
Chartridge *Bucks* 18 A6
Charvil *Wokingham* 18 D4
Charwelton *Northants* 28 C2
Chasetown *Staffs* 34 E6
Chastleton *Oxon* 27 F9
Chasty *Devon* 6 F2
Chatburn *Lancs* 50 E3
Chatcull *Staffs* 34 B3
Chatham *Medway* 20 E4
Chathill *Northum* 71 H10
Chattenden *Medway* 20 D4
Chatteris *Cambs* 37 G9
Chattisham *Suffolk* 31 D7
Chatto *Scot Borders* 62 B3
Chatton *Northum* 71 H9
Chawleigh *Devon* 6 E6
Chawley *Oxon* 17 A11
Chawston *Beds* 29 C8
Chawton *Hants* 18 H4
Cheadle *Gtr Man* 44 D2
Cheadle *Staffs* 34 A6
Cheadle Heath *Gtr Man* 44 D2
Cheadle Hulme *Gtr Man* 44 D2
Cheam *London* 19 E9
Cheapside *Surrey* 19 F7
Chearsley *Bucks* 28 G4
Chebsey *Staffs* 34 C4
Checkendon *Oxon* 18 C3
Checkley *Ches* 43 H10
Checkley *Heref'd* 26 E2
Checkley *Staffs* 34 B6
Chedburgh *Suffolk* 30 C4
Cheddar *Som'set* 15 F10
Cheddington *Bucks* 28 G6
Cheddleton *Staffs* 44 G3
Cheddon Fitzpaine *Som'set* 8 B1
Chedglow *Wilts* 16 B6
Chedgrave *Norfolk* 39 F9
Chedington *Dorset* 8 D3
Chediston *Suffolk* 39 H9
Chedworth *Glos* 27 G7
Chedzoy *Som'set* 15 H9
Cheeklaw *Scot Borders* 70 E6
Cheeseman's Green *Kent* 13 C9
Cheglinch *Devon* 6 B4
Cheldon *Devon* 7 E6
Chelford *Ches* 44 E2
Chell Heath *Stoke* 44 G2
Chellaston *Derby C* 35 B9
Chellington *Beds* 28 C6
Chelmarsh *Shrops* 34 G3
Chelmer Village *Essex* 30 H4
Chelmondiston *Suffolk* 31 E9
Chelmorton *Derby* 44 F5
Chelmsford *Essex* 30 H4
Chelsea *London* 19 D9
Chelsfield *London* 19 E11
Chelsworth *Suffolk* 30 D6
Cheltenham *Glos* 26 F6
Chelveston *Northants* 28 B6
Chelvey *N Som'set* 15 E10
Chelwood *Bath/NE Som'set* 16 E3
Chelwood Common *E Sussex* 12 D3
Chelwood Gate *E Sussex* 12 D3
Chelworth *Wilts* 16 B6
Chelworth Green *Wilts* 17 B7
Chemistry *Shrops* 33 A11
Chenies *Bucks* 19 B7
Cheny Longville *Shrops* 33 G10
Chepstow = Cas-gwent *Monmouths* 15 B11
Chequerfield *W Yorks* 51 G10
Cherhill *Wilts* 17 D7
Cherington *Glos* 16 B6
Cherington *Warwick* 27 E9
Cheriton *Devon* 7 B6
Cheriton *Hants* 10 B4
Cheriton *Kent* 21 H8
Cheriton *Swan* 23 G9
Cheriton Bishop *Devon* 7 G6
Cheriton Fitzpaine *Devon* 7 F7
Cheriton or Stackpole Elidor *Pembs* 22 G4
Cherrington *Telford* 34 C2
Cherry Burton *ER Yorks* 52 E5
Cherry Hinton *Cambs* 29 C11
Cherry Orchard *Worcs* 26 C5
Cherry Willingham *Lincs* 46 E4
Cherrybank *Perth/Kinr* 76 E4
Chertsey *Surrey* 19 E7
Cheselbourne *Dorset* 9 E6
Chesham *Bucks* 18 A6
Chesham Bois *Bucks* 18 B6
Cheshunt *Herts* 19 A10
Cheslyn Hay *Staffs* 34 E5
Chessington *London* 19 E8
Chester *Ches* 43 F7
Chester-Le-Street *Durham* 58 A3
Chester Moor *Durham* 58 B3
Chesterblade *Som'set* 16 G3
Chesterfield *Derby* 45 E7
Chesters *Scot Borders* 62 B2
Chesters *Scot Borders* 62 A2
Chesterton *Cambs* 37 F7
Chesterton *Cambs* 29 B11
Chesterton *Glos* 17 A7
Chesterton *Oxon* 28 F2
Chesterton *Shrops* 34 F3
Chesterton *Staffs* 44 H2
Chesterton *Warwick* 27 C10
Chesterwood *Northum* 62 G4
Chestfield *Kent* 21 E8
Cheston *Devon* 5 F7
Cheswardine *Shrops* 34 C3
Cheswick *Northum* 71 F9
Chetnole *Dorset* 8 D5
Chettiscombe *Devon* 7 E8
Chettisham *Cambs* 37 G11
Chettle *Dorset* 9 C8
Chetton *Shrops* 34 F2
Chetwode *Bucks* 28 F3
Chetwynd Aston *Telford* 34 D3
Cheveley *Cambs* 30 B3
Chevening *Kent* 19 F11
Chevington *Suffolk* 30 C4
Chevithorne *Devon* 7 E8
Chew Magna *Bath/NE Som'set* 16 E2
Chew Stoke *Bath/NE Som'set* 16 E2
Chewton Keynsham *Bath/NE Som'set* 16 E3
Chewton Mendip *Som'set* 16 F2
Chicheley *M/Keynes* 28 D6
Chichester *W Sussex* 11 D7
Chickerell *Dorset* 8 F5
Chicklade *Wilts* 9 A8
Chicksgrove *Wilts* 9 A8
Chidden *Hants* 10 C5
Chiddingfold *Surrey* 18 H6
Chiddingly *E Sussex* 12 E4
Chiddingstone *Kent* 19 G11
Chiddingstone Causeway *Kent* 20 G2
Chiddingstone Hoath *Kent* 12 B3
Chideock *Dorset* 8 E3
Chidham *W Sussex* 11 D6
Chidswell *W Yorks* 51 G8
Chieveley *W Berks* 17 D11
Chignall St James *Essex* 30 H3
Chignall Smealy *Essex* 30 G3
Chigwell *Essex* 19 B11
Chigwell Row *Essex* 19 B11
Chilbolton *Hants* 17 H10
Chilcomb *Hants* 10 B4
Chilcombe *Dorset* 8 E4
Chilcompton *Som'set* 16 F3
Chilcote *Leics* 35 D8
Child Okeford *Dorset* 9 C7
Childer Thornton *Ches* 42 E6
Childrey *Oxon* 17 C10
Child's Ercall *Shrops* 34 C2
Childswickham *Worcs* 27 E7
Childwall *Mersey* 43 D7
Childwick Green *Herts* 29 G8
Chilfrome *Dorset* 8 E4
Chilgrove *W Sussex* 11 C7
Chilham *Kent* 21 F7
Chilhampton *Wilts* 9 A9
Chilla *Devon* 6 F3
Chillaton *Devon* 4 C5
Chillenden *Kent* 21 F9
Chillerton *I/Wight* 10 F3
Chillesford *Suffolk* 31 C10
Chillingham *Northum* 71 H9
Chillington *Devon* 5 G8
Chillington *Som'set* 8 C2
Chilmark *Wilts* 9 A8
Chilson *Oxon* 27 G10
Chilsworthy *Cornw'l* 4 D5
Chilsworthy *Devon* 6 F2
Chilthorne Domer *Som'set* 8 C4
Chiltington *E Sussex* 12 E2
Chilton *Bucks* 28 G3
Chilton *Durham* 58 D3
Chilton *Oxon* 17 C11
Chilton Cantelo *Som'set* 8 B4
Chilton Foliat *Wilts* 17 D10
Chilton Lane *Durham* 58 C4
Chilton Polden *Som'set* 15 H9
Chilton Street *Suffolk* 30 D4
Chilton Trinity *Som'set* 15 H8
Chilvers Coton *Warwick* 35 F9
Chilwell *Notts* 35 B11
Chilworth *Hants* 10 C3
Chilworth *Surrey* 19 G7
Chimney *Oxon* 17 A10
Chineham *Hants* 18 F3
Chingford *London* 19 B10
Chinley *Derby* 44 D4
Chinley Head *Derby* 44 D4
Chinnor *Oxon* 18 A4
Chipnall *Shrops* 34 B3
Chippenhall Green *Suffolk* 39 H8
Chippenham *Cambs* 30 B3
Chippenham *Wilts* 16 D6
Chipperfield *Herts* 19 A7
Chipping *Herts* 29 E10
Chipping *Lancs* 50 E2
Chipping Campden *Glos* 27 E8
Chipping Hill *Essex* 30 G5
Chipping Norton *Oxon* 27 F10
Chipping Ongar *Essex* 20 A2
Chipping Sodbury *S Gloucs* 16 C4
Chipping Warden *Northants* 27 D11
Chipstable *Som'set* 7 D9
Chipstead *Kent* 19 F11
Chipstead *Surrey* 19 F9
Chirbury *Shrops* 33 F8
Chirk = Y Waun *Wrex* 33 B8
Chirk Bank *Shrops* 33 B8
Chirmorrie *S Ayrs* 54 B5
Chirnside *Scot Borders* 71 E7
Chirnsidebridge *Scot Borders* 71 E7
Chirton *Wilts* 17 F7
Chisbury *Wilts* 17 E9
Chiselborough *Som'set* 8 C3
Chiseldon *Swindon* 17 D8
Chiserley *W Yorks* 50 G6
Chislehampton *Oxon* 18 B2
Chislehurst *London* 19 D11
Chislet *Kent* 21 E9
Chiswell Green *Herts* 19 A8
Chiswick *London* 19 D9
Chiswick End *Cambs* 29 D10
Chisworth *Derby* 44 C3
Chithurst *W Sussex* 11 B7
Chittering *Cambs* 29 A11
Chitterne *Wilts* 16 G6
Chittlehamholt *Devon* 6 D5
Chittlehampton *Devon* 6 D5
Chittoe *Wilts* 16 E6
Chivenor *Devon* 6 C4
Chobham *Surrey* 18 E6
Choicelee *Scot Borders* 70 E6
Cholderton *Wilts* 17 G9
Cholesbury *Bucks* 28 H6
Chollerford *Northum* 62 F5
Chollerton *Northum* 62 F5
Cholmondeston *Ches* 43 F9
Cholsey *Oxon* 18 C2
Cholstrey *Heref'd* 25 C11
Chop Gate *N Yorks* 59 G6
Choppington *Northum* 63 E8
Chopwell *Tyne/Wear* 63 H7
Chorley *Ches* 43 G8
Chorley *Lancs* 50 H1
Chorley *Shrops* 34 G2
Chorley *Staffs* 35 D6
Chorleywood *Herts* 19 B7
Chorlton cum Hardy *Gtr Man* 44 C2
Chorlton Lane *Ches* 43 H7
Choulton *Shrops* 33 G9
Chowdene *Tyne/Wear* 63 H8
Chowley *Ches* 43 G7
Chrishall *Essex* 29 E11
Christchurch *Cambs* 37 F10
Christchurch *Dorset* 9 E10
Christchurch *Glos* 26 G2
Christchurch *Newp* 15 C9
Christian Malford *Wilts* 16 D6
Christleton *Ches* 43 F7
Christmas Common *Oxon* 18 B4
Christon *N Som'set* 15 F9
Christon Bank *Northum* 63 A8
Christow *Devon* 5 C9
Chryston *N Lanarks* 68 C5
Chudleigh *Devon* 5 D9
Chudleigh Knighton *Devon* 5 D9
Chulmleigh *Devon* 6 E5
Chunal *Derby* 44 C4
Church *Lancs* 50 G3
Church Aston *Telford* 34 D3
Church Brampton *Northants* 28 B4
Church Broughton *Derby* 35 B8
Church Crookham *Hants* 18 F5
Church Eaton *Staffs* 34 D4
Church End *Beds* 28 F6
Church End *Beds* 29 E8
Church End *Beds* 28 E6
Church End *Cambs* 37 G8
Church End *Cambs* 37 E9
Church End *ER Yorks* 53 D6
Church End *Essex* 30 D2
Church End *Essex* 30 F4
Church End *Hants* 18 F3
Church End *Lincs* 37 B8
Church End *Warwick* 35 F8
Church End *Warwick* 35 F8
Church End *Wilts* 17 D7
Church Enstone *Oxon* 27 F10
Church Fenton *N Yorks* 51 F11
Church Green *Devon* 7 G10
Church Green *Norfolk* 39 F6
Church Gresley *Derby* 35 D8
Church Hanborough *Oxon* 27 G11
Church Hill *Ches* 43 F9
Church Houses *N Yorks* 59 G7
Church Knowle *Dorset* 9 F8
Church Laneham *Notts* 46 E2
Church Langton *Leics* 36 F3
Church Lawford *Warwick* 35 H10
Church Lawton *Ches* 44 G2
Church Leigh *Staffs* 34 B6
Church Lench *Worcs* 27 C7
Church Mayfield *Staffs* 35 A7
Church Minshull *Ches* 43 F9
Church Norton *W Sussex* 11 E7
Church Preen *Shrops* 33 F11
Church Pulverbatch *Shrops* 33 E10
Church Stoke *Powys* 33 F8
Church Stowe *Northants* 28 C3
Church Street *Kent* 20 D4
Church Stretton *Shrops* 33 F10
Church Town *N Lincs* 45 B11
Church Town *Surrey* 19 F10
Church Village *Rh Cyn Taff* 14 C6
Church Warsop *Notts* 45 F9
Churcham *Glos* 26 G4
Churchbank *Shrops* 33 H8
Churchbridge *Staffs* 34 E5
Churchdown *Glos* 26 G5
Churchend *Essex* 30 F3
Churchend *Essex* 21 B7
Churchend *S Gloucs* 16 B4
Churchfield *W Midlands* 34 F6
Churchgate Street *Essex* 29 G11
Churchill *Devon* 6 B4
Churchill *Devon* 8 D2
Churchill *N Som'set* 15 F10
Churchill *Oxon* 27 F9
Churchill *Worcs* 34 H4
Churchill *Worcs* 26 C6
Churchinford *Som'set* 7 E11
Churchover *Warwick* 35 G11
Churchstanton *Som'set* 7 E10
Churchstow *Devon* 5 G8
Churchtown *Derby* 44 F6
Churchtown *I/Man* 48 C4
Churchtown *Lancs* 49 E4
Churchtown *Mersey* 49 H3
Churnsike Lodge *Northum* 62 F2
Churston Ferrers *Torbay* 5 F10
Churt *Surrey* 18 H5
Churton *Ches* 43 G7
Churwell *W Yorks* 51 G8
Chute Standen *Wilts* 17 F10
Chwilog *Gwyn* 40 G6
Chyandour *Cornw'l* 2 F3
Cilan Uchaf *Gwyn* 40 H4
Cilcain *Flints* 42 F4
Cilcennin *Ceredig'n* 24 B2
Cilfor *Gwyn* 41 G8
Cilfrew *Neath P Talb* 14 A3
Cilfynydd *Rh Cyn Taff* 14 B6
Cilgerran *Pembs* 22 B6
Cilgwyn *Carms* 24 F4
Cilgwyn *Gwyn* 40 E6
Cilgwyn *Pembs* 22 C5
Ciliau Aeron *Ceredig'n* 23 A9
Cill Donnain *W Isles* 84 F2
Cille Bhrighde *W Isles* 84 G2
Cille Pheadair *W Isles* 84 G2
Cilmery *Powys* 25 C7
Cilsan *Carms* 23 D10
Ciltalgarth *Gwyn* 41 F10
Cilwendeg *Pembs* 23 C7
Cilybebyll *Neath P Talb* 14 A3
Cilycwm *Carms* 24 E4
Cimla *Neath P Talb* 14 B3
Cinderford *Glos* 26 G3
Cippyn *Pembs* 22 B6
Circebost *W Isles* 90 D6
Cirencester *Glos* 17 A7
Ciribhig *W Isles* 90 C6
City *London* 19 C10
City *Powys* 33 G8
City Dulas *Angl* 40 B6
Clachaig *Arg/Bute* 73 E10
Clachan *Arg/Bute* 72 H6
Clachan *Arg/Bute* 72 B6
Clachan *Arg/Bute* 79 G11
Clachan *Arg/Bute* 74 F4
Clachan *H'land* 85 E10
Clachan *W Isles* 84 D2
Clachan na Luib *W Isles* 84 B3
Clachan of Campsie *E Dunb* 68 C5
Clachan of Glendaruel *Arg/Bute* 73 E8
Clachan-Seil *Arg/Bute* 72 B6
Clachan Strachur *Arg/Bute* 73 C9
Clachaneasy *Dumf/Gal* 54 B6
Clachanmore *Dumf/Gal* 54 E3
Clachbreck *Arg/Bute* 72 F6
Clachnabrain *Angus* 82 G5
Clachtoll *H'land* 92 G3
Clackmannan *Clack* 69 A8
Clacton-on-Sea *Essex* 31 G8
Cladach Chireboist *W Isles* 84 B2
Claddach-knockline *W Isles* 84 B2
Cladich *Arg/Bute* 74 E3
Claggan *H'land* 79 G9
Claggan *H'land* 80 F3
Claigan *H'land* 84 C7
Claines *Worcs* 26 C5
Clandown *Bath/NE Som'set* 16 F3
Clanfield *Hants* 10 C5
Clanfield *Oxon* 17 A9
Clanville *Hants* 17 G10
Claonaig *Arg/Bute* 73 H7
Claonel *H'land* 93 J8
Clap Hill *Kent* 13 C9
Clapgate *Dorset* 9 D9
Clapgate *Herts* 29 F11
Clapham *Beds* 29 C7
Clapham *London* 19 D9
Clapham *N Yorks* 50 C3
Clapham *W Sussex* 11 D9
Clappers *Scot Borders* 71 E8
Clappersgate *Cumb* 56 F5
Clapton *Som'set* 8 D3
Clapton-in-Gordano *N Som'set* 15 D10
Clapton-on-the-Hill *Glos* 27 G8
Clapworthy *Devon* 6 D5
Clara Vale *Tyne/Wear* 63 G7
Clarach *Ceredig'n* 32 G2
Clarbeston *Pembs* 22 D5
Clarbeston Road *Pembs* 22 D5
Clarborough *Notts* 45 D11
Clardon *H'land* 94 D3
Clare *Suffolk* 30 D4
Clarebrand *Dumf/Gal* 55 C10
Clarencefield *Dumf/Gal* 60 G6
Clarilaw *Scot Borders* 61 B11
Clark's Green *Surrey* 19 H8
Clarkston *E Renf* 68 E4
Clashandorran *H'land* 87 G8
Clashcoig *H'land* 87 B9
Clashindarroch *Aberds* 88 E4
Clashmore *H'land* 92 F3
Clashmore *H'land* 87 C10
Clashnessie *H'land* 92 F3
Clashnoir *Moray* 82 A4
Clate *Shetl'd* 96 G7
Clathy *Perth/Kinr* 76 F2
Clatt *Aberds* 83 A7
Clatter *Powys* 32 F5
Clatterford *I/Wight* 10 F3
Clatterin Bridge *Aberds* 83 F8
Clatworthy *Som'set* 7 C9
Claughton *Lancs* 49 E5
Claughton *Lancs* 50 C1
Claughton *Mersey* 42 D6
Claverdon *Warwick* 27 B8
Claverham *N Som'set* 15 E10
Clavering *Essex* 29 E11
Claverley *Shrops* 34 F3
Claverton *Bath/NE Som'set* 16 E4
Clawdd-newydd *Denbs* 42 G3
Clawthorpe *Cumb* 49 B5
Clawton *Devon* 6 G2
Claxby *Lincs* 46 C5
Claxby *Lincs* 47 E8
Claxton *Norfolk* 39 E9
Claxton *N Yorks* 52 C2
Clay Common *Suffolk* 39 G10
Clay Coton *Northants* 36 H1
Clay Cross *Derby* 45 F7
Clay Hill *W Berks* 18 D2
Clay Lake *Lincs* 37 C8

Crosshill *E Ayrs* 67 D7
Crosshill *Fife* 76 H4
Crosshill *S Ayrs* 66 F6
Crosshouse *E Ayrs* 67 C6
Crossings *Cumb* 61 F11
Crosskeys *Caerph* 15 B8
Crosskirk *H'land* 93 B13
Crosslanes *Shrops* 33 D9
Crosslee *Scot Borders* 61 B9
Crosslee *Renf* 68 D3
Crossmichael *Dumf/Gal* 55 C10
Crossmoor *Lancs* 49 F4
Crossroads *Aberds* 83 D9
Crossroads *E Ayrs* 67 C7
Crossway *Heref'd* 26 E3
Crossway *Monmouths* 25 G11
Crossway *Powys* 25 C7
Crossway Green *Worcs* 26 B5
Crossways *Dorset* 9 F6
Crosswell *Pembs* 22 C6
Crosswood *Ceredig'n* 24 A3
Crosthwaite *Cumb* 56 G6
Croston *Lancs* 49 H4
Crostwick *Norfolk* 39 D8
Crostwight *Norfolk* 39 C9
Crothair *W Isles* 90 D6
Crouch *Kent* 20 F3
Crouch Hill *Dorset* 8 C6
Crouch House Green *Kent* 19 G11
Croucheston *Wilts* 9 B9
Croughton *Northants* 28 E2
Crovie *Aberds* 89 B8
Crow Edge *S Yorks* 44 B5
Crow Hill *Heref'd* 26 F3
Crowan *Cornw'l* 2 F5
Crowborough *E Sussex* 12 C4
Crowcombe *Som'set* 7 C10
Crowdecote *Derby* 44 F5
Crowden *Derby* 44 C4
Crowell *Oxon* 18 B4
Crowfield *Northants* 28 D3
Crowfield *Suffolk* 31 C8
Crowhurst *E Sussex* 13 E6
Crowhurst *Surrey* 19 G10
Crowhurst Lane End *Surrey* 19 G10
Crowland *Lincs* 37 D8
Crowlas *Cornw'l* 2 F4
Crowle *N Lincs* 45 A11
Crowle *Worcs* 26 C6
Crowmarsh Gifford *Oxon* 18 C3
Crown Corner *Suffolk* 31 A9
Crownhill *Plym'th* 4 F5
Crownland *Suffolk* 31 B7
Crownthorpe *Norfolk* 39 E6
Crowntown *Cornw'l* 2 F5
Crows-an-wra *Cornw'l* 2 G2
Crowshill *Norfolk* 38 E5
Crowsnest *Shrops* 33 E9
Crowthorne *Brackn'l* 18 E5
Crowton *Ches* 43 E8
Croxall *Staffs* 35 D7
Croxby *Lincs* 46 C5
Croxdale *Durham* 58 C3
Croxden *Staffs* 35 B6
Croxley Green *Herts* 19 B7
Croxton *Cambs* 29 B9
Croxton *N Lincs* 46 A4
Croxton *Norfolk* 38 G4
Croxton *Staffs* 34 B3
Croxton Kerrial *Leics* 36 C4
Croxtonbank *Staffs* 34 B3
Croy *H'land* 87 G10
Croy *N Lanarks* 68 C6
Croyde *Devon* 6 C3
Croydon *Cambs* 29 D10
Croydon *London* 19 E10
Crubenmore Lodge *H'land* 81 D8
Cruckmeole *Shrops* 33 E10
Cruckton *Shrops* 33 D10
Cruden Bay *Aberds* 89 E10
Crudgington *Telford* 34 D2
Crudwell *Wilts* 16 B6
Crug *Powys* 25 A8
Crugmeer *Cornw'l* 3 B8
Crugybar *Carms* 24 E3
Crulabhig *W Isles* 90 D6
Crumlin = Crymlyn *Caerph* 15 B8
Crumpsall *Gtr Man* 44 B2
Crundale *Kent* 21 G7
Crundale *Pembs* 22 E4
Cruwys Morchard *Devon* 7 E7
Crux Easton *Hants* 17 F11
Crwbin *Carms* 23 E9
Crya *Orkney* 95 H4
Cryers Hill *Bucks* 18 B5
Crymlyn *Gwyn* 41 C8
Crymlyn = Crumlin *Caerph* 15 B8
Crymych *Pembs* 22 C6
Crynant *Neath P Talb* 14 A3
Crynfryn *Ceredig'n* 24 B2
Cuaig *H'land* 85 C12
Cuan *Arg/Bute* 72 B6
Cubbington *Warwick* 27 B10
Cubeck *N Yorks* 57 H11
Cubert *Cornw'l* 3 D6
Cubley *S Yorks* 44 B6
Cubley Common *Derby* 35 B7
Cublington *Bucks* 28 F5
Cublington *Heref'd* 25 E11
Cuckfield *W Sussex* 12 D2
Cucklington *Som'set* 9 B6
Cuckney *Notts* 45 E9
Cuckoo Hill *Notts* 45 C11
Cuddesdon *Oxon* 18 A3
Cuddington *Bucks* 28 G4
Cuddington *Ches* 43 E9
Cuddington Heath *Ches* 43 H7
Cuddy Hill *Lancs* 49 F4
Cudham *London* 19 F11
Cudliptown *Devon* 4 D6
Cudworth *Som'set* 8 C2
Cudworth *S Yorks* 45 B7
Cuffley *Herts* 19 A10
Cuiashader *W Isles* 91 B10
Cuidhir *W Isles* 84 H1
Cuidhtinis *W Isles* 90 J5
Culbo *H'land* 87 E9
Culbokie *H'land* 87 F9
Culburnie *H'land* 86 G7
Culcabock *H'land* 87 G9
Culcairn *H'land* 87 E9
Culcharry *H'land* 87 F11
Culcheth *Warrington* 43 C9
Culdrain *Aberds* 88 E5
Culduie *H'land* 85 D12
Culford *Suffolk* 30 A5
Culgaith *Cumb* 57 D8
Culham *Oxon* 18 B2
Culkein *H'land* 92 F3
Culkein Drumbeg *H'land* 92 F4
Culkerton *Glos* 16 B6
Cullachie *H'land* 81 A11
Cullen *Moray* 88 B5
Cullercoats *Tyne/Wear* 63 F9
Cullicudden *H'land* 87 E9
Cullingworth *W Yorks* 51 F6
Cullipool *Arg/Bute* 72 B6
Cullivoe *Shetl'd* 96 C7
Culloch *Perth/Kinr* 75 F10
Culloden *H'land* 87 G10
Cullompton *Devon* 7 F9
Culmaily *H'land* 87 B11
Culmazie *Dumf/Gal* 54 D6
Culmington *Shrops* 33 G10
Culmstock *Devon* 7 E10
Culnacraig *H'land* 92 J3
Culnaknock *H'land* 85 B10
Culpho *Suffolk* 31 D9
Culrain *H'land* 87 B8
Culross *Fife* 69 B8
Culroy *S Ayrs* 66 E6
Culsh *Aberds* 89 D8
Culsh *Aberds* 82 D5
Culshabbin *Dumf/Gal* 54 D6
Culswick *Shetl'd* 96 J4
Cultercullen *Aberds* 89 F9
Cults *Aberd C* 83 C10
Cults *Aberds* 88 E5
Cults *Dumf/Gal* 55 E7
Culverstone Green *Kent* 20 E3
Culverthorpe *Lincs* 36 A6
Culworth *Northants* 28 D2
Culzie Lodge *H'land* 87 D8
Cumbernauld *N Lanarks* 68 C6
Cumbernauld Village *N Lanarks* 68 C6
Cumberworth *Lincs* 47 E9
Cuminestown *Aberds* 89 C8
Cumlewick *Shetl'd* 96 L6
Cummersdale *Cumb* 56 A5
Cummertrees *Dumf/Gal* 61 G7
Cummingston *Moray* 88 B1
Cumnock *E Ayrs* 67 D8
Cumnor *Oxon* 17 A11
Cumrew *Cumb* 57 A7
Cumwhinton *Cumb* 56 A6
Cumwhitton *Cumb* 57 A7
Cundall *N Yorks* 51 B10
Cunninghamhead *N Ayrs* 67 B6
Cunnister *Shetl'd* 96 D7
Cupar *Fife* 76 F6
Cupar Muir *Fife* 76 F6
Cupernham *Hants* 10 B2
Curbar *Derby* 44 E6
Curbridge *Hants* 10 C4
Curbridge *Oxon* 27 H10
Curdridge *Hants* 10 C4
Curdworth *Warwick* 35 F7
Curland *Som'set* 8 C1
Curlew Green *Suffolk* 31 B10
Currarie *S Ayrs* 66 G4
Curridge *W Berks* 17 D11
Currie *C/Edinb* 69 D10
Curry Mallet *Som'set* 8 B2
Curry Rivel *Som'set* 8 B2
Curtisden Green *Kent* 12 B6
Curtisknowle *Devon* 5 F8
Cury *Cornw'l* 2 G5
Cushnie *Aberds* 89 B7
Cushuish *Som'set* 7 C10
Cusop *Heref'd* 25 D9
Cutcloy *Dumf/Gal* 55 F7
Cutcombe *Som'set* 7 C8
Cutgate *Gtr Man* 44 A2
Cutiau *Gwyn* 32 D2
Cutlers Green *Essex* 30 E2
Cutnall Green *Worcs* 26 B5
Cutsdean *Glos* 27 E7
Cutthorpe *Derby* 45 E7
Cutts *Shetl'd* 96 K6
Cuxham *Oxon* 18 B3
Cuxton *Medway* 20 E4
Cuxwold *Lincs* 46 B5
Cwm *Bl Gwent* 25 H8
Cwm *Denbs* 42 E3
Cwm *Swan* 14 B2
Cwm-byr *Carms* 24 E3
Cwm-Cewydd *Gwyn* 32 D4
Cwm-cou *Ceredig'n* 23 B7
Cwm-Dulais *Swan* 14 A2
Cwm-felin-fach *Caerph* 15 B7
Cwm Ffrwd-oer *Torf* 15 A8
Cwm-hesgen *Gwyn* 32 C3
Cwm-hwnt *Rh Cyn Taff* 24 H6
Cwm Irfon *Powys* 24 D5
Cwm-Llinau *Powys* 32 E4
Cwm-mawr *Carms* 23 E10
Cwm-parc *Rh Cyn Taff* 14 B5
Cwm Penmachno *Conwy* 41 F9
Cwm-y-glo *Carms* 23 E10
Cwm-y-glo *Gwyn* 41 D7
Cwmafan *Neath P Talb* 14 B3
Cwmaman *Rh Cyn Taff* 14 B6
Cwmann *Carms* 23 B10
Cwmavon *Torf* 25 H9
Cwmbach *Carms* 23 D7
Cwmbach *Carms* 23 F9
Cwmbach *Powys* 25 C7
Cwmbach *Powys* 25 E8
Cwmbâch *Rh Cyn Taff* 14 A6
Cwmbelan *Powys* 32 G5
Cwmbran = Cwmbrân *Torf* 15 B8
Cwmbrân = Cwmbran *Torf* 15 B8
Cwmbrwyno *Ceredig'n* 32 G3
Cwmcarn *Caerph* 15 B8
Cwmcarvan *Monmouths* 25 H11
Cwmcych *Pembs* 23 C7
Cwmdare *Rh Cyn Taff* 14 A5
Cwmderwen *Powys* 32 E5
Cwmdu *Carms* 24 E3
Cwmdu *Powys* 25 F8
Cwmdu *Swan* 14 B2
Cwmduad *Carms* 23 C8
Cwmdwr *Carms* 24 E4
Cwmfelin *Bridg* 14 C4
Cwmfelin *Merth Tyd* 14 A6
Cwmfelin Boeth *Carms* 22 E6
Cwmfelin Mynach *Carms* 23 D7
Cwmffrwd *Carms* 23 E9
Cwmgiedd *Powys* 24 G4
Cwmgors *Neath P Talb* 24 G4
Cwmgwili *Carms* 23 E10
Cwmgwrach *Neath P Talb* 14 A4
Cwmhiraeth *Carms* 23 C8
Cwmifor *Carms* 24 F3
Cwmisfael *Carms* 23 E9
Cwmllynfell *Neath P Talb* 24 G4
Cwmorgan *Carms* 23 C7
Cwmpengraig *Carms* 23 C8
Cwmrhos *Powys* 25 F8
Cwmsychpant *Ceredig'n* 23 B9
Cwmtillery *Bl Gwent* 25 H9
Cwmwysg *Powys* 24 F5
Cwmyoy *Monmouths* 25 F9
Cwmystwyth *Ceredig'n* 24 A4
Cwrt *Gwyn* 32 E2
Cwrt-newydd *Ceredig'n* 23 B9
Cwrt-y-cadno *Carms* 24 D3
Cwrt-y-gollen *Powys* 25 G9
Cydweli = Kidwelly *Carms* 23 F9
Cyffordd Llandudno = Llandudno Junction *Conwy* 41 C9
Cyffylliog *Denbs* 42 G3
Cyfronydd *Powys* 33 E7
Cymer *Neath P Talb* 14 B4
Cyncoed *Card* 15 C7
Cynghordy *Carms* 24 D5
Cynheidre *Carms* 23 F9
Cynwyd *Denbs* 33 A6
Cynwyl Elfed *Carms* 23 D8
Cywarch *Gwyn* 32 D4

D

Dacre *Cumb* 56 D6
Dacre *N Yorks* 51 C7
Dacre Banks *N Yorks* 51 C7
Daddry Shield *Durham* 57 C10
Dadford *Bucks* 28 E3
Dadlington *Leics* 35 F10
Dafarn Faig *Gwyn* 40 F6
Dafen *Carms* 23 F10
Daffy Green *Norfolk* 38 E5
Dagenham *London* 19 C11
Daglingworth *Glos* 26 H6
Dagnall *Bucks* 28 G6
Dail Beag *W Isles* 90 C7
Dail bho Dheas *W Isles* 91 A9
Dail bho Thuath *W Isles* 91 A9
Dail Mor *W Isles* 90 C7
Daill *Arg/Bute* 64 B4
Dailly *S Ayrs* 66 F5
Dairsie or Osnaburgh *Fife* 77 F7
Daisy Hill *Gtr Man* 43 B9
Dalabrog *W Isles* 84 F2
Dalavich *Arg/Bute* 73 B8
Dalbeattie *Dumf/Gal* 55 C11
Dalblair *E Ayrs* 67 E9
Dalbog *Angus* 83 F7
Dalbury *Derby* 35 B8
Dalby *I/Man* 48 E2
Dalby *N Yorks* 52 B2
Dalchalloch *Perth/Kinr* 75 A10
Dalchalm *H'land* 93 J12
Dalchenna *Arg/Bute* 73 C9
Dalchirach *Moray* 88 E1
Dalchork *H'land* 93 H8
Dalchreichart *H'land* 80 B4
Dalchruin *Perth/Kinr* 75 F10
Dalderby *Lincs* 46 F6
Dale *Pembs* 22 F3
Dale Abbey *Derby* 35 B10
Dale Head *Cumb* 56 E6
Dale of Walls *Shetl'd* 96 H3
Dalelia *H'land* 79 E10
Daless *H'land* 87 H11
Dalfaber *H'land* 81 B11
Dalgarven *N Ayrs* 66 B5
Dalgety Bay *Fife* 69 B10
Dalginross *Perth/Kinr* 75 E10
Dalguise *Perth/Kinr* 76 C2
Dalhalvaig *H'land* 93 D11
Dalham *Suffolk* 30 B4
Dalinlongart *Arg/Bute* 73 E10
Dalkeith *Midloth* 70 D2
Dallam *Warrington* 43 C8
Dallas *Moray* 87 F14
Dalleagles *E Ayrs* 67 E8
Dallinghoo *Suffolk* 31 C9
Dallington *E Sussex* 12 E5
Dallington *Northants* 28 B4
Dallow *N Yorks* 51 B7
Dalmadilly *Aberds* 83 B9
Dalmally *Arg/Bute* 74 E4
Dalmarnock *C/Glasg* 68 D5
Dalmary *Stirl* 75 H8
Dalmellington *E Ayrs* 67 F7
Dalmeny *C/Edinb* 69 C10
Dalmigavie *H'land* 81 B9
Dalmigavie Lodge *H'land* 81 A9
Dalmore *H'land* 87 E9
Dalmuir *W Dunb* 68 C3
Dalnabreck *H'land* 79 E9
Dalnacardoch Lodge *Perth/Kinr* 81 F9
Dalnacroich *H'land* 86 F6
Dalnaglar Castle *Perth/Kinr* 76 A4
Dalnahaitnach *H'land* 81 A10
Dalnaspidal Lodge *Perth/Kinr* 81 F8
Dalnavaid *Perth/Kinr* 76 A3
Dalnavie *H'land* 87 D9
Dalnawillan Lodge *H'land* 93 E13
Dalness *H'land* 74 B4
Dalnessie *H'land* 93 H9
Dalqueich *Perth/Kinr* 76 G3
Dalreavoch *H'land* 93 J10
Dalry *N Ayrs* 66 B5
Dalrymple *E Ayrs* 67 E6
Dalserf *S Lanarks* 69 E7
Dalston *Cumb* 56 A5
Dalswinton *Dumf/Gal* 60 E5
Dalton *Dumf/Gal* 61 F7
Dalton *Lancs* 43 B7
Dalton *Northum* 62 H5
Dalton *Northum* 63 F7
Dalton *N Yorks* 51 B10
Dalton *N Yorks* 58 F2
Dalton *S Yorks* 45 C8
Dalton-in-Furness *Cumb* 49 B2
Dalton-le-Dale *Durham* 58 B5
Dalton-on-Tees *N Yorks* 58 F3
Dalton Piercy *Hartlep'l* 58 C5
Dalveich *Stirl* 75 E9
Dalvina Lodge *H'land* 93 E9
Dalwhinnie *H'land* 81 E8
Dalwood *Devon* 8 D1
Dalwyne *S Ayrs* 66 G6
Dam Green *Norfolk* 39 G6
Dam Side *Lancs* 49 E4
Damerham *Hants* 9 C10
Damgate *Norfolk* 39 E10
Damnaglaur *Dumf/Gal* 54 F4
Damside *Scot Borders* 69 F10
Danbury *Essex* 30 H4
Danby *N Yorks* 59 F8
Danby Wiske *N Yorks* 58 G4
Dandaleith *Moray* 88 D2
Danderhall *Midloth* 70 D2
Dane End *Herts* 29 F10
Danebridge *Ches* 44 F3
Danehill *E Sussex* 12 D3
Danemoor Green *Norfolk* 39 E6
Danesford *Shrops* 34 F3
Daneshill *Hants* 18 F3
Dangerous Corner *Lancs* 43 A8
Danskine *E Loth* 70 D4
Darcy Lever *Gtr Man* 43 B10
Darenth *Kent* 20 D2
Daresbury *Halton* 43 D8
Darfield *S Yorks* 45 B8
Darfoulds *Notts* 45 E9
Dargate *Kent* 21 E7
Darite *Cornw'l* 4 E3
Darlaston *W Midlands* 34 F5
Darley *N Yorks* 51 D8
Darley Bridge *Derby* 44 F6
Darley Head *N Yorks* 51 D7
Darlingscott *Warwick* 27 D9
Darlington *D'lington* 58 E3
Darliston *Shrops* 34 B1
Darlton *Notts* 45 E11
Darnall *S Yorks* 45 D7
Darnick *Scot Borders* 70 G4
Darowen *Powys* 32 E4
Darra *Aberds* 89 D7
Darracott *Devon* 6 C3
Darras Hall *Northum* 63 F7
Darrington *W Yorks* 51 G10
Darsham *Suffolk* 31 B11
Dartford *Kent* 20 D2
Dartford Crossing *Kent* 20 D2
Dartington *Devon* 5 E8
Dartmeet *Devon* 5 D7
Dartmouth *Devon* 5 F9
Darton *S Yorks* 45 B7
Darvel *E Ayrs* 68 G4
Darwell Hole *E Sussex* 12 E5
Darwen *Blackb'n* 50 G2
Datchet *Windsor* 18 D6
Datchworth *Herts* 29 G9
Datchworth Green *Herts* 29 G9
Daubhill *Gtr Man* 43 B10
Daugh of Kinermony *Moray* 88 D2
Dauntsey *Wilts* 16 C6
Dava *Moray* 87 H13
Davenham *Ches* 43 E9
Davenport Green *Ches* 44 E2
Daventry *Northants* 28 B2
David's Well *Powys* 33 H6
Davidson's Mains *C/Edinb* 69 C11
Davidstow *Cornw'l* 4 C2
Davington *Dumf/Gal* 61 C8
Daviot *Aberds* 83 A9
Daviot *H'land* 87 H10
Davoch of Grange *Moray* 88 C4
Davyhulme *Gtr Man* 43 C10
Dawley *Telford* 34 E2
Dawlish *Devon* 5 D10
Dawlish Warren *Devon* 5 D10
Dawn *Conwy* 41 C10
Daws Heath *Essex* 20 C5
Daw's House *Cornw'l* 4 C4
Dawsmere *Lincs* 37 B10
Dayhills *Staffs* 34 B5
Daylesford *Glos* 27 F9
Ddôl-Cownwy *Powys* 32 D6
Ddrydwy *Angl* 40 C5
Deadwater *Northum* 62 D2
Deaf Hill *Durham* 58 C4
Deal *Kent* 21 F10
Deal Hall *Essex* 21 B7
Dean *Cumb* 56 D2
Dean *Devon* 5 E8
Dean *Devon* 6 B4
Dean *Dorset* 9 C8
Dean *Hants* 10 C4
Dean *Som'set* 16 G3
Dean Prior *Devon* 5 E8
Dean Row *Ches* 44 D2
Deanburnhaugh *Scot Borders* 61 B9
Deane *Gtr Man* 43 B9
Deane *Hants* 18 F2
Deanich Lodge *H'land* 86 C6
Deanland *Dorset* 9 C8
Deans *W Loth* 69 D9
Deanscales *Cumb* 56 D2
Deanshanger *Northants* 28 E4
Deanston *Stirl* 75 G10
Dearham *Cumb* 56 C2
Debach *Suffolk* 31 C9
Debden *Essex* 30 E2
Debden *Essex* 19 B11
Debden Cross *Essex* 30 E2
Debenham *Suffolk* 31 B8
Dechmont *W Loth* 69 C9
Deddington *Oxon* 27 E11
Dedham *Essex* 31 E7
Dedham Heath *Essex* 31 E7
Deebank *Aberds* 83 D8
Deene *Northants* 36 F5
Deenethorpe *Northants* 36 F5
Deepcar *S Yorks* 44 C6
Deepcut *Surrey* 18 F6
Deepdale *Cumb* 50 A3
Deeping Gate *Lincs* 37 E7
Deeping St James *Lincs* 37 E7
Deeping St Nicholas *Lincs* 37 D8
Deerhill *Moray* 88 C4
Deerhurst *Glos* 26 F5
Deerness *Orkney* 95 H6
Defford *Worcs* 26 D6
Defynnog *Powys* 24 F6
Deganwy *Conwy* 41 C9
Deighton *N Yorks* 58 F4
Deighton *W Yorks* 51 H7
Deighton *C/York* 52 E2
Deiniolen *Gwyn* 41 D7
Delabole *Cornw'l* 4 C1
Delamere *Ches* 43 F8
Delfrigs *Aberds* 89 F9
Dell Lodge *H'land* 82 B2
Delliefure *H'land* 87 H13
Delnabo *Moray* 82 B3
Delnadamph *Aberds* 82 C4
Delph *Gtr Man* 44 B3
Delves *Durham* 58 B2
Delvine *Perth/Kinr* 76 C4
Dembleby *Lincs* 36 B6
Denaby Main *S Yorks* 45 C8
Denbigh = Dinbych *Denbs* 42 F3
Denbury *Devon* 5 E9
Denby *Derby* 45 H7
Denby Dale *W Yorks* 44 B6
Denchworth *Oxon* 17 B10
Dendron *Cumb* 49 B2
Denel End *Beds* 29 E7
Denend *Aberds* 88 E6
Denford *Northants* 36 H5
Dengie *Essex* 20 A6
Denham *Bucks* 19 C7
Denham *Suffolk* 30 B4
Denham *Suffolk* 31 A8
Denham Green *Bucks* 19 C7
Denham Street *Suffolk* 31 A8
Denhead *Aberds* 89 C9
Denhead *Fife* 77 F7
Denhead of Arbilot *Angus* 77 C8
Denhead of Gray *Dundee C* 76 D6
Denholm *Scot Borders* 61 B11
Denholme *W Yorks* 51 F6
Denholme Clough *W Yorks* 51 F6
Denio *Gwyn* 40 G5
Denmead *Hants* 10 C5
Denmore *Aberd C* 83 B11
Denmoss *Aberds* 89 D6
Dennington *Suffolk* 31 B9
Denny *Falk* 69 B7
Denny Lodge *Hants* 10 D2
Dennyloanhead *Falk* 69 B7
Denshaw *Gtr Man* 44 A3
Denside *Aberds* 83 D10
Densole *Kent* 21 G9
Denston *Suffolk* 30 C4
Denstone *Staffs* 35 A7
Dent *Cumb* 57 H9
Denton *Cambs* 37 G7
Denton *D'lington* 58 E3
Denton *E Sussex* 12 F3
Denton *Gtr Man* 44 C3
Denton *Kent* 21 G9
Denton *Lincs* 36 B4
Denton *Norfolk* 39 G8
Denton *Northants* 28 C5
Denton *N Yorks* 51 E7
Denton *Oxon* 18 A2
Denton's Green *Mersey* 43 C7
Denver *Norfolk* 38 E2
Denwick *Northum* 63 B8
Deopham *Norfolk* 39 E6
Deopham Green *Norfolk* 38 F6
Depden *Suffolk* 30 C4
Depden Green *Suffolk* 30 C4
Deptford *London* 19 D10
Deptford *Wilts* 17 H7
Derby *Derby C* 35 B9
Derbyhaven *I/Man* 48 F2
Dereham *Norfolk* 38 D5
Deri *Caerph* 15 A7
Derril *Devon* 6 F2
Derringstone *Kent* 21 G9
Derrington *Staffs* 34 C4
Derriton *Devon* 6 F2
Derry Hill *Wilts* 16 D6
Derryguaig *Arg/Bute* 78 H7
Derrythorpe *N Lincs* 46 B2
Dersingham *Norfolk* 38 B2
Dervaig *Arg/Bute* 78 F7
Derwen *Denbs* 42 G3
Derwenlas *Powys* 32 F3
Desborough *Northants* 36 G4
Desford *Leics* 35 E10
Detchant *Northum* 71 G9
Detling *Kent* 20 F4
Deuddwr *Powys* 33 D8
Devauden *Monmouths* 15 B10
Devil's Bridge *Ceredig'n* 32 H3
Devizes *Wilts* 17 E7
Devol *Invercl* 68 C2
Devonport *Plym'th* 4 F5
Devonside *Clack* 76 H2
Devoran *Cornw'l* 3 F6
Dewar *Scot Borders* 70 F2
Dewlish *Dorset* 9 E6
Dewsbury *W Yorks* 51 G8
Dewsbury Moor *W Yorks* 51 G8
Dewshall Court *Heref'd* 25 E11
Dhoon *I/Man* 48 D4
Dhoor *I/Man* 48 C4
Dhowin *I/Man* 48 B4
Dial Post *W Sussex* 11 C10
Dibden *Hants* 10 D3
Dibden Purlieu *Hants* 10 D3
Dickleburgh *Norfolk* 39 G7
Didbrook *Glos* 27 E7
Didcot *Oxon* 18 C2
Diddington *Cambs* 29 B8
Diddlebury *Shrops* 33 G11
Didley *Heref'd* 25 E11
Didling *W Sussex* 11 C7
Didmarton *Glos* 16 C5
Didsbury *Gtr Man* 44 C2
Didworthy *Devon* 5 E7
Digby *Lincs* 46 G4
Digg *H'land* 85 B9
Diggle *Gtr Man* 44 B4
Digmoor *Lancs* 43 B7
Digswell Park *Herts* 29 G9
Dihewid *Ceredig'n* 23 A9
Dilham *Norfolk* 39 C9
Dilhorne *Staffs* 34 A5
Dillarburn *S Lanarks* 69 F7
Dillington *Cambs* 29 B8
Dilston *Northum* 62 G5
Dilton Marsh *Wilts* 16 G5
Dilwyn *Heref'd* 25 C11
Dinas *Carms* 23 C7
Dinas *Gwyn* 40 G4
Dinas Cross *Pembs* 22 C5
Dinas Dinlle *Gwyn* 40 E6
Dinas-Mawddwy *Gwyn* 32 D4
Dinas Powys *V/Glam* 15 D7
Dinbych = Denbigh *Denbs* 42 F3
Dinbych-y-Pysgod = Tenby *Pembs* 22 F6
Dinder *Som'set* 16 G2
Dinedor *Heref'd* 26 E2
Dingestow *Monmouths* 25 G11
Dingle *Mersey* 42 D6
Dingleden *Kent* 13 C7
Dingley *Northants* 36 G3
Dingwall *H'land* 87 F8
Dinlabyre *Scot Borders* 61 D11
Dinmael *Conwy* 32 A6
Dinnet *Aberds* 82 D6
Dinnington *Som'set* 8 C3
Dinnington *S Yorks* 45 D9
Dinnington *Tyne/Wear* 63 F8
Dinorwic *Gwyn* 41 D7
Dinton *Bucks* 28 G4
Dinton *Wilts* 9 A9
Dinwoodie Mains *Dumf/Gal* 61 D7
Dinworthy *Devon* 6 E2
Dippen *N Ayrs* 66 D3
Dippenhall *Surrey* 18 G5
Dipple *Moray* 88 C3
Dipple *S Ayrs* 66 F5
Diptford *Devon* 5 F8
Dipton *Durham* 58 A2
Dirdhu *H'land* 82 A2
Dirleton *E Loth* 70 B4
Dirt Pot *Northum* 57 B10
Discoed *Powys* 25 B9
Diseworth *Leics* 35 C10
Dishes *Orkney* 95 F7
Dishforth *N Yorks* 51 B9
Disley *Ches* 44 D3
Diss *Norfolk* 39 H7
Disserth *Powys* 25 C7
Distington *Cumb* 56 D2
Ditchampton *Wilts* 9 A9
Ditcheat *Som'set* 16 H3
Ditchingham *Norfolk* 39 F9
Ditchling *E Sussex* 12 E2
Ditherington *Shrops* 33 D11
Dittisham *Devon* 5 F9
Ditton *Halton* 43 D7
Ditton *Kent* 20 F4
Ditton Green *Cambs* 30 C3
Ditton Priors *Shrops* 34 G2
Divach *H'land* 81 A6
Divlyn *Carms* 24 E4
Dixton *Glos* 26 E6
Dixton *Monmouths* 26 G2
Dobcross *Gtr Man* 44 B3
Dobwalls *Cornw'l* 4 E3
Doc Penfro = Pembroke Dock *Pembs* 22 F4
Doccombe *Devon* 5 C8
Dochfour Ho. *H'land* 87 H9
Dochgarroch *H'land* 87 G9
Docking *Norfolk* 38 B3
Docklow *Heref'd* 26 C2
Dockray *Cumb* 56 D5
Dockroyd *W Yorks* 50 F6
Dodburn *Scot Borders* 61 C10
Doddinghurst *Essex* 20 B2
Doddington *Cambs* 37 F9
Doddington *Kent* 20 F6
Doddington *Lincs* 46 E3
Doddington *Northum* 71 G8
Doddington *Shrops* 34 H2
Doddiscombsleigh *Devon* 5 C9
Dodford *Northants* 28 B3
Dodford *Worcs* 26 A6
Dodington *S Gloucs* 16 C4
Dodleston *Ches* 42 F6
Dods Leigh *Staffs* 34 B6
Dodworth *S Yorks* 45 B7
Doe Green *Warrington* 43 D8
Doe Lea *Derby* 45 F8
Dog Village *Devon* 7 G8
Dogdyke *Lincs* 46 G6
Dogmersfield *Hants* 18 F4
Dogridge *Wilts* 17 C7
Dogsthorpe *Peterbro* 37 E7
Dol-fôr *Powys* 32 E4
Dôl-y-Bont *Ceredig'n* 32 G2
Dol-y-cannau *Powys* 25 D9
Dolanog *Powys* 33 D6
Dolau *Powys* 25 B8
Dolau *Rh Cyn Taff* 14 C5
Dolbenmaen *Gwyn* 41 F7
Dolfach *Powys* 32 E5
Dolfor *Powys* 33 G7
Dolgarrog *Conwy* 41 D9
Dolgellau *Gwyn* 32 D3
Dolgran *Carms* 23 C9
Dolhendre *Gwyn* 41 G10
Doll *H'land* 93 J11
Dollar *Clack* 76 H2
Dolley Green *Powys* 25 B9
Dollwen *Ceredig'n* 32 G2
Dolphin *Flints* 42 E4
Dolphinholme *Lancs* 49 D5
Dolphinton *S Lanarks* 69 F10
Dolton *Devon* 6 E4
Dolwen *Conwy* 41 C10
Dolwen *Powys* 32 E5
Dolwyd *Conwy* 41 C10
Dolwyddelan *Conwy* 41 E9
Dolyhir *Powys* 25 C9
Doncaster *S Yorks* 45 B9
Dones Green *Ches* 43 E9
Donhead St Andrew *Wilts* 9 B8
Donhead St Mary *Wilts* 9 B8
Donibristle *Fife* 69 B10
Donington *Lincs* 37 B8
Donington on Bain *Lincs* 46 D6
Donington South Ing *Lincs* 37 B8
Donisthorpe *Leics* 35 D9
Donkey Town *Surrey* 18 E6
Donnington *Glos* 27 F8
Donnington *Heref'd* 26 E4
Donnington *Shrops* 34 E1
Donnington *Telford* 34 D3
Donnington *W Berks* 17 E11
Donnington *W Sussex* 11 D7
Donnington Wood *Telford* 34 D3
Donyatt *Som'set* 8 C2
Doonfoot *S Ayrs* 66 E6
Dorback Lodge *H'land* 82 B2
Dorchester *Dorset* 8 E5
Dorchester *Oxon* 18 B2
Dordon *Warwick* 35 E8
Dore *S Yorks* 45 D7
Dores *H'land* 87 H8
Dorking *Surrey* 19 G8
Dormansland *Surrey* 12 B3
Dormanstown *Redcar/Clevel'd* 59 D6
Dormington *Heref'd* 26 D2
Dormston *Worcs* 26 C6
Dornal *S Ayrs* 54 B5
Dorney *Bucks* 18 D6
Dornie *H'land* 85 F13
Dornoch *H'land* 87 C10
Dornock *Dumf/Gal* 61 G8
Dorrery *H'land* 94 E2
Dorridge *W Midlands* 35 H7
Dorrington *Lincs* 46 G4
Dorrington *Shrops* 33 E10
Dorsington *Warwick* 27 D8
Dorstone *Heref'd* 25 D10
Dorton *Bucks* 28 G3
Dorusduain *H'land* 80 A1
Dosthill *Staffs* 35 F8
Dottery *Dorset* 8 E3
Doublebois *Cornw'l* 4 E2
Dougarie *N Ayrs* 66 C1
Doughton *Glos* 16 B5
Douglas *I/Man* 48 E3
Douglas *S Lanarks* 69 G7
Douglas & Angus *Dundee C* 77 D7
Douglas Water *S Lanarks* 69 G7
Douglas West *S Lanarks* 69 G7
Douglastown *Angus* 77 C7
Doulting *Som'set* 16 G3
Dounby *Orkney* 95 F3
Doune *H'land* 92 J7
Doune *Stirl* 75 G10
Doune Park *Aberds* 89 B7
Douneside *Aberds* 82 C6
Dounie *H'land* 87 B8
Dounreay *H'land* 93 C12
Dousland *Devon* 4 E6
Dovaston *Shrops* 33 C9
Dove Holes *Derby* 44 E4
Dovenby *Cumb* 56 C2
Dover *Kent* 21 G10
Dovercourt *Essex* 31 E9
Doverdale *Worcs* 26 B5
Doveridge *Derby* 35 B7
Doversgreen *Surrey* 19 G9
Dowally *Perth/Kinr* 76 C3
Dowbridge *Lancs* 49 F4
Dowdeswell *Glos* 26 G6
Dowlais *Merth Tyd* 25 H7
Dowland *Devon* 6 E4
Dowlish Wake *Som'set* 8 C2
Down Ampney *Glos* 17 B8
Down Hatherley *Glos* 26 F5
Down St Mary *Devon* 7 F6
Down Thomas *Devon* 4 F6
Downcraig Ferry *N Ayrs* 73 H10
Downderry *Cornw'l* 4 F4
Downe *London* 19 E11
Downend *I/Wight* 10 F4
Downend *S Gloucs* 16 D3
Downend *W Berks* 17 D11
Downfield *Dundee C* 76 D6
Downgate *Cornw'l* 4 D4
Downham *Essex* 20 B4
Downham *Lancs* 50 E3
Downham *Northum* 71 G7
Downham Market *Norfolk* 38 E2
Downhead *Som'set* 16 G3
Downhill *Perth/Kinr* 76 D3
Downhill *Tyne/Wear* 63 H9
Downholland Cross *Lancs* 42 B6
Downholme *N Yorks* 58 G2
Downies *Aberds* 83 D11
Downley *Bucks* 18 B5
Downside *Som'set* 16 G3
Downside *Surrey* 19 F8
Downton *Hants* 10 E1
Downton *Wilts* 9 B10
Downton on the Rock *Heref'd* 25 A11
Dowsby *Lincs* 37 C7
Dowsdale *Lincs* 37 D8
Dowthwaitehead *Cumb* 56 D5
Doxey *Staffs* 34 C5
Doxford *Northum* 63 A7
Doxford Park *Tyne/Wear* 58 A4
Doynton *S Gloucs* 16 D4
Draffan *S Lanarks* 68 F6
Dragonby *N Lincs* 46 A3
Drakeland Corner *Devon* 5 F6
Drakemyre *N Ayrs* 66 A5
Drake's Broughton *Worcs* 26 D6
Drakes Cross *Worcs* 35 H6
Drakewalls *Cornw'l* 4 D5
Draughton *Northants* 36 H3
Draughton *N Yorks* 50 D6
Drax *N Yorks* 52 G2
Draycote *Warwick* 27 A11
Draycott *Derby* 35 B10
Draycott *Glos* 27 E8
Draycott *Som'set* 15 F10
Draycott in the Clay *Staffs* 35 C7
Draycott in the Moors *Staffs* 34 A5
Drayford *Devon* 7 E6
Drayton *Leics* 36 F4
Drayton *Lincs* 37 B8
Drayton *Norfolk* 39 D7
Drayton *Oxon* 27 D11
Drayton *Oxon* 17 B11
Drayton *Portsm'th* 10 D5
Drayton *Som'set* 8 B3
Drayton *Worcs* 34 H5
Drayton Bassett *Staffs* 35 E7
Drayton Beauchamp *Bucks* 28 G6
Drayton Parslow *Bucks* 28 F5
Drayton St Leonard *Oxon* 18 B2
Dre-fach *Ceredig'n* 23 B10
Dre-fach *Carms* 24 G3
Drebley *N Yorks* 51 D6
Dreemskerry *I/Man* 48 C4
Dreenhill *Pembs* 22 E4
Drefach *Carms* 23 C8
Drefach *Carms* 23 E10
Drefelin *Carms* 23 C8
Dreghorn *N Ayrs* 67 C6
Drellingore *Kent* 21 G9
Drem *E Loth* 70 C4
Dresden *Stoke* 34 A5
Dreumasdal *W Isles* 84 E2
Drewsteignton *Devon* 7 G6
Driby *Lincs* 47 E7
Driffield *ER Yorks* 52 D6
Driffield *Glos* 17 B7
Drigg *Cumb* 56 G2
Drighlington *W Yorks* 51 G8
Drimnin *H'land* 79 F8
Drimpton *Dorset* 8 D3
Drimsynie *Arg/Bute* 74 G4
Drinisiadar *W Isles* 90 H6
Drinkstone *Suffolk* 30 B6
Drinkstone Green *Suffolk* 30 B6
Drishaig *Arg/Bute* 74 F4
Drissaig *Arg/Bute* 73 B8
Drochil *Scot Borders* 69 F10
Drointon *Staffs* 34 C6
Droitwich Spa *Worcs* 26 B5
Droman *H'land* 92 D4
Dron *Perth/Kinr* 76 F4
Dronfield *Derby* 45 E7
Dronfield Woodhouse *Derby* 45 E7
Drongan *E Ayrs* 67 E7
Dronley *Angus* 76 D6
Droxford *Hants* 10 C5
Droylsden *Gtr Man* 44 C3
Druid *Denbs* 32 A6
Druidston *Pembs* 22 E3
Druimarbin *H'land* 80 F2
Druimavuic *Arg/Bute* 74 C3
Druimdrishaig *Arg/Bute* 72 F6
Druimindarroch *H'land* 79 C9
Druimyeon More *Arg/Bute* 65 C7
Drum *Arg/Bute* 73 F8
Drum *Perth/Kinr* 76 G3
Drumbeg *H'land* 92 F4
Drumblade *Aberds* 88 D5
Drumblair *Aberds* 89 D6
Drumbuie *Dumf/Gal* 55 A8
Drumbuie *H'land* 85 E12
Drumburgh *Cumb* 61 H8
Drumburn *Dumf/Gal* 60 G5
Drumchapel *C/Glasg* 68 C4
Drumchardine *H'land* 87 G8
Drumchork *H'land* 91 J13
Drumclog *S Lanarks* 68 G5
Drumderfit *H'land* 87 F9
Drumeldrie *Fife* 77 G7
Drumelzier *Scot Borders* 69 G10
Drumfearn *H'land* 85 G11
Drumgask *H'land* 81 D8
Drumgley *Angus* 77 B7
Drumguish *H'land* 81 D9
Drumin *Moray* 88 E1
Drumlasie *Aberds* 83 C8
Drumlemble *Arg/Bute* 65 G7
Drumligair *Aberds* 83 B11
Drumlithie *Aberds* 83 E9
Drummoddie *Dumf/Gal* 54 E6
Drummond *H'land* 87 E9
Drummore *Dumf/Gal* 54 F4
Drummuir *Moray* 88 D3
Drummuir Castle *Moray* 88 D3
Drumnadrochit *H'land* 81 A7
Drumnagorrach *Moray* 88 C5
Drumoak *Aberds* 83 D9
Drumpark *Dumf/Gal* 60 E4
Drumphail *Dumf/Gal* 54 C5
Drumrash *Dumf/Gal* 55 B9
Drumrunie *H'land* 92 J4
Drums *Aberds* 89 F9
Drumsallie *H'land* 80 F1
Drumstinchall *Dumf/Gal* 55 D11
Drumsturdy *Angus* 77 D7
Drumtochty Castle *Aberds* 83 F8
Drumtroddan *Dumf/Gal* 54 E6
Drumuie *H'land* 85 D9
Drumuillie *H'land* 81 A11
Drumvaich *Stirl* 75 G9
Drumwhindle *Aberds* 89 E9
Drunkendub *Angus* 77 C9
Drury *Flints* 42 F5
Drury Square *Norfolk* 38 D5
Dry Doddington *Lincs* 46 H2
Dry Drayton *Cambs* 29 B10
Drybeck *Cumb* 57 E8
Drybridge *Moray* 88 B4
Drybridge *N Ayrs* 67 C6
Drybrook *Glos* 26 G3
Dryburgh *Scot Borders* 70 G4
Dryhope *Scot Borders* 61 A8
Drylaw *C/Edinb* 69 C11
Drym *Cornw'l* 2 F5
Drymen *Stirl* 68 B3
Drymuir *Aberds* 89 D9
Drynoch *H'land* 85 E9
Dryslwyn *Carms* 23 D10
Dryton *Shrops* 34 E1
Dubford *Aberds* 89 B8
Dubton *Angus* 77 B8
Duchally *H'land* 92 H6
Duchlage *Arg/Bute* 68 B2
Duck Corner *Suffolk* 31 D10
Ducklington *Ches* 43 G7
Ducklington *Oxon* 27 H10
Duckmanton *Derby* 45 E8
Duck's Cross *Beds* 29 C8
Duddenhoe End *Essex* 29 E11
Duddingston *C/Edinb* 69 C11
Duddington *Northants* 36 E5
Duddleswell *E Sussex* 12 D3
Duddo *Northum* 71 F8
Duddon *Ches* 43 F8
Duddon Bridge *Cumb* 56 H4
Dudleston *Shrops* 33 B9
Dudleston Heath *Shrops* 33 B9
Dudley *Tyne/Wear* 63 F8
Dudley *W Midlands* 34 F5
Dudley Port *W Midlands* 34 F5
Duffield *Derby* 35 A9
Duffryn *Newp* 15 C8
Duffryn *Neath P Talb* 14 B4
Dufftown *Moray* 88 E3
Duffus *Moray* 88 B1
Dufton *Cumb* 57 D8
Duggleby *N Yorks* 52 C4
Duirinish *H'land* 85 E12
Duisdalemore *H'land* 85 G12
Duisky *H'land* 80 F2
Dukestown *Bl Gwent* 25 G8
Dukinfield *Gtr Man* 44 C3
Dulas *Angl* 40 B6
Dulcote *Som'set* 16 G2
Dulford *Devon* 7 F9
Dull *Perth/Kinr* 75 C11
Dullatur *N Lanarks* 68 C6
Dullingham *Cambs* 30 C3
Dulnain Bridge *H'land* 82 A1
Duloe *Beds* 29 B8
Duloe *Cornw'l* 4 F3
Dulsie *H'land* 87 G12
Dulverton *Som'set* 7 D8
Dulwich *London* 19 D10
Dumbarton *W Dunb* 68 C2
Dumbleton *Glos* 27 E7
Dumcrieff *Dumf/Gal* 61 C7
Dumfries *Dumf/Gal* 60 F5
Dumgoyne *Stirl* 68 B4
Dummer *Hants* 18 G2
Dumpford *W Sussex* 11 B7
Dumpton *Kent* 21 E10
Dun *Angus* 77 B9
Dun Charlabhaigh *W Isles* 90 C6
Dunain Ho. *H'land* 87 G9
Dunalastair *Perth/Kinr* 75 B10
Dunan *H'land* 85 F10
Dunans *Arg/Bute* 73 D9
Dunball *Som'set* 15 G9
Dunbar *E Loth* 70 C5
Dunbeath *H'land* 94 H3
Dunbeg *Arg/Bute* 79 H11
Dunblane *Stirl* 75 G10
Dunbog *Fife* 76 F5
Duncanston *Aberds* 83 A7
Duncanston *H'land* 87 F8
Dunchurch *Warwick* 27 A11
Duncote *Northants* 28 C3
Duncow *Dumf/Gal* 60 E5
Duncraggan *Stirl* 75 G8
Duncrievie *Perth/Kinr* 76 G4
Duncton *W Sussex* 11 C8
Dundas Ho. *Orkney* 95 K5
Dundee *Dundee C* 77 D7
Dundeugh *Dumf/Gal* 67 H8
Dundon *Som'set* 8 A3
Dundonald *S Ayrs* 67 C6
Dundonnell *H'land* 86 C3
Dundonnell Hotel *H'land* 86 C3
Dundonnell House *H'land* 86 C4
Dundraw *Cumb* 56 B4
Dundreggan *H'land* 80 B5
Dundreggan Lodge *H'land* 80 B5
Dundrennan *Dumf/Gal* 55 E10
Dundry *N Som'set* 16 E2
Dunecht *Aberds* 83 C9
Dunfermline *Fife* 69 B9
Dunfield *Glos* 17 B8
Dunford Bridge *S Yorks* 44 B5
Dungworth *S Yorks* 44 D6
Dunham *Notts* 46 E2
Dunham-on-the-Hill *Ches* 43 E7
Dunham Town *Gtr Man* 43 D10
Dunhampton *Worcs* 26 B5
Dunholme *Lincs* 46 E4
Dunino *Fife* 77 F8
Dunipace *Falk* 69 B7
Dunira *Perth/Kinr* 75 E10
Dunkeld *Perth/Kinr* 76 C3
Dunkerton *Bath/NE Som'set* 16 F4
Dunkeswell *Devon* 7 F10
Dunkeswick *N Yorks* 51 E9
Dunkirk *Kent* 21 F7
Dunkirk *Norfolk* 39 C8
Dunk's Green *Kent* 20 F3
Dunlappie *Angus* 83 G7
Dunley *Hants* 17 F11
Dunley *Worcs* 26 B4
Dunlichity Lodge *H'land* 87 H9
Dunlop *E Ayrs* 67 B7
Dunmaglass Lodge *H'land* 81 A7
Dunmore *Arg/Bute* 72 G6
Dunmore *Falk* 69 B7
Dunnet *H'land* 94 C4
Dunnichen *Angus* 77 C8
Dunninald *Angus* 77 B10
Dunning *Perth/Kinr* 76 F3
Dunnington *ER Yorks* 53 D7
Dunnington *Warwick* 27 C7
Dunnington *C/York* 52 D2
Dunnockshaw *Lancs* 50 G4
Dunollie *Arg/Bute* 79 H11
Dunoon *Arg/Bute* 73 F10
Dunragit *Dumf/Gal* 54 D4
Dunrostan *Arg/Bute* 72 E6
Duns *Scot Borders* 70 E6
Duns Tew *Oxon* 27 F11
Dunsby *Lincs* 37 C7
Dunscore *Dumf/Gal* 60 E4
Dunscroft *S Yorks* 45 B10
Dunsdale *Redcar/Clevel'd* 59 E7
Dunsden Green *Oxon* 18 D4
Dunsfold *Surrey* 19 H7
Dunsford *Devon* 5 C9
Dunshalt *Fife* 76 F5
Dunshillock *Aberds* 89 D9
Dunskey Ho. *Dumf/Gal* 54 D3
Dunsley *N Yorks* 59 E9
Dunsmore *Bucks* 28 H5
Dunsop Bridge *Lancs* 50 D2
Dunstable *Beds* 29 F7
Dunstall *Staffs* 35 C7
Dunstall Common *Worcs* 26 D5
Dunstall Green *Suffolk* 30 B4
Dunstan *Northum* 63 B8
Dunstan Steads *Northum* 63 A8
Dunster *Som'set* 7 B8
Dunston *Lincs* 46 F4
Dunston *Norfolk* 39 E8
Dunston *Staffs* 34 D5
Dunston *Tyne/Wear* 63 G8
Dunsville *S Yorks* 45 B10
Dunswell *ER Yorks* 53 F6
Dunsyre *S Lanarks* 69 F9
Dunterton *Devon* 4 D4
Duntisbourne Abbots *Glos* 26 H6
Duntisbourne Leer *Glos* 26 H6
Duntisbourne Rouse *Glos* 26 H6
Duntish *Dorset* 8 D5
Duntocher *W Dunb* 68 C3
Dunton *Beds* 29 D9
Dunton *Bucks* 28 F5
Dunton *Norfolk* 38 B4
Dunton Bassett *Leics* 35 F11
Dunton Green *Kent* 20 F2

Dunton Wayletts Essex 20 B3
Duntulm H'land 85 A9
Dunure S Ayrs 66 E5
Dunvant Swan 23 G10
Dunvegan H'land 84 D7
Dunwich Suffolk 31 A11
Dunwood Staffs 44 G3
Dupplin Castle Perth/Kinr 76 F3
Durdar Cumb 56 A6
Durgates E Sussex 12 C5
Durham Durham 58 B3
Durisdeer Dumf/Gal 60 C4
Durisdeermill Dumf/Gal 60 C4
Durkar W Yorks 51 H9
Durleigh Som'set 15 H8
Durley Hants 10 C4
Durley Wilts 17 E9
Durnamuck H'land 86 B3
Durness H'land 92 C7
Durno Aberds 83 A9
Duror H'land 74 B2
Durran Arg/Bute 73 C8
Durran H'land 94 D3
Durrington Wilts 17 G8
Durrington W Sussex 11 D10
Dursley Glos 16 B4
Durston Som'set 8 B1
Durweston Dorset 9 D7
Dury Shetl'd 96 G6
Duston Northants 28 B4
Duthil H'land 81 A11
Dutlas Powys 33 H8
Duton Hill Essex 30 F3
Dutson Cornw'l 4 C4
Dutton Ches 43 E8
Duxford Cambs 29 D11
Duxford Oxon 17 B10
Dwygyfylchi Conwy 41 C9
Dwyran Angl 40 D6
Dyce Aberd C 83 B10
Dye House Northum 62 H5
Dyffryn Bridg 14 B4
Dyffryn Carms 23 D8
Dyffryn Pembs 22 C4
Dyffryn Ardudwy Gwyn 32 C1
Dyffryn Castell Ceredig'n 32 G3
Dyffryn Ceidrych Carms 24 F4
Dyffryn Cellwen Neath P Talb 24 H5
Dyke Lincs 37 C7
Dyke Moray 87 F12
Dykehead Angus 76 A6
Dykehead N Lanarks 69 E7
Dykehead Stirl 75 H8
Dykelands Aberds 83 G9
Dykends Angus 76 B5
Dykeside Aberds 89 D7
Dykesmains N Ayrs 66 B5
Dylife Powys 32 F4
Dymchurch Kent 13 D9
Dymock Glos 26 E4
Dyrham S Glouc 16 D4
Dysart Fife 70 A2
Dyserth Denbs 42 E3

E

Eachwick Northum 63 F7
Eadar Dha Fhadhail W Isles 90 D5
Eagland Hill Lancs 49 E4
Eagle Lincs 46 F2
Eagle Barnsdale Lincs 46 F2
Eagle Moor Lincs 46 F2
Eaglescliffe Stockton 58 E5
Eaglesfield Cumb 56 D2
Eaglesfield Dumf/Gal 61 F8
Eaglesham E Renf 68 E4
Eaglethorpe Northants 37 F6
Eairy I/Man 48 E2
Eakley Lanes M/Keynes 28 C5
Eakring Notts 45 F10
Ealand N Lincs 45 A11
Ealing London 19 C8
Eals Northum 62 H2
Eamont Bridge Cumb 57 D7
Earby Lancs 50 E5
Earcroft Blackb'n 50 G2
Eardington Shrops 34 F3
Eardisland Heref'd 25 C11
Eardisley Heref'd 25 D10
Eardiston Shrops 33 C9
Eardiston Worcs 26 B3
Earith Cambs 29 A10
Earl Shilton Leics 35 F10
Earl Soham Suffolk 31 B9
Earl Sterndale Derby 44 F4
Earl Stonham Suffolk 31 C8
Earle Northum 71 H8
Earley Wokingham 18 D4
Earlham Norfolk 39 E8
Earlish H'land 85 B8
Earls Barton Northants 28 B5
Earls Colne Essex 30 F5
Earl's Croome Worcs 26 D5
Earl's Green Suffolk 31 B7
Earlsdon W Midlands 35 H9
Earlsferry Fife 77 H7
Earlsfield Lincs 36 B5
Earlsford Aberds 89 E8
Earlsheaton W Yorks 51 G8
Earlsmill Moray 87 F12
Earlston Scot Borders 70 G4
Earlston E Ayrs 67 C7
Earlswood Monmouths 15 B10
Earlswood Surrey 19 G9
Earlswood Warwick 27 A8
Earnley W Sussex 11 E7
Earsairidh W Isles 84 J2
Earsdon Tyne/Wear 63 F9
Earsham Norfolk 39 G9
Earswick C/York 52 D2
Eartham W Sussex 11 D8
Easby N Yorks 59 F6
Easby N Yorks 58 F2
Easdale Arg/Bute 72 B6
Easebourne W Sussex 11 B7
Easenhall Warwick 35 H10
Eashing Surrey 18 G6
Easington Bucks 28 G3
Easington Durham 58 B5
Easington ER Yorks 53 H9
Easington Northum 71 G10
Easington Oxon 27 E11
Easington Oxon 18 B3
Easington Redcar/Clevel'd 59 E8
Easington Colliery Durham 58 B5
Easington Lane Tyne/Wear 58 B4
Easingwold N Yorks 51 C11
Easole Street Kent 21 F9
Eassie Angus 76 C6
East Aberthaw V/Glam 14 E6
East Adderbury Oxon 27 E11
East Allington Devon 5 G8
East Anstey Devon 7 D7
East Appleton N Yorks 58 G3
East Ardsley W Yorks 51 G9
East Ashling W Sussex 11 D7
East Auchronie Aberds 83 C10
East Ayton N Yorks 59 H10
East Bank Bl Gwent 25 H9
East Barkwith Lincs 46 D5
East Barming Kent 20 F4
East Barnby N Yorks 59 E9
East Barnet London 19 B9
East Barns E Loth 70 C6
East Barsham Norfolk 38 B5
East Beckham Norfolk 39 B7
East Bedfont London 19 D7
East Bergholt Suffolk 31 E7
East Bilney Norfolk 38 D5
East Blatchington E Sussex 12 F3
East Boldre Hants 10 D2
East Brent Som'set 15 F9
East Bridgford Notts 36 A2
East Buckland Devon 6 C5
East Budleigh Devon 7 H9
East Burrafirth Shetl'd 96 H5
East Burton Dorset 9 F7
East Butsfield Durham 58 B2
East Butterwick N Lincs 46 B2
East Cairnbeg Aberds 83 F9
East Calder W Loth 69 D9
East Carleton Norfolk 39 E7
East Carlton Northants 36 G4
East Carlton W Yorks 51 E8
East Chaldon Dorset 9 F6
East Challow Oxon 17 C10
East Chiltington E Sussex 12 E2
East Chinnock Som'set 8 C3
East Chisenbury Wilts 17 F8
East Clandon Surrey 19 F7
East Claydon Bucks 28 F4
East Clyne H'land 93 J12
East Coker Som'set 8 C4
East Combe Som'set 7 C10
East Common N Yorks 52 F2
East Compton Som'set 16 G3
East Cottingwith ER Yorks 52 E3
East Cowes I/Wight 10 E4
East Cowick ER Yorks 52 G2
East Cowton N Yorks 58 F4
East Cramlington Northum 63 F8
East Cranmore Som'set 16 G3
East Creech Dorset 9 F8
East Croachy H'land 81 A8
East Croftmore H'land 81 B11
East Curthwaite Cumb 56 B5
East Dean E Sussex 12 G4
East Dean Hants 10 B1
East Dean W Sussex 11 C8
East Down Devon 6 B5
East Drayton Notts 45 E11
East Ella Kingston/Hull 53 G6
East End Dorset 9 E8
East End ER Yorks 53 G8
East End Hants 10 E2
East End Hants 10 B5
East End Hants 17 E11
East End Herts 29 F11
East End Kent 13 C7
East End N Som'set 15 D10
East End Oxon 27 G10
East Farleigh Kent 20 F4
East Farndon Northants 36 G3
East Ferry Lincs 46 C2
East Fortune E Loth 70 C4
East Garston W Berks 17 D10
East Ginge Oxon 17 C11
East Goscote Leics 36 D2
East Grafton Wilts 17 E9
East Grimstead Wilts 9 B11
East Grinstead W Sussex 12 C2
East Guldeford E Sussex 13 D8
East Haddon Northants 28 B3
East Hagbourne Oxon 18 C2
East Halton N Lincs 53 H7
East Ham London 19 C11
East Hanney Oxon 17 B11
East Hanningfield Essex 20 A4
East Hardwick W Yorks 51 H10
East Harling Norfolk 38 G5
East Harlsey N Yorks 58 G5
East Harnham Wilts 9 B10
East Harptree Bath/NE Som'set 16 F2
East Hartford Northum 63 F8
East Harting W Sussex 11 C6
East Hatley Cambs 29 C9
East Hauxwell N Yorks 58 G2
East Haven Angus 77 D8
East Heckington Lincs 37 A7
East Hedleyhope Durham 58 B2
East Hendred Oxon 17 C11
East Herrington Tyne/Wear 58 A4
East Heslerton N Yorks 52 B5
East Hoathly E Sussex 12 E4
East Horrington Som'set 16 G2
East Horsley Surrey 19 F7
East Horton Northum 71 G9
East Huntspill Som'set 15 G9
East Hyde Beds 29 G8
East Ilkerton Devon 6 B6
East Ilsley W Berks 17 C11
East Keal Lincs 47 F7
East Kennett Wilts 17 E8
East Keswick W Yorks 51 E9
East Kilbride S Lanarks 68 E5
East Kirkby Lincs 47 F7
East Knapton N Yorks 52 B4
East Knighton Dorset 9 F7
East Knoyle Wilts 9 A7
East Kyloe Northum 71 G9
East Lambrook Som'set 8 C3
East Lamington H'land 87 D10
East Langdon Kent 21 G10
East Langton Leics 36 F3
East Langwell H'land 93 J10
East Lavant W Sussex 11 D7
East Lavington W Sussex 11 C8
East Layton N Yorks 58 F2
East Leake Notts 36 C1
East Learmouth Northum 71 G7
East Leigh Devon 6 F5
East Lexham Norfolk 38 D4
East Lilburn Northum 62 A6
East Linton E Loth 70 C4
East Liss Hants 11 B6
East Looe Cornw'l 4 F3
East Lound N Lincs 45 C11
East Lulworth Dorset 9 F7
East Lutton N Yorks 52 C5
East Lydford Som'set 8 A4
East Mains Aberds 83 D8
East Malling Kent 20 F4
East March Angus 77 D7
East Marden W Sussex 11 C7
East Markham Notts 45 E11
East Marton N Yorks 50 D5
East Meon Hants 10 B5
East Mere Devon 7 E8
East Mersea Essex 31 G7
East Mey H'land 94 C5
East Molesey Surrey 19 E8
East Morden Dorset 9 E8
East Morton W Yorks 51 E6
East Ness N Yorks 52 B2
East Newton ER Yorks 53 F8
East Norton Leics 36 E3
East Nynehead Som'set 7 D10
East Oakley Hants 18 F2
East Ogwell Devon 5 D9
East Orchard Dorset 9 C7
East Ord Northum 71 E8
East Panson Devon 6 G2
East Peckham Kent 20 G3
East Pennard Som'set 16 H2
East Perry Cambs 29 B8
East Portlemouth Devon 5 H8
East Prawle Devon 5 H8
East Preston W Sussex 11 D9
East Putford Devon 6 E2
East Quantoxhead Som'set 7 B10
East Rainton Tyne/Wear 58 B4
East Ravendale NE Lincs 46 C6
East Raynham Norfolk 38 C4
East Rhidorroch Lodge H'land 86 B5
East Rigton W Yorks 51 E9
East Rounton N Yorks 58 F5
East Row N Yorks 59 E9
East Rudham Norfolk 38 C4
East Runton Norfolk 39 A7
East Ruston Norfolk 39 C9
East Saltoun E Loth 70 D3
East Sleekburn Northum 63 E8
East Somerton Norfolk 39 D10
East Stockwith Lincs 45 C11
East Stoke Dorset 9 F7
East Stoke Notts 45 H11
East Stour Dorset 9 B7
East Stourmouth Kent 21 E9
East Stowford Devon 6 D5
East Stratton Hants 18 H2
East Studdal Kent 21 G10
East Suisnish H'land 85 E10
East Taphouse Cornw'l 4 E2
East-the-Water Devon 6 D3
East Thirston Northum 63 D7
East Tilbury Thurr'k 20 D3
East Tisted Hants 10 A6
East Torrington Lincs 46 D5
East Tuddenham Norfolk 39 D6
East Tytherley Hants 10 B1
East Tytherton Wilts 16 D6
East Village Devon 7 F7
East Wall Shrops 33 F11
East Walton Norfolk 38 D3
East Wellow Hants 10 B2
East Wemyss Fife 76 H6
East Whitburn W Loth 69 D8
East Williamston Pembs 22 F5
East Winch Norfolk 38 D2
East Winterslow Wilts 9 A11
East Wittering W Sussex 11 E6
East Witton N Yorks 58 H2
East Woodburn Northum 62 E5
East Woodhay Hants 17 E11
East Worldham Hants 18 H4
East Worlington Devon 7 E6
East Worthing W Sussex 11 D10
Eastbourne E Sussex 12 G5
Eastbridge Suffolk 31 B11
Eastburn W Yorks 50 E6
Eastbury Herts 19 B7
Eastbury W Berks 17 D10
Eastby N Yorks 50 D6
Eastchurch Kent 20 D6
Eastcombe Glos 16 A5
Eastcote London 19 C8
Eastcote Northants 28 C3
Eastcote W Midlands 35 H7
Eastcott Cornw'l 6 E1
Eastcott Wilts 17 F7
Eastcourt Wilts 16 B6
Eastcourt Wilts 17 E9
Easter Ardross H'land 87 D9
Easter Balmoral Aberds 82 D4
Easter Boleskine H'land 81 A7
Easter Compton S Glouc 16 C2
Easter Cringate Stirl 68 B6
Easter Davoch Aberds 82 C6
Easter Earshaig Dumf/Gal 60 C6
Easter Fearn H'land 87 C9
Easter Galcantray H'land 87 G11
Easter Howgate Midloth 69 D11
Easter Howlaws Scot Borders 70 F6
Easter Kinkell H'land 87 F8
Easter Lednathie Angus 76 A6
Easter Milton H'land 87 F12
Easter Moniack H'land 87 G8
Easter Ord Aberds 83 C10
Easter Quarff Shetl'd 96 K6
Easter Rhynd Perth/Kinr 76 F4
Easter Row Stirl 75 H10
Easter Silverford Aberds 89 B7
Easter Skeld Shetl'd 96 J5
Easter Whyntie Aberds 88 B6
Eastergate W Sussex 11 D8
Easterhouse C/Glasg 68 D5
Eastern Green W Midlands 35 G8
Easterton Wilts 17 F7
Eastertown Som'set 15 F9
Eastertown of Auchleuchries Aberds 89 E10
Eastfield N Lanarks 69 D7
Eastfield N Yorks 52 A6
Eastfield Hall Northum 63 C8
Eastgate Durham 57 C11
Eastgate Norfolk 39 C7
Eastham Mersey 42 D6
Eastham Ferry Mersey 42 D6
Easthampstead Brackn'l 18 E5
Easthope Shrops 34 F1
Easthorpe Essex 30 F6
Easthorpe Leics 36 B4
Easthorpe Notts 45 G11
Easthouses Midloth 70 D2
Eastington Devon 7 F6
Eastington Glos 26 H4
Eastington Glos 27 G8
Eastleach Martin Glos 27 H9
Eastleach Turville Glos 27 H8
Eastleigh Devon 6 D3
Eastleigh Hants 10 C3
Eastling Kent 20 F6
Eastmoor Derby 45 E7
Eastmoor Norfolk 38 E3
Eastney Portsm'th 10 E5
Eastnor Heref'd 26 E4
Eastoft N Lincs 52 H4
Eastoke Hants 10 E6
Easton Cambs 29 A8
Easton Cumb 61 F10
Easton Devon 5 C8
Easton Dorset 8 G5
Easton Hants 10 A4
Easton Lincs 36 C5
Easton Norfolk 39 D7
Easton Som'set 15 G11
Easton Suffolk 31 C9
Easton Wilts 16 D5
Easton Grey Wilts 16 C5
Easton-in-Gordano N Som'set 15 D11
Easton Maudit Northants 28 C5
Easton on the Hill Northants 36 E6
Easton Royal Wilts 17 E9
Eastpark Dumf/Gal 60 G6
Eastrea Cambs 37 F8
Eastriggs Dumf/Gal 61 G8
Eastrington ER Yorks 52 G3
Eastry Kent 21 F10
Eastville Bristol 16 D3
Eastville Lincs 47 G8
Eastwell Leics 36 C3
Eastwick Herts 29 G11
Eastwick Shetl'd 96 F5
Eastwood Notts 45 H8
Eastwood Southend 20 C5
Eastwood W Yorks 50 G5
Eathorpe Warwick 27 B10
Eaton Ches 43 F8
Eaton Ches 44 F2
Eaton Leics 36 C3
Eaton Norfolk 39 E8
Eaton Oxon 17 A11
Eaton Shrops 33 G9
Eaton Shrops 33 G11
Eaton Bishop Heref'd 25 E11
Eaton Bray Beds 28 F6
Eaton Constantine Shrops 34 E1
Eaton Green Beds 28 F6
Eaton Hastings Oxon 17 B9
Eaton on Tern Shrops 34 C2
Eaton Socon Cambs 29 C8
Eavestone N Yorks 51 C8
Ebberston N Yorks 52 A4
Ebbesbourne Wake Wilts 9 B8
Ebbw Vale = Glyn Ebwy Bl Gwent 25 H8
Ebchester Durham 63 H7
Ebford Devon 5 C10
Ebley Glos 26 H5
Ebnal Ches 43 H7
Ebrington Glos 27 D8
Ecchinswell Hants 17 F11
Ecclaw Scot Borders 70 D6
Ecclefechan Dumf/Gal 61 F7
Eccles Scot Borders 70 F6
Eccles Gtr Man 43 C10
Eccles Kent 20 E4
Eccles on Sea Norfolk 39 C10
Eccles Road Norfolk 38 F6
Ecclesall S Yorks 45 D7
Ecclesfield S Yorks 45 C7
Ecclesgreig Aberds 83 G9
Eccleshall Staffs 34 C4
Eccleshill W Yorks 51 F7
Ecclesmachan W Loth 69 C9
Eccleston Ches 43 F7
Eccleston Lancs 49 H5
Eccleston Mersey 43 C7
Eccleston Park Mersey 43 C7
Eccup W Yorks 51 E8
Echt Aberds 83 C9
Eckford Scot Borders 70 H6
Eckington Derby 45 E8
Eckington Worcs 26 D6
Ecton Northants 28 B5
Edale Derby 44 D5
Edburton W Sussex 11 C11
Edderside Cumb 56 B2
Edderton H'land 87 C10
Eddistone Devon 6 D1
Eddleston Scot Borders 69 F11
Eden Park London 19 E10
Edenbridge Kent 19 G11
Edenfield Lancs 50 H3
Edenhall Cumb 57 C7
Edenham Lincs 37 C6
Edensor Derby 44 F6
Edentaggart Arg/Bute 68 A2
Edenthorpe S Yorks 45 B10
Edentown Cumb 61 H9
Ederline Arg/Bute 73 C7
Edern Gwyn 40 G4
Edgarley Som'set 15 H11
Edgbaston W Midlands 35 G6
Edgcott Bucks 28 F3
Edgcott Som'set 7 C7
Edge Shrops 33 E9
Edge End Glos 26 G2
Edge Green Ches 43 G7
Edge Hill Mersey 42 D6
Edgebolton Shrops 34 C1
Edgefield Norfolk 39 B6
Edgefield Street Norfolk 39 B6
Edgeside Lancs 50 G4
Edgeworth Glos 26 H6
Edgmond Telford 34 D3
Edgmond Marsh Telford 34 C3
Edgton Shrops 33 G9
Edgware London 19 B8
Edgworth Blackb'n 50 H3
Edinample Stirl 75 E8
Edinbane H'land 85 C8
Edinburgh C/Edinb 69 C11
Edingale Staffs 35 D8
Edingight Ho. Moray 88 C5
Edingley Notts 45 G10
Edingthorpe Norfolk 39 B9
Edingthorpe Green Norfolk 39 B9
Edington Som'set 15 H9
Edington Wilts 16 F6
Edintore Moray 88 D4
Edith Weston Rutl'd 36 E5
Edithmead Som'set 15 G9
Edlesborough Bucks 28 G6
Edlingham Northum 63 C7
Edlington Lincs 46 E6
Edmondsham Dorset 9 C9
Edmondsley Durham 58 B3
Edmondthorpe Leics 36 D4
Edmonstone Orkney 95 F6
Edmonton London 19 B10
Edmundbyers Durham 58 A1
Ednam Scot Borders 70 G6
Ednaston Derby 35 A8
Edradynate Perth/Kinr 75 B11
Edrom Scot Borders 71 E7
Edstaston Shrops 33 B11
Edstone Warwick 27 B8
Edvin Loach Heref'd 26 C3
Edwalton Notts 36 B1
Edwardstone Suffolk 30 D6
Edwinsford Carms 24 E3
Edwinstowe Notts 45 F10
Edworth Beds 29 D9
Edwyn Ralph Heref'd 26 C3
Edzell Angus 83 G7
Efail Isaf Rh Cyn Taff 14 C6
Efailnewydd Gwyn 40 G5
Efailwen Carms 22 D6
Efenechtyd Denbs 42 G4
Effingham Surrey 19 F8
Effirth Shetl'd 96 H5
Efford Devon 7 F7
Egdon Worcs 26 C6
Egerton Gtr Man 43 A10
Egerton Kent 20 G6
Egerton Forstal Kent 20 G5
Eggborough N Yorks 52 G1
Eggbuckland Plym'th 4 F6
Eggington Beds 28 F6
Egginton Derby 35 C8
Egglescliffe Stockton 58 E5
Eggleston Durham 57 D11
Egham Surrey 19 D7
Egleton Rutl'd 36 E4
Eglingham Northum 63 B7
Egloshayle Cornw'l 3 B8
Egloskerry Cornw'l 4 C3
Eglwys-Brewis V/Glam 14 E6
Eglwys Cross Wrex 33 A10
Eglwys Fach Ceredig'n 32 F2
Eglwysbach Conwy 41 C10
Eglwyswen Pembs 22 C6
Eglwyswrw Pembs 22 C6
Egmanton Notts 45 F11
Egremont Cumb 56 E2
Egremont Mersey 42 C6
Egton N Yorks 59 F9
Egton Bridge N Yorks 59 F9
Eight Ash Green Essex 30 F6
Eignaig H'land 79 G10
Eil H'land 81 B10
Eilanreach H'land 85 G13
Eilean Darach H'land 86 C4
Eileanach Lodge H'land 87 E8
Einacleite W Isles 90 E6
Eisgean W Isles 91 F8
Eisingrug Gwyn 41 G8
Elan Village Powys 24 B6
Elberton S Glouc 16 C3
Elburton Plym'th 4 F6
Elcho Perth/Kinr 76 E4
Elcombe Swindon 17 C8
Eldernell Cambs 37 F9
Eldersfield Worcs 26 E5
Elderslie Renf 68 D3
Eldon Durham 58 D3
Eldrick S Ayrs 54 A5
Eldroth N Yorks 50 C3
Eldwick W Yorks 51 E7
Elfhowe Cumb 56 G6
Elford Northum 71 G10
Elford Staffs 35 D7
Elgin Moray 88 B2
Elgol H'land 85 G10
Elham Kent 21 G8
Elie Fife 77 G7
Elim Angl 40 B5
Eling Hants 10 C2
Elishader H'land 85 B10
Elishaw Northum 62 D4
Elkesley Notts 45 E10
Elkstone Glos 26 G6
Ellan H'land 81 A10
Elland W Yorks 51 G7
Ellary Arg/Bute 72 F6
Ellastone Staffs 35 A7
Ellemford Scot Borders 70 D6
Ellenbrook I/Man 48 E3
Ellenhall Staffs 34 C4
Ellen's Green Surrey 19 H7
Ellerbeck N Yorks 58 G5
Ellerburn N Yorks 52 A4
Ellerby N Yorks 59 E8
Ellerdine Heath Telford 34 C2
Ellerhayes Devon 7 F8
Elleric Arg/Bute 74 C3
Ellerker ER Yorks 52 G5
Ellerton ER Yorks 52 F3
Ellerton Shrops 34 C3
Ellesborough Bucks 28 H5
Ellesmere Shrops 33 B10
Ellesmere Port Ches 43 E7
Ellingham Norfolk 39 F9
Ellingham Northum 71 H10
Ellingstring N Yorks 51 A7
Ellington Cambs 29 A8
Ellington Northum 63 D8
Elliot Angus 77 D9
Ellisfield Hants 18 G3
Ellistown Leics 35 D10
Ellon Aberds 89 E9
Ellonby Cumb 56 C6
Ellough Suffolk 39 G10
Elloughton ER Yorks 52 G5
Ellwood Glos 26 H2
Elm Cambs 37 E10
Elm Hill Dorset 9 B7
Elm Park London 20 C2
Elmbridge Worcs 26 B6
Elmdon Essex 29 E11
Elmdon W Midlands 35 G7
Elmdon Heath W Midlands 35 G7
Elmers End London 19 E10
Elmesthorpe Leics 35 F10
Elmfield I/Wight 10 E5
Elmhurst Staffs 35 D7
Elmley Castle Worcs 26 D6
Elmley Lovett Worcs 26 B5
Elmore Glos 26 G4
Elmore Back Glos 26 G4
Elmscott Devon 6 D1
Elmsett Suffolk 31 D7
Elmstead Market Essex 31 F7
Elmsted Kent 13 B10
Elmstone Kent 21 E9
Elmstone Hardwicke Glos 26 F6
Elmswell ER Yorks 52 D5
Elmswell Suffolk 30 B6
Elmton Derby 45 E9
Elphin H'land 92 H5
Elphinstone E Loth 70 C2
Elrick Aberds 83 C10
Elrig Dumf/Gal 54 E6
Elsdon Northum 62 D5
Elsecar S Yorks 45 C7
Elsenham Essex 30 F2
Elsfield Oxon 28 G2
Elsham N Lincs 46 A4
Elsing Norfolk 39 D6
Elslack N Yorks 50 E5
Elson Shrops 33 B9
Elsrickle S Lanarks 69 F9
Elstead Surrey 18 G6
Elsted W Sussex 11 C7
Elsthorpe Lincs 37 C6
Elstob Durham 58 D4
Elston Notts 45 H11
Elston Wilts 17 G7
Elstone Devon 6 E5
Elstow Beds 29 D7
Elstree Herts 19 B8
Elstronwick ER Yorks 53 F8
Elswick Lancs 49 F4
Elsworth Cambs 29 B10
Elterwater Cumb 56 F5
Eltham London 19 D11
Eltisley Cambs 29 C9
Elton Cambs 37 F6
Elton Ches 43 E7
Elton Derby 44 F6
Elton Glos 26 G4
Elton Heref'd 25 A11
Elton Notts 36 B3
Elton Stockton 58 E5
Elton Green Ches 43 E7
Elvanfoot S Lanarks 60 B5
Elvaston Derby 35 B10
Elveden Suffolk 38 H4
Elvingston E Loth 70 C3
Elvington Kent 21 F9
Elvington C/York 52 E2
Elwick Hartlep'l 58 C5
Elwick Northum 71 G10
Elworth Ches 43 F10
Elworthy Som'set 7 C9
Ely Cambs 37 G11
Ely Card 15 D7
Emberton M/Keynes 28 D5
Embleton Cumb 56 C3
Embleton Northum 63 A8
Embo H'land 87 B11
Embo Street H'land 87 B11
Emborough Som'set 16 F3
Embsay N Yorks 50 D6
Emery Down Hants 10 D1
Emley W Yorks 44 A6
Emmbrook Wokingham 18 E4
Emmer Green Reading 18 D4
Emmington Oxon 18 A4
Emneth Norfolk 37 E10
Emneth Hungate Norfolk 37 E11
Empingham Rutl'd 36 E5
Empshott Hants 11 A6
Emstrey Shrops 33 D11
Emsworth Hants 10 D6
Enborne W Berks 17 E11
Enchmarsh Shrops 33 F11
Enderby Leics 35 F11
Endmoor Cumb 49 A5
Endon Staffs 44 G3
Endon Bank Staffs 44 G3
Enfield London 19 B10
Enfield Wash London 19 B10
Enford Wilts 17 F8
Engamoor Shetl'd 96 H4
Engine Common S Glouc 16 C3
Englefield W Berks 18 D3
Englefield Green Surrey 18 D6
Englesea-brook Ches 43 G10
English Bicknor Glos 26 G2
English Frankton Shrops 33 C10
Englishcombe Bath/NE Som'set 16 E4
Enham-Alamein Hants 17 G10
Enmore Som'set 8 A1
Ennerdale Bridge Cumb 56 E2
Enoch Dumf/Gal 60 C4
Enochdhu Perth/Kinr 76 A3
Ensay Arg/Bute 78 G6
Ensbury Bournem'th 9 E9
Ensdon Shrops 33 D10
Ensis Devon 6 D4
Enstone Oxon 27 F10
Enterkinfoot Dumf/Gal 60 C4
Enterpen N Yorks 58 F5
Enville Staffs 34 G4
Eolaigearraidh W Isles 84 H2
Eorabus Arg/Bute 78 J6
Eòropaidh W Isles 91 A10
Epperstone Notts 45 H10
Epping Essex 19 A11
Epping Green Essex 29 H11
Epping Green Herts 29 H9
Epping Upland Essex 19 A11
Eppleby N Yorks 58 E2
Eppleworth ER Yorks 52 F6
Epsom Surrey 19 E9
Epwell Oxon 27 D10
Epworth N Lincs 45 B11
Epworth Turbary N Lincs 45 B11
Erbistock Wrex 33 A9
Erbusaig H'land 85 F12
Erchless Castle H'land 86 G7
Erdington W Midlands 35 F7
Eredine Arg/Bute 73 C8
Eriboll H'land 92 D7
Ericstane Dumf/Gal 60 B6
Eridge Green E Sussex 12 C4
Erines Arg/Bute 73 F7
Eriswell Suffolk 38 H3
Erith London 20 D2
Erlestoke Wilts 16 F6
Ermine Lincs 46 E3
Ermington Devon 5 F7
Erpingham Norfolk 39 B7
Errogie H'land 81 A7
Errol Perth/Kinr 76 E5
Erskine Renf 68 C3
Erskine Bridge Renf 68 C3
Ervie Dumf/Gal 54 C3
Erwarton Suffolk 31 E9
Erwood Powys 25 D7
Eryholme N Yorks 58 F4
Eryrys Denbs 42 G5
Escomb Durham 58 D2
Escrick N Yorks 52 E2
Esgairdawe Carms 24 D3
Esgairgeiliog Powys 32 E3
Esh Durham 58 B2
Esh Winning Durham 58 B2
Esher Surrey 19 E8
Esholt W Yorks 51 E7
Eshott Northum 63 D8
Eshton N Yorks 50 D5
Esk Valley N Yorks 59 F9
Eskadale H'land 86 H7
Eskbank Midloth 70 D2
Eskdale Green Cumb 56 F3
Eskdalemuir Dumf/Gal 61 D8
Eske ER Yorks 53 E6
Eskham Lincs 47 C7
Esprick Lancs 49 F4
Essendine Rutl'd 36 D6
Essendon Herts 29 H9
Essich H'land 87 H9
Essington Staffs 34 E5
Esslemont Aberds 89 F9
Eston Redcar/Clevel'd 59 E6
Eswick Shetl'd 96 H6
Etal Northum 71 G8
Etchilhampton Wilts 17 E7
Etchingham E Sussex 12 D6
Etchinghill Kent 21 H8
Etchinghill Staffs 34 D6
Ethie Castle Angus 77 C9
Ethie Mains Angus 77 C9
Etling Green Norfolk 38 D6
Eton Windsor 18 D6
Eton Wick Windsor 18 D6
Etteridge H'land 81 D8
Ettersgill Durham 57 D10
Ettingshall W Midlands 34 F5
Ettington Warwick 27 D9
Etton ER Yorks 52 E5
Etton Peterbro 37 E7
Ettrick Scot Borders 61 B8
Ettrickbridge Scot Borders 61 A9
Ettrickhill Scot Borders 61 B8
Etwall Derby 35 B8
Euston Suffolk 38 H4
Euximoor Drove Cambs 37 F10
Euxton Lancs 50 H1
Evanstown Bridg 14 C5
Evanton H'land 87 E9
Evedon Lincs 46 H4
Evelix H'land 87 B10
Evenjobb Powys 25 B9
Evenley Northants 28 E2
Evenlode Glos 27 F9
Evenwood Durham 58 D2
Evenwood Gate Durham 58 D2
Everbay Orkney 95 F7
Evercreech Som'set 16 H3
Everdon Northants 28 C2
Everingham ER Yorks 52 E4
Everleigh Wilts 17 F9
Everley N Yorks 59 H10
Eversholt Beds 28 E6
Evershot Dorset 8 D4
Eversley Hants 18 E4
Eversley Cross Hants 18 E4
Everthorpe ER Yorks 52 F5
Everton Beds 29 C9
Everton Hants 10 E1
Everton Mersey 42 C6
Everton Notts 45 C10
Evertown Dumf/Gal 61 F9
Evesbatch Heref'd 26 D3
Evesham Worcs 27 D7
Evington Leics C 36 E2
Ewden Village S Yorks 44 C6
Ewell Surrey 19 E9
Ewell Minnis Kent 21 G9
Ewelme Oxon 18 B3
Ewen Glos 17 B7
Ewenny V/Glam 14 D5
Ewerby Lincs 46 H5
Ewerby Thorpe Lincs 46 H5
Ewes Dumf/Gal 61 D9
Ewesley Northum 62 D6
Ewhurst Surrey 19 G7
Ewhurst Green E Sussex 13 D6
Ewhurst Green Surrey 19 H7
Ewloe Flints 42 F6
Ewloe Green Flints 42 F5
Ewood Blackb'n 50 G2
Eworthy Devon 6 G3
Ewshot Hants 18 G5
Ewyas Harold Heref'd 25 F10
Exbourne Devon 6 F5
Exbury Hants 10 E3
Exebridge Som'set 7 D8
Exelby N Yorks 58 H3
Exeter Devon 7 G8
Exford Som'set 7 C7
Exhall Warwick 27 C8
Exley Head W Yorks 50 F6
Exminster Devon 5 C10
Exmouth Devon 5 C11
Exnaboe Shetl'd 96 M5
Exning Suffolk 30 B3
Exton Devon 5 C10
Exton Hants 10 B5
Exton Rutl'd 36 D5
Exton Som'set 7 C8
Exwick Devon 7 G8
Eyam Derby 44 E6
Eydon Northants 28 C2
Eye Heref'd 25 B11
Eye Peterbro 37 E8
Eye Suffolk 31 A8
Eye Green Peterbro 37 E8
Eyemouth Scot Borders 71 D8
Eyeworth Beds 29 D9
Eyhorne Street Kent 20 F5
Eyke Suffolk 31 C10
Eynesbury Cambs 29 C8
Eynort H'land 85 F8
Eynsford Kent 20 E2
Eynsham Oxon 27 H11
Eype Dorset 8 E3
Eyre H'land 85 C9
Eyre H'land 85 E10
Eythorne Kent 21 G9
Eyton Heref'd 25 B11
Eyton Shrops 33 G9
Eyton Wrex 33 A9
Eyton upon the Weald Moors Telford 34 D2

F

Faccombe Hants 17 F10
Faceby N Yorks 58 F5
Facit Lancs 50 H4
Faddiley Ches 43 G8
Fadmoor N Yorks 59 H7
Faerdre Swan 14 A2
Failford S Ayrs 67 D7
Failsworth Gtr Man 44 B2
Fain H'land 86 D4
Fair Green Norfolk 38 D2
Fair Hill Cumb 57 C7
Fair Oak Hants 10 C3
Fair Oak Green Hants 18 E3
Fairbourne Gwyn 32 D2
Fairburn N Yorks 51 G10
Fairfield Derby 44 E4
Fairfield Stockton 58 E5
Fairfield Worcs 27 D7
Fairfield Worcs 34 H5
Fairford Glos 17 A8
Fairhaven Lancs 49 G3
Fairlie N Ayrs 73 H11
Fairlight E Sussex 13 E7
Fairlight Cove E Sussex 13 E7
Fairmile Devon 7 G9
Fairmilehead C/Edinb 69 D11
Fairoak Staffs 34 B3
Fairseat Kent 20 E3
Fairstead Essex 30 G4
Fairstead Norfolk 38 D2
Fairwarp E Sussex 12 D3
Fairy Cottage I/Man 48 D4
Fairy Cross Devon 6 D3
Fakenham Norfolk 38 C5
Fala Midloth 70 D3
Fala Dam Midloth 70 D3
Falahill Scot Borders 70 E2
Falcon Heref'd 26 E3
Faldingworth Lincs 46 D4
Falfield S Glouc 16 B3
Falkenham Suffolk 31 E9
Falkirk Falk 69 C7
Falkland Fife 76 G5
Falla Scot Borders 62 B3
Fallgate Derby 45 F7
Fallin Stirl 69 A7
Fallowfield Gtr Man 44 C2
Fallsidehill Scot Borders 70 F5
Falmer E Sussex 12 F2
Falmouth Cornw'l 3 F7
Falsgrave N Yorks 59 H11
Falstone Northum 62 E3
Fanagmore H'land 92 E4
Fangdale Beck N Yorks 59 G6
Fangfoss ER Yorks 52 D3
Fankerton Falk 68 B6
Fanmore Arg/Bute 78 G7
Fannich Lodge H'land 86 E5
Fans Scot Borders 70 F5
Far Bank S Yorks 45 A10
Far Bletchley M/Keynes 28 E5
Far Cotton Northants 28 C4
Far Forest Worcs 26 A4
Far Laund Derby 45 H7
Far Sawrey Cumb 56 G5
Farcet Cambs 37 F8
Farden Shrops 34 H1
Fareham Hants 10 D4
Farewell Staffs 35 D6
Farforth Lincs 47 E7
Faringdon Oxon 17 B9
Farington Lancs 49 G5
Farlam Cumb 61 H11
Farlary H'land 93 J10
Farleigh N Som'set 15 E10
Farleigh Surrey 19 E10
Farleigh Hungerford Som'set 16 F5
Farleigh Wallop Hants 18 G3
Farlesthorpe Lincs 47 E8
Farleton Cumb 49 A5
Farleton Lancs 50 C1
Farley Shrops 33 E9
Farley Staffs 35 A6
Farley Wilts 9 B11
Farley Green Surrey 19 G7
Farley Hill Luton 29 F7
Farley Hill Wokingham 18 E4
Farleys End Glos 26 G4
Farlington N Yorks 52 C2
Farlow Shrops 34 G2
Farmborough Bath/NE Som'set 16 E3
Farmcote Glos 27 F7
Farmcote Shrops 34 F3
Farmington Glos 27 G8
Farmoor Oxon 27 H11
Farmtown Moray 88 C5
Farnborough London 19 E11
Farnborough Hants 18 F5
Farnborough Warwick 27 D11
Farnborough W Berks 17 C11
Farnborough Green Hants 18 F5
Farncombe Surrey 18 G6
Farndish Beds 28 B6
Farndon Ches 43 G7
Farndon Notts 45 G11
Farnell Angus 77 B9
Farnham Dorset 9 C8
Farnham Essex 29 F11
Farnham N Yorks 51 C9
Farnham Suffolk 31 B10
Farnham Surrey 18 G5
Farnham Common Bucks 18 C6
Farnham Green Essex 29 F11
Farnham Royal Bucks 18 C6
Farnhill N Yorks 50 E6
Farningham Kent 20 E2
Farnley N Yorks 51 E8
Farnley W Yorks 51 F8
Farnley Tyas W Yorks 44 A5
Farnsfield Notts 45 G10
Farnworth Gtr Man 43 B10
Farnworth Halton 43 D8
Farr H'land 87 H9
Farr H'land 81 C10
Farr H'land 93 C10
Farr House H'land 87 H9
Farringdon Devon 7 G9
Farrington Gurney Bath/NE Som'set 16 F3
Farsley W Yorks 51 F8
Farthinghoe Northants 28 E2
Farthingloe Kent 21 G9
Farthingstone Northants 28 C3
Fartown W Yorks 51 H7
Farway Devon 7 G10
Fasag H'land 85 C13
Fascadale H'land 79 D8
Faslane Port Arg/Bute 73 E11
Fasnacloich Arg/Bute 74 C3
Fasnakyle Ho. H'land 80 A5
Fassfern H'land 80 F2
Fatfield Tyne/Wear 58 A4
Fattahead Aberds 89 C6
Faugh Cumb 57 A7
Fauldhouse W Loth 69 D8
Faulkbourne Essex 30 G4
Faulkland Som'set 16 F4
Fauls Shrops 34 B1
Faversham Kent 21 E7
Favillar Moray 88 E2
Fawdington N Yorks 51 B10
Fawfieldhead Staffs 44 F4
Fawkham Green Kent 20 E2
Fawler Oxon 27 G10
Fawley Bucks 18 C4
Fawley Hants 10 D3
Fawley W Berks 17 C10
Fawley Chapel Heref'd 26 F2
Faxfleet ER Yorks 52 G4
Faygate W Sussex 11 A11
Fazakerley Mersey 43 C6
Fazeley Staffs 35 E8
Fearby N Yorks 51 A7
Fearn H'land 87 D11
Fearn Lodge H'land 87 C9
Fearn Station H'land 87 D11
Fearnan Perth/Kinr 75 C10
Fearnbeg H'land 85 C12
Fearnhead Warrington 43 C9
Fearnmore H'land 85 B12
Featherstone Staffs 34 E5
Featherstone W Yorks 51 G10
Featherwood Northum 62 C4
Feckenham Worcs 27 B7
Feering Essex 30 F5
Feetham N Yorks 57 G11
Feizor N Yorks 50 C3
Felbridge Surrey 12 C2
Felbrigg Norfolk 39 B8
Felcourt Surrey 12 B2
Felden Herts 19 A7
Felin-Crai Powys 24 F5
Felindre Ceredig'n 23 A10
Felindre Carms 23 D10
Felindre Carms 24 E3
Felindre Carms 24 F4
Felindre Carms 23 C8
Felindre Powys 33 G7
Felindre Swan 14 A2
Felindre Farchog Pembs 22 C6
Felinfach Ceredig'n 23 A10
Felinfach Powys 25 E7
Felinfoel Carms 23 F10
Felingwm isaf Carms 23 D10
Felingwm uchaf Carms 23 D10
Felinwynt Ceredig'n 23 A7
Felixkirk N Yorks 51 A10
Felixstowe Suffolk 31 E9
Felixstowe Ferry Suffolk 31 E10
Felkington Northum 71 F8
Felkirk W Yorks 45 A7
Fell Side Cumb 56 C5
Felling Tyne/Wear 63 G8
Felmersham Beds 28 C6
Felmingham Norfolk 39 C8
Felpham W Sussex 11 E8
Felsham Suffolk 30 C6
Felsted Essex 30 F3
Feltham London 19 D8
Felthorpe Norfolk 39 D7
Felton Heref'd 26 D2
Felton Northum 63 C7
Felton N Som'set 15 E11
Felton Butler Shrops 33 D9
Feltwell Norfolk 38 F3
Fen Ditton Cambs 29 B11
Fen Drayton Cambs 29 B10
Fen End W Midlands 35 H8
Fen Side Lincs 47 G7

Godolphin Cross Cornw'l 2 F5
Godre'r-graig Neath P Talb 24 H4
Godshill Hants 9 C10
Godshill I/Wight 10 F4
Godstone Surrey 19 F10
Godwinscroft Hants 9 E10
Goetre Monmouths 25 H10
Goferydd Angl 40 B4
Goff's Oak Herts 19 A10
Gogar C/Edinb 69 C10
Goginan Ceredig'n 32 G2
Golan Gwyn 41 F7
Golant Cornw'l 4 F2
Golberdon Cornw'l 4 D4
Golborne Gtr Man 43 C9
Golcar W Yorks 51 H7
Gold Hill Norfolk 37 F11
Goldcliff Newp 15 C9
Golden Cross E Sussex 12 E4
Golden Green Kent 20 G3
Golden Grove Carms 23 E10
Golden Hill Hants 10 E1
Golden Pot Hants 18 G4
Golden Valley Glos 26 F6
Goldenhill Stoke 44 G2
Golders Green London 19 C9
Goldhanger Essex 30 H6
Golding Shrops 33 E11
Goldington Beds 29 C7
Goldsborough N Yorks 51 D9
Goldsborough N Yorks 59 E9
Goldsithney Cornw'l 2 F4
Goldsworthy Devon 6 D2
Goldthorpe S Yorks 45 B8
Gollanfield H'land 87 F11
Golspie H'land 93 J11
Golval H'land 93 C11
Gomeldon Wilts 17 H8
Gomersal W Yorks 51 G8
Gomshall Surrey 19 G7
Gonalston Notts 45 H10
Gonfirth Shetl'd 96 G5
Good Easter Essex 30 G3
Gooderstone Norfolk 38 E3
Goodleigh Devon 6 C5
Goodmanham ER Yorks 52 E4
Goodnestone Kent 21 E7
Goodnestone Kent 21 F9
Goodrich Heref'd 26 G2
Goodrington Torbay 5 F9
Goodshaw Lancs 50 G4
Goodwick = Wdig Pembs 22 C4
Goodworth Clatford Hants 17 G10
Goole ER Yorks 52 G3
Goonbell Cornw'l 2 E6
Goonhavern Cornw'l 3 D6
Goose Eye W Yorks 50 E6
Goose Green Gtr Man 43 B8
Goose Green Norfolk 39 G7
Goose Green W Sussex 11 C10
Gooseham Cornw'l 6 E1
Goosey Oxon 17 B10
Goosnargh Lancs 50 F1
Goostrey Ches 43 E10
Gorcott Hill Warwick 27 B7
Gord Shetl'd 96 L6
Gordon Scot Borders 70 F5
Gordonbush H'land 93 J11
Gordonsburgh Moray 88 B4
Gordonstoun Moray 88 B1
Gordonstown Aberds 88 C5
Gordonstown Aberds 89 E7
Gore Kent 21 F10
Gore Cross Wilts 17 F7
Gore Pit Essex 30 G5
Gorebridge Midloth 70 D2
Gorefield Cambs 37 D10
Gorey Jersey 11
Gorgie C/Edinb 69 C11
Goring Oxon 18 C3
Goring-by-Sea W Sussex 11 D10
Goring Heath Oxon 18 D3
Gorleston-on-Sea Norfolk 39 E11
Gornalwood W Midlands 34 F5
Gorrachie Aberds 89 C7
Gorran Churchtown Cornw'l 3 E8
Gorran Haven Cornw'l 3 E9
Gorrenberry Scot Borders 61 D10
Gors Ceredig'n 32 H2
Gorse Hill Swindon 17 C8
Gorsedd Flints 42 E4
Gorseinon Swan 23 G10
Gorseness Orkney 95 G5
Gorsgoch Ceredig'n 23 A9
Gorslas Carms 23 E10
Gorsley Glos 26 F3
Gorstan H'land 86 E6
Gorstanvorran H'land 79 D11
Gorsteyhill Staffs 43 G10
Gorsty Hill Staffs 35 C7
Gortantaoid Arg/Bute 64 A4
Gorton Gtr Man 44 C2
Gosbeck Suffolk 31 C8
Gosberton Lincs 37 B8
Gosberton Clough Lincs 37 C7
Gosfield Essex 30 F4
Gosford Heref'd 26 B2
Gosforth Cumb 56 F2
Gosforth Tyne/Wear 63 G8
Gosmore Herts 29 F8
Gosport Hants 10 E5
Gossabrough Shetl'd 96 E7
Gossington Glos 16 A4
Goswick Northum 71 F9
Gotham Notts 35 B11
Gotherington Glos 26 F6
Gott Shetl'd 96 J6
Goudhurst Kent 12 C6
Goulceby Lincs 46 E6
Gourdas Aberds 89 D7
Gourdon Aberds 83 F10
Gourock Inverc'l 73 F11
Govan C/Glasg 68 D4
Govanhill C/Glasg 68 D4
Goveton Devon 5 G8
Govilon Monmouths 25 G9
Gowanhill Aberds 89 B10
Gowdall ER Yorks 52 G2
Gowerton Swan 23 G10
Gowkhall Fife 69 B9
Gowthorpe ER Yorks 52 D3
Goxhill ER Yorks 53 E7
Goxhill N Lincs 53 G7
Goxhill Haven N Lincs 53 G7
Goybre Neath P Talb 14 C3
Grabhair W Isles 91 F8
Graby Lincs 37 C6
Grade Cornw'l 2 H6
Graffham W Sussex 11 C8
Grafham Cambs 29 B8
Grafham Surrey 19 G7
Grafton Heref'd 25 E11
Grafton N Yorks 51 C10
Grafton Oxon 17 A9
Grafton Shrops 33 D10
Grafton Worcs 26 B2
Grafton Flyford Worcs 26 C6
Grafton Regis Northants 28 D4
Grafton Underwood Northants 36 G5
Grafty Green Kent 20 G5
Graianrhyd Denb 42 G5
Graig Conwy 41 C10
Graig Denb 42 E3
Graig-fechan Denbs 42 G4
Grain Medway 20 D5
Grainsby Lincs 46 C6
Grainthorpe Lincs 47 C7
Grampound Cornw'l 3 E8
Grampound Road Cornw'l 3 D8
Gramsdal W Isles 84 C3
Granborough Bucks 28 F4
Granby Notts 36 B3
Grandborough Warwick 27 B11
Grandtully Perth/Kinr 76 B2
Grange Cumb 56 E4
Grange E Ayrs 67 C7
Grange Medway 20 E4
Grange Mersey 42 D5
Grange Perth/Kinr 76 E5
Grange Crossroads Moray 88 C4
Grange Hall Moray 87 E13
Grange Hill Essex 19 B11
Grange Moor W Yorks 51 H8
Grange of Lindores Fife 76 F5
Grange-over-Sands Cumb 49 B4
Grange Villa Durham 58 A3
Grangemill Derby 44 G6
Grangemouth Falk 69 B8
Grangepans Falk 69 B9
Grangetown Card 15 D7
Grangetown Redcar/Clevel'd 59 D6
Granish H'land 81 B11
Gransmoor ER Yorks 53 D7
Granston Pembs 22 C3
Grantchester Cambs 29 C11
Grantham Lincs 36 B5
Grantley N Yorks 51 C8
Grantlodge Aberds 83 B9
Granton Dumf/Gal 60 C6
Granton C/Edinb 69 C11
Grantown-on-Spey H'land 82 A2
Grantshouse Scot Borders 71 D7
Grappenhall Warrington 43 D9
Grasby Lincs 46 B4
Grasmere Cumb 56 F5
Grasscroft Gtr Man 44 B3
Grassendale Mersey 43 D6
Grassholme Durham 57 D11
Grassington N Yorks 50 C6
Grassmoor Derby 45 F8
Grassthorpe Notts 45 F11
Grateley Hants 17 G9
Gratwich Staffs 34 B6
Graveley Cambs 29 B9
Graveley Herts 29 F9
Gravelly Hill W Midlands 35 F7
Gravels Shrops 33 E9
Graven Shetl'd 96 F6
Graveney Kent 21 E7
Gravesend Kent 20 D3
Grayingham Lincs 46 C3
Grayrigg Cumb 57 G7
Grays Thurr'k 20 D3
Grayshott Hants 18 H5
Grayswood Surrey 11 A8
Graythorp Hartlep'l 58 D6
Grazeley Wokingham 18 E3
Greasbrough S Yorks 45 C8
Greasby Mersey 42 D5
Great Abington Cambs 30 D2
Great Addington Northants 28 A6
Great Alne Warwick 27 C8
Great Altcar Lancs 42 B6
Great Amwell Herts 29 G10
Great Asby Cumb 57 E8
Great Ashfield Suffolk 30 B6
Great Ayton N Yorks 59 E6
Great Baddow Essex 20 A4
Great Bardfield Essex 30 E3
Great Barford Beds 29 C8
Great Barr W Midlands 34 F6
Great Barrington Glos 27 G9
Great Barrow Ches 43 F7
Great Barton Suffolk 30 B5
Great Barugh N Yorks 52 B3
Great Bavington Northum 62 E5
Great Bealings Suffolk 31 D9
Great Bedwyn Wilts 17 E9
Great Bentley Essex 31 F8
Great Billing Northants 28 B5
Great Bircham Norfolk 38 B3
Great Blakenham Suffolk 31 C8
Great Blencow Cumb 56 C6
Great Bolas Telford 34 C2
Great Bookham Surrey 19 F8
Great Bourton Oxon 27 D11
Great Bowden Leics 36 G3
Great Bradley Suffolk 30 C3
Great Braxted Essex 30 G5
Great Bricett Suffolk 31 C7
Great Brickhill Bucks 28 E6
Great Bridge W Midlands 34 F5
Great Bridgeford Staffs 34 C4
Great Brington Northants 28 B3
Great Bromley Essex 31 F7
Great Broughton Cumb 56 C2
Great Broughton N Yorks 59 F6
Great Budworth Ches 43 E9
Great Burdon D'lington 58 E4
Great Burgh Surrey 19 F9
Great Burstead Essex 20 B3
Great Busby N Yorks 58 F6
Great Canfield Essex 30 G2
Great Carlton Lincs 47 D8
Great Casterton Rutl'd 36 E6
Great Chart Kent 13 B8
Great Chatwell Staffs 34 D3
Great Chesterford Essex 30 D2
Great Cheverell Wilts 16 F6
Great Chishill Cambs 29 E11
Great Clacton Essex 31 G8
Great Cliff W Yorks 51 H9
Great Clifton Cumb 56 D2
Great Coates NE Lincs 46 B6
Great Comberton Worcs 26 D6
Great Corby Cumb 56 A6
Great Cornard Suffolk 30 D5
Great Cowden ER Yorks 53 E8
Great Coxwell Oxon 17 B9
Great Crakehall N Yorks 58 G3
Great Cransley Northants 36 H4
Great Cressingham Norfolk 38 E4
Great Crosby Mersey 42 C6
Great Cubley Derby 35 B7
Great Dalby Leics 36 D3
Great Doddington Northants 28 B5
Great Dunham Norfolk 38 D4
Great Dunmow Essex 30 F3
Great Durnford Wilts 17 H8
Great Easton Essex 30 F3
Great Easton Leics 36 F4
Great Eccleston Lancs 49 E4
Great Edstone N Yorks 52 A3
Great Ellingham Norfolk 38 F6
Great Elm Som'set 16 G4
Great Eversden Cambs 29 C10
Great Fencote N Yorks 58 G3
Great Finborough Suffolk 31 C7
Great Fransham Norfolk 38 D4
Great Gaddesden Herts 29 G7
Great Gidding Cambs 37 G7
Great Givendale ER Yorks 52 D4
Great Glemham Suffolk 31 B10
Great Glen Leics 36 F2
Great Gonerby Lincs 36 B4
Great Gransden Cambs 29 C9
Great Green Norfolk 39 G8
Great Green Suffolk 30 C6
Great Habton N Yorks 52 B3
Great Hale Lincs 37 A7
Great Hallingbury Essex 30 G2
Great Hampden Bucks 18 A5
Great Harrowden Northants 28 A5
Great Harwood Lancs 50 F3
Great Haseley Oxon 18 A3
Great Hatfield ER Yorks 53 E7
Great Haywood Staffs 34 C4
Great Heath W Midlands 35 G9
Great Heck N Yorks 52 G1
Great Henny Essex 30 E5
Great Hinton Wilts 16 F6
Great Hockham Norfolk 38 F5
Great Holland Essex 31 G9
Great Horkesley Essex 30 E6
Great Hormead Herts 29 F10
Great Horton W Yorks 51 F7
Great Horwood Bucks 28 E4
Great Houghton Northants 28 C4
Great Houghton S Yorks 45 B8
Great Hucklow Derby 44 E5
Great Kelk ER Yorks 53 D7
Great Kimble Bucks 18 A5
Great Kingshill Bucks 18 B5
Great Langton N Yorks 58 G3
Great Leighs Essex 30 G4
Great Lever Gtr Man 43 B10
Great Limber Lincs 46 B5
Great Linford M/Keynes 28 D5
Great Livermere Suffolk 30 A5
Great Longstone Derby 44 E6
Great Lumley Durham 58 B3
Great Lyth Shrops 33 E10
Great Malvern Worcs 26 D4
Great Maplestead Essex 30 E5
Great Marton Blackp'l 49 F3
Great Massingham Norfolk 38 C3
Great Melton Norfolk 39 E7
Great Milton Oxon 18 A3
Great Missenden Bucks 18 A5
Great Mitton Lancs 50 F3
Great Mongeham Kent 21 F10
Great Moulton Norfolk 39 F7
Great Munden Herts 29 F10
Great Musgrave Cumb 57 E9
Great Ness Shrops 33 D9
Great Notley Essex 30 F4
Great Oakley Essex 31 F8
Great Oakley Northants 36 G4
Great Offley Herts 29 F8
Great Ormside Cumb 57 E9
Great Orton Cumb 56 A5
Great Ouseburn N Yorks 51 C10
Great Oxendon Northants 36 G3
Great Oxney Green Essex 30 H3
Great Palgrave Norfolk 38 D4
Great Parndon Essex 29 H11
Great Paxton Cambs 29 B9
Great Plumpton Lancs 49 F3
Great Plumstead Norfolk 39 D9
Great Ponton Lincs 36 B5
Great Preston W Yorks 51 G10
Great Raveley Cambs 37 G8
Great Rissington Glos 27 G8
Great Rollright Oxon 27 E10
Great Ryburgh Norfolk 38 C5
Great Ryle Northum 62 B6
Great Ryton Shrops 33 E10
Great Saling Essex 30 F4
Great Salkeld Cumb 57 C7
Great Sampford Essex 30 E3
Great Sankey Warrington 43 D8
Great Saxham Suffolk 30 B4
Great Shefford W Berks 17 D10
Great Shelford Cambs 29 C11
Great Smeaton N Yorks 58 F4
Great Snoring Norfolk 38 B5
Great Somerford Wilts 16 C6
Great Stainton D'lington 58 D4
Great Stambridge Essex 20 B5
Great Staughton Cambs 29 B8
Great Steeping Lincs 47 F8
Great Stonar Kent 21 F10
Great Strickland Cumb 57 D7
Great Stukeley Cambs 29 A9
Great Sturton Lincs 46 E6
Great Sutton Ches 43 E6
Great Sutton Shrops 33 G11
Great Swinburne Northum 62 F5
Great Tew Oxon 27 F10
Great Tey Essex 30 F5
Great Thurkleby N Yorks 51 B10
Great Thurlow Suffolk 30 C3
Great Torrington Devon 6 E3
Great Tosson Northum 62 C6
Great Totham Essex 30 G5
Great Totham Essex 30 G5
Great Tows Lincs 46 C6
Great Urswick Cumb 49 B2
Great Wakering Essex 20 C6
Great Waldingfield Suffolk 30 D6
Great Walsingham Norfolk 38 B5
Great Waltham Essex 30 G3
Great Warley Essex 20 B2
Great Washbourne Glos 26 E6
Great Weldon Northants 36 G5
Great Welnetham Suffolk 30 C5
Great Wenham Suffolk 31 E7
Great Whittington Northum 62 F6
Great Wigborough Essex 30 G6
Great Wilbraham Cambs 30 C2
Great Wishford Wilts 17 H7
Great Witcombe Glos 26 G6
Great Witley Worcs 26 B4
Great Wolford Warwick 27 E9
Great Wratting Suffolk 30 D3
Great Wymondley Herts 29 F9
Great Wyrley Staffs 34 E5
Great Wytheford Shrops 34 D1
Great Yarmouth Norfolk 39 E11
Great Yeldham Essex 30 E4
Greater Doward Heref'd 26 G2
Greatford Lincs 37 D6
Greatgate Staffs 35 A6
Greatham Hants 11 A6
Greatham Hartlep'l 58 D5
Greatham W Sussex 11 C9
Greatstone on Sea Kent 13 D9
Greatworth Northants 28 D2
Greave Lancs 50 G4
Greeba I/Man 48 D3
Green Denbs 42 F3
Green End Beds 29 C8
Green Hammerton N Yorks 51 D10
Green Lane Powys 33 F7
Green Ore Som'set 16 F2
Green St Green London 19 E11
Green Street Herts 19 B8
Greenbank Shetl'd 96 C7
Greenburn W Loth 69 D8
Greendikes Northum 71 H9
Greenfield Beds 29 E7
Greenfield Flints 42 E4
Greenfield Gtr Man 44 B3
Greenfield H'land 80 C4
Greenfield Oxon 18 B4
Greenford London 19 C8
Greengairs N Lanarks 68 C6
Greenham W Berks 17 E11
Greenhaugh Northum 62 E3
Greenhead Northum 62 G2
Greenhill Falk 69 C7
Greenhill London 19 C8
Greenhill Kent 21 E8
Greenhill Leics 35 D10
Greenhills N Ayrs 67 A6
Greenhithe Kent 20 D2
Greenholm E Ayrs 67 C8
Greenholme Cumb 57 F7
Greenhouse Scot Borders 61 A11
Greenhow Hill N Yorks 51 C7
Greenigoe Orkney 95 H5
Greenland H'land 94 D4
Greenlands Bucks 18 C4
Greenlaw Aberds 89 C6
Greenlaw Scot Borders 70 F6
Greenlea Dumf/Gal 60 F6
Greenloaning Perth/Kinr 75 G11
Greenmount Gtr Man 43 A10
Greenmow Shetl'd 96 L6
Greenock Inverc'l 73 F11
Greenock West Inverc'l 73 F11
Greenodd Cumb 49 A3
Greenrow Cumb 56 A3
Greens Norton Northants 28 D3
Greenside Tyne/Wear 63 G7
Greensidehill Northum 62 B5
Greenstead Green Essex 30 F5
Greensted Essex 20 A2
Greenwich London 19 D10
Greet Glos 27 E7
Greete Shrops 26 A2
Greetham Lincs 47 E7
Greetham Rutl'd 36 D5
Greetland W Yorks 51 G6
Gregg Hall Cumb 56 G6
Gregson Lane Lancs 50 G1
Greinetobht W Isles 84 A3
Greinton Som'set 15 H10
Gremista Shetl'd 96 J6
Grenaby I/Man 48 E2
Grendon Northants 28 B5
Grendon Warwick 35 E8
Grendon Common Warwick 35 F8
Grendon Green Heref'd 26 C2
Grendon Underwood Bucks 28 F3
Grenofen Devon 4 D5
Grenoside S Yorks 45 C7
Greosabhagh W Isles 90 H6
Gresford Wrex 42 G6
Gresham Norfolk 39 B7
Gressenhall Norfolk 38 D5
Gressingham Lancs 50 C1
Gresty Green Ches 43 G10
Greta Bridge Durham 58 E1
Gretna Dumf/Gal 61 G9
Gretna Green Dumf/Gal 61 G9
Gretton Glos 27 E7
Gretton Northants 36 F4
Gretton Shrops 33 F11
Grewelthorpe N Yorks 51 B8
Grey Green N Lincs 45 B11
Greygarth N Yorks 51 B7
Greynor Carms 23 F10
Greysouthen Cumb 56 D2
Greystoke Cumb 56 C6
Greystone Angus 77 C8
Greystone Dumf/Gal 60 F5
Greywell Hants 18 F4
Griais W Isles 91 C9
Grianan W Isles 91 D9
Gribthorpe ER Yorks 52 F3
Gridley Corner Devon 6 G2
Griff Warwick 35 G9
Griffithstown Torf 15 B8
Grimbister Orkney 95 G4
Grimblethorpe Lincs 46 D6
Grimeford Village Lancs 43 A9
Grimethorpe S Yorks 45 B8
Griminis W Isles 84 C2
Grimister Shetl'd 96 D6
Grimley Worcs 26 B5
Grimness Orkney 95 J5
Grimoldby Lincs 47 D7
Grimpo Shrops 33 C9
Grimsargh Lancs 50 F1
Grimsbury Oxon 27 D11
Grimsby NE Lincs 46 A6
Grimscote Northants 28 C3
Grimscott Cornw'l 6 F1
Grimsthorpe Lincs 36 C6
Grimston ER Yorks 53 F8
Grimston Leics 36 C2
Grimston Norfolk 38 C3
Grimston C/York 52 D2
Grimstone Dorset 8 E5
Grinacombe Moor Devon 6 G3
Grindale ER Yorks 53 B7
Grindigar Orkney 95 H6
Grindiscol Shetl'd 96 K6
Grindle Shrops 34 E3
Grindleford Derby 44 E6
Grindleton Lancs 50 E3
Grindley Staffs 34 C6
Grindley Brook Shrops 33 A11
Grindlow Derby 44 E5
Grindon Northum 71 F8
Grindon Staffs 44 G4
Grindonmoor Gate Staffs 44 G4
Gringley on the Hill Notts 45 C11
Grinsdale Cumb 61 H9
Grinshill Shrops 33 C11
Grinton N Yorks 58 G1
Griomsidar W Isles 91 E8
Grishipoll Arg/Bute 78 F4
Grisling Common E Sussex 12 D3
Gristhorpe N Yorks 53 A6
Griston Norfolk 38 F5
Gritley Orkney 95 H6
Grittenham Wilts 17 C7
Grittleton Wilts 16 C5
Grizebeck Cumb 49 A2
Grizedale Cumb 56 G5
Grobister Orkney 95 F7
Groby Leics 35 E11
Groes Conwy 42 F3
Groes Neath P Talb 14 C3
Groes-faen Rh Cyn Taff 14 C6
Groes-lwyd Powys 33 D8
Groesffordd Marli Denbs 42 E3
Groeslon Gwyn 41 D7
Groeslon Gwyn 40 E6
Grogport Arg/Bute 65 D9
Gromford Suffolk 31 C10
Gronant Flints 42 D3
Groombridge E Sussex 12 C4
Grosmont Monmouths 25 F11
Grosmont N Yorks 59 F9
Groton Suffolk 30 D6
Grougfoot Falk 69 C9
Grouville Jersey 11
Grove Dorset 8 G6
Grove Kent 21 E9
Grove Notts 45 E11
Grove Oxon 17 B11
Grove Park London 19 D11
Grove Vale W Midlands 34 F6
Grovesend Swan 23 F10
Grudie H'land 86 E6
Gruids H'land 93 J8
Gruinard House H'land 86 B2
Grula H'land 85 F8
Gruline Arg/Bute 79 G8
Grunasound Shetl'd 96 K5
Grundisburgh Suffolk 31 C9
Grunsagill Lancs 50 D3
Gruting Shetl'd 96 J4
Grutness Shetl'd 96 N6
Gualachulain H'land 74 C4
Gualin Ho. H'land 92 D6
Guardbridge Fife 77 F7
Guarlford Worcs 26 D5
Guay Perth/Kinr 76 C3
Guestling Green E Sussex 13 E7
Guestling Thorn E Sussex 13 E7
Guestwick Norfolk 39 C6
Guestwick Green Norfolk 39 C6
Guide Blackb'n 50 G3
Guide Post Northum 63 E8
Guilden Morden Cambs 29 D9
Guilden Sutton Ches 43 F7
Guildford Surrey 18 G6
Guildtown Perth/Kinr 76 D4
Guilsborough Northants 28 A3
Guilsfield Powys 33 D8
Guilton Kent 21 F9
Guineaford Devon 6 C4
Guisborough Redcar/Clevel'd 59 E7
Guiseley W Yorks 51 E7
Guist Norfolk 38 C5
Guith Orkney 95 E6
Guiting Power Glos 27 F7
Gulberwick Shetl'd 96 K6
Gullane E Loth 70 B3
Gulval Cornw'l 2 F3
Gulworthy Devon 4 D5
Gumfreston Pembs 22 F6
Gumley Leics 36 F2
Gummow's Shop Cornw'l 3 D7
Gun Hill E Sussex 12 E4
Gunby ER Yorks 52 F3
Gunby Lincs 36 C5
Gundleton Hants 10 A5
Gunn Devon 6 C5
Gunnerside N Yorks 57 G11
Gunnerton Northum 62 F5
Gunness N Lincs 46 A2
Gunnislake Cornw'l 4 D5
Gunnista Shetl'd 96 J7
Gunthorpe Norfolk 38 B6
Gunthorpe Notts 36 A2
Gunthorpe Peterbro 37 E7
Gunville I/Wight 10 F3
Gunwalloe Cornw'l 2 G5
Gurnard I/Wight 10 E3
Gurnett Ches 44 E3
Gurney Slade Som'set 16 G3
Gurnos Powys 24 H4
Gussage All Saints Dorset 9 C9
Gussage St Michael Dorset 9 C8
Guston Kent 21 G10
Gutcher Shetl'd 96 D7
Guthrie Angus 77 B8
Guyhirn Cambs 37 E9
Guyhirn Gull Cambs 37 E9
Guy's Head Lincs 37 C10
Guy's Marsh Dorset 9 B7
Guyzance Northum 63 C8
Gwaenysgor Flints 42 D3
Gwalchmai Angl 40 C5
Gwaun-Cae-Gurwen Neath P Talb 24 G4
Gwaun-Leision Neath P Talb 24 G4
Gwbert Ceredig'n 22 B6
Gweek Cornw'l 2 G6
Gwehelog Monmouths 15 A9
Gwenddwr Powys 25 D7
Gwennap Cornw'l 2 F6
Gwenter Cornw'l 2 H6
Gwernaffield Flints 42 F5
Gwernesney Monmouths 15 A10
Gwernogle Carms 23 C10
Gwernymynydd Flints 42 F5
Gwersyllt Wrex 42 G6
Gwespyr Flints 42 D4
Gwithian Cornw'l 2 E4
Gwredog Angl 40 B6
Gwyddelwern Denbs 42 H3
Gwyddgrug Carms 23 C9
Gwydyr Uchaf Conwy 41 D9
Gwynfryn Wrex 42 G5
Gwystre Powys 25 B7
Gwytherin Conwy 41 D10
Gyfelia Wrex 42 H6
Gyffin Conwy 41 C9
Gyre Orkney 95 H4
Gyrn-goch Gwyn 40 F6

H

Habberley Shrops 33 E9
Habergham Lancs 50 F4
Habrough NE Lincs 46 A5
Haceby Lincs 36 B6
Hacheston Suffolk 31 C10
Hackbridge London 19 E9
Hackenthorpe S Yorks 45 D8
Hackford Norfolk 39 E6
Hackforth N Yorks 58 G3
Hackland Orkney 95 F4
Hackleton Northants 28 C5
Hackness N Yorks 59 G10
Hackness Orkney 95 J4
Hackney London 19 C10
Hackthorn Lincs 46 D3
Hackthorpe Cumb 57 D7
Haconby Lincs 37 C7
Hacton London 20 C2
Hadden Scot Borders 70 G6
Haddenham Bucks 28 H4
Haddenham Cambs 37 H10
Haddington E Loth 70 C4
Haddington Lincs 46 F3
Haddiscoe Norfolk 39 F10
Haddon Cambs 37 F7
Haddon Ches 44 F3
Hade Edge W Yorks 44 B5
Hademore Staffs 35 E7
Hadfield Derby 44 C4
Hadham Cross Herts 29 G11
Hadham Ford Herts 29 F11
Hadleigh Essex 20 C5
Hadleigh Suffolk 31 D7
Hadley Telford 34 D2
Hadley End Staffs 35 C7
Hadlow Kent 20 G3
Hadlow Down E Sussex 12 D4
Hadnall Shrops 33 D11
Hadstock Essex 30 D2
Hady Derby 45 E7
Hadzor Worcs 26 B6
Haffenden Quarter Kent 13 B7
Hafod-Dinbych Conwy 41 E10
Hafod-Iom Conwy 41 C10
Haggate Lancs 50 F4
Haggbeck Cumb 61 F10
Haggerston Northum 71 F9
Haggrister Shetl'd 96 F5
Hagley Heref'd 26 D2
Hagley Worcs 34 G5
Hagworthingham Lincs 47 F7
Haigh Gtr Man 43 B9
Haigh S Yorks 44 A6
Haigh Moor W Yorks 51 G8
Haighton Green Lancs 50 F1
Hail Weston Cambs 29 B8
Haile Cumb 56 F2
Hailes Glos 27 E7
Hailey Herts 29 G10
Hailey Oxon 27 G10
Hailsham E Sussex 12 F4
Haimer H'land 94 D3
Hainault London 19 B11
Hainford Norfolk 39 D8
Hainton Lincs 46 D5
Hairmyres S Lanarks 68 E5
Haisthorpe ER Yorks 53 C7
Hakin Pembs 22 F3
Halam Notts 45 G10
Halbeath Fife 69 B10
Halberton Devon 7 E9
Halcro H'land 94 D4
Hale Gtr Man 43 D10
Hale Halton 43 D7
Hale Hants 9 C10
Hale Bank Halton 43 D7
Hale Street Kent 20 G3
Halebarns Gtr Man 43 D10
Hales Norfolk 39 F9
Hales Staffs 34 B3
Hales Place Kent 21 F8
Halesfield Telford 34 E3
Halesgate Lincs 37 C9
Halesowen W Midlands 34 G5
Halesworth Suffolk 39 H9
Halewood Mersey 43 D7
Halford Shrops 33 G10
Halford Warwick 27 D9
Halfpenny Furze Carms 23 E7
Halfpenny Green Staffs 34 F4
Halfway Carms 24 E3
Halfway Carms 24 E5
Halfway W Berks 17 E11
Halfway Bridge W Sussex 11 B8
Halfway House Shrops 33 D9
Halfway Houses Kent 20 D6
Halifax W Yorks 51 G6
Halket E Ayrs 67 A7
Halkirk H'land 94 E3
Halkyn Flints 42 E5
Hall Dunnerdale Cumb 56 G4
Hall Green W Midlands 35 G7
Hall Green W Yorks 51 H9
Hall Grove Herts 29 G9
Hall of Tankerness Orkney 95 H6
Hall of the Forest Shrops 33 G8
Halland E Sussex 12 E3
Hallaton Leics 36 F3
Hallatrow Bath/NE Som'set 16 F3
Hallbankgate Cumb 61 H11
Hallen S Gloucs 15 C11
Halliburton Scot Borders 70 F5
Hallin H'land 84 C7
Halling Medway 20 E4
Hallington Lincs 47 D7
Hallington Northum 62 F5
Halliwell Gtr Man 43 A10
Halloughton Notts 45 G10
Hallow Worcs 26 C5
Hallrule Scot Borders 61 B11
Halls E Loth 70 C5
Hall's Green Herts 29 F9
Hallsands Devon 5 H9
Hallthwaites Cumb 56 H3
Hallworthy Cornw'l 4 C2
Hallyburton House Perth/Kinr 76 D5
Hallyne Scot Borders 69 F10
Halmer End Staffs 43 H10
Halmore Glos 16 A3
Halmyre Mains Scot Borders 69 F10
Halnaker W Sussex 11 D8
Halsall Lancs 42 A6
Halse Northants 28 D2
Halse Som'set 7 D10
Halsetown Cornw'l 2 F4
Halsham ER Yorks 53 G8
Halsinger Devon 6 C4
Halstead Essex 30 E5
Halstead Kent 19 E11
Halstead Leics 36 E3
Halstock Dorset 8 D4
Haltham Lincs 46 F6
Haltoft End Lincs 47 H7
Halton Bucks 28 G5
Halton Halton 43 D8
Halton Lancs 49 C5
Halton Northum 62 G5
Halton Wrex 33 B9
Halton W Yorks 51 F9
Halton East N Yorks 50 D6
Halton Gill N Yorks 50 B5
Halton Holegate Lincs 47 F8
Halton Lea Gate Northum 62 H2
Halton West N Yorks 50 D4
Haltwhistle Northum 62 G3
Halvergate Norfolk 39 E10
Halwell Devon 5 F8
Halwill Devon 6 G3
Halwill Junction Devon 6 F3
Ham Devon 7 F11
Ham Glos 16 B3
Ham London 19 D8
Ham H'land 94 C4
Ham Kent 21 F10
Ham Shetl'd 96 K1
Ham Wilts 17 E10
Ham Common Dorset 9 B7
Ham Green Heref'd 26 D4
Ham Green Kent 13 D7
Ham Green Kent 20 E5
Ham Green N Som'set 15 D11
Ham Green Worcs 27 B7
Ham Street Som'set 8 A4
Hamble-le-Rice Hants 10 D3
Hambleden Bucks 18 C4
Hambledon Hants 10 C5
Hambledon Surrey 18 H6
Hambleton Lancs 49 E3
Hambleton N Yorks 52 F1
Hambridge Som'set 8 B2
Hambrook S Gloucs 16 D3
Hambrook W Sussex 11 D6
Hameringham Lincs 47 F7
Hamerton Cambs 37 H7
Hametoun Shetl'd 96 K1
Hamilton S Lanarks 68 E6
Hammer W Sussex 11 A7
Hammerpot W Sussex 11 D9
Hammersmith London 19 D9
Hammerwich Staffs 35 E6
Hammerwood E Sussex 12 C3
Hammond Street Herts 19 A10
Hammoon Dorset 9 C7
Hamnavoe Shetl'd 96 E4
Hamnavoe Shetl'd 96 K5
Hamnavoe Shetl'd 96 E6
Hamnavoe Shetl'd 96 F6
Hampden Park E Sussex 12 F5
Hamperden End Essex 30 E2
Hampnett Glos 27 G7
Hampole S Yorks 45 A9
Hampreston Dorset 9 E9
Hampstead London 19 C9
Hampstead Norreys W Berks 18 D2
Hampsthwaite N Yorks 51 D8
Hampton London 19 E8
Hampton Shrops 34 G3
Hampton Worcs 27 D7
Hampton Bishop Heref'd 26 E2
Hampton Heath Ches 43 H7
Hampton in Arden W Midlands 35 G8
Hampton Loade Shrops 34 G3
Hampton Lovett Worcs 26 B5
Hampton Lucy Warwick 27 C9
Hampton on the Hill Warwick 27 B9
Hampton Poyle Oxon 28 G2
Hamrow Norfolk 38 C5
Hamsey E Sussex 12 E3
Hamsey Green Surrey 19 F10
Hamstall Ridware Staffs 35 D7
Hamstead I/Wight 10 E3
Hamstead W Midlands 34 F6
Hamstead Marshall W Berks 17 E11
Hamsterley Durham 58 C2
Hamsterley Durham 63 H7
Hamstreet Kent 13 C9
Hamworthy Poole 9 E8
Hanbury Staffs 35 C7
Hanbury Worcs 26 B6
Hanbury Woodend Staffs 35 C7
Hanby Lincs 36 B6
Hanchurch Staffs 34 A4
Handbridge Ches 43 F7
Handcross W Sussex 12 D1
Handforth Ches 44 D2
Handley Ches 43 G7
Handsacre Staffs 35 D6
Handsworth S Yorks 45 D8
Handsworth W Midlands 34 F6
Handy Cross Devon 6 D3
Hanford Stoke 34 A4
Hanging Langford Wilts 17 H7
Hangleton W Sussex 11 D9
Hanham S Gloucs 16 D3
Hankelow Ches 43 H9
Hankerton Wilts 16 B6
Hankham E Sussex 12 F5
Hanley Stoke 44 H2
Hanley Castle Worcs 26 D5
Hanley Child Worcs 26 B3
Hanley Swan Worcs 26 D5
Hanley William Worcs 26 B3
Hanlith N Yorks 50 C5
Hanmer Wrex 33 B10
Hannah Lincs 47 E9
Hannington Hants 18 F2
Hannington Northants 28 A5
Hannington Swindon 17 B8
Hannington Wick Swindon 17 B8
Hansel Village S Ayrs 67 C6
Hanslope M/Keynes 28 D5
Hanthorpe Lincs 37 C6
Hanwell London 19 C8
Hanwell Oxon 27 D11
Hanwood Shrops 33 E10
Hanworth London 19 D8
Hanworth Norfolk 39 B7
Happendon S Lanarks 69 G7
Happisburgh Norfolk 39 B9
Happisburgh Common Norfolk 39 C9
Hapsford Ches 43 E7
Hapton Lancs 50 F3
Hapton Norfolk 39 F7
Harberton Devon 5 F8
Harbertonford Devon 5 F8
Harbledown Kent 21 F8
Harborne W Midlands 34 G6
Harborough Magna Warwick 35 H10
Harbottle Northum 62 C5
Harbury Warwick 27 C10
Harby Leics 36 B3
Harby Notts 46 E2
Harcombe Devon 7 G10
Harden W Midlands 34 E6
Harden W Yorks 51 F6
Hardenhuish Wilts 16 D6
Hardgate Aberds 83 C9
Hardham W Sussex 11 C9
Hardingham Norfolk 38 E6
Hardingstone Northants 28 C4
Hardington Som'set 16 F4
Hardington Mandeville Som'set 8 C4
Hardington Marsh Som'set 8 D4
Hardley Hants 10 D3
Hardley Street Norfolk 39 E9
Hardmead M/Keynes 28 D6
Hardrow N Yorks 57 G10
Hardstoft Derby 45 F8
Hardway Hants 10 D5
Hardway Som'set 8 A6
Hardwick Bucks 28 G5
Hardwick Cambs 29 C10
Hardwick Norfolk 38 D2
Hardwick Norfolk 39 G8
Hardwick Notts 45 E10
Hardwick Northants 28 B5
Hardwick Oxon 27 H10
Hardwick Oxon 28 F2
Hardwick W Midlands 35 F6
Hardwicke Glos 26 G4
Hardwicke Glos 26 F6
Hardwicke Heref'd 25 D9
Hardy's Green Essex 30 F6
Hare Green Essex 31 F7
Hare Hatch Wokingham 18 D5
Hare Street Herts 29 F10
Hareby Lincs 47 F7
Hareden Lancs 50 D2
Harefield London 19 B7
Harehills W Yorks 51 F9
Harehope Northum 62 A6
Haresceugh Cumb 57 B8
Harescombe Glos 26 G5
Haresfield Glos 26 G5
Hareshaw N Lanarks 69 D7
Hareshaw Head Northum 62 E4
Harewood W Yorks 51 E9
Harewood End Heref'd 26 F2
Harford Carms 24 D3
Harford Devon 5 F7
Hargate Norfolk 39 F7
Hargatewall Derby 44 E5
Hargrave Ches 43 F7
Hargrave Northants 29 A7
Hargrave Suffolk 30 C4
Harker Cumb 61 G9
Harkland Shetl'd 96 E6
Harkstead Suffolk 31 E8
Harlaston Staffs 35 D8
Harlaw Ho. Aberds 83 A9
Harlaxton Lincs 36 B4
Harle Syke Lancs 50 F4
Harlech Gwyn 41 G7
Harlequin Notts 36 B2
Harlescott Shrops 33 D11
Harlesden London 19 C9
Harleston Devon 5 G8
Harleston Norfolk 39 G8
Harleston Suffolk 31 C7
Harlestone Northants 28 B4
Harley Shrops 34 E1
Harley S Yorks 45 C7
Harleyholm S Lanarks 69 G8
Harlington Beds 29 E7
Harlington London 19 D7
Harlington S Yorks 45 B8
Harlosh H'land 85 D7
Harlow Essex 29 G11
Harlow Hill Northum 62 G6
Harlow Hill N Yorks 51 D8
Harlthorpe ER Yorks 52 F3
Harlton Cambs 29 C10
Harman's Cross Dorset 9 F8
Harmby N Yorks 58 H2
Harmer Green Herts 29 G9
Harmer Hill Shrops 33 C10
Harmondsworth London 19 D7
Harmston Lincs 46 F3
Harnham Northum 62 F6
Harnhill Glos 17 A7
Harold Hill London 20 B2
Harold Wood London 20 B2
Haroldston West Pembs 22 E3
Haroldswick Shetl'd 96 B8
Harome N Yorks 52 A2
Harpenden Herts 29 G8
Harpford Devon 7 G9
Harpham ER Yorks 53 C6
Harpley Norfolk 38 C3
Harpley Worcs 26 B3
Harpole Northants 28 B3
Harpsdale H'land 94 E3
Harpsden Oxon 18 C4
Harpswell Lincs 46 D3
Harpur Hill Derby 44 E4
Harpurhey Gtr Man 44 B2
Harraby Cumb 56 A6
Harrapool H'land 85 F11
Harrier Shetl'd 96 J1
Harrietfield Perth/Kinr 76 E2
Harrietsham Kent 20 F5
Harrington Cumb 56 D1
Harrington Lincs 47 E7
Harrington Northants 36 G3
Harringworth Northants 36 F5
Harris H'land 78 B6
Harrogate N Yorks 51 D9
Harrold Beds 28 C6
Harrow London 19 C8
Harrow on the Hill London 19 C8
Harrow Street Suffolk 30 E6
Harrow Weald London 19 B8
Harrowbarrow Cornw'l 4 E4
Harrowden Beds 29 D7
Harrowgate Hill D'lington 58 E3
Harston Cambs 29 C11
Harston Leics 36 B4
Harswell ER Yorks 52 E4
Hart Hartlep'l 58 C5
Hart Common Gtr Man 43 B9
Hart Hill Luton 29 F8
Hart Station Hartlep'l 58 C5
Hartburn Northum 62 E6
Hartburn Stockton 58 E5
Hartest Suffolk 30 C5
Hartfield E Sussex 12 C3
Hartford Cambs 29 A9
Hartford Ches 43 E9
Hartford End Essex 30 G3
Hartfordbridge Hants 18 F4
Hartforth N Yorks 58 F2
Harthill Ches 43 G8
Harthill N Lanarks 69 D8
Harthill S Yorks 45 D8
Hartington Derby 44 F5
Hartland Devon 6 D1
Hartlebury Worcs 26 A5
Hartlepool Hartlep'l 58 C6
Hartley Cumb 57 F9
Hartley Kent 20 E3
Hartley Kent 13 C6
Hartley Northum 63 F9
Hartley Westpall Hants 18 F3
Hartley Wintney Hants 18 F4
Hartlip Kent 20 E5
Harton N Yorks 52 C3
Harton Shrops 33 G10
Harton Tyne/Wear 63 G9
Hartpury Glos 26 F4
Hartshead W Yorks 51 G7
Hartshill Warwick 35 F9
Hartshorne Derby 35 C9
Hartsop Cumb 56 E6
Hartwell Northants 28 C4
Hartwood N Lanarks 69 E7
Harviestoun Stirl 68 B4
Harvington Worcs 27 D7
Harvington Cross Worcs 27 D7
Harwell Oxon 17 C11
Harwich Essex 31 E9
Harwood Durham 57 C10
Harwood Gtr Man 43 A10
Harwood Dale N Yorks 59 G10
Harworth Notts 45 C10
Hasbury W Midlands 34 G5
Hascombe Surrey 18 G6
Haselbech Northants 36 H3
Haselbury Plucknett Som'set 8 C3
Haseley Warwick 27 B9
Haselor Warwick 27 C8
Hasfield Glos 26 F5
Hasguard Pembs 22 F3
Haskayne Lancs 42 B6
Hasketon Suffolk 31 C9
Hasland Derby 45 F7
Haslemere Surrey 11 A8
Haslingden Lancs 50 G3
Haslingfield Cambs 29 C11
Haslington Ches 43 G10
Hassall Ches 43 G10
Hassall Green Ches 43 G10
Hassell Street Kent 21 G7
Hassendean Scot Borders 61 A11
Hassingham Norfolk 39 E9
Hassocks W Sussex 12 E1
Hassop Derby 44 E6
Hastigrow H'land 94 D4
Hastingleigh Kent 13 B9
Hastings E Sussex 13 F7

Kirkandrews Dumf/Gal 55 E9
Kirkandrews upon Eden Cumb 61 H9
Kirkbampton Cumb 61 H9
Kirkbean Dumf/Gal 60 H5
Kirkbride Cumb 61 H8
Kirkbuddo Angus 77 C8
Kirkburn Scot Borders 69 G11
Kirkburn ER Yorks 52 D5
Kirkburton W Yorks 44 A5
Kirkby Lincs 46 C4
Kirkby Mersey 43 C7
Kirkby N Yorks 59 F6
Kirkby Fleetham N Yorks 58 G3
Kirkby Green Lincs 46 G4
Kirkby In Ashfield Notts 45 G9
Kirkby-in-Furness Cumb 49 A2
Kirkby la Thorpe Lincs 46 H5
Kirkby Lonsdale Cumb 50 B2
Kirkby Malham N Yorks 50 C4
Kirkby Mallory Leics 35 E10
Kirkby Malzeard N Yorks 51 B8
Kirkby Mills N Yorks 59 H8
Kirkby on Bain Lincs 46 F6
Kirkby Stephen Cumb 57 F9
Kirkby Thore Cumb 57 D8
Kirkby Underwood Lincs 37 C6
Kirkby Wharfe N Yorks 51 E11
Kirkbymoorside N Yorks 59 H7
Kirkcaldy Fife 69 A11
Kirkcambeck Cumb 61 G11
Kirkcarswell Dumf/Gal 55 E10
Kirkcolm Dumf/Gal 54 C3
Kirkconnel Dumf/Gal 60 B3
Kirkconnell Dumf/Gal 60 G5
Kirkcowan Dumf/Gal 54 C6
Kirkcudbright Dumf/Gal 55 D9
Kirkdale Mersey 42 C6
Kirkfieldbank S Lanarks 69 F7
Kirkgunzeon Dumf/Gal 55 C11
Kirkham Lancs 49 F4
Kirkham N Yorks 52 C3
Kirkhamgate W Yorks 51 G8
Kirkharle Northum 62 E6
Kirkheaton Northum 62 F6
Kirkheaton W Yorks 51 H7
Kirkhill Angus 77 A9
Kirkhill H'land 87 G8
Kirkhill Midloth 69 D11
Kirkhill Moray 88 E2
Kirkhope Scot Borders 61 A9
Kirkhouse Scot Borders 70 G2
Kirkiboll H'land 93 D8
Kirkibost H'land 85 G10
Kirkinch Angus 76 C6
Kirkinner Dumf/Gal 55 D7
Kirkintilloch E Dunb 68 C5
Kirkland Cumb 56 E2
Kirkland Cumb 57 C8
Kirkland Dumf/Gal 60 D4
Kirkland Dumf/Gal 60 B3
Kirkleatham Redcar/Clevel'd 59 D6
Kirklevington Stockton 58 F5
Kirkley Suffolk 39 F11
Kirklington Notts 45 G10
Kirklington N Yorks 51 A9
Kirklinton Cumb 61 G10
Kirkliston C/Edinb 69 C10
Kirkmaiden Dumf/Gal 54 F4
Kirkmichael Perth/Kinr 76 B3
Kirkmichael S Ayrs 66 F6
Kirkmuirhill S Lanarks 68 F6
Kirknewton Northum 71 G8
Kirknewton W Loth 69 D10
Kirkney Aberds 88 E5
Kirkoswald Cumb 57 B7
Kirkoswald S Ayrs 66 F5
Kirkpatrick Durham Dumf/Gal 60 F3
Kirkpatrick-Fleming Dumf/Gal 61 F8
Kirksanton Cumb 49 A1
Kirkstall W Yorks 51 F8
Kirkstead Lincs 46 F5
Kirkstile Aberds 88 E5
Kirkstyle H'land 94 C5
Kirkton Aberds 83 A8
Kirkton Aberds 89 D6
Kirkton Angus 77 C7
Kirkton Angus 77 D7
Kirkton Scot Borders 61 B11
Kirkton Dumf/Gal 60 E5
Kirkton Fife 76 E6
Kirkton H'land 85 F13
Kirkton H'land 86 G2
Kirkton H'land 87 B10
Kirkton H'land 87 F10
Kirkton Perth/Kinr 76 F2
Kirkton S Lanarks 60 A5
Kirkton Stirl 75 G8
Kirkton Manor Scot Borders 69 G11
Kirkton of Airlie Angus 76 B6
Kirkton of Auchterhouse Angus 76 D6
Kirkton of Auchterless Aberds 89 D7
Kirkton of Barevan H'land 87 G11
Kirkton of Bourtie Aberds 89 F8
Kirkton of Collace Perth/Kinr 76 D4
Kirkton of Craig Angus 77 B10
Kirkton of Culsalmond Aberds 89 E6
Kirkton of Durris Aberds 83 D9
Kirkton of Glenbuchat Aberds 82 B5
Kirkton of Glenisla Angus 76 A5
Kirkton of Kingoldrum Angus 76 B6
Kirkton of Largo Fife 77 G7
Kirkton of Lethendy Perth/Kinr 76 C4
Kirkton of Logie Buchan Aberds 89 F9
Kirkton of Maryculter Aberds 83 D10
Kirkton of Menmuir Angus 77 A8
Kirkton of Monikie Angus 77 D8
Kirkton of Oyne Aberds 83 A8
Kirkton of Rayne Aberds 83 A8
Kirkton of Skene Aberds 83 C10
Kirkton of Tough Aberds 83 B8
Kirktonhill Scot Borders 70 E3
Kirktown Aberds 89 C10
Kirktown of Alvah Aberds 89 B6
Kirktown of Deskford Moray 88 B5
Kirktown of Fetteresso Aberds 83 E10
Kirktown of Mortlach Moray 88 E3
Kirktown of Slains Aberds 89 F10
Kirkurd Scot Borders 69 F10
Kirkwall Orkney 95 G5
Kirkwhelpington Northum 62 E5
Kirmington N Lincs 46 A5
Kirmond le Mire Lincs 46 C5
Kirn Arg/Bute 73 F10
Kirriemuir Angus 76 B6
Kirstead Green Norfolk 39 F8
Kirtlebridge Dumf/Gal 61 F8
Kirtleton Dumf/Gal 61 E8
Kirtling Cambs 30 C3
Kirtling Green Cambs 30 C3
Kirtlington Oxon 27 G11
Kirtomy H'land 93 C10
Kirton Lincs 37 B9
Kirton Notts 45 F10
Kirton Suffolk 31 E9
Kirton End Lincs 37 A8
Kirton Holme Lincs 37 A8
Kirton in Lindsey N Lincs 46 C3
Kislingbury Northants 28 C3
Kites Hardwick Warwick 27 B11
Kittisford Som'set 7 D9
Kittle Swan 23 H10
Kitt's Green W Midlands 35 G7
Kitt's Moss Gtr Man 44 D2
Kittybrewster Aberd C 83 C11
Kitwood Hants 10 A5
Kivernoll Heref'd 25 E11
Kiveton Park S Yorks 45 D8
Knaith Lincs 46 D2
Knaith Park Lincs 46 D2
Knap Corner Dorset 9 B7
Knaphill Surrey 18 F6
Knapp Perth/Kinr 76 D5
Knapp Som'set 8 B2
Knapthorpe Notts 45 G11
Knapton Norfolk 39 B9
Knapton C/York 52 D1
Knapton Green Heref'd 25 C11
Knapwell Cambs 29 B10
Knaresborough N Yorks 51 D9
Knarsdale Northum 57 A8
Knauchland Moray 88 C5
Knaven Aberds 89 D8
Knayton N Yorks 58 H5
Knebworth Herts 29 F9
Knedlington ER Yorks 52 G3
Kneesall Notts 45 F11
Kneesworth Cambs 29 D10
Kneeton Notts 45 H11
Knelston Swan 23 H9
Knenhall Staffs 34 B5
Knettishall Suffolk 38 G5
Knightacott Devon 6 C5
Knightcote Warwick 27 C10
Knightley Dale Staffs 34 C4
Knighton Devon 4 G6
Knighton Leics C 36 E1
Knighton Staffs 34 C3
Knighton Staffs 34 A3
Knighton = Tref-y-Clawdd Powys 25 A9
Knightswood C/Glasg 68 D4
Knightwick Worcs 26 C4
Knill Heref'd 25 B9
Knipton Leics 36 B4
Knitsley Durham 58 B2
Kniveton Derby 44 G6
Knock Arg/Bute 79 H8
Knock Cumb 57 D8
Knock Moray 88 C5
Knockally H'land 94 H3
Knockan H'land 92 H5
Knockandhu Moray 82 A4
Knockando Moray 88 D1
Knockando Ho. Moray 88 D2
Knockbain H'land 87 F9
Knockbreck H'land 84 B7
Knockbrex Dumf/Gal 55 E8
Knockdee H'land 94 D3
Knockdolian S Ayrs 66 H4
Knockenkelly N Ayrs 66 D3
Knockentiber E Ayrs 67 C6
Knockespock Ho. Aberds 83 A7
Knockfarrel H'land 87 F8
Knockglass Dumf/Gal 54 D3
Knockholt Kent 19 F11
Knockholt Pound Kent 19 F11
Knockie Lodge H'land 80 B6
Knockin Shrops 33 C9
Knockinlaw E Ayrs 67 C7
Knocklearn Dumf/Gal 60 F3
Knocknaha Arg/Bute 65 G7
Knocknain Dumf/Gal 54 C2
Knockrome Arg/Bute 72 F4
Knocksharry I/Man 48 D2
Knodishall Suffolk 31 B11
Knolls Green Ches 44 E2
Knolton Wrex 33 B9
Knolton Bryn Wrex 33 B9
Knook Wilts 16 G6
Knossington Leics 36 E4
Knott End-on-Sea Lancs 49 E3
Knotting Beds 29 B7
Knotting Green Beds 29 B7
Knottingley W Yorks 51 G11
Knotts Cumb 56 D6
Knotts Lancs 50 D3
Knotty Ash Mersey 43 C7
Knotty Green Bucks 18 B6
Knowbury Shrops 26 A2
Knowe Dumf/Gal 54 B6
Knowehead Dumf/Gal 67 G9
Knowes of Elrick Aberds 88 C6
Knowesgate Northum 62 E5
Knoweton N Lanarks 68 E6
Knowhead Aberds 89 C9
Knowl Hill Windsor 18 D5
Knowle Bristol 16 D3
Knowle Devon 7 F6
Knowle Devon 7 H9
Knowle Devon 6 C3
Knowle Shrops 26 A2
Knowle W Midlands 35 H7
Knowle Green Lancs 50 F2
Knowle Park W Yorks 51 E6
Knowlton Dorset 9 C9
Knowlton Kent 21 F9
Knowsley Mersey 43 C7
Knowstone Devon 7 D7
Knox Bridge Kent 13 B6
Knucklas Powys 25 A9
Knuston Northants 28 B6
Knutsford Ches 43 E10
Knutton Staffs 44 H2
Knypersley Staffs 44 G2
Kuggar Cornw'l 2 H6
Kyle of Lochalsh H'land 85 F12
Kyleakin H'land 85 F12
Kylerhea H'land 85 F12
Kylesknoydart H'land 79 B11
Kylesku H'land 92 F5
Kylesmorar H'land 79 B11
Kylestrome H'land 92 F5
Kyllachy House H'land 81 A9
Kynaston Shrops 33 C9
Kynnersley Telford 34 D2
Kyre Magna Worcs 26 B3

L

La Fontenelle Guernsey 11
La Planque Guernsey 11
Labost W Isles 91 C7
Lacasaidh W Isles 91 E8
Lacasdal W Isles 91 D9
Laceby NE Lincs 46 B6
Lacey Green Bucks 18 B5
Lach Dennis Ches 43 E10
Lackford Suffolk 30 A4
Lacock Wilts 16 E6
Ladbroke Warwick 27 C11
Laddingford Kent 20 G3
Lade Bank Lincs 47 G7
Ladock Cornw'l 3 D7
Lady Orkney 95 D7
Ladybank Fife 76 F6
Ladykirk Scot Borders 71 F7
Ladysford Aberds 89 B9
Laga H'land 79 E9
Lagalochan Arg/Bute 73 B7
Lagavulin Arg/Bute 64 D5
Lagg Arg/Bute 72 F4
Lagg N Ayrs 66 D2
Laggan Arg/Bute 64 C3
Laggan H'land 80 D4
Laggan H'land 81 D8
Laggan H'land 79 D10
Laggan S Ayrs 54 A5
Lagganulva Arg/Bute 78 G7
Laide H'land 91 H13
Laigh Fenwick E Ayrs 67 B7
Laigh Glengall S Ayrs 66 E6
Laighmuir E Ayrs 67 B7
Laindon Essex 20 C3
Lair H'land 86 G3
Lairg H'land 93 J8
Lairg Lodge H'land 93 J8
Lairg Muir H'land 93 J8
Lairgmore H'land 87 H8
Laisterdyke W Yorks 51 F7
Laithes Cumb 56 C6
Lake I/Wight 10 F4
Lake Wilts 17 H8
Lakenham Norfolk 39 E8
Lakenheath Suffolk 38 G3
Lakesend Norfolk 37 F11
Lakeside Cumb 56 H5
Laleham Surrey 19 E7
Laleston Bridg 14 D4
Lamarsh Essex 30 E5
Lamas Norfolk 39 C8
Lambden Scot Borders 70 F6
Lamberhurst Kent 12 C5
Lamberhurst Quarter Kent 12 C5
Lamberton Scot Borders 71 E8
Lambeth London 19 D10
Lambhill C/Glasg 68 D4
Lambley Notts 45 H10
Lambley Northum 62 H2
Lamborough Hill Oxon 17 A11
Lambourn W Berks 17 D10
Lambourne End Essex 19 B11
Lambs Green W Sussex 19 H9
Lambston Pembs 22 E4
Lambton Tyne/Wear 58 A3
Lamerton Devon 4 D5
Lamesley Tyne/Wear 63 H8
Laminess Orkney 95 E7
Lamington H'land 87 D10
Lamington S Lanarks 69 G8
Lamlash N Ayrs 66 C3
Lamloch Dumf/Gal 67 G8
Lamonby Cumb 56 C6
Lamorna Cornw'l 2 G3
Lamorran Cornw'l 3 E7
Lampardbrook Suffolk 31 B9
Lampeter = Llanbedr Pont Steffan Ceredig'n 23 B10
Lampeter Velfrey Pembs 22 E6
Lamphey Pembs 22 F5
Lamplugh Cumb 56 D2
Lamport Northants 28 A4
Lamyatt Som'set 16 H3
Lana Devon 6 G2
Lanark S Lanarks 69 F7
Lancaster Lancs 49 C4
Lanchester Durham 58 B2
Lancing W Sussex 11 D10
Landbeach Cambs 29 B11
Landcross Devon 6 D3
Landerberry Aberds 83 C9
Landford Wilts 10 C1
Landford Manor Wilts 10 B1
Landimore Swan 23 G9
Landkey Devon 6 C4
Landore Swan 14 B2
Landrake Cornw'l 4 E4
Landscove Devon 5 E8
Landshipping Pembs 22 E5
Landshipping Quay Pembs 22 E5
Landulph Cornw'l 4 E5
Landwade Suffolk 30 B3
Lane Cornw'l 3 C7
Lane End Bucks 18 B5
Lane End Cumb 56 G3
Lane End Dorset 9 E7
Lane End Hants 10 B4
Lane End I/Wight 10 F5
Lane End Lancs 50 E4
Lane Ends Lancs 50 F3
Lane Ends Lancs 50 D3
Lane Ends N Yorks 50 E5
Lane Head Derby 44 E5
Lane Head Durham 58 E2
Lane Head Gtr Man 43 C9
Lane Head W Yorks 44 B5
Lane Side Lancs 50 G3
Laneast Cornw'l 4 C3
Laneham Notts 46 E2
Lanehead Durham 57 B10
Lanehead Northum 62 E3
Lanercost Cumb 61 G11
Laneshaw Bridge Lancs 50 E5
Lanfach Caerph 15 B8
Langar Notts 36 B3
Langbank Renf 68 C2
Langbar N Yorks 51 D6
Langburnshiels Scot Borders 61 C11
Langcliffe N Yorks 50 C4
Langdale H'land 93 E9
Langdale End N Yorks 59 G10
Langdon Cornw'l 4 C4
Langdon Beck Durham 57 C10
Langdon Hills Essex 20 C3
Langdyke Fife 76 G6
Langenhoe Essex 31 G7
Langford Beds 29 D8
Langford Devon 7 F9
Langford Essex 30 H5
Langford Notts 46 G2
Langford Oxon 17 A9
Langford Budville Som'set 7 D10
Langham Essex 31 E7
Langham Norfolk 38 A6
Langham Rutl'd 36 D4
Langham Suffolk 30 B6
Langhaugh Scot Borders 69 G11
Langho Lancs 50 F3
Langholm Dumf/Gal 61 E9
Langleeford Northum 62 A5
Langley Ches 44 E3
Langley Hants 10 D3
Langley Herts 29 F9
Langley Kent 20 F5
Langley Northum 62 G4
Langley Slough 19 D7
Langley Warwick 27 B8
Langley W Sussex 11 B7
Langley Burrell Wilts 16 D6
Langley Common Derby 35 B8
Langley Heath Kent 20 F5
Langley Lower Green Essex 29 E11
Langley Marsh Som'set 7 D9
Langley Park Durham 58 B3
Langley Street Norfolk 39 E9
Langley Upper Green Essex 29 E11
Langney E Sussex 12 F5
Langold Notts 45 D9
Langore Cornw'l 4 C4
Langport Som'set 8 B3
Langrick Lincs 46 H6
Langridge Bath/NE Som'set 16 E4
Langridge Ford Devon 6 D4
Langrigg Cumb 56 B3
Langrish Hants 10 B6
Langsett S Yorks 44 B6
Langshaw Scot Borders 70 G4
Langside Perth/Kinr 75 F10
Langskaill Orkney 95 D5
Langstone Hants 10 D6
Langstone Newp 15 B9
Langthorne N Yorks 58 G3
Langthorpe N Yorks 51 C9
Langthwaite N Yorks 58 F1
Langtoft ER Yorks 52 C6
Langtoft Lincs 37 D7
Langton Durham 58 E2
Langton Lincs 46 F6
Langton Lincs 47 E7
Langton N Yorks 52 C3
Langton by Wragby Lincs 46 E5
Langton Green Kent 12 C4
Langton Green Suffolk 31 A8
Langton Herring Dorset 8 F5
Langton Matravers Dorset 9 G9
Langtree Devon 6 E3
Langwathby Cumb 57 C7
Langwell Ho. H'land 94 H3
Langwell Lodge H'land 92 J4
Langwith Derby 45 F9
Langwith Junction Derby 45 F9
Langworth Lincs 46 E4
Lanivet Cornw'l 3 C9
Lanlivery Cornw'l 4 F1
Lanner Cornw'l 2 F6
Lanreath Cornw'l 4 F2
Lansallos Cornw'l 4 F2
Lansdown Glos 26 F6
Lanteglos Highway Cornw'l 4 F2
Lanton Scot Borders 62 A2
Lanton Northum 71 G8
Lapford Devon 7 F6
Laphroaig Arg/Bute 64 D4
Lapley Staffs 34 D4
Lapworth Warwick 27 A8
Larachbeg H'land 79 G9
Larbert Falk 69 B7
Larden Green Ches 43 G8
Largie Aberds 88 E6
Largiemore Arg/Bute 73 E8
Largoward Fife 77 G7
Largs N Ayrs 73 H11
Largybeg N Ayrs 66 D3
Largymore N Ayrs 66 D3
Larkfield Invercl 73 F11
Larkhall S Lanarks 68 E6
Larkhill Wilts 17 G8
Larling Norfolk 38 G5
Larriston Scot Borders 61 D11
Lartington Durham 58 E1
Lary Aberds 82 C5
Lasham Hants 18 G3
Lashenden Kent 13 B7
Lassington Glos 26 F4
Lassodie Fife 69 A10
Lastingham N Yorks 59 G8
Latcham Som'set 15 G10
Latchford Herts 29 F10
Latchford Warrington 43 D9
Latchingdon Essex 20 A5
Latchley Cornw'l 4 D5
Lately Common Warrington 43 C9
Lathbury M/Keynes 28 D5
Latheron H'land 94 G3
Latheronwheel H'land 94 G3
Latheronwheel Ho. H'land 94 G3
Lathones Fife 77 G7
Latimer Bucks 19 B7
Latteridge S Gloucs 16 C3
Lattiford Som'set 8 B5
Latton Wilts 17 B7
Latton Bush Essex 29 H11
Lauchintilly Aberds 83 B9
Lauder Scot Borders 70 F4
Laugharne Carms 23 E8
Laughterton Lincs 46 E2
Laughton E Sussex 12 E4
Laughton Leics 36 G2
Laughton Lincs 37 B6
Laughton Lincs 46 C2
Laughton Common S Yorks 45 D9
Laughton en le Morthen S Yorks 45 D9
Launcells Cornw'l 6 F1
Launceston Cornw'l 4 C4
Launton Oxon 28 F3
Laurencekirk Aberds 83 F9
Laurieston Dumf/Gal 55 C9
Laurieston Falk 69 C8
Lavendon M/Keynes 28 C6
Lavenham Suffolk 30 D6
Laverhay Dumf/Gal 61 D7
Laversdale Cumb 61 G10
Laverstock Wilts 9 A10
Laverstoke Hants 17 G11
Laverton Glos 27 E7
Laverton N Yorks 51 B8
Laverton Som'set 16 F4
Lavister Wrex 42 G6
Law S Lanarks 69 E7
Lawers Perth/Kinr 75 D9
Lawers Perth/Kinr 75 E10
Lawford Essex 31 E7
Lawhitton Cornw'l 4 C4
Lawkland N Yorks 50 C3
Lawley Telford 34 E2
Lawnhead Staffs 34 C4
Lawrenny Pembs 22 F5
Lawshall Suffolk 30 C5
Lawton Heref'd 25 C11
Laxey I/Man 48 D4
Laxfield Suffolk 31 A9
Laxfirth Shetl'd 96 J6
Laxfirth Shetl'd 96 H6
Laxford Bridge H'land 92 E5
Laxo Shetl'd 96 G6
Laxobigging Shetl'd 96 F6
Laxton ER Yorks 52 G3
Laxton Notts 45 F11
Laxton Northants 36 F5
Laycock W Yorks 50 E6
Layer Breton Essex 30 G6
Layer de la Haye Essex 30 G6
Layer Marney Essex 30 G6
Layham Suffolk 31 D7
Laylands Green W Berks 17 E10
Laytham ER Yorks 52 F3
Layton Blackp'l 49 F3
Lazenby Redcar/Clevel'd 59 D6
Lazonby Cumb 57 C7
Le Planel Guernsey 11
Le Villocq Guernsey 11
Lea Derby 45 G7
Lea Heref'd 26 F3
Lea Lincs 46 D2
Lea Shrops 33 G9
Lea Shrops 33 E10
Lea Wilts 16 C6
Lea Marston Warwick 35 F8
Lea Town Lancs 49 F4
Leabrooks Derby 45 G8
Leac a Li W Isles 90 H6
Leachkin H'land 87 G9
Leadburn Midloth 69 E11
Leaden Roding Essex 30 G2
Leadenham Lincs 46 G3
Leadgate Cumb 57 B9
Leadgate Durham 58 A2
Leadgate Northum 63 H7
Leadhills S Lanarks 60 B4
Leafield Oxon 27 G10
Leagrave Luton 29 F7
Leake N Yorks 58 G5
Leake Commonside Lincs 47 G7
Lealholm N Yorks 59 F8
Lealt Arg/Bute 72 D5
Lealt H'land 85 B10
Leamington Hastings Warwick 27 B11
Leamonsley Staffs 35 E7
Leamside Durham 58 B4
Leanaig H'land 87 F8
Leargybreck Arg/Bute 72 F4
Leasgill Cumb 49 A4
Leasingham Lincs 46 H4
Leasingthorne Durham 58 D3
Leasowe Mersey 42 C5
Leatherhead Surrey 19 F8
Leatherhead Common Surrey 19 F8
Leathley N Yorks 51 E8
Leaton Shrops 33 D10
Leaveland Kent 21 F7
Leavening N Yorks 52 C3
Leaves Green London 19 E11
Leazes Durham 63 H7
Lebberston N Yorks 53 A6
Lechlade-on-Thames Glos 17 B9
Leck Lancs 50 B2
Leckford Hants 17 H10
Leckfurin H'land 93 D10
Leckgruinart Arg/Bute 64 B3
Leckhampstead Bucks 28 E4
Leckhampstead W Berks 17 D11
Leckhampstead Thicket W Berks 17 D11
Leckhampton Glos 26 G6
Leckie H'land 86 E3
Leckmelm H'land 86 B4
Leckwith V/Glam 15 D7
Leconfield ER Yorks 52 E6
Ledaig Arg/Bute 74 D2
Ledburn Bucks 28 F6
Ledbury Heref'd 26 E4
Ledcharrie Stirl 75 E8
Ledgemoor Heref'd 25 C11
Ledicot Heref'd 25 B11
Ledmore H'land 92 H5
Lednagullin H'land 93 C10
Ledsham Ches 42 E6
Ledsham W Yorks 51 G10
Ledston W Yorks 51 G10
Ledston Luck W Yorks 51 F10
Ledwell Oxon 27 F11
Lee Arg/Bute 78 J7
Lee Devon 6 B3
Lee Hants 10 C2
Lee Lancs 50 D1
Lee Shrops 33 B10
Lee Brockhurst Shrops 33 C11
Lee Clump Bucks 18 A6
Lee Mill Devon 5 F7
Lee Moor Devon 5 E6
Lee-on-the-Solent Hants 10 D4
Leeans Shetl'd 96 J5
Leebotten Shetl'd 96 L6
Leebotwood Shrops 33 F10
Leece Cumb 49 C2
Leechpool Pembs 22 E4
Leeds Kent 20 F5
Leeds W Yorks 51 F8
Leedstown Cornw'l 2 F5
Leek Staffs 44 G3
Leek Wootton Warwick 27 B9
Leekbrook Staffs 44 G3
Leeming N Yorks 58 H3
Leeming Bar N Yorks 58 G3
Lees Derby 35 B8
Lees Gtr Man 44 B3
Lees W Yorks 50 F6
Leeswood Flints 42 F5
Legbourne Lincs 47 D7
Legerwood Scot Borders 70 F4
Legsby Lincs 46 D5
Leicester Leics C 36 E1
Leicester Forest East Leics 35 E11
Leigh Dorset 8 D5
Leigh Glos 26 F5
Leigh Gtr Man 43 B9
Leigh Kent 20 G2
Leigh Shrops 33 E9
Leigh Surrey 19 G9
Leigh Wilts 17 B7
Leigh Worcs 26 C4
Leigh Beck Essex 20 C5
Leigh Common Som'set 8 B6
Leigh Delamere Wilts 16 D5
Leigh Green Kent 13 C8
Leigh on Sea Southend 20 C5
Leigh Park Hants 10 D6
Leigh Sinton Worcs 26 C4
Leigh upon Mendip Som'set 16 G3
Leigh Woods N Som'set 16 D2
Leighswood W Midlands 35 E6
Leighterton Glos 16 B5
Leighton N Yorks 51 B7
Leighton Powys 33 E8
Leighton Shrops 34 E2
Leighton Som'set 16 G4
Leighton Bromswold Cambs 37 H7
Leighton Buzzard Beds 28 F6
Leinthall Earls Heref'd 25 B11
Leinthall Starkes Heref'd 25 B11
Leintwardine Heref'd 25 A11
Leire Leics 35 F11
Leirinmore H'land 92 C7
Leiston Suffolk 31 B11
Leitfie Perth/Kinr 76 C5
Leith C/Edinb 69 C11
Leitholm Scot Borders 70 F6
Lelant Cornw'l 2 F4
Lelley ER Yorks 53 F8
Lem Hill Worcs 26 A4
Lemmington Hall Northum 63 B7
Lempitlaw Scot Borders 70 G6
Lenchwick Worcs 27 D7
Lendalfoot S Ayrs 66 H4
Lendrick Lodge Stirl 75 G8
Lenham Kent 20 F5
Lenham Heath Kent 20 G6
Lennel Scot Borders 71 F7
Lennoxtown E Dunb 68 C5
Lenton Lincs 36 B6
Lenton Nott'ham 36 B1
Lentran H'land 87 G8
Lenwade Norfolk 39 D6
Leny Ho. Stirl 75 G9
Lenzie E Dunb 68 C5
Leoch Angus 76 D6
Leochel-Cushnie Aberds 83 B7
Leominster Heref'd 25 C11
Leonard Stanley Glos 16 A5
Leorin Arg/Bute 64 D4
Lepe Hants 10 E3
Lephin H'land 84 D6
Lephinchapel Arg/Bute 73 D8
Lephinmore Arg/Bute 73 D8
Leppington N Yorks 52 C3
Lepton W Yorks 51 H8
Lerryn Cornw'l 4 F2
Lerwick Shetl'd 96 J6
Lesbury Northum 63 B8
Leslie Aberds 83 A7
Leslie Fife 76 G5
Lesmahagow S Lanarks 69 G7
Lesnewth Cornw'l 4 B2
Lessendrum Aberds 88 D5
Lessingham Norfolk 39 C9
Lessonhall Cumb 56 A4
Leswalt Dumf/Gal 54 C3
Letchmore Heath Herts 19 B8
Letchworth Herts 29 E9
Letcombe Bassett Oxon 17 C10
Letcombe Regis Oxon 17 C10
Letham Angus 77 C8
Letham Falk 69 B7
Letham Fife 76 F6
Letham Perth/Kinr 76 E3
Letham Grange Angus 77 C9
Lethenty Aberds 89 D8
Letheringham Suffolk 31 C9
Letheringsett Norfolk 39 B6
Lettaford Devon 5 C8
Lettan Orkney 95 D8
Letterewe H'land 86 D2
Letterfearn H'land 85 F13
Letterfinlay H'land 80 D4
Lettermorar H'land 79 C10
Lettermore Arg/Bute 78 G7
Letters H'land 86 C4
Letterston Pembs 22 D4
Lettoch H'land 82 A2
Lettoch H'land 87 H13
Letton Heref'd 25 D10
Letton Heref'd 25 A10
Letton Green Norfolk 38 E5
Letty Green Herts 29 G9
Letwell S Yorks 45 D9
Leuchars Fife 77 E7
Leuchars Ho. Moray 88 B2
Leumrabhagh W Isles 91 F8
Levan Invercl 73 F11
Levaneap Shetl'd 96 G6
Levedale Staffs 34 D4
Leven ER Yorks 53 E7
Leven Fife 76 G6
Levencorroch N Ayrs 66 D3
Levens Cumb 57 H6
Levens Green Herts 29 F10
Levenshulme Gtr Man 44 C2
Levenwick Shetl'd 96 L6
Leverburgh = An t-Ob W Isles 90 J5
Leverington Cambs 37 D10
Leverton Lincs 47 H8
Leverton Highgate Lincs 47 H8
Leverton Lucasgate Lincs 47 H8
Leverton Outgate Lincs 47 H8
Levington Suffolk 31 E9
Levisham N Yorks 59 G9
Levishie H'land 80 B6
Lew Oxon 27 H10
Lewannick Cornw'l 4 C3
Lewdown Devon 4 C5
Lewes E Sussex 12 E3
Leweston Pembs 22 D4
Lewisham London 19 D10
Lewiston H'land 81 A7
Lewistown Bridg 14 C5
Lewknor Oxon 18 B4
Leworthy Devon 6 F2
Leworthy Devon 6 C5
Lewtrenchard Devon 4 C5
Lexden Essex 30 F6
Ley Aberds 83 B7
Ley Cornw'l 4 E2
Leybourne Kent 20 F3
Leyburn N Yorks 58 G2
Leyfields Staffs 35 E8
Leyhill Bucks 18 A6
Leyland Lancs 49 G5
Leylodge Aberds 83 B9
Leymoor W Yorks 51 H7
Leys Aberds 89 C10
Leys Perth/Kinr 76 D5
Leys Castle H'land 87 G9
Leys of Cossans Angus 76 C6
Leysdown-on-Sea Kent 21 D7
Leysmill Angus 77 C9
Leysters Pole Heref'd 26 B2
Leyton London 19 C10
Leytonstone London 19 C10
Lezant Cornw'l 4 D4
Leziate Norfolk 38 D2
Lhanbryde Moray 88 B2
Liatrie H'land 86 H5
Libanus Powys 24 F6
Libberton S Lanarks 69 F8
Liberton C/Edinb 69 D11
Liceasto W Isles 90 H6
Lichfield Staffs 35 E7
Lickey Worcs 34 H5
Lickey End Worcs 26 A6
Lickfold W Sussex 11 B8
Liddel Orkney 95 K5
Liddesdale H'land 79 F10
Liddington Swindon 17 C9
Lidgate Suffolk 30 C4
Lidget S Yorks 45 B10
Lidget Green W Yorks 51 F7
Lidgett Notts 45 F10
Lidlington Beds 28 E6
Lidstone Oxon 27 F10
Lieurary H'land 94 D2
Liff Angus 76 D6
Lifton Devon 4 C4
Liftondown Devon 4 C4
Lighthorne Warwick 27 C10
Lightwater Surrey 18 E6
Lightwood Stoke 34 A5
Lightwood Green Ches 34 A2
Lightwood Green Wrex 33 A9
Lilbourne Northants 36 H1
Lilburn Tower Northum 62 A6
Lilleshall Telford 34 D3
Lilley Herts 29 F8
Lilley W Berks 17 D11
Lilliesleaf Scot Borders 61 A11
Lillingstone Dayrell Bucks 28 E4
Lillingstone Lovell Bucks 28 D4
Lillington Dorset 8 C5
Lillington Warwick 27 B10
Lilliput Poole 9 E9
Lilstock Som'set 7 B10
Lilyhurst Shrops 34 D3
Limbury Luton 29 F7
Limebrook Heref'd 25 B10
Limefield Gtr Man 44 A2
Limekilnburn S Lanarks 68 E6
Limekilns Fife 69 B9
Limerigg Falk 69 C7
Limerstone I/Wight 10 F3
Limington Som'set 8 B4
Limpenhoe Norfolk 39 E9
Limpley Stoke Wilts 16 E4
Limpsfield Surrey 19 F11
Limpsfield Chart Surrey 19 F11
Linby Notts 45 G9
Linchmere W Sussex 11 A7
Lincluden Dumf/Gal 60 F5
Lincoln Lincs 46 E3
Lincomb Worcs 26 B5
Lincombe Devon 5 F8
Lindal in Furness Cumb 49 B2
Lindale Cumb 49 A4
Lindean Scot Borders 70 G3
Lindfield W Sussex 12 D2
Lindford Hants 18 H5
Lindifferon Fife 76 F6
Lindley W Yorks 51 H7
Lindley Green N Yorks 51 E8
Lindores Fife 76 F5
Lindridge Worcs 26 B3
Lindsell Essex 30 F3
Lindsey Suffolk 30 D6
Linford Hants 9 D10
Linford Thurr'k 20 D3
Lingague I/Man 48 E2
Lingards Wood W Yorks 44 A4
Lingbob W Yorks 51 F6
Lingdale Redcar/Clevel'd 59 E7
Lingen Heref'd 25 B10
Lingfield Surrey 12 B2
Lingreabhagh W Isles 90 J5
Lingwood Norfolk 39 E9
Linicro H'land 85 B8
Linkenholt Hants 17 F10
Linkhill Kent 13 D7
Linkinhorne Cornw'l 4 D4
Linklater Orkney 95 K5
Linksness Orkney 95 H3
Linktown Fife 69 A11
Linley Shrops 33 F9
Linley Green Heref'd 26 C3
Linlithgow W Loth 69 C9
Linlithgow Bridge W Loth 69 C8
Linshiels Northum 62 C4
Linsiadar W Isles 90 D7
Linsidemore H'land 87 B8
Linslade Beds 28 F6
Linstead Parva Suffolk 39 H9
Linstock Cumb 61 H10
Linthwaite W Yorks 44 A5
Lintlaw Scot Borders 71 E7
Lintmill Moray 88 B5
Linton Scot Borders 70 H6
Linton Cambs 30 D2
Linton Derby 35 D8
Linton Heref'd 26 F3
Linton Kent 20 G4
Linton Northum 63 D8
Linton N Yorks 50 C5
Linton W Yorks 51 E9
Linton-on-Ouse N Yorks 51 C10
Linwood Hants 9 D10
Linwood Lincs 46 D5
Linwood Renf 68 D3
Lionacleit W Isles 84 D2
Lional W Isles 91 A10
Liphook Hants 11 A7
Liscard Mersey 42 C6
Liscombe Som'set 7 C7
Liskeard Cornw'l 4 E3
L'Islet Guernsey 11
Liss Hants 11 B6
Liss Forest Hants 11 B6
Lissett ER Yorks 53 D7
Lissington Lincs 46 D5
Lisvane Card 15 C7
Liswerry Newp 15 C9
Litcham Norfolk 38 D4
Litchborough Northants 28 C3
Litchfield Hants 17 F11
Litherland Mersey 42 C6
Litlington Cambs 29 D10
Litlington E Sussex 12 F4
Little Abington Cambs 30 D2
Little Addington Northants 28 A6
Little Alne Warwick 27 B8
Little Altcar Mersey 42 B6
Little Asby Cumb 57 F8
Little Assynt H'land 92 G4
Little Aston Staffs 35 E6
Little Atherfield I/Wight 10 F3
Little Ayre Orkney 95 J4
Little-ayre Shetl'd 96 G5
Little Ayton N Yorks 59 E6
Little Baddow Essex 30 H4
Little Badminton S Gloucs 16 C5
Little Ballinluig Perth/Kinr 76 B2
Little Bampton Cumb 61 H8
Little Bardfield Essex 30 E3
Little Barford Beds 29 C8
Little Barningham Norfolk 39 B7
Little Barrington Glos 27 G9
Little Barrow Ches 43 F7
Little Barugh N Yorks 52 B3
Little Bavington Northum 62 F5
Little Bealings Suffolk 31 D9
Little Bedwyn Wilts 17 E9
Little Bentley Essex 31 F8
Little Berkhamsted Herts 29 H9
Little Billing Northants 28 B5
Little Birch Heref'd 26 E2
Little Blakenham Suffolk 31 D8
Little Blencow Cumb 56 C6
Little Bollington Ches 43 D10
Little Bookham Surrey 19 F8
Little Bowden Leics 36 G3
Little Bradley Suffolk 30 C3
Little Brampton Shrops 33 G9
Little Brechin Angus 77 A8
Little Brickhill M/Keynes 28 E6
Little Brington Northants 28 B3
Little Bromley Essex 31 F7
Little Broughton Cumb 56 C2
Little Budworth Ches 43 F8
Little Burstead Essex 20 B3
Little Bytham Lincs 36 D6
Little Carlton Lincs 47 D7
Little Carlton Notts 45 G11
Little Casterton Rutl'd 36 E6
Little Cawthorpe Lincs 47 D7
Little Chalfont Bucks 18 B6
Little Chart Kent 20 G6
Little Chesterford Essex 30 D2
Little Cheverell Wilts 16 F6
Little Chishill Cambs 29 E11
Little Clacton Essex 31 G8
Little Clifton Cumb 56 D2
Little Colp Aberds 89 D7
Little Comberton Worcs 26 D6
Little Common E Sussex 12 F6
Little Compton Warwick 27 E9
Little Cornard Suffolk 30 E5
Little Cowarne Heref'd 26 C3
Little Coxwell Oxon 17 B9
Little Crakehall N Yorks 58 G3
Little Cressingham Norfolk 38 E4
Little Crosby Mersey 42 B6
Little Dalby Leics 36 D3
Little Dawley Telford 34 E2
Little Dens Aberds 89 D10
Little Dewchurch Heref'd 26 E2
Little Downham Cambs 37 G11
Little Driffield ER Yorks 52 D6
Little Dunham Norfolk 38 D4
Little Dunkeld Perth/Kinr 76 C3
Little Dunmow Essex 30 F3
Little Easton Essex 30 F3
Little Eaton Derby 35 A9
Little Eccleston Lancs 49 E4
Little Ellingham Norfolk 38 F6
Little End Essex 20 A2
Little Eversden Cambs 29 C10
Little Fakenham Suffolk 38 H5
Little Faringdon Oxon 17 A9
Little Fencote N Yorks 58 G3
Little Fenton N Yorks 51 F11
Little Finborough Suffolk 31 C7
Little Fransham Norfolk 38 D5
Little Gaddesden Herts 28 G6
Little Gidding Cambs 37 G7
Little Glemham Suffolk 31 C10
Little Glenshee Perth/Kinr 76 D2
Little Gransden Cambs 29 C9
Little Green Som'set 16 G4
Little Grimsby Lincs 47 C7
Little Gruinard H'land 86 C2
Little Habton N Yorks 52 B3
Little Hadham Herts 29 F11
Little Hale Lincs 37 A7
Little Hallingbury Essex 29 G11
Little Hampden Bucks 18 A5
Little Harrowden Northants 28 A5
Little Haseley Oxon 18 A3
Little Hatfield ER Yorks 53 E7
Little Hautbois Norfolk 39 C8
Little Haven Pembs 22 E3
Little Hay Staffs 35 E7
Little Hayfield Derby 44 D4
Little Haywood Staffs 34 C6
Little Heath W Midlands 35 G9
Little Hereford Heref'd 26 B2
Little Horkesley Essex 30 E6
Little Horsted E Sussex 12 E3
Little Horton W Yorks 51 F7
Little Horwood Bucks 28 E4
Little Houghton Northants 28 C5
Little Houghton S Yorks 45 B8
Little Hucklow Derby 44 E5
Little Hulton Gtr Man 43 B10
Little Humber ER Yorks 53 G7
Little Hungerford W Berks 18 D2
Little Irchester Northants 28 B6
Little Kimble Bucks 28 H5
Little Kineton Warwick 27 C10
Little Kingshill Bucks 18 B5
Little Langdale Cumb 56 F5
Little Langford Wilts 17 H7
Little Laver Essex 30 H2
Little Leigh Ches 43 E9
Little Leighs Essex 30 G4
Little Lever Gtr Man 43 B10
Little London Bucks 28 G3
Little London E Sussex 12 E4
Little London Hants 17 G10
Little London Hants 18 F3
Little London Lincs 37 C8
Little London Lincs 37 C10
Little London Norfolk 39 C7
Little London Powys 32 G6
Little Longstone Derby 44 E5
Little Lynturk Aberds 83 B7
Little Malvern Worcs 26 D4
Little Maplestead Essex 30 E5
Little Marcle Heref'd 26 E3
Little Marlow Bucks 18 C5
Little Marsden Lancs 50 F4
Little Massingham Norfolk 38 C3
Little Melton Norfolk 39 E7
Little Mill Monmouths 15 A9
Little Milton Oxon 18 A3
Little Missenden Bucks 18 B6
Little Musgrave Cumb 57 E9
Little Ness Shrops 33 D10
Little Neston Ches 42 E5
Little Newcastle Pembs 22 D4
Little Newsham Durham 58 E2
Little Oakley Essex 31 F9
Little Oakley Northants 36 G4
Little Orton Cumb 61 H9
Little Ouseburn N Yorks 51 C10
Little Paxton Cambs 29 B8
Little Petherick Cornw'l 3 B8
Little Pitlurg Moray 88 D4
Little Plumpton Lancs 49 F3
Little Plumstead Norfolk 39 D9
Little Ponton Lincs 36 B5
Little Raveley Cambs 37 H8
Little Reedness ER Yorks 52 G4
Little Ribston N Yorks 51 D9
Little Rissington Glos 27 G8
Little Ryburgh Norfolk 38 C5
Little Ryle Northum 62 B6
Little Salkeld Cumb 57 C7
Little Sampford Essex 30 E3
Little Sandhurst Brackn'l 18 E5
Little Saxham Suffolk 30 B4
Little Scatwell H'land 86 F6
Little Sessay N Yorks 51 B10
Little Shelford Cambs 29 C11
Little Singleton Lancs 49 F3
Little Skillymarno Aberds 89 C9
Little Smeaton N Yorks 51 H11
Little Snoring Norfolk 38 B5
Little Sodbury S Gloucs 16 C4
Little Somborne Hants 10 A2
Little Somerford Wilts 16 C6
Little Stainforth N Yorks 50 C4
Little Stainton D'lington 58 D4
Little Stanney Ches 43 E7
Little Staughton Beds 29 B8
Little Steeping Lincs 47 F8
Little Stoke Staffs 34 B5
Little Stonham Suffolk 31 B8
Little Stretton Leics 36 E2
Little Stretton Shrops 33 F10
Little Strickland Cumb 57 E7
Little Stukeley Cambs 37 H8
Little Sutton Ches 42 E6
Little Tew Oxon 27 F10
Little Thetford Cambs 37 H11
Little Thirkleby N Yorks 51 B10
Little Thurlow Suffolk 30 C3
Little Thurrock Thurr'k 20 D3
Little Torboll H'land 87 B10
Little Torrington Devon 6 E3

Morton Lincs 37 C6
Morton Lincs 46 C2
Morton Lincs 46 F2
Morton Norfolk 39 D7
Morton Notts 45 G11
Morton Shrops 33 C8
Morton S Gloucs 16 B3
Morton Bagot Warwick 27 B8
Morton-on-Swale N Yorks 58 G4
Morvah Cornw'l 2 F3
Morval Cornw'l 4 F3
Morvich H'land 80 A1
Morvich H'land 93 J10
Morville Shrops 34 F2
Morville Heath Shrops 34 F2
Morwenstow Cornw'l 6 E1
Mosborough S Yorks 45 D8
Moscow E Ayrs 67 B7
Mosedale Cumb 56 C5
Moseley W Midlands 35 G6
Moseley W Midlands 34 F5
Moseley Worcs 26 C5
Moss Arg/Bute 78 G2
Moss H'land 79 F9
Moss S Yorks 45 A9
Moss Wrex 42 G6
Moss Bank Mersey 43 C8
Moss Edge Lancs 49 E4
Moss End Brackn'l 18 D5
Moss of Barmuckity Moray 88 B2
Moss Pit Staffs 34 C5
Moss-side H'land 87 F11
Moss Side Lancs 49 F3
Mossat Aberds 82 B6
Mossbank Shetl'd 96 F6
Mossbay Cumb 60 B3
Mossblown S Ayrs 67 D7
Mossbrow Gtr Man 43 D10
Mossburnford Scot Borders 62 B2
Mossdale Dumf/Gal 55 B9
Mossend N Lanarks 68 D6
Mosser Cumb 56 D3
Mossfield H'land 87 D9
Mossgiel E Ayrs 67 D7
Mosside Angus 77 B7
Mossley Ches 44 F2
Mossley Gtr Man 44 B3
Mossley Hill Mersey 43 D6
Mosstodloch Moray 88 C3
Mosston Angus 77 C8
Mossy Lea Lancs 43 A8
Mosterton Dorset 8 D3
Moston Gtr Man 44 B2
Moston Shrops 34 C1
Moston Green Ches 43 F10
Mostyn Flints 42 D4
Mostyn Quay Flints 42 D4
Motcombe Dorset 9 B7
Mothecombe Devon 5 G7
Motherby Cumb 56 D6
Motherwell N Lanarks 68 E6
Mottingham London 19 D11
Mottisfont Hants 10 B2
Mottistone I/Wight 10 F3
Mottram in Longdendale Gtr Man 44 C3
Mottram St Andrew Ches 44 E2
Mouilpied Guernsey 11
Mouldsworth Ches 43 E8
Moulin Perth/Kinr 76 B2
Moulsecoomb Brighton/Hove 12 F2
Moulsford Oxon 18 C2
Moulsoe M/Keynes 28 D6
Moulton Ches 43 F9
Moulton Lincs 37 C9
Moulton Northants 28 B4
Moulton N Yorks 58 F3
Moulton Suffolk 30 B3
Moulton V/Glam 14 D6
Moulton Chapel Lincs 37 D8
Moulton Eaugate Lincs 37 D9
Moulton St Mary Norfolk 39 E9
Moulton Seas End Lincs 37 C9
Mounie Castle Aberds 83 A9
Mount Cornw'l 3 D6
Mount Cornw'l 4 E2
Mount H'land 87 G12
Mount Bures Essex 30 E6
Mount Canisp H'land 87 D10
Mount Hawke Cornw'l 2 E6
Mount Pleasant Ches 44 G2
Mount Pleasant Derby 45 H7
Mount Pleasant Derby 35 D8
Mount Pleasant Flints 42 E5
Mount Pleasant Hants 10 E1
Mount Pleasant W Yorks 51 G8
Mount Sorrel Wilts 9 B9
Mount Tabor W Yorks 51 G6
Mountain W Yorks 51 F6
Mountain Ash = Aberpennar Rh Cyn Taff 14 B6
Mountain Cross Scot Borders 69 F10
Mountain Water Pembs 22 D4
Mountbenger Scot Borders 70 H2
Mountfield E Sussex 12 D6
Mountgerald H'land 87 E8
Mountjoy Cornw'l 3 C7
Mountnessing Essex 20 B3
Mounton Monmouths 15 B11
Mountsorrel Leics 36 D1
Mousehole Cornw'l 2 G3
Mousen Northum 71 G10
Mouswald Dumf/Gal 60 F6
Mow Cop Ches 44 G2
Mowhaugh Scot Borders 62 A4
Mowsley Leics 36 G2
Moxley W Midlands 34 F5
Moy H'land 80 E6
Moy H'land 87 H10
Moy Hall H'land 87 H10
Moy Ho. Moray 87 E13
Moy Lodge H'land 80 E6
Moyles Court Hants 9 D10
Moylgrove Pembs 22 B6
Muasdale Arg/Bute 65 D7
Much Birch Heref'd 26 E2
Much Cowarne Heref'd 26 D3
Much Dewchurch Heref'd 25 E11
Much Hadham Herts 29 G11
Much Hoole Lancs 49 G4
Much Marcle Heref'd 26 E3
Much Wenlock Shrops 34 E2
Muchalls Aberds 83 D11
Muchelney Som'set 8 B3
Muchlarnick Cornw'l 4 F3
Muchrachd H'land 86 H5
Muckernich H'land 87 F8
Mucking Thurr'k 20 C3
Muckleford Dorset 8 E5
Mucklestone Staffs 34 B3
Muckleton Shrops 34 C1
Muckletown Aberds 83 A7
Muckley Corner Staffs 35 E6
Muckton Lincs 47 D7
Mudale H'land 93 F8
Muddiford Devon 6 C4
Mudeford Dorset 9 E10
Mudford Som'set 8 C4
Mudgley Som'set 15 G10
Mugdock Stirl 68 C4
Mugeary H'land 85 E9
Mugginton Derby 35 A8
Muggleswick Durham 58 B1
Muie H'land 93 J9
Muir Aberds 82 E2
Muir of Fairburn H'land 86 F7
Muir of Fowlis Aberds 83 B7
Muir of Ord H'land 87 F8
Muir of Pert Angus 77 D7
Muirden Aberds 89 C7
Muirdrum Angus 77 D8
Muirhead Angus 76 D6
Muirhead Fife 76 G5
Muirhead N Lanarks 68 D5
Muirhead S Ayrs 66 C6
Muirhouselaw Scot Borders 70 H5
Muirhouses Falk 69 B9
Muirkirk E Ayrs 68 H5
Muirmill Stirl 68 B6
Muirshearlich H'land 80 E3
Muirskie Aberds 83 D10
Muirtack Aberds 89 E9
Muirton H'land 87 E10
Muirton Perth/Kinr 76 E4
Muirton Perth/Kinr 76 F2
Muirton Mains H'land 86 F7
Muirton of Ardblair Perth/Kinr 76 C4
Muirton of Ballochy Angus 77 A9
Muiryfold Aberds 89 C7
Muker N Yorks 57 G11
Mulbarton Norfolk 39 E7
Mulben Moray 88 C3
Mulindry Arg/Bute 64 C4
Mullardoch House H'land 86 H5
Mullion Cornw'l 2 H5
Mullion Cove Cornw'l 2 H5
Mumby Lincs 47 E9
Munderfield Row Heref'd 26 C3
Munderfield Stocks Heref'd 26 C3
Mundesley Norfolk 39 B9
Mundford Norfolk 38 F4
Mundham Norfolk 39 F9
Mundon Essex 20 A5
Mundurno Aberd C 83 B11
Munerigie H'land 80 C4
Muness Shetl'd 96 C8
Mungasdale H'land 86 B2
Mungrisdale Cumb 56 C5
Munlochy H'land 87 F9
Munsley Heref'd 26 D3
Munslow Shrops 33 G11
Murchington Devon 5 C7
Murcott Oxon 28 G2
Murkle H'land 94 D3
Murlaggan H'land 80 D2
Murlaggan H'land 80 E5
Murra Orkney 95 H3
Murrayfield C/Edinb 69 C11
Murrow Cambs 37 E9
Mursley Bucks 28 F5
Murthill Angus 77 B7
Murthly Perth/Kinr 76 D3
Murton Cumb 57 D9
Murton Durham 58 B4
Murton Northum 71 F8
Murton C/York 52 D2
Musbury Devon 8 E1
Muscoates N Yorks 52 A2
Musdale Arg/Bute 74 E2
Musselburgh E Loth 70 C2
Muston Leics 36 B4
Muston N Yorks 53 B6
Mustow Green Worcs 26 A5
Mutehill Dumf/Gal 55 E9
Mutford Suffolk 39 G10
Muthill Perth/Kinr 75 F11
Mutterton Devon 7 F9
Muxton Telford 34 D3
Mybster H'land 94 E3
Myddfai Carms 24 F4
Myddle Shrops 33 C10
Mydroilyn Ceredig'n 23 A9
Myerscough Lancs 49 F4
Mylor Bridge Cornw'l 3 F7
Mynachlog-ddu Pembs 22 C6
Myndtown Shrops 33 G9
Mynydd Bach Ceredig'n 32 H3
Mynydd-bach Monmouths 15 B10
Mynydd Bodafon Angl 40 B6
Mynydd-isa Flints 42 F5
Mynyddygarreg Carms 23 F9
Mynytho Gwyn 40 G5
Myrebird Aberds 83 D9
Myrelandhorn H'land 94 E4
Myreside Perth/Kinr 76 E5
Myrtle Hill Carms 24 E4
Mytchett Surrey 18 F5
Mytholm W Yorks 50 G5
Mytholmroyd W Yorks 50 G6
Myton-on-Swale N Yorks 51 C10
Mytton Shrops 33 D10

N

Na Gearrannan W Isles 90 C6
Naast H'land 91 J13
Naburn C/York 52 E1
Nackington Kent 21 F8
Nacton Suffolk 31 D9
Nafferton ER Yorks 53 D6
Nailbridge Glos 26 G3
Nailsbourne Som'set 7 D11
Nailsea N Som'set 15 D10
Nailstone Leics 35 E10
Nailsworth Glos 16 B5
Nairn H'land 87 F11
Nalderswood Surrey 19 G9
Nancegollan Cornw'l 2 F5
Nancledra Cornw'l 2 F3
Nanhoron Gwyn 40 G4
Nannau Gwyn 32 C3
Nannerch Flints 42 F4
Nanpantan Leics 35 D11
Nanpean Cornw'l 3 D8
Nanstallon Cornw'l 3 C9
Nant-ddu Powys 25 G7
Nant-glas Powys 24 B6
Nant Peris Gwyn 41 E8
Nant Uchaf Denbs 42 G3
Nant-y-Bai Carms 24 D4
Nant-y-cafn Neath P Talb 24 H5
Nant-y-derry Monmouths 25 H10
Nant-y-ffin Carms 23 C10
Nant-y-moel Bridg 14 B5
Nant-y-pandy Conwy 41 C8
Nanternis Ceredig'n 23 A8
Nantgaredig Carms 23 D9
Nantgarw Rh Cyn Taff 15 C7
Nantglyn Denbs 42 F3
Nantgwyn Powys 32 H5
Nantlle Gwyn 41 E7
Nantmawr Shrops 33 C8
Nantmel Powys 25 B7
Nantmor Gwyn 41 F8
Nantwich Ches 43 G9
Nantycaws Carms 23 E9
Nantyffyllon Bridg 14 B4
Nantyglo Bl Gwent 25 G8
Naphill Bucks 18 B5
Nappa N Yorks 50 D4
Napton on the Hill Warwick 27 B11
Narberth = Arberth Pembs 22 D6
Narborough Leics 35 F11
Narborough Norfolk 38 D3
Nasareth Gwyn 40 E6
Naseby Northants 36 H2
Nash Bucks 28 E4
Nash Heref'd 25 B10
Nash Newp 15 C9
Nash Shrops 26 A3
Nash Lee Bucks 28 H5
Nassington Northants 37 F6
Nasty Herts 29 F10
Nateby Cumb 57 F9
Nateby Lancs 49 E4
Natland Cumb 57 H7
Naughton Suffolk 31 D7
Naunton Glos 27 F8
Naunton Worcs 26 E5
Naunton Beauchamp Worcs 26 C6
Navenby Lincs 46 G3
Navestock Heath Essex 20 B2
Navestock Side Essex 20 B2
Navidale H'land 93 H13
Nawton N Yorks 52 A2
Nayland Suffolk 30 E6
Nazeing Essex 29 H11
Neacroft Hants 9 E10
Neal's Green Warwick 35 G9
Neap Shetl'd 96 H7
Near Sawrey Cumb 56 G5
Neasham D'lington 58 E4
Neath = Castell-Nedd Neath P Talb 14 B3
Neath Abbey Neath P Talb 14 B3
Neatishead Norfolk 39 C9
Nebo Angl 40 A6
Nebo Ceredig'n 24 B2
Nebo Conwy 41 E10
Nebo Gwyn 40 E6
Necton Norfolk 38 E4
Nedd H'land 92 F4
Nedderton Northum 63 E8
Nedging Tye Suffolk 31 D7
Needham Norfolk 39 G8
Needham Market Suffolk 31 C7
Needingworth Cambs 29 A10
Needwood Staffs 35 C7
Neen Savage Shrops 34 H2
Neen Sollars Shrops 26 A3
Neenton Shrops 34 G2
Nefyn Gwyn 40 F5
Neilston E Renf 68 E3
Neinthirion Powys 32 E5
Neithrop Oxon 27 D11
Nelly Andrews Green Powys 33 E8
Nelson Caerph 15 B7
Nelson Lancs 50 F4
Nelson Village Northum 63 F8
Nemphlar S Lanarks 69 F7
Nempnett Thrubwell Bath/NE Som'set 15 E11
Nene Terrace Lincs 37 E8
Nenthall Cumb 57 B9
Nenthead Cumb 57 B9
Nenthorn Scot Borders 70 G5
Nerabus Arg/Bute 64 C3
Nercwys Flints 42 F5
Nerston S Lanarks 68 E5
Nesbit Northum 71 G8
Ness Ches 42 E6
Nesscliffe Shrops 33 D9
Neston Ches 42 E5
Neston Wilts 16 E5
Nether Alderley Ches 44 E2
Nether Blainslie Scot Borders 70 F4
Nether Booth Derby 44 D5
Nether Broughton Leics 36 C2
Nether Burrow Lancs 50 B2
Nether Cerne Dorset 8 E5
Nether Compton Dorset 8 C4
Nether Crimond Aberds 89 F8
Nether Dalgliesh Scot Borders 61 C8
Nether Dallachy Moray 88 B3
Nether Exe Devon 7 F8
Nether Glasslaw Aberds 89 C8
Nether Handwick Angus 76 C6
Nether Haugh S Yorks 45 C8
Nether Heage Derby 45 G7
Nether Heyford Northants 28 C3
Nether Hindhope Scot Borders 62 B3
Nether Howecleuch S Lanarks 60 B6
Nether Kellet Lancs 49 C5
Nether Kinmundy Aberds 89 D10
Nether Langwith Notts 45 E9
Nether Leask Aberds 89 E10
Nether Lenshie Aberds 89 D6
Nether Monynut Scot Borders 70 D6
Nether Padley Derby 44 E6
Nether Park Aberds 89 C10
Nether Poppleton C/York 52 D1
Nether Silton N Yorks 58 G5
Nether Stowey Som'set 7 C10
Nether Urquhart Fife 76 G4
Nether Wallop Hants 17 H10
Nether Wasdale Cumb 56 F3
Nether Whitacre Warwick 35 F8
Nether Worton Oxon 27 E11
Netheravon Wilts 17 G8
Netherbrae Aberds 89 C7
Netherbrough Orkney 95 G4
Netherburn S Lanarks 69 F7
Netherbury Dorset 8 E3
Netherby Cumb 61 F9
Netherby N Yorks 51 E9
Nethercote Warwick 28 B2
Nethercott Devon 6 C3
Netherend Glos 16 A2
Netherfield E Sussex 12 E6
Netherhampton Wilts 9 B10
Netherlaw Dumf/Gal 55 E10
Netherley Aberds 83 D10
Netherley Mersey 43 D7
Nethermill Dumf/Gal 60 E6
Nethermuir Aberds 89 D9
Netherplace E Renf 68 E4
Netherseal Derby 35 D8
Netherthird E Ayrs 67 E8
Netherthong W Yorks 44 B5
Netherthorpe S Yorks 45 D9
Netherton Angus 77 B8
Netherton Devon 5 D9
Netherton Hants 17 F10
Netherton Mersey 42 B6
Netherton Northum 62 C5
Netherton Oxon 17 B11
Netherton Perth/Kinr 76 B4
Netherton Stirl 68 C4
Netherton W Midlands 34 G5
Netherton Worcs 26 D6
Netherton W Yorks 44 A5
Netherton W Yorks 51 H8
Nethertown Cumb 56 F1
Nethertown H'land 94 C5
Netherwitton Northum 63 D7
Netherwood E Ayrs 68 H5
Nethy Bridge H'land 82 A2
Netley Hants 10 D3
Netley Marsh Hants 10 C2
Netteswell Essex 29 G11
Nettlebed Oxon 18 C4
Nettlebridge Som'set 16 G3
Nettlecombe Dorset 8 E4
Nettleden Herts 29 G7
Nettleham Lincs 46 E4
Nettlestead Kent 20 F3
Nettlestead Green Kent 20 F3
Nettlestone I/Wight 10 E5
Nettlesworth Durham 58 B3
Nettleton Lincs 46 B5
Nettleton Wilts 16 D5
Neuadd Carms 24 F3
Nevendon Essex 20 B4
Nevern Pembs 22 B5
New Abbey Dumf/Gal 60 G5
New Aberdour Aberds 89 B8
New Addington London 19 E10
New Alresford Hants 10 A4
New Alyth Perth/Kinr 76 C5
New Arley Warwick 35 G8
New Ash Green Kent 20 E3
New Barn Kent 20 E3
New Barnetby N Lincs 46 A4
New Barton Northants 28 B5
New Bewick Northum 62 A6
New-bigging Angus 76 C5
New Bilton Warwick 35 H10
New Bolingbroke Lincs 47 G7
New Boultham Lincs 46 E3
New Bradwell M/Keynes 28 D5
New Brancepeth Durham 58 B3
New Bridge Wrex 33 A8
New Brighton Flints 42 F5
New Brighton Mersey 42 C6
New Brinsley Notts 45 G8
New Broughton Wrex 42 G6
New Buckenham Norfolk 39 F6
New Byth Aberds 89 C8
New Catton Norfolk 39 D8
New Cheriton Hants 10 B4
New Costessy Norfolk 39 D7
New Cowper Cumb 56 B3
New Cross Ceredig'n 32 H2
New Cross London 19 D10
New Cumnock E Ayrs 67 E9
New Deer Aberds 89 D8
New Delaval Northum 63 F9
New Duston Northants 28 B4
New Earswick C/York 52 D2
New Edlington S Yorks 45 C9
New Elgin Moray 88 B2
New Ellerby ER Yorks 53 F7
New Eltham London 19 D11
New End Worcs 27 C7
New Farnley W Yorks 51 F8
New Ferry Mersey 42 D6
New Fryston W Yorks 51 G10
New Galloway Dumf/Gal 55 B9
New Gilston Fife 77 G7
New Grimsby I/Scilly 2 C2
New Hainford Norfolk 39 D8
New Hartley Northum 63 F9
New Haw Surrey 19 E7
New Hedges Pembs 22 F6
New Herrington Tyne/Wear 58 A4
New Hinksey Oxon 18 A2
New Holkham Norfolk 38 B4
New Holland N Lincs 53 G6
New Houghton Derby 45 F8
New Houghton Norfolk 38 C3
New Houses N Yorks 50 B4
New Humberstone Leics C 36 E2
New Hutton Cumb 57 G7
New Hythe Kent 20 F4
New Inn Carms 23 C9
New Inn Monmouths 15 A10
New Inn Torf 15 B9
New Invention Shrops 33 H8
New Invention W Midlands 34 E5
New Kelso H'land 86 G2
New Kingston Notts 35 C11
New Lanark S Lanarks 69 F7
New Lane Lancs 43 A7
New Lane End Warrington 43 C9
New Leake Lincs 47 G8
New Leeds Aberds 89 C9
New Longton Lancs 49 G5
New Luce Dumf/Gal 54 C4
New Malden London 19 E9
New Marske Redcar/Clevel'd 59 D7
New Marton Shrops 33 B9
New Micklefield W Yorks 51 F10
New Mill Aberds 83 E9
New Mill Herts 28 G6
New Mill Wilts 17 E8
New Mill W Yorks 44 B5
New Mills Ches 43 D10
New Mills Cornw'l 3 D7
New Mills Derby 44 D3
New Mills Powys 33 E6
New Milton Hants 9 E11
New Moat Pembs 22 D5
New Ollerton Notts 45 F10
New Oscott W Midlands 35 F6
New Park N Yorks 51 D8
New Pitsligo Aberds 89 C8
New Polzeath Cornw'l 3 B8
New Quay = Ceinewydd Ceredig'n 23 A8
New Rackheath Norfolk 39 D8
New Radnor Powys 25 B9
New Rent Cumb 56 C6
New Ridley Northum 62 H6
New Road Side N Yorks 50 E5
New Romney Kent 13 D9
New Rossington S Yorks 45 C10
New Row Ceredig'n 24 A4
New Row Lancs 50 F2
New Row N Yorks 59 E7
New Sarum Wilts 9 A10
New Silksworth Tyne/Wear 58 A4
New Stevenston N Lanarks 68 E6
New Street Staffs 44 G4
New Street Lane Shrops 34 B2
New Swanage Dorset 9 F9
New Totley S Yorks 45 E7
New Town E Loth 70 C3
New Tredegar = Tredegar Newydd Caerph 15 A7
New Trows S Lanarks 69 G7
New Ulva Arg/Bute 72 E6
New Walsoken Cambs 37 E10
New Waltham NE Lincs 46 B6
New Whittington Derby 45 E7
New Wimpole Cambs 29 D10
New Winton E Loth 70 C3
New Yatt Oxon 27 G10
New York Lincs 46 G6
New York N Yorks 51 C7
Newall W Yorks 51 E7
Newark Orkney 95 D8
Newark Peterbo 37 E8
Newark-on-Trent Notts 45 G11
Newarthill N Lanarks 68 E6
Newbarns Cumb 49 B2
Newbattle Midloth 70 D2
Newbiggin Cumb 56 G2
Newbiggin Cumb 49 C2
Newbiggin Cumb 56 D6
Newbiggin Cumb 57 B7
Newbiggin Cumb 57 D8
Newbiggin Durham 57 D11
Newbiggin N Yorks 57 G11
Newbiggin N Yorks 57 H11
Newbiggin-by-the-Sea Northum 63 E9
Newbiggin-on-Lune Cumb 57 F9
Newbigging Angus 77 D7
Newbigging Angus 77 D8
Newbigging S Lanarks 69 F9
Newbold Derby 45 E7
Newbold Leics 35 D10
Newbold on Avon Warwick 35 H10
Newbold on Stour Warwick 27 D9
Newbold Pacey Warwick 27 C9
Newbold Verdon Leics 35 E10
Newborough Angl 40 D6
Newborough Peterbo 37 E8
Newborough Staffs 35 C7
Newbottle Northants 28 E2
Newbottle Tyne/Wear 58 A4
Newbourne Suffolk 31 D9
Newbridge Caerph 15 B8
Newbridge Ceredig'n 23 A10
Newbridge Cornw'l 2 F3
Newbridge Cornw'l 4 E4
Newbridge Dumf/Gal 60 F5
Newbridge C/Edinb 69 C10
Newbridge Hants 10 C1
Newbridge I/Wight 10 F3
Newbridge Pembs 22 C4
Newbridge Green Worcs 26 E5
Newbridge-on-Usk Monmouths 15 B9
Newbridge on Wye Powys 25 C7
Newbrough Northum 62 G4
Newbuildings Devon 7 F6
Newburgh Aberds 89 F9
Newburgh Aberds 89 C9
Newburgh Scot Borders 61 B9
Newburgh Fife 76 F5
Newburgh Lancs 43 A7
Newburn Tyne/Wear 63 G7
Newbury W Berks 17 E11
Newbury Park London 19 C11
Newby Cumb 57 D7
Newby Lancs 50 E4
Newby N Yorks 50 B3
Newby N Yorks 58 E6
Newby N Yorks 59 G11
Newby Bridge Cumb 56 H5
Newby East Cumb 61 H10
Newby West Cumb 56 A5
Newby Wiske N Yorks 58 H4
Newcastle Monmouths 25 G11
Newcastle Shrops 33 G8
Newcastle Emlyn = Castell Newydd Emlyn Carms 23 B8
Newcastle-under-Lyme Staffs 44 H2
Newcastle Upon Tyne Tyne/Wear 63 G8
Newcastleton Scot Borders 61 E10
Newchapel Pembs 23 C7
Newchapel Powys 32 G5
Newchapel Staffs 44 G2
Newchapel Surrey 12 B2
Newchurch Carms 23 D8
Newchurch I/Wight 10 F4
Newchurch Kent 13 C9
Newchurch Lancs 50 F4
Newchurch Monmouths 15 B10
Newchurch Powys 25 C9
Newchurch Staffs 35 C7
Newcott Devon 7 F11
Newcraighall C/Edinb 70 C2
Newdigate Surrey 19 G8
Newell Green Brackn'l 18 D5
Newenden Kent 13 D7
Newent Glos 26 F4
Newerne Glos 16 A3
Newfield Durham 58 C3
Newfield H'land 87 D10
Newford I/Scilly 2 C3
Newfound Hants 18 F2
Newgale Pembs 22 D3
Newgate Norfolk 39 A6
Newgate Street Herts 19 A10
Newhall Ches 43 H9
Newhall Derby 35 C8
Newhall House H'land 87 E9
Newhall Point H'land 87 E10
Newham Northum 71 H10
Newham Hall Northum 71 H10
Newhaven Derby 44 G5
Newhaven C/Edinb 69 C11
Newhaven E Sussex 12 F3
Newhey Gtr Man 44 A3
Newholm N Yorks 59 E9
Newhouse N Lanarks 68 D6
Newick E Sussex 12 D3
Newingreen Kent 13 C10
Newington Kent 20 E5
Newington Kent 21 H8
Newington Kent 21 E10
Newington Notts 45 C10
Newington Oxon 18 B3
Newington Shrops 33 G10
Newland Glos 26 H2
Newland Kingston/Hull 53 F6
Newland N Yorks 52 G2
Newland Worcs 26 D4
Newlandrig Midloth 70 D2
Newlands Scot Borders 61 D11
Newlands H'land 87 G10
Newlands Moray 88 C3
Newlands Northum 62 H6
Newland's Corner Surrey 19 G7
Newlands of Geise H'land 94 D2
Newlands of Tynet Moray 88 B3
Newlands Park Angl 40 B4
Newlandsmuir S Lanarks 68 E5
Newlot Orkney 95 G6
Newlyn Cornw'l 2 G3
Newmachar Aberds 83 B10
Newmains N Lanarks 69 E7
Newmarket Suffolk 30 B3
Newmarket W Isles 91 D9
Newmill Scot Borders 61 B10
Newmill Cornw'l 2 F3
Newmill Moray 88 C4
Newmill of Inshewan Angus 77 A7
Newmills Monmouths 26 H2
Newmills of Boyne Aberds 88 C5
Newmiln Perth/Kinr 76 D4
Newmilns E Ayrs 67 C8
Newnham Cambs 29 C11
Newnham Glos 26 G3
Newnham Hants 18 F4
Newnham Herts 29 E9
Newnham Kent 20 F6
Newnham Northants 28 C2
Newnham Bridge Worcs 26 B3
Newpark Fife 77 F7
Newport Devon 6 C4
Newport ER Yorks 52 F4
Newport Essex 30 E2
Newport H'land 94 H3
Newport I/Wight 10 F4
Newport Norfolk 39 D11
Newport Telford 34 D3
Newport = Casnewydd Newp 15 C9
Newport = Trefdraeth Pembs 22 C5
Newport-on-Tay Fife 77 E7
Newport Pagnell M/Keynes 28 D5
Newpound Common W Sussex 11 B9
Newquay Cornw'l 3 C7
Newsbank Ches 44 F2
Newseat Aberds 89 E7
Newseat Aberds 89 D10
Newsham Northum 63 F9
Newsham N Yorks 58 E2
Newsham N Yorks 51 A9
Newsholme ER Yorks 52 G3
Newsholme Lancs 50 D4
Newsome W Yorks 44 A5
Newstead Scot Borders 70 G4
Newstead Notts 45 G9
Newstead Northum 71 H10
Newthorpe N Yorks 51 F10
Newton Arg/Bute 73 D9
Newton Scot Borders 62 A2
Newton Bridg 14 D4
Newton Cambs 29 D11
Newton Cambs 37 D10
Newton Card 15 D8
Newton Ches 43 G8
Newton Ches 43 F7
Newton Ches 43 E8
Newton Cumb 49 B2
Newton Derby 45 G8
Newton Dorset 9 C6
Newton Dumf/Gal 61 D7
Newton Dumf/Gal 61 F8
Newton Gtr Man 44 C3
Newton Heref'd 25 E10
Newton Heref'd 26 C2
Newton H'land 87 E10
Newton H'land 92 F5
Newton H'land 94 F5
Newton H'land 87 G10
Newton Lancs 49 F4
Newton Lancs 50 D2
Newton Lancs 50 B1
Newton Lincs 36 B6
Newton Moray 88 B1
Newton Norfolk 38 D4
Newton Notts 36 A2
Newton Northants 36 G4
Newton Northum 62 G6
Newton Perth/Kinr 75 D11
Newton S Lanarks 68 D5
Newton S Lanarks 69 G8
Newton Staffs 34 C6
Newton Suffolk 30 D6
Newton Swan 14 C2
Newton S Yorks 45 B9
Newton Warwick 35 H11
Newton Wilts 9 B11
Newton W Loth 69 C9
Newton Abbot Devon 5 D9
Newton Arlosh Cumb 61 H7
Newton Aycliffe Durham 58 D3
Newton Bewley Hartlep'l 58 D5
Newton Blossomville M/Keynes 28 C6
Newton Bromswold Northants 28 B6
Newton Burgoland Leics 35 E9
Newton by Toft Lincs 46 D4
Newton Ferrers Devon 4 G6
Newton Flotman Norfolk 39 F8
Newton Hall Northum 62 G6
Newton Harcourt Leics 36 F2
Newton Heath Gtr Man 44 B2
Newton Ho. Aberds 83 A8
Newton Kyme N Yorks 51 E10
Newton-le-Willows Mersey 43 C8
Newton-le-Willows N Yorks 58 H3
Newton Longville Bucks 28 E5
Newton Mearns E Renf 68 E4
Newton Morrell N Yorks 58 F3
Newton Mulgrave N Yorks 59 E8
Newton of Ardtoe H'land 79 D9
Newton of Balcanquhal Perth/Kinr 76 F4
Newton of Falkland Fife 76 G5
Newton on Ayr S Ayrs 66 D6
Newton on Ouse N Yorks 51 D11
Newton-on-Rawcliffe N Yorks 59 G9
Newton-on-the-Moor Northum 63 C7
Newton on Trent Lincs 46 E2
Newton Park Arg/Bute 73 G10
Newton Poppleford Devon 7 H9
Newton Purcell Oxon 28 E3
Newton Regis Warwick 35 E8
Newton Reigny Cumb 57 C6
Newton St Cyres Devon 7 G7
Newton St Faith Norfolk 39 D8
Newton St Loe Bath/NE Som'set 16 E4
Newton St Petrock Devon 6 E3
Newton Solney Derby 35 C8
Newton Stacey Hants 17 G11
Newton Stewart Dumf/Gal 55 C7
Newton Tony Wilts 17 G9
Newton Tracey Devon 6 D4
Newton under Roseberry Redcar/Clevel'd 59 E6
Newton upon Derwent ER Yorks 52 E3
Newton Valence Hants 10 A6
Newtonairds Dumf/Gal 60 E4
Newtongrange Midloth 70 D2
Newtonhill Aberds 83 D11
Newtonhill H'land 87 G8
Newtonmill Angus 77 A9
Newtonmore H'land 81 D9
Newtown Arg/Bute 73 C9
Newtown Ches 43 E8
Newtown Cornw'l 2 G6
Newtown Cumb 56 B2
Newtown Cumb 61 G11
Newtown Derby 44 D3
Newtown Devon 7 D6
Newtown Glos 16 A3
Newtown Glos 26 E6
Newtown Hants 10 C1
Newtown Hants 10 B2
Newtown Hants 10 C5
Newtown Hants 17 E11
Newtown Hants 10 C4
Newtown Hants 10 D3
Newtown Heref'd 26 D3
Newtown H'land 80 C5
Newtown I/Man 48 E3
Newtown I/Wight 10 E3
Newtown Northum 62 C6
Newtown Northum 71 H9
Newtown Northum 71 G8
Newtown Poole 9 E9
Newtown Shrops 33 B10
Newtown Staffs 44 F3
Newtown Staffs 44 F4
Newtown Wilts 9 B8
Newtown = Y Drenewydd Powys 33 F7
Newtown Linford Leics 35 E11
Newtown St Boswells Scot Borders 70 G4
Newtown Unthank Leics 35 E10
Newtyle Angus 76 C5
Neyland Pembs 22 F4
Niarbyl I/Man 48 E2
Nibley S Glos 16 C3
Nibley Green Glos 16 B4
Nibon Shetl'd 96 F5
Nicholashayne Devon 7 E10
Nicholaston Swan 23 H10
Nidd N Yorks 51 C9
Nigg Aberd C 83 C11
Nigg H'land 87 D11
Nigg Ferry H'land 87 E10
Nightcott Som'set 7 D7
Nilig Denbs 42 G3
Nine Ashes Essex 20 A2
Nine Mile Burn Midloth 69 E10
Nine Wells Pembs 22 D2
Ninebanks Northum 57 A9
Ninfield E Sussex 12 E6
Ningwood I/Wight 10 F2
Nisbet Scot Borders 70 H5
Nisthouse Orkney 95 G4
Nisthouse Shetl'd 96 G7
Niton I/Wight 10 G4
Nitshill C/Glasg 68 D4
No Man's Heath Ches 43 H8
No Man's Heath Warwick 35 E8
Noak Hill London 20 B2
Noblethorpe S Yorks 44 B6
Nobottle Northants 28 B3
Nocton Lincs 46 F4
Noke Oxon 28 G2
Nolton Pembs 22 E3
Nolton Haven Pembs 22 E3
Nomansland Devon 7 E7
Nomansland Wilts 10 C1
Noneley Shrops 33 C10
Nonikiln H'land 87 D9
Nonington Kent 21 F9
Noonsbrough Shetl'd 96 H4
Norbreck Blackp'l 49 E3
Norbridge Heref'd 26 D4
Norbury Ches 43 H8
Norbury Derby 35 A7
Norbury Shrops 33 F9
Norbury Staffs 34 C3
Nordelph Norfolk 38 E1
Norden Gtr Man 44 A2
Norden Heath Dorset 9 F8
Nordley Shrops 34 F2
Norham Northum 71 F8
Norley Ches 43 E8
Norleywood Hants 10 E2
Norman Cross Cambs 37 F7
Normanby N Lincs 52 H4
Normanby N Yorks 52 A3
Normanby Redcar/Clevel'd 59 E6
Normanby-by-Spital Lincs 46 D4
Normanby by Stow Lincs 46 D2
Normanby le Wold Lincs 46 C5
Normandy Surrey 18 F6
Norman's Bay E Sussex 12 F5
Norman's Green Devon 7 F9
Normanstone Suffolk 39 F11
Normanton Derby C 35 B9
Normanton Leics 36 A4
Normanton Lincs 46 H3
Normanton Notts 45 G11
Normanton Rutl'd 36 E5
Normanton W Yorks 51 G9
Normanton le Heath Leics 35 D9
Normanton on Soar Notts 35 C11
Normanton-on-the-Wolds Notts 36 B2
Normanton on Trent Notts 45 F11
Normoss Lancs 49 F3
Norney Surrey 18 G6
Norrington Common Wilts 16 E5
Norris Green Mersey 43 C6
Norris Hill Leics 35 D9
North Anston S Yorks 45 D9
North Aston Oxon 27 F11
North Baddesley Hants 10 C2
North Ballachulish H'land 74 A3
North Barrow Som'set 8 B5
North Barsham Norfolk 38 B5
North Benfleet Essex 20 C4
North Bersted W Sussex 11 D8
North Berwick E Loth 70 B4
North Boarhunt Hants 10 C5
North Bovey Devon 5 C8
North Bradley Wilts 16 F5
North Brentor Devon 4 C5
North Brewham Som'set 16 H4
North Buckland Devon 6 B3
North Burlingham Norfolk 39 D9
North Cadbury Som'set 8 B5
North Cairn Dumf/Gal 54 B2
North Carlton Lincs 46 E3
North Carrine Arg/Bute 65 H7
North Cave ER Yorks 52 F4
North Cerney Glos 27 H7
North Charford Wilts 9 C10
North Charlton Northum 63 A7
North Cheriton Som'set 8 B5
North Cliff ER Yorks 53 E8
North Cliffe ER Yorks 52 F4
North Clifton Notts 46 E2
North Cockerington Lincs 47 C7
North Coker Som'set 8 C4
North Collafirth Shetl'd 96 E5
North Common E Sussex 12 D2
North Connel Arg/Bute 74 D2
North Cornelly Bridg 14 C4
North Cove Suffolk 39 G10
North Cowton N Yorks 58 F3
North Crawley M/Keynes 28 D6
North Cray London 19 D11
North Creake Norfolk 38 B4
North Curry Som'set 8 B2
North Dalton ER Yorks 52 D5
North Dawn Orkney 95 H5
North Deighton N Yorks 51 D9
North Duffield N Yorks 52 F2
North Elkington Lincs 46 C6
North Elmham Norfolk 38 C5
North Elmshall W Yorks 45 A8
North End Bucks 28 F5
North End ER Yorks 53 F8
North End Essex 30 G3
North End Hants 17 E11
North End Lincs 37 A8
North End N Som'set 15 E10
North End Portsm'th 10 D5
North End Som'set 8 B1
North End W Sussex 11 D10
North Erradale H'land 91 J12
North Fambridge Essex 20 B5
North Fearns H'land 85 E10
North Featherstone W Yorks 51 G10
North Ferriby ER Yorks 52 G5
North Frodingham ER Yorks 53 D7
North Gluss Shetl'd 96 F5
North Gorley Hants 9 C10
North Green Norfolk 39 G8
North Green Suffolk 31 B10
North Greetwell Lincs 46 E4
North Grimston N Yorks 52 C4
North Halley Orkney 95 H6
North Halling Medway 20 E4
North Hayling Hants 10 D6
North Hazelrigg Northum 71 G9
North Heasley Devon 7 C6
North Heath W Sussex 11 B9
North Hill Cambs 37 H10
North Hill Cornw'l 4 D3
North Hinksey Oxon 27 H11
North Holmwood Surrey 19 G8
North Howden ER Yorks 52 F3
North Huish Devon 5 F8
North Hykeham Lincs 46 F3
North Johnston Pembs 22 E4
North Kelsey Lincs 46 B4
North Kelsey Moor Lincs 46 B4
North Kessock H'land 87 G9
North Killingholme N Lincs 53 H7
North Kilvington N Yorks 58 H5
North Kilworth Leics 36 G2
North Kirkton Aberds 89 C11
North Kiscadale N Ayrs 66 D3
North Kyme Lincs 46 G5
North Lancing W Sussex 11 D10
North Lee Bucks 28 H5
North Leigh Oxon 27 G10
North Leverton with Habblesthorpe Notts 45 D11
North Littleton Worcs 27 D7
North Lopham Norfolk 38 G6
North Luffenham Rutl'd 36 E5
North Marden W Sussex 11 C7
North Marston Bucks 28 F4
North Middleton Midloth 70 E2
North Middleton Northum 62 A6
North Molton Devon 7 D6
North Moreton Oxon 18 C2
North Mundham W Sussex 11 D7
North Muskham Notts 45 G11
North Newbald ER Yorks 52 F5
North Newington Oxon 27 E11
North Newnton Wilts 17 F8
North Newton Som'set 8 A1
North Nibley Glos 16 B4
North Oakley Hants 18 F2
North Ockendon London 20 C2
North Ormesby Middlesbro' 58 D6
North Ormsby Lincs 46 C6
North Otterington N Yorks 58 H4
North Owersby Lincs 46 C4
North Perrott Som'set 8 D3
North Petherton Som'set 8 A1
North Petherwin Cornw'l 4 C3
North Pickenham Norfolk 38 E4
North Piddle Worcs 26 C6
North Poorton Dorset 8 E4
North Port Arg/Bute 74 E3
North Queensferry Fife 69 B10
North Radworthy Devon 7 C6
North Rauceby Lincs 46 H4
North Reston Lincs 47 D7
North Rigton N Yorks 51 E8
North Rode Ches 44 F2
North Roe Shetl'd 96 E5
North Runcton Norfolk 38 D2
North Sandwick Shetl'd 96 D7
North Scale Cumb 49 C1
North Scarle Lincs 46 F2
North Seaton Northum 63 E8
North Shian Arg/Bute 74 C2
North Shields Tyne/Wear 63 G9
North Shoebury Southend 20 C6
North Shore Blackp'l 49 F3
North Side Cumb 56 D2
North Side Peterbo 37 F8
North Skelton Redcar/Clevel'd 59 E7
North Somercotes Lincs 47 C8
North Stainley N Yorks 51 B8
North Stainmore Cumb 57 E10
North Stifford Thurr'k 20 C3
North Stoke Bath/NE Som'set 16 E4
North Stoke Oxon 18 C3
North Stoke W Sussex 11 C9
North Street Hants 10 A5
North Street Kent 21 F7
North Street Medway 20 D5
North Street W Berks 18 D3
North Sunderland Northum 71 G11
North Tamerton Cornw'l 6 G2
North Tawton Devon 6 F5
North Thoresby Lincs 46 C6
North Tidworth Wilts 17 G9
North Togston Northum 63 C8
North Tuddenham Norfolk 38 D6
North Walbottle Tyne/Wear 63 G7
North Walsham Norfolk 39 B8
North Waltham Hants 18 G2
North Warnborough Hants 18 F4
North Water Bridge Angus 83 G8
North Watten H'land 94 E4
North Weald Bassett Essex 19 A11
North Wheatley Notts 45 D11
North Whilborough Devon 5 E9
North Wick Bath/NE Som'set 16 E2
North Willingham Lincs 46 D5
North Wingfield Derby 45 F8
North Witham Lincs 36 C5
North Woolwich London 19 D11
North Wootton Dorset 8 C5
North Wootton Norfolk 38 C2
North Wootton Som'set 16 G2
North Wraxall Wilts 16 D5
North Wroughton Swindon 17 C8
Northacre Norfolk 38 F5
Northallerton N Yorks 58 G4
Northam Devon 6 D3
Northam S'thampton 10 C3
Northampton Northants 28 B4
Northaw Herts 19 A9
Northbeck Lincs 37 A6
Northborough Peterbo 37 E7
Northbourne Kent 21 F10
Northbridge Street E Sussex 12 D6
Northchapel W Sussex 11 B8
Northchurch Herts 28 H6
Northcott Devon 6 G2
Northdown Kent 21 D10
Northdyke Orkney 95 F3
Northend Bath/NE Som'set 16 E4
Northend Bucks 18 B4
Northend Warwick 27 C10
Northenden Gtr Man 44 C2
Northfield Aberd C 83 C11
Northfield Scot Borders 71 D8
Northfield ER Yorks 52 G6

Northfield *W Midlands* 34 H6
Northfields *Lincs* 36 E6
Northfleet *Kent* 20 D3
Northgate *Lincs* 37 C7
Northhouse *Scot Borders* 61 C10
Northiam *E Sussex* 13 D7
Northill *Beds* 29 D8
Northington *Hants* 18 H2
Northlands *Lincs* 47 G7
Northlea *Durham* 58 A5
Northleach *Glos* 27 G8
Northleigh *Devon* 7 G10
Northlew *Devon* 6 G4
Northmoor *Oxon* 17 A11
Northmoor Green or Moorland *Som'set* 8 A2
Northmuir *Angus* 76 B6
Northney *Hants* 10 D6
Northolt *London* 19 C8
Northop *Flints* 42 F5
Northop Hall *Flints* 42 F5
Northorpe *Lincs* 37 D6
Northorpe *Lincs* 37 B8
Northorpe *Lincs* 46 C2
Northover *Som'set* 15 H10
Northover *Som'set* 8 B4
Northowram *W Yorks* 51 G7
Northport *Dorset* 9 F8
Northpunds *Shetl'd* 96 L6
Northrepps *Norfolk* 39 B8
Northtown *Orkney* 95 J5
Northway *Glos* 26 E6
Northwich *Ches* 43 E9
Northwick *S Gloucs* 16 C2
Northwold *Norfolk* 38 F3
Northwood *Derby* 44 F6
Northwood *London* 19 B7
Northwood *I/Wight* 10 E3
Northwood *Kent* 21 E10
Northwood *Shrops* 33 B10
Northwood Green *Glos* 26 G4
Norton *E Sussex* 12 F3
Norton *Glos* 26 F5
Norton *Halton* 43 D8
Norton *Herts* 29 E9
Norton *I/Wight* 10 F2
Norton *Monmouths* 25 G11
Norton *Notts* 45 E9
Norton *Northants* 28 B3
Norton *N Yorks* 52 B3
Norton *Powys* 25 B10
Norton *Shrops* 33 G10
Norton *Shrops* 34 E1
Norton *Shrops* 34 E3
Norton *Stockton* 58 D5
Norton *Suffolk* 30 B6
Norton *S Yorks* 51 H11
Norton *Wilts* 16 C5
Norton *Worcs* 26 C5
Norton *Worcs* 27 D7
Norton *W Sussex* 11 E7
Norton *W Sussex* 11 D8
Norton Bavant *Wilts* 16 G6
Norton Bridge *Staffs* 34 B4
Norton Canes *Staffs* 34 E6
Norton Canon *Heref'd* 25 D10
Norton Corner *Norfolk* 39 C6
Norton Disney *Lincs* 46 G2
Norton East *Staffs* 34 E6
Norton Ferris *Wilts* 16 H4
Norton Fitzwarren *Som'set* 7 D10
Norton Green *I/Wight* 10 F2
Norton Hawkfield *Bath/NE Som'set* 16 E2
Norton Heath *Essex* 20 A3
Norton in Hales *Shrops* 34 B3
Norton-in-the-Moors *Stoke* 44 G2
Norton-Juxta-Twycross *Leics* 35 E9
Norton-le-Clay *N Yorks* 51 B10
Norton Lindsey *Warwick* 27 B9
Norton Malreward *Bath/NE Som'set* 16 E3
Norton Mandeville *Essex* 20 A2
Norton St Philip *Som'set* 16 F4
Norton sub Hamdon *Som'set* 8 C3
Norton Woodseats *S Yorks* 45 D7
Norwell *Notts* 45 F11
Norwell Woodhouse *Notts* 45 F11
Norwich *Norfolk* 39 E8
Norwick *Shetl'd* 96 B8
Norwood *Derby* 45 D8
Norwood Hill *Surrey* 19 G9
Norwoodside *Cambs* 37 F10
Noseley *Leics* 36 F3
Noss *Shetl'd* 96 M5
Noss Mayo *Devon* 4 G6
Nosterfield *N Yorks* 51 A8
Nostie *H'land* 85 F13
Notgrove *Glos* 27 F8
Nottage *Bridg* 14 D4
Nottingham *Nott'ham* 36 B1
Nottington *Dorset* 8 F5
Notton *Wilts* 16 E6
Notton *W Yorks* 45 A7
Nounsley *Essex* 30 G4
Noutard's Green *Worcs* 26 B4
Novar House *H'land* 87 E9
Nox *Shrops* 33 D10
Nuffield *Oxon* 18 C3
Nun Hills *Lancs* 50 G4
Nun Monkton *N Yorks* 51 D11
Nunburnholme *ER Yorks* 52 E4
Nuncargate *Notts* 45 G9
Nuneaton *Warwick* 35 F9
Nuneham Courtenay *Oxon* 18 B2
Nunney *Som'set* 16 G4
Nunnington *N Yorks* 52 B2
Nunnykirk *Northum* 62 D6
Nunsthorpe *NE Lincs* 46 B6
Nunthorpe *Middlesbro'* 59 E6
Nunthorpe *C/York* 52 D2
Nunton *Wilts* 9 B10
Nunwick *N Yorks* 51 B9
Nupend *Glos* 26 H4
Nursling *Hants* 10 C2
Nursted *Hants* 11 B6
Nutbourne *W Sussex* 11 C9
Nutbourne *W Sussex* 11 D6
Nutfield *Surrey* 19 F10
Nuthall *Notts* 35 A11
Nuthampstead *Herts* 29 E11
Nuthurst *W Sussex* 11 B10
Nutley *E Sussex* 12 D3
Nutley *Hants* 18 G3
Nutwell *S Yorks* 45 B10
Nybster *H'land* 94 D5
Nyetimber *W Sussex* 11 E7
Nyewood *W Sussex* 11 B7
Nymet Rowland *Devon* 6 F6
Nymet Tracey *Devon* 7 F6
Nympsfield *Glos* 16 A5
Nynehead *Som'set* 7 D10
Nyton *W Sussex* 11 D8

O

Oad Street *Kent* 20 E5
Oadby *Leics* 36 E2
Oak Cross *Devon* 6 G4
Oakamoor *Staffs* 35 A6
Oakbank *W Loth* 69 D9
Oakdale *Caerph* 15 B7
Oake *Som'set* 7 D10
Oaken *Staffs* 34 E4
Oakenclough *Lancs* 49 E5
Oakengates *Telford* 34 D3
Oakenholt *Flints* 42 E5
Oakenshaw *Durham* 58 C3
Oakenshaw *W Yorks* 51 G7
Oakerthorpe *Derby* 45 G7
Oakes *W Yorks* 51 H7
Oakfield *Torf* 15 B9
Oakford *Ceredig'n* 23 A9
Oakford *Devon* 7 D8
Oakfordbridge *Devon* 7 D8
Oakgrove *Ches* 44 F3
Oakham *Rutl'd* 36 E4
Oakhanger *Hants* 18 H4
Oakhill *Som'set* 16 G3
Oakhurst *Kent* 20 F2
Oakington *Cambs* 29 B11
Oaklands *Herts* 29 G9
Oaklands *Powys* 25 C7
Oakle Street *Glos* 26 G4
Oakley *Beds* 29 C7
Oakley *Bucks* 28 G3
Oakley *Fife* 69 B9
Oakley *Hants* 18 F2
Oakley *Oxon* 18 A4
Oakley *Poole* 9 E9
Oakley *Suffolk* 39 H7
Oakley Green *Windsor* 18 D6
Oakley Park *Powys* 32 G5
Oakmere *Ches* 43 F8
Oakridge *Glos* 16 A6
Oakridge *Hants* 18 F3
Oaks *Shrops* 33 E10
Oaks Green *Derby* 35 B7
Oaksey *Wilts* 16 B6
Oakthorpe *Leics* 35 D9
Oakwoodhill *Surrey* 19 H8
Oakworth *W Yorks* 50 F6
Oape *H'land* 92 J7
Oare *Kent* 21 E7
Oare *Som'set* 7 B7
Oare *W Berks* 18 D2
Oare *Wilts* 17 E8
Oasby *Lincs* 36 B6
Oathlaw *Angus* 77 B7
Oatlands *N Yorks* 51 D9
Oban *Arg/Bute* 79 J11
Oban *H'land* 79 C11
Oborne *Dorset* 8 C5
Obthorpe *Lincs* 37 D6
Occlestone Green *Ches* 43 F9
Occold *Suffolk* 31 A8
Ochil Hills Hospital *Perth/Kinr* 76 G3
Ochiltree *E Ayrs* 67 D8
Ochtermuthill *Perth/Kinr* 75 F11
Ochtertyre *Perth/Kinr* 75 E11
Ockbrook *Derby* 35 B10
Ockham *Surrey* 19 F7
Ockle *H'land* 79 D8
Ockley *Surrey* 19 H8
Ocle Pychard *Heref'd* 26 D2
Octon *ER Yorks* 52 C6
Octon Cross Roads *ER Yorks* 52 C6
Odcombe *Som'set* 8 C4
Odd Down *Bath/NE Som'set* 16 E4
Oddendale *Cumb* 57 E7
Odder *Lincs* 46 E3
Oddingley *Worcs* 26 C6
Oddington *Glos* 27 F9
Oddington *Oxon* 28 G2
Odell *Beds* 28 C6
Odie *Orkney* 95 F7
Odiham *Hants* 18 F4
Odstock *Wilts* 9 B10
Odstone *Leics* 35 E9
Offchurch *Warwick* 27 B10
Offenham *Worcs* 27 D7
Offham *E Sussex* 12 E2
Offham *Kent* 20 F3
Offham *W Sussex* 11 D9
Offord Cluny *Cambs* 29 B9
Offord Darcy *Cambs* 29 B9
Offton *Suffolk* 31 D7
Offwell *Devon* 7 G10
Ogbourne Maizey *Wilts* 17 D8
Ogbourne St Andrew *Wilts* 17 D8
Ogbourne St George *Wilts* 17 D9
Ogil *Angus* 77 A7
Ogle *Northum* 63 F7
Ogmore *V/Glam* 14 D4
Ogmore-by-Sea *V/Glam* 14 D4
Ogmore Vale *Bridg* 14 B5
Okeford Fitzpaine *Dorset* 9 C7
Okehampton *Devon* 6 G4
Okehampton Camp *Devon* 6 G4
Okraquoy *Shetl'd* 96 K6
Old *Northants* 28 A4
Old Aberdeen *Aberd C* 83 C11
Old Alresford *Hants* 10 A4
Old Arley *Warwick* 35 F8
Old Basford *Nott'ham* 35 A11
Old Basing *Hants* 18 F3
Old Bewick *Northum* 62 A6
Old Bolingbroke *Lincs* 47 F7
Old Bramhope *W Yorks* 51 E8
Old Brampton *Derby* 45 E7
Old Bridge of Tilt *Perth/Kinr* 81 G10
Old Bridge of Urr *Dumf/Gal* 55 C10
Old Buckenham *Norfolk* 39 F6
Old Burghclere *Hants* 17 F11
Old Byland *N Yorks* 59 H6
Old Cassop *Durham* 58 C4
Old Castleton *Scot Borders* 61 D11
Old Catton *Norfolk* 39 D8
Old Clee *NE Lincs* 46 B6
Old Cleeve *Som'set* 7 B9
Old Clipstone *Notts* 45 F10
Old Colwyn *Conwy* 41 C10
Old Coulsdon *London* 19 F10
Old Crombie *Aberds* 88 C5
Old Dailly *S Ayrs* 66 G5
Old Dalby *Leics* 36 C2
Old Deer *Aberds* 89 D9
Old Denaby *S Yorks* 45 C8
Old Edlington *S Yorks* 45 C9
Old Eldon *Durham* 58 D3
Old Ellerby *ER Yorks* 53 F7
Old Felixstowe *Suffolk* 31 E10
Old Fletton *Peterbro* 37 F7
Old Glossop *Derby* 44 C4
Old Goole *ER Yorks* 52 G3
Old Hall *Powys* 32 G5
Old Heath *Essex* 31 F7
Old Heathfield *E Sussex* 12 D4
Old Hill *W Midlands* 34 G5
Old Hunstanton *Norfolk* 38 A2
Old Hurst *Cambs* 37 H8
Old Hutton *Cumb* 57 H7
Old Kea *Cornw'l* 3 E7
Old Kilpatrick *W Dunb* 68 C3
Old Kinnernie *Aberds* 83 C9
Old Knebworth *Herts* 29 F9
Old Langho *Lancs* 50 F3
Old Laxey *I/Man* 48 D4
Old Leake *Lincs* 47 G8
Old Malton *N Yorks* 52 B3
Old Micklefield *W Yorks* 51 F10
Old Milton *Hants* 9 E11
Old Milverton *Warwick* 27 B9
Old Monkland *N Lanarks* 68 D6
Old Netley *Hants* 10 D3
Old Philpstoun *W Loth* 69 C9
Old Quarrington *Durham* 58 C4
Old Radnor *Powys* 25 C9
Old Rattray *Aberds* 89 C10
Old Rayne *Aberds* 83 A8
Old Romney *Kent* 13 D9
Old Sodbury *S Gloucs* 16 C4
Old Somerby *Lincs* 36 B5
Old Stratford *Northants* 28 D4
Old Thirsk *N Yorks* 51 A10
Old Town *Cumb* 57 B6
Old Town *Cumb* 50 A1
Old Town *Northum* 62 D4
Old Town *I/Scilly* 2 C3
Old Trafford *Gtr Man* 44 C2
Old Tupton *Derby* 45 F7
Old Warden *Beds* 29 D8
Old Weston *Cambs* 37 H6
Old Whittington *Derby* 45 E7
Old Wick *H'land* 94 E5
Old Windsor *Windsor* 18 D6
Old Wives Lees *Kent* 21 F7
Old Woking *Surrey* 19 F7
Old Woodhall *Lincs* 46 F6
Oldany *H'land* 92 F4
Oldberrow *Warwick* 27 B8
Oldborough *Devon* 7 F6
Oldbury *Shrops* 34 F3
Oldbury *Warwick* 35 F9
Oldbury *W Midlands* 34 G5
Oldbury-on-Severn *S Gloucs* 16 B3
Oldbury on the Hill *Glos* 16 C5
Oldcastle *Bridg* 14 D5
Oldcastle *Monmouths* 25 F10
Oldcotes *Notts* 45 D9
Oldfallow *Staffs* 34 D5
Oldfield *Worcs* 26 B5
Oldford *Som'set* 16 F4
Oldham *Gtr Man* 44 B3
Oldhamstocks *E Loth* 70 C6
Oldland *S Gloucs* 16 D3
Oldmeldrum *Aberds* 89 F8
Oldshore Beg *H'land* 92 D4
Oldshoremore *H'land* 92 D5
Oldstead *N Yorks* 51 A11
Oldtown *Aberds* 83 A7
Oldtown of Ord *Aberds* 88 C6
Oldway *Swan* 23 H10
Oldways End *Devon* 7 D7
Oldwhat *Aberds* 89 C8
Olgrinmore *H'land* 94 E2
Oliver's Battery *Hants* 10 B3
Ollaberry *Shetl'd* 96 E5
Ollerton *Ches* 43 E10
Ollerton *Notts* 45 F10
Ollerton *Shrops* 34 C2
Olmarch *Ceredig'n* 24 C3
Olney *M/Keynes* 28 C5
Olrig Ho. *H'land* 94 D3
Olton *W Midlands* 35 G7
Olveston *S Gloucs* 16 C3
Olwen *Ceredig'n* 23 B10
Ombersley *Worcs* 26 B5
Ompton *Notts* 45 F10
Onchan *I/Man* 48 E3
Onecote *Staffs* 44 G4
Onen *Monmouths* 25 G11
Ongar Hill *Norfolk* 38 C1
Ongar Street *Heref'd* 25 B10
Onibury *Shrops* 33 H10
Onich *H'land* 74 A3
Onllwyn *Neath P Talb* 24 G5
Onneley *Staffs* 34 A3
Onslow Village *Surrey* 18 G6
Onthank *E Ayrs* 67 B7
Openwoodgate *Derby* 45 H7
Opinan *H'land* 91 H13
Opinan *H'land* 85 A12
Orange Lane *Scot Borders* 70 F6
Orange Row *Norfolk* 37 C11
Orasaigh *W Isles* 91 F8
Orbliston *Moray* 88 C3
Orbost *H'land* 84 D7
Orby *Lincs* 47 F8
Orchard Hill *Devon* 6 D3
Orchard Portman *Som'set* 8 B1
Orcheston *Wilts* 17 G7
Orcop *Heref'd* 25 F11
Orcop Hill *Heref'd* 25 F11
Ord *H'land* 85 G11
Ordhead *Aberds* 83 B8
Ordie *Aberds* 82 C6
Ordiequish *Moray* 88 C3
Ordsall *Notts* 45 D10
Ore *E Sussex* 13 E7
Oreton *Shrops* 34 G2
Orford *Suffolk* 31 D11
Orford *Warrington* 43 C9
Orgreave *Staffs* 35 D7
Orlestone *Kent* 13 C8
Orleton *Heref'd* 25 B11
Orleton *Worcs* 26 B3
Orlingbury *Northants* 28 A5
Ormesby *Redcar/Clevel'd* 59 E6
Ormesby St Margaret *Norfolk* 39 D10
Ormesby St Michael *Norfolk* 39 D10
Ormiclate Castle *W Isles* 84 E2
Ormiscaig *H'land* 91 H13
Ormiston *E Loth* 70 D3
Ormsaigbeg *H'land* 78 E7
Ormsaigmore *H'land* 78 E7
Ormsary *Arg/Bute* 72 F6
Ormsgill *Cumb* 49 B1
Ormskirk *Lancs* 43 B7
Orpington *London* 19 E11
Orrell *Gtr Man* 43 B8
Orrell *Mersey* 42 C6
Orrisdale *I/Man* 48 C3
Orroland *Dumf/Gal* 55 E10
Orsett *Thurr'k* 20 C3
Orslow *Staffs* 34 D4
Orston *Notts* 36 A3
Orthwaite *Cumb* 56 C4
Ortner *Lancs* 49 D5
Orton *Cumb* 57 F8
Orton *Northants* 36 H4
Orton Longueville *Peterbro* 37 F7
Orton-on-the-Hill *Leics* 35 E9
Orton Waterville *Peterbro* 37 F7
Orwell *Cambs* 29 C10
Osbaldeston *Lancs* 50 F2
Osbaldwick *C/York* 52 D2
Osbaston *Shrops* 33 C9
Osbournby *Lincs* 37 B6
Oscroft *Ches* 43 F8
Ose *H'land* 85 D8
Osgathorpe *Leics* 35 D10
Osgodby *Lincs* 46 C4
Osgodby *N Yorks* 52 F2
Osgodby *N Yorks* 53 A6
Oskaig *H'land* 85 E10
Oskamull *Arg/Bute* 78 G7
Osmaston *Derby* 35 A8
Osmaston *Derby C* 35 B9
Osmington *Dorset* 8 F6
Osmington Mills *Dorset* 8 F6
Osmotherley *N Yorks* 58 G5
Ospisdale *H'land* 87 C10
Ospringe *Kent* 21 E7
Ossett *W Yorks* 51 G8
Ossington *Notts* 45 F11
Ostend *Essex* 20 B6
Oswaldkirk *N Yorks* 52 B2
Oswaldtwistle *Lancs* 50 G3
Oswestry *Shrops* 33 C8
Otford *Kent* 20 F2
Otham *Kent* 20 F4
Othery *Som'set* 8 A2
Otley *Suffolk* 31 C9
Otley *W Yorks* 51 E8
Otter Ferry *Arg/Bute* 73 E8
Otterbourne *Hants* 10 B3
Otterburn *Northum* 62 D4
Otterburn *N Yorks* 50 D4
Otterburn Camp *Northum* 62 D4
Otterham *Cornw'l* 4 B2
Otterhampton *Som'set* 15 G8
Ottershaw *Surrey* 19 E7
Otterswick *Shetl'd* 96 E7
Otterton *Devon* 7 H9
Ottery St Mary *Devon* 7 G10
Ottinge *Kent* 21 G8
Ottringham *ER Yorks* 53 G8
Oughterby *Cumb* 61 H8
Oughtershaw *N Yorks* 50 A4
Oughterside *Cumb* 56 B3
Oughtibridge *S Yorks* 45 C7
Oughtrington *Warrington* 43 D9
Oulston *N Yorks* 51 B11
Oulton *Cumb* 56 A4
Oulton *Norfolk* 39 C7
Oulton *Staffs* 34 B5
Oulton *Suffolk* 39 F11
Oulton *W Yorks* 51 G9
Oulton Broad *Suffolk* 39 F11
Oulton Street *Norfolk* 39 C7
Oundle *Northants* 36 G6
Ousby *Cumb* 57 C8
Ousdale *H'land* 94 H2
Ousden *Suffolk* 30 C4
Ousefleet *ER Yorks* 52 G4
Ouston *Durham* 58 A3
Ouston *Northum* 62 F6
Out Newton *ER Yorks* 53 G9
Out Rawcliffe *Lancs* 49 E4
Outertown *Orkney* 95 G3
Outgate *Cumb* 56 G5
Outhgill *Cumb* 57 F9
Outlane *W Yorks* 51 H6
Outwell *Norfolk* 37 E11
Outwick *Hants* 9 C10
Outwood *Surrey* 19 G10
Outwood *W Yorks* 51 G9
Outwoods *Staffs* 34 D3
Ovenden *W Yorks* 51 G6
Ovenscloss *Scot Borders* 70 G3
Over *Cambs* 29 A10
Over *Ches* 43 F9
Over *S Gloucs* 16 C2
Over Compton *Dorset* 8 C4
Over Green *W Midlands* 35 F7
Over Haddon *Derby* 44 F6
Over Hulton *Gtr Man* 43 B9
Over Kellet *Lancs* 49 B5
Over Kiddington *Oxon* 27 F11
Over Knutsford *Ches* 43 E10
Over Monnow *Monmouths* 26 G2
Over Norton *Oxon* 27 F10
Over Peover *Ches* 43 E10
Over Silton *N Yorks* 58 G5
Over Stowey *Som'set* 7 C10
Over Stratton *Som'set* 8 C3
Over Tabley *Ches* 43 D10
Over Wallop *Hants* 17 H9
Over Whitacre *Warwick* 35 F8
Over Worton *Oxon* 27 F11
Overbister *Orkney* 95 D7
Overbury *Worcs* 26 E6
Overcombe *Dorset* 8 F5
Overgreen *Derby* 45 E7
Overleigh *Som'set* 15 H10
Overley Green *Warwick* 27 C7
Overpool *Ches* 43 E6
Overscaig Hotel *H'land* 92 G7
Overseal *Derby* 35 D8
Oversland *Kent* 21 F7
Overstone *Northants* 28 B5
Overstrand *Norfolk* 39 A8
Overthorpe *Northants* 27 D11
Overton *Aberd C* 83 B10
Overton *Ches* 43 E8
Overton *Dumf/Gal* 60 G5
Overton *Hants* 18 G2
Overton *Lancs* 49 D4
Overton *N Yorks* 52 D1
Overton *Shrops* 26 A2
Overton *Swan* 23 H9
Overton *W Yorks* 51 H8
Overton = Owrtyn *Wrex* 33 A9
Overton Bridge *Wrex* 33 A9
Overtown *N Lanarks* 69 E7
Oving *Bucks* 28 F4
Oving *W Sussex* 11 D8
Ovingdean *Brighton/Hove* 12 F2
Ovingham *Northum* 62 G6
Ovington *Durham* 58 E2
Ovington *Essex* 30 D4
Ovington *Hants* 10 A4
Ovington *Norfolk* 38 E5
Ovington *Northum* 62 G6
Ower *Hants* 10 C2
Owermoigne *Dorset* 9 F6
Owlbury *Shrops* 33 F9
Owler Bar *Derby* 44 E6
Owlerton *S Yorks* 45 D7
Owl's Green *Suffolk* 31 B9
Owlswick *Bucks* 28 H4
Owmby *Lincs* 46 B4
Owmby-by-Spital *Lincs* 46 D4
Owrtyn = Overton *Wrex* 33 A9
Owslebury *Hants* 10 B4
Owston *Leics* 36 E3
Owston *S Yorks* 45 A9
Owston Ferry *N Lincs* 46 B2
Owstwick *ER Yorks* 53 F8
Owthorne *ER Yorks* 53 G9
Owthorpe *Notts* 36 B2
Oxborough *Norfolk* 38 E3
Oxcombe *Lincs* 47 E7
Oxen Park *Cumb* 56 H5
Oxenholme *Cumb* 57 H7
Oxenhope *W Yorks* 50 F6
Oxenton *Glos* 26 E6
Oxenwood *Wilts* 17 F10
Oxford *Oxon* 28 H2
Oxhey *Herts* 19 B8
Oxhill *Warwick* 27 D10
Oxley *W Midlands* 34 E5
Oxley Green *Essex* 30 G6
Oxley's Green *E Sussex* 12 D5
Oxnam *Scot Borders* 62 B3
Oxshott *Surrey* 19 E8
Oxspring *S Yorks* 44 B6
Oxted *Surrey* 19 F10
Oxton *Scot Borders* 70 E3
Oxton *Notts* 45 G10
Oxwich *Swan* 23 H9
Oxwick *Norfolk* 38 C5
Oykel Bridge *H'land* 92 J6
Oyne *Aberds* 83 A8

P

Pabail Iarach *W Isles* 91 D10
Pabail Uarach *W Isles* 91 D10
Pace Gate *N Yorks* 51 D7
Packington *Leics* 35 D9
Padanaram *Angus* 77 B7
Padbury *Bucks* 28 E4
Paddington *London* 19 C9
Paddlesworth *Kent* 21 H8
Paddock Wood *Kent* 12 B5
Paddockhaugh *Moray* 88 C2
Paddockhole *Dumf/Gal* 61 E8
Padfield *Derby* 44 C4
Padiham *Lancs* 50 F3
Padog *Conwy* 41 E10
Padside *N Yorks* 51 D7
Padstow *Cornw'l* 3 B8
Padworth *W Berks* 18 E3
Page Bank *Durham* 58 C3
Pagelsham Eastend *Essex* 20 B6
Pagham *W Sussex* 11 E7
Paglesham Churchend *Essex* 20 B6
Paibeil *W Isles* 84 B2
Paible *W Isles* 90 H5
Paignton *Torbay* 5 E9
Pailton *Warwick* 35 G10
Painscastle *Powys* 25 D8
Painshawfield *Northum* 62 G6
Painsthorpe *ER Yorks* 52 D4
Painswick *Glos* 26 H5
Pairc Shiaboist *W Isles* 90 C7
Paisley *Renf* 68 D3
Pakefield *Suffolk* 39 F11
Pakenham *Suffolk* 30 B6
Pale *Gwyn* 32 B5
Palestine *Hants* 17 G9
Paley Street *Windsor* 18 D5
Palfrey *W Midlands* 34 F6
Palgowan *Dumf/Gal* 54 A6
Palgrave *Suffolk* 39 H7
Pallion *Tyne/Wear* 63 H9
Palmarsh *Kent* 13 C10
Palnackie *Dumf/Gal* 55 D11
Palnure *Dumf/Gal* 55 C7
Palterton *Derby* 45 F8
Pamber End *Hants* 18 F3
Pamber Green *Hants* 18 F3
Pamber Heath *Hants* 18 E3
Pamphill *Dorset* 9 D8
Pampisford *Cambs* 29 D11
Pan *Orkney* 95 J4
Panbride *Angus* 77 D8
Pancrasweek *Devon* 6 F1
Pandy *Gwyn* 32 E2
Pandy *Monmouths* 25 F10
Pandy *Powys* 32 E5
Pandy *Wrex* 33 B7
Pandy Tudur *Conwy* 41 D10
Panfield *Essex* 30 F4
Pangbourne *W Berks* 18 D3
Pannal *N Yorks* 51 D9
Panshanger *Herts* 29 G9
Pant *Shrops* 33 C8
Pant-glas *Carms* 23 D10
Pant-glas *Gwyn* 40 F6
Pant-glâs *Powys* 32 F3
Pant-glas *Shrops* 33 B8
Pant gwyn *Carms* 23 D10
Pant Mawr *Powys* 32 G4
Pant-teg *Carms* 23 D9
Pant-y-Caws *Carms* 22 D6
Pant-y-dwr *Powys* 32 H5
Pant-y-ffridd *Powys* 33 E7
Pant-y-Wacco *Flints* 42 E4
Pant-yr-awel *Bridg* 14 C5
Pantgwyn *Ceredig'n* 23 B7
Pantlasau *Swan* 14 B2
Panton *Lincs* 46 E5
Pantperthog *Gwyn* 32 F3
Pantyffynnon *Carms* 24 G3
Pantymwyn *Flints* 42 F4
Panxworth *Norfolk* 39 D9
Papcastle *Cumb* 56 C3
Papigoe *H'land* 94 E5
Papil *Shetl'd* 96 K5
Papley *Orkney* 95 J5
Papple *E Loth* 70 C4
Papplewick *Notts* 45 G9
Papworth Everard *Cambs* 29 B9
Papworth St Agnes *Cambs* 29 B9
Par *Cornw'l* 4 F1
Parbold *Lancs* 43 A7
Parbrook *Som'set* 16 H2
Parbrook *W Sussex* 11 B9
Parc *Gwyn* 41 G10
Parc-Seymour *Newp* 15 B10
Parc-y-rhôs *Carms* 23 B10
Parcllyn *Ceredig'n* 23 A7
Pardshaw *Cumb* 56 D2
Parham *Suffolk* 31 B10
Park *Dumf/Gal* 60 D5
Park Corner *Oxon* 18 C3
Park Corner *Windsor* 18 C5
Park End *Middlesbro'* 58 E6
Park End *Northum* 62 F4
Park Gate *Hants* 10 D4
Park Hill *Notts* 45 G10
Park Hill *N Yorks* 51 C9
Park Street *W Sussex* 11 A10
Parkend *Glos* 26 H3
Parkeston *Essex* 31 E9
Parkgate *Ches* 42 E5
Parkgate *Dumf/Gal* 60 E6
Parkgate *Kent* 13 C7
Parkgate *Surrey* 19 G9
Parkham *Devon* 6 D2
Parkham Ash *Devon* 6 D2
Parkhill Ho. *Aberds* 83 B10
Parkhouse *Monmouths* 15 A10
Parkhouse Green *Derby* 45 F8
Parkhurst *I/Wight* 10 E3
Parkmill *Swan* 23 H10
Parkneuk *Aberds* 83 F9
Parkstone *Poole* 9 E9
Parley Cross *Dorset* 9 E9
Parracombe *Devon* 6 B5
Parrog *Pembs* 22 C5
Parsley Hay *Derby* 44 F5
Parson Cross *S Yorks* 45 C7
Parson Drove *Cambs* 37 E9
Parsonage Green *Essex* 30 H4
Parsonby *Cumb* 56 C3
Parson's Heath *Essex* 31 F7
Partick *C/Glasg* 68 D4
Partington *Gtr Man* 43 C10
Partney *Lincs* 47 F8
Parton *Cumb* 56 D1
Parton *Dumf/Gal* 55 B9
Parton *Glos* 26 F5
Partridge Green *W Sussex* 11 C10
Parwich *Derby* 44 G5
Passenham *Northants* 28 E4
Paston *Norfolk* 39 B9
Patchacott *Devon* 6 G3
Patcham *Brighton/Hove* 12 F2
Patching *W Sussex* 11 D9
Patchole *Devon* 6 B5
Patchway *S Gloucs* 16 C3
Pateley Bridge *N Yorks* 51 C7
Paternoster Heath *Essex* 30 G6
Path of Condie *Perth/Kinr* 76 F3
Pathe *Som'set* 8 A2
Pathhead *Aberds* 77 A10
Pathhead *E Ayrs* 67 E9
Pathhead *Fife* 69 A11
Pathhead *Midloth* 70 D2
Pathstruie *Perth/Kinr* 76 F3
Patmore Heath *Herts* 29 F11
Patna *E Ayrs* 67 E7
Patney *Wilts* 17 F7
Patrick *I/Man* 48 D2
Patrick Brompton *N Yorks* 58 G3
Patrington *ER Yorks* 53 G9
Patrixbourne *Kent* 21 F8
Patterdale *Cumb* 56 E5
Pattingham *Staffs* 34 F4
Pattishall *Northants* 28 C3
Pattiswick Green *Essex* 30 F5
Patton Bridge *Cumb* 57 G7
Paul *Cornw'l* 2 G3
Paulerspury *Northants* 28 D4
Paull *ER Yorks* 53 G7
Paulton *Bath/NE Som'set* 16 F3
Pavenham *Beds* 28 C6
Pawlett *Som'set* 15 G9
Pawston *Northum* 71 G7
Paxford *Glos* 27 E8
Paxton *Scot Borders* 71 E8
Payhembury *Devon* 7 F9
Paythorne *Lancs* 50 D4
Peacehaven *E Sussex* 12 F3
Peak Dale *Derby* 44 E4
Peak Forest *Derby* 44 E5
Peakirk *Peterbro* 37 E7
Pearsie *Angus* 76 B6
Pease Pottage *W Sussex* 12 C1
Peasedown St John *Bath/NE Som'set* 16 F4
Peasemore *W Berks* 17 D11
Peasenhall *Suffolk* 31 B10
Peaslake *Surrey* 19 G7
Peasley Cross *Mersey* 43 C8
Peasmarsh *E Sussex* 13 D7
Peaston *E Loth* 70 D3
Peastonbank *E Loth* 70 D3
Peat Inn *Fife* 77 G7
Peathill *Aberds* 89 B9
Peatling Magna *Leics* 36 F1
Peatling Parva *Leics* 36 G1
Peaton *Shrops* 33 G11
Peats Corner *Suffolk* 31 B8
Pebmarsh *Essex* 30 E5
Pebworth *Worcs* 27 D8
Pecket Well *W Yorks* 50 G5
Peckforton *Ches* 43 G8
Peckham *London* 19 D10
Peckleton *Leics* 35 E10
Pedlinge *Kent* 13 C10
Pedmore *W Midlands* 34 G5
Pedwell *Som'set* 15 H10
Peebles *Scot Borders* 69 F11
Peel *I/Man* 48 D2
Peel Common *Hants* 10 D4
Peel Park *S Lanarks* 68 E5
Peening Quarter *Kent* 13 D7
Pegsdon *Beds* 29 E8
Pegswood *Northum* 63 E8
Pegwell *Kent* 21 E10
Peinchorran *H'land* 85 E10
Peinlich *H'land* 85 C9
Pelaw *Tyne/Wear* 63 G8
Pelcomb Bridge *Pembs* 22 E4
Pelcomb Cross *Pembs* 22 E4
Peldon *Essex* 30 G6
Pellon *W Yorks* 51 G6
Pelsall *W Midlands* 34 E6
Pelton *Durham* 58 A3
Pelutho *Cumb* 56 B3
Pelynt *Cornw'l* 4 F3
Pemberton *Gtr Man* 43 B8
Pembrey *Carms* 23 F9
Pembridge *Heref'd* 25 C10
Pembroke = Penfro *Pembs* 22 F4
Pembroke Dock = Doc Penfro *Pembs* 22 F4
Pembury *Kent* 12 B5
Pen-bont Rhydybeddau *Ceredig'n* 32 G2
Pen-clawdd *Swan* 23 G10
Pen-ffordd *Pembs* 22 D5
Pen-groes-oped *Monmouths* 25 H10
Pen-llyn *Angl* 40 B5
Pen-lon *Angl* 40 D6
Pen-sarn *Gwyn* 40 F6
Pen-sarn *Gwyn* 32 C1
Pen-twyn *Monmouths* 26 H2
Pen-y-banc *Carms* 24 F3
Pen-y-bont *Carms* 23 D8
Pen-y-bont *Gwyn* 32 E3
Pen-y-bont *Gwyn* 32 C2
Pen-y-bont *Powys* 33 C8
Pen-y-bont ar Ogwr = Bridgend *Bridg* 14 D5
Pen-y-bryn *Gwyn* 32 D2
Pen-y-bryn *Pembs* 22 B6
Pen-y-cae *Powys* 24 G5
Pen-y-cae-mawr *Monmouths* 15 B10
Pen-y-cefn *Flints* 42 E4
Pen-y-clawdd *Monmouths* 25 H11
Pen-y-coedcae *Rh Cyn Taff* 14 C6
Pen-y-fai *Bridg* 14 C4
Pen-y-garn *Ceredig'n* 32 G2
Pen-y-garn *Carms* 23 C10
Pen-y-garnedd *Angl* 41 C7
Pen-y-gop *Conwy* 32 A5
Pen-y-graig *Gwyn* 40 G3
Pen-y-groes *Carms* 23 E10
Pen-y-groeslon *Gwyn* 40 G4
Pen-y-Gwryd Hotel *Gwyn* 41 E8
Pen-y-stryt *Denbs* 42 G4
Pen-yr-heol *Monmouths* 25 G11
Pen-yr-Heolgerrig *Merth Tyd* 25 H7
Penallt *Monmouths* 26 G2
Penally *Pembs* 22 G6
Penalt *Heref'd* 26 F2
Penare *Cornw'l* 3 E8
Penarlâg = Hawarden *Flints* 42 F6
Penarth *V/Glam* 15 D7
Penbryn *Ceredig'n* 23 A7
Pencader *Carms* 23 C9
Pencaenewydd *Gwyn* 40 F6
Pencaitland *E Loth* 70 D3
Pencarnisiog *Angl* 40 C5
Pencarreg *Carms* 23 B10
Pencelli *Powys* 25 F7
Pencoed *Bridg* 14 C5
Pencombe *Heref'd* 26 C2
Pencoyd *Heref'd* 26 F2
Pencraig *Heref'd* 26 F2
Pencraig *Powys* 32 C6
Pendeen *Cornw'l* 2 F2
Penderyn *Rh Cyn Taff* 24 H6
Pendine *Carms* 23 F7
Pendlebury *Gtr Man* 43 B10
Pendleton *Lancs* 50 F3
Pendock *Worcs* 26 E4
Pendoggett *Cornw'l* 3 B9
Pendomer *Som'set* 8 C4
Pendoylan *V/Glam* 14 D6
Pendre *Bridg* 14 C5
Penegoes *Powys* 32 E3
Penfro = Pembroke *Pembs* 22 F4
Pengam *Caerph* 15 B7
Penge *London* 19 D10
Pengenffordd *Powys* 25 E8
Pengorffwysfa *Angl* 40 A6
Pengover Green *Cornw'l* 4 E3
Penhale *Cornw'l* 2 H5
Penhale *Cornw'l* 3 D8
Penhalvaen *Cornw'l* 2 F6
Penhill *Swindon* 17 C8
Penhow *Newp* 15 B10
Penhurst *E Sussex* 12 E5
Peniarth *Gwyn* 32 E2
Penicuik *Midloth* 69 D11
Peniel *Carms* 23 D9
Peniel *Denbs* 42 F3
Penifiler *H'land* 85 D9
Peninver *Arg/Bute* 65 F8
Penisarwaun *Gwyn* 41 D7
Penistone *S Yorks* 44 B6
Penjerrick *Cornw'l* 3 F6
Penketh *Warrington* 43 D8
Penkill *S Ayrs* 66 G5
Penkridge *Staffs* 34 D5
Penley *Wrex* 33 B10
Penllergaer *Swan* 14 B2
Penllyn *V/Glam* 14 D5
Penmachno *Conwy* 41 E9
Penmaen *Swan* 23 H10
Penmaenan *Conwy* 41 C9
Penmaenmawr *Conwy* 41 C9
Penmaenpool *Gwyn* 32 D2
Penmark *V/Glam* 14 E6
Penmarth *Cornw'l* 2 F6
Penmon *Angl* 41 B8
Penmore Mill *Arg/Bute* 78 F7
Penmorfa *Ceredig'n* 23 A8
Penmorfa *Gwyn* 41 F7
Penmynydd *Angl* 41 C7
Penn *Bucks* 18 B6
Penn *W Midlands* 34 F4
Penn Street *Bucks* 18 B6
Pennal *Gwyn* 32 E3
Pennan *Aberds* 89 B8
Pennant *Ceredig'n* 24 B2
Pennant *Denbs* 32 B6
Pennant *Denbs* 42 G3
Pennant *Powys* 32 F4
Pennant Melangell *Powys* 32 C6
Pennar *Pembs* 22 F4
Pennard *Swan* 23 H10
Pennerley *Shrops* 33 F9
Pennington *Cumb* 49 B2
Pennington *Gtr Man* 43 C9
Pennington *Hants* 10 E2
Penny Bridge *Cumb* 49 A3
Pennycross *Arg/Bute* 79 J8
Pennygate *Norfolk* 39 C9
Pennygown *Arg/Bute* 79 G8
Pennymoor *Devon* 7 E7
Pennywell *Tyne/Wear* 63 H9
Penparc *Ceredig'n* 23 B7
Penparc *Pembs* 22 C3
Penparcau *Ceredig'n* 32 G1
Penperlleni *Monmouths* 15 A9
Penpillick *Cornw'l* 4 F1
Penpol *Cornw'l* 3 F7
Penpoll *Cornw'l* 4 F2
Penpont *Dumf/Gal* 60 D4
Penpont *Powys* 24 F6
Penrherber *Carms* 23 C7
Penrhiw goch *Carms* 23 E10
Penrhiw-llan *Ceredig'n* 23 B8
Penrhiw-pâl *Ceredig'n* 23 B8
Penrhiwceiber *Rh Cyn Taff* 14 B6
Penrhos *Gwyn* 40 G5
Penrhôs *Monmouths* 25 G11
Penrhos *Powys* 24 G4
Penrhosfeilwo *Angl* 40 B4
Penrhyn Bay *Conwy* 41 B10
Penrhyn-coch *Ceredig'n* 32 G2
Penrhyndeudraeth *Gwyn* 41 G8
Penrhynside *Conwy* 41 B10
Penrice *Swan* 23 H9
Penrith *Cumb* 57 C7
Penrose *Cornw'l* 3 B7
Penruddock *Cumb* 56 D6
Penryn *Cornw'l* 3 F6
Pensarn *Carms* 23 E9
Pensarn *Conwy* 42 E2
Pensax *Worcs* 26 B4
Pensby *Mersey* 42 D5
Penselwood *Som'set* 9 A6
Pensford *Bath/NE Som'set* 16 E3
Penshaw *Tyne/Wear* 58 A4
Penshurst *Kent* 12 B4
Pensilva *Cornw'l* 4 E3
Penston *E Loth* 70 C3
Pentewan *Cornw'l* 3 E9
Pentir *Gwyn* 41 D7
Pentire *Cornw'l* 3 C6
Pentlow *Essex* 30 D5
Pentney *Norfolk* 38 D3
Penton Mewsey *Hants* 17 G10
Pentraeth *Angl* 41 C7
Pentre *Carms* 23 E10
Pentre *Powys* 33 G6
Pentre *Powys* 33 F8
Pentre *Rh Cyn Taff* 14 B5
Pentre *Shrops* 33 D9
Pentre *Wrex* 33 A8
Pentre *Wrex* 33 B7
Pentre-bâch *Ceredig'n* 23 B10
Pentre-bach *Powys* 24 E6
Pentre Berw *Angl* 40 C6
Pentre-bont *Conwy* 41 E9
Pentre-celyn *Denbs* 42 G4
Pentre-Celyn *Powys* 32 E4
Pentre-chwyth *Swan* 14 B2
Pentre-cwrt *Carms* 23 C8
Pentre Dolau-Honddu *Powys* 24 D6
Pentre-dwr *Swan* 14 B2
Pentre-galar *Pembs* 22 C6
Pentre-Gwenlais *Carms* 24 G3
Pentre Gwynfryn *Gwyn* 32 C1
Pentre Halkyn *Flints* 42 E5
Pentre-Isaf *Conwy* 41 D10
Pentre Llanrhaeadr *Denbs* 42 F3
Pentre-llwyn-llŵyd *Powys* 24 C6
Pentre-llyn *Ceredig'n* 24 A3
Pentre-llyn cymmer *Conwy* 42 G2
Pentre Meyrick *V/Glam* 14 D5
Pentre-poeth *Newp* 15 C8
Pentre-rhew *Ceredig'n* 24 C3
Pentre-tafarn-y-fedw *Conwy* 41 D10
Pentre-ty-gwyn *Carms* 24 E5
Pentrebach *Merth Tyd* 14 A6
Pentrebach *Swan* 24 H3
Pentrebeirdd *Powys* 33 D7
Pentrecagal *Carms* 23 B8
Pentredwr *Denbs* 42 H4
Pentrefelin *Ceredig'n* 24 D3
Pentrefelin *Carms* 23 D10
Pentrefelin *Conwy* 41 C10
Pentrefelin *Gwyn* 41 G7
Pentrefoelas *Conwy* 41 E10
Pentregat *Ceredig'n* 23 A8
Pentreheyling *Shrops* 33 F8
Pentre'r Felin *Conwy* 41 D10
Pentre'r-felin *Powys* 24 E6
Pentrich *Derby* 45 G7
Pentridge *Dorset* 9 C9
Pentyrch *Card* 15 C7
Penuchadre *V/Glam* 14 D4
Penuwch *Ceredig'n* 24 B2
Penwithick *Cornw'l* 3 D9
Penwyllt *Powys* 24 G5
Penybanc *Carms* 24 G3
Penybont *Powys* 25 B8
Penybontfawr *Powys* 33 C6
Penycae *Wrex* 42 H5
Penycwm *Pembs* 22 D3
Penyffordd *Flints* 42 F6
Penyffridd *Gwyn* 41 E7
Penygarnedd *Powys* 33 C7
Penygraig *Rh Cyn Taff* 14 B5
Penygroes *Gwyn* 40 E6
Penygroes *Pembs* 22 C6
Penyrheol *Caerph* 15 C7
Penysarn *Angl* 40 A6
Penywaun *Rh Cyn Taff* 14 A5
Penzance *Cornw'l* 2 F3
Peopleton *Worcs* 26 C6
Peover Heath *Ches* 43 E10
Peper Harow *Surrey* 18 G6
Perceton *N Ayrs* 67 B6
Percie *Aberds* 83 D7
Percyhorner *Aberds* 89 B9
Periton *Som'set* 7 B8
Perivale *London* 19 C8
Perkinsville *Durham* 58 A3
Perlethorpe *Notts* 45 E10
Perranarworthal *Cornw'l* 3 F6
Perranporth *Cornw'l* 3 D6
Perranuthnoe *Cornw'l* 2 G4
Perranzabuloe *Cornw'l* 3 D6
Perry Barr *W Midlands* 35 F6
Perry Green *Herts* 29 G11
Perry Green *Wilts* 16 C6
Perry Street *Kent* 20 D3
Perryfoot *Derby* 44 D5
Pershall *Staffs* 34 B4
Pershore *Worcs* 26 D6
Pert *Angus* 83 G8
Pertenhall *Beds* 29 B7
Perth *Perth/Kinr* 76 E4
Perthy *Shrops* 33 B9
Perton *Staffs* 34 F4
Pertwood *Wilts* 16 H5
Peter Tavy *Devon* 4 D6
Peterborough *Peterbro* 37 F7
Peterburn *H'land* 91 J12
Peterchurch *Heref'd* 25 E10
Peterculter *Aberd C* 83 C10
Peterhead *Aberds* 89 D11
Peterlee *Durham* 58 B5
Peter's Green *Herts* 29 G8
Peters Marland *Devon* 6 E3
Petersfield *Hants* 10 B6
Peterston super-Ely *V/Glam* 14 D6
Peterstone Wentlooge *Newp* 15 C8
Peterstow *Heref'd* 26 F2
Petertown *Orkney* 95 H4
Petham *Kent* 21 F8
Petrockstow *Devon* 6 F4
Pett *E Sussex* 13 E7
Pettaugh *Suffolk* 31 C8
Petteridge *Kent* 12 B5
Pettinain *S Lanarks* 69 F8
Pettistree *Suffolk* 31 C9
Petton *Devon* 7 D9
Petton *Shrops* 33 C10
Petts Wood *London* 19 E11
Petty *Aberds* 89 E7
Pettycur *Fife* 69 B11
Pettymuick *Aberds* 89 F9
Petworth *W Sussex* 11 B8
Pevensey *E Sussex* 12 F5
Pevensey Bay *E Sussex* 12 F5
Pewsey *Wilts* 17 E8
Philham *Devon* 6 D1
Philiphaugh *Scot Borders* 70 H3
Phillack *Cornw'l* 2 F4
Philleigh *Cornw'l* 3 F7
Philpstoun *W Loth* 69 C9
Phocle Green *Heref'd* 26 F3
Phoenix Green *Hants* 18 F4
Pica *Cumb* 56 D2
Piccotts End *Herts* 29 H7
Pickering *N Yorks* 52 A3
Picket Piece *Hants* 17 G10
Picket Post *Hants* 9 D10
Pickhill *N Yorks* 51 A9
Picklescott *Shrops* 33 F10
Pickletillem *Fife* 77 E7
Pickmere *Ches* 43 E9
Pickney *Som'set* 7 D10
Pickstock *Telford* 34 C3
Pickwell *Devon* 6 B3
Pickwell *Leics* 36 D3
Pickworth *Lincs* 36 B6
Pickworth *Rutl'd* 36 D5
Picton *Ches* 43 E7
Picton *Flints* 42 D4
Picton *N Yorks* 58 F5
Piddinghoe *E Sussex* 12 F3
Piddington *Northants* 28 C5
Piddington *Oxon* 28 G3
Piddlehinton *Dorset* 8 E6
Piddletrenthide *Dorset* 8 E6
Pidley *Cambs* 37 H9
Piercebridge *D'lington* 58 E3
Pierowall *Orkney* 95 D5
Pigdon *Northum* 63 E7
Pikehall *Derby* 44 G5
Pilgrims Hatch *Essex* 20 B2
Pilham *Lincs* 46 C2
Pill *N Som'set* 15 D11
Pillaton *Cornw'l* 4 E4
Pillerton Hersey *Warwick* 27 D10
Pillerton Priors *Warwick* 27 D9
Pilleth *Powys* 25 B9
Pilley *Hants* 10 E2
Pilley *S Yorks* 45 B7
Pilling *Lancs* 49 E4
Pilling Lane *Lancs* 49 E3
Pillowell *Glos* 26 H3
Pillwell *Dorset* 9 C6
Pilning *S Gloucs* 16 C2

Pilsbury Derby 44 F5
Pilsdon Dorset 8 E3
Pilsgate Peterbro 37 E6
Pilsley Derby 44 G6
Pilsley Derby 6 C4
Pilton Devon 6 C4
Pilton Northants 36 G6
Pilton Rutl'd 36 E5
Pilton Green Swan 16 G2
Pimperne Dorset 9 D8
Pinchbeck Lincs 37 C8
Pinchbeck Bars Lincs 37 C7
Pinchbeck West Lincs 37 C7
Pincheon Green S Yorks 52 H2
Pinehurst Swindon 17 C8
Pinfold Lancs 43 A6
Pinged Carms 23 F9
Pinhoe Devon 7 G8
Pinkneys Green Windsor 18 C4
Pinley W Midlands 35 H9
Pinmill Suffolk 31 E9
Pinminnoch S Ayrs 66 G4
Pinmore S Ayrs 66 G5
Pinmore Mains S Ayrs 66 G5
Pinner London 19 C8
Pinvin Worcs 26 D6
Pinwherry S Ayrs 66 H4
Pinxton Derby 45 G8
Pipe and Lyde Heref'd 26 D2
Pipe Gate Shrops 34 A3
Piperhill H'land 87 F11
Piper's Pool Cornw'l 4 E3
Pipewell Northants 36 G4
Pippacott Devon 6 C4
Pipton Powys 25 E8
Pirbright Surrey 18 F6
Pirnmill N Ayrs 66 B11
Pirton Herts 29 E8
Pirton Worcs 26 D5
Pisgah Ceredig'n 24 A3
Pisgah Stirl 75 G10
Pishill Oxon 18 C4
Pistyll Gwyn 40 F5
Pitagowan Perth/Kinr 81 F10
Pitblae Aberds 89 B9
Pitcairngreen Perth/Kinr 76 E3
Pitcalnie H'land 87 D11
Pitcaple Aberds 83 A9
Pitch Green Bucks 18 A4
Pitch Place Surrey 18 F6
Pitchcombe Glos 26 H5
Pitchcott Bucks 28 F4
Pitchford Shrops 33 E11
Pitcombe Som'set 8 A5
Pitcorthie Fife 77 G8
Pitcox E Loth 70 C5
Pitcur Perth/Kinr 76 D5
Pitfichie Aberds 83 B8
Pitforthie Aberds 83 F10
Pitgrudy H'land 87 B10
Pitkennedy Angus 77 B8
Pitkevy Fife 76 G5
Pitkierie Fife 77 G8
Pitlessie Fife 76 G6
Pitlochry Perth/Kinr 76 B2
Pitmachie Aberds 83 A8
Pitmain H'land 81 C9
Pitmedden Aberds 89 F8
Pitminster Som'set 7 E11
Pitmuies Angus 77 C8
Pitmunie Aberds 83 B8
Pitney Som'set 8 B3
Pitscottie Fife 77 F7
Pitsea Essex 20 C4
Pitsford Northants 28 B4
Pitsmoor S Yorks 45 D7
Pitstone Bucks 28 G6
Pitstone Green Bucks 28 G6
Pittendreich Moray 88 B1
Pittentrail H'land 93 J10
Pittenweem Fife 77 G8
Pittodrie Aberds 83 A8
Pitton Wilts 9 A11
Pittswood Kent 20 G3
Pittulie Aberds 89 B9
Pity Me Durham 58 B3
Pityme Cornw'l 3 B8
Pityoulish H'land 81 B11
Pixey Green Suffolk 39 H8
Pixham Surrey 19 F8
Pixley Heref'd 26 E3
Place Newton N Yorks 52 B4
Plaidy Aberds 89 C7
Plains N Lanarks 68 D6
Plaish Shrops 33 F11
Plaistow W Sussex 11 A9
Plaitford Hants 10 C1
Plank Lane Gtr Man 43 C9
Plâs Carms 23 E10
Plas-canol Gwyn 32 D1
Plas Gogerddan Ceredig'n 32 G2
Plas Llwyngwern Powys 32 E3
Plas Nantyr Wrex 33 B7
Plas-yn-Cefn Denbs 42 E3
Plastow Green Hants 18 E2
Platt Kent 20 F3
Platt Bridge Gtr Man 43 B9
Platts Common S Yorks 45 B7
Plawsworth Durham 58 B3
Plaxtol Kent 20 F3
Play Hatch Oxon 18 D4
Playden E Sussex 13 D8
Playford Suffolk 31 D9
Playing Place Cornw'l 3 E7
Playley Green Glos 26 E4
Plealey Shrops 33 E10
Plean Stirl 69 B7
Pleasington Blackb'n 50 G2
Pleasley Derby 45 F9
Pleckgate Blackb'n 50 F2
Plenmeller Northum 62 G3
Pleshey Essex 30 G3
Plockton H'land 85 E13
Plocrapol W Isles 90 H6
Ploughfield Heref'd 25 D10
Plowden Shrops 33 G9
Ploxgreen Shrops 33 E9
Pluckley Kent 20 G6
Pluckley Thorne Kent 13 B8
Plumbland Cumb 56 C3
Plumley Ches 43 E10
Plumpton Cumb 57 C6
Plumpton E Sussex 12 E2
Plumpton Green E Sussex 12 E2
Plumpton Head Cumb 57 C7
Plumstead London 19 D11
Plumstead Norfolk 39 B7
Plumtree Notts 36 B2
Plungar Leics 36 B3
Plush Dorset 8 D6
Plwmp Ceredig'n 23 A8
Plymouth Plym'th 4 F6
Plympton Plym'th 4 F6
Plymstock Plym'th 4 F6
Plymtree Devon 7 F9
Pockley N Yorks 59 H7
Pocklington ER Yorks 52 E4
Pode Hole Lincs 37 C8
Podimore Som'set 8 B4
Podington Beds 28 B6
Podmore Staffs 34 B3
Point Clear Essex 31 G7
Pointon Lincs 37 B7
Pokesdown Bournem'th 9 E10
Pol a Charra W Isles 84 G2
Polbae Dumf/Gal 54 B5
Polbain H'land 92 H2
Polbathic Cornw'l 4 F4
Polbeth W Loth 69 D9
Polchar H'land 81 C10
Pole Elm Worcs 26 D5
Polebrook Northants 37 G6
Polegate E Sussex 12 F4
Poles H'land 87 B10
Polesworth Warwick 35 E8
Polglass H'land 92 H2
Polgooth Cornw'l 3 D8
Poling W Sussex 11 D9
Polla H'land 92 D6

Pollington ER Yorks 52 H2
Polloch H'land 79 E10
Pollok C/Glasg 68 D4
Pollokshields C/Glasg 68 D4
Polmassick Cornw'l 3 E8
Polmont Falk 69 C8
Polnessan E Ayrs 67 E7
Polperro Cornw'l 4 F3
Polruan Cornw'l 4 F2
Polsham Som'set 15 G11
Polstead Suffolk 30 E6
Poltalloch Arg/Bute 73 D7
Poltimore Devon 7 G8
Polton Midloth 69 D11
Polwarth Scot Borders 70 E6
Polyphant Cornw'l 4 C3
Polzeath Cornw'l 3 B8
Ponders End London 19 B10
Pondersbridge Cambs 37 F8
Pondtail Hants 18 F5
Ponsanooth Cornw'l 3 F6
Ponsonby Cumb 56 F2
Ponsworthy Devon 5 D8
Pont Aber Carms 24 F4
Pont Aber-Geirw Gwyn 32 C3
Pont-ar-gothi Carms 23 D10
Pont-ar-Hydfer Powys 24 F5
Pont-ar-llechau Carms 24 F4
Pont Cwm Pydew Denbs 32 B6
Pont Cyfyng Conwy 41 E9
Pont Cysyllte Wrex 33 A8
Pont Dolydd Prysor Gwyn 41 G9
Pont-faen Powys 24 E6
Pont Fronwydd Gwyn 32 C4
Pont-gareg Pembs 22 B6
Pont-Henri Carms 23 F9
Pont Llogel Powys 32 D6
Pont Pen-y-benglog Gwyn 41 D8
Pont Rhyd-goch Conwy 41 D8
Pont Rhyd-sarn Gwyn 32 C4
Pont-Rhyd-y-cyff Bridg 14 C4
Pont-rhyd-y-groes Ceredig'n 24 A4
Pont-rug Gwyn 41 D7
Pont Senni = Sennybridge Powys
Pont-siân Ceredig'n 23 B9
Pont-y-gwaith Rh Cyn Taff 14 B6
Pont-y-pant Conwy 41 E9
Pont y Pennant Gwyn 32 C5
Pont yclun Rh Cyn Taff 14 C6
Pont yr Afon-Gam Gwyn 41 F9
Pont-y-hafod Pembs 22 D4
Pontamman Carms 24 G3
Pontantwn Carms 23 E9
Pontardawe Neath P Talb 14 A3
Pontarddulais Swan 23 F10
Pontarsais Carms 23 D9
Pontblyddyn Flints 42 F5
Pontbren Araeth Carms 24 F3
Pontbren Llwyd Rh Cyn Taff 24 H6
Pontefract W Yorks 51 G10
Ponteland Northum 63 F7
Ponterwyd Ceredig'n 32 G3
Pontesbury Shrops 33 E9
Pontfadog Wrex 33 B8
Pontfaen Pembs 22 C5
Pontgarreg Ceredig'n 23 A8
Ponthir Torf 15 B9
Ponthirwaun Ceredig'n 23 B7
Pontllanfraith Caerph 15 B7
Pontlliw Swan 23 F10
Pontllyfni Gwyn 40 E6
Pontlottyn Caerph 25 H8
Pontneddfechan Powys 24 H6
Pontnewydd Torf 15 B8
Pontrhydfendigaid Ceredig'n 24 B4
Pontrhydyfen Neath P Talb 14 B3
Pontrilas Heref'd 25 F10
Pontrobert Powys 33 D7
Ponts Green E Sussex 12 E5
Pontshill Heref'd 26 F3
Pontsticill Merthyr Tyd 25 G7
Pontyates Carms 23 F9
Pontyberem Carms 23 E10
Pontycymer Bridg 14 B5
Pontyglasier Pembs 22 C6
Pontypool = Pont-y-Pŵl Torf 15 A8
Pontypridd Rh Cyn Taff 14 C6
Pontywaun Caerph 15 B8
Pooksgreen Hants 10 C2
Pool Cornw'l 3 F6
Pool W Yorks 51 E8
Pool o' Muckhart Clack 76 G3
Pool Quay Powys 33 D8
Poole Poole 9 E9
Poole Keynes Glos 16 B6
Poolend Staffs 44 G3
Poolewe H'land 91 J13
Pooley Bridge Cumb 56 D6
Poolfold Staffs 44 G2
Poolhill Glos 26 F4
Poolsbrook Derby 45 E8
Pootings Kent 19 G11
Pope Hill Pembs 22 E4
Popeswood Brack'll 18 E5
Popham Hants 18 G2
Poplar London 19 C10
Popley Hants 18 F3
Porchester Notts 36 A1
Porchfield I/Wight 10 E3
Porin H'land 86 F6
Poringland Norfolk 39 E8
Porkellis Cornw'l 3 F6
Porlock Som'set 7 B7
Porlock Weir Som'set 7 B7
Port Ann Arg/Bute 73 E8
Port Appin Arg/Bute 74 C2
Port Askaig Arg/Bute 64 B5
Port Bannatyne Arg/Bute 73 G9
Port Carlisle Cumb 61 G9
Port Charlotte Arg/Bute 64 C3
Port Clarence Stockton 58 D5
Port Driseach Arg/Bute 73 F8
Port e Vullen I/Man 48 C4
Port Ellen Arg/Bute 64 D4
Port Elphinstone Aberds 83 B9
Port Erin I/Man 48 F1
Port Erroll Aberds 89 E10
Port Eynon Swan 23 H9
Port Gaverne Cornw'l 3 A9
Port Glasgow Invercl 68 C3
Port Henderson H'land 85 A12
Port Isaac Cornw'l 3 A8
Port Lamont Arg/Bute 73 F9
Port Lion Pembs 22 F4
Port Logan Dumf/Gal 54 E3
Port Mholair W Isles 91 D10
Port Mor H'land 78 D7
Port Mulgrave N Yorks 59 E8
Port nan Giúran W Isles 91 D10
Port nan Long W Isles 84 A3
Port Nis W Isles 91 A10
Port of Menteith Stirl 75 G8
Port Quin Cornw'l 3 A8
Port Ramsay Arg/Bute 79 G11
Port St Mary I/Man 48 F2
Port Sunlight Mersey 42 D6
Port Talbot Neath P Talb 14 B3
Port Wemyss Arg/Bute 64 C2
Port William Dumf/Gal 54 E6
Portachoillan Arg/Bute 72 H6
Portavadie Arg/Bute 73 G8
Portbury N Som'set 15 D11
Portchester Hants 10 D5
Portclair H'land 80 B6
Portencalzie Dumf/Gal 54 B3
Portencross N Ayrs 66 B4
Portesham Dorset 8 F5
Portessie Moray 88 B4
Portfield Gate Pembs 22 E4
Portgate Devon 4 C5
Portgordon Moray 88 B3
Portgower H'land 93 H13
Porth Cornw'l 3 C7
Porth Rh Cyn Taff 14 B6

Porth Navas Cornw'l 3 G6
Porth Tywyn = Burry Port Carms 23 F9
Porth-y-waen Shrops 33 C8
Porthaethwy = Menai Bridge Angl 41 C7
Porthallow Cornw'l 3 B7
Porthallow Cornw'l 3 G6
Porthcawl Bridg 14 D4
Porthcothan Cornw'l 3 B7
Porthcurno Cornw'l 2 G2
Porthgain Pembs 22 C3
Porthill Shrops 33 D10
Porthkerry V/Glam 14 E6
Porthleven Cornw'l 2 G5
Porthllechog Angl 40 A6
Porthmadog Gwyn 41 G7
Porthmeor Cornw'l 2 F3
Portholland Cornw'l 3 E8
Porthoustock Cornw'l 3 G7
Porthpean Cornw'l 3 D9
Porthtowan Cornw'l 2 E5
Porthyrhyd Carms 23 E10
Porthyrhyd Carms 24 E4
Portincaple Arg/Bute 73 D11
Portington ER Yorks 52 F3
Portinnisherrich Arg/Bute 73 B8
Portinscale Cumb 56 D4
Portishead N Som'set 15 D10
Portkil Arg/Bute 73 E11
Portlethen Aberds 83 D11
Portling Dumf/Gal 55 D11
Portloe Cornw'l 3 F8
Portmahomack H'land 87 C12
Portmeirion Gwyn 41 G7
Portmellon Cornw'l 3 E9
Portmore Hants 10 E2
Portnacroish Arg/Bute 74 C2
Portnahaven Arg/Bute 64 C2
Portnalong H'land 85 E8
Portnaluchaig H'land 79 C9
Portnancon H'land 92 C7
Portnellan Stirl 75 E7
Portobello C/Edinb 70 C2
Porton Wilts 9 A10
Portpatrick Dumf/Gal 54 D3
Portreath Cornw'l 2 E5
Portree H'land 85 D9
Portscatho Cornw'l 3 F7
Portsea Portsm'th 10 D5
Portskerra H'land 93 C11
Portskewett Monmouths 15 C11
Portslade Brighton/Hove 12 F1
Portslade-by-Sea Brighton/Hove 12 F1
Portsmouth Portsm'th 10 D5
Portsmouth W Yorks 50 G5
Portsonachan Arg/Bute 74 E3
Portsoy Aberds 88 B5
Portswood S'thampton 10 C3
Porttanaby Moray 88 B1
Portuairk H'land 78 E7
Portway Heref'd 25 D11
Portway Worcs 27 A7
Portwrinkle Cornw'l 4 F4
Poslingford Suffolk 30 D4
Postbridge Devon 5 D7
Postcombe Oxon 18 B4
Postling Kent 13 C10
Postwick Norfolk 39 E8
Potholm Dumf/Gal 61 E9
Potsgrove Beds 28 F6
Pott Row Norfolk 38 C3
Pott Shrigley Ches 44 E3
Potten End Herts 29 H7
Potter Brompton N Yorks 52 B5
Potter Heigham Norfolk 39 D10
Potter Street Essex 29 H11
Potterhanworth Lincs 46 F4
Potterhanworth Booths Lincs 46 F4
Potterne Wilts 16 F6
Potterne Wick Wilts 17 F7
Potternewton W Yorks 51 F9
Potters Bar Herts 19 A9
Potter's Cross Staffs 34 G4
Potterspury Northants 28 D4
Potterton Aberds 83 B11
Potterton W Yorks 51 F10
Potto N Yorks 58 F5
Potton Beds 29 D9
Poughill Cornw'l 6 F1
Poughill Devon 7 F7
Poulshot Wilts 16 F6
Poulton Glos 17 A8
Poulton Mersey 42 C6
Poulton-le-Fylde Lancs 49 F3
Pound Bank Worcs 26 A4
Pound Green E Sussex 12 D4
Pound Green I/Wight 10 F1
Pound Hill W Sussex 12 C1
Poundfield E Sussex 12 C4
Poundland S Ayrs 66 H4
Poundon Bucks 28 F3
Poundsgate Devon 5 D8
Poundstock Cornw'l 4 B3
Powburn Northum 62 B6
Powderham Devon 5 C10
Powerstock Dorset 8 E4
Powfoot Dumf/Gal 61 G7
Powick Worcs 26 D5
Powmill Perth/Kinr 76 H3
Poxwell Dorset 8 F6
Poyle Slough 19 D7
Poynings W Sussex 12 E1
Poyntington Dorset 8 C5
Poynton Ches 44 D3
Poynton Green Telford 34 D1
Poystreet Green Suffolk 30 C6
Praa Sands Cornw'l 2 G4
Pratt's Bottom London 19 E11
Praze Cornw'l 2 F5
Praze-an-Beeble Cornw'l 2 F5
Predannack Wollas Cornw'l 2 H5
Prees Shrops 33 B11
Prees Green Shrops 33 B11
Prees Heath Shrops 34 B1
Prees Higher Heath Shrops 33 B11
Prees Lower Heath Shrops 33 B11
Preesall Lancs 49 E3
Preesgweene Shrops 33 B8
Prendergast Pembs 22 E4
Prendwick Northum 62 B6
Prengwyn Ceredig'n 23 B9
Prenteg Gwyn 41 F7
Prenton Mersey 42 D6
Prescot Mersey 43 C7
Prescott Shrops 33 C10
Pressen Northum 71 G7
Prestatyn Denbs 42 D4
Prestbury Ches 44 E3
Prestbury Glos 26 F6
Presteigne = Llanandras Powys 25 B10
Presthope Shrops 34 F1
Prestleigh Som'set 16 G3
Preston Scot Borders 70 E6
Preston Brighton/Hove 12 F2
Preston Devon 5 D9
Preston Dorset 8 F6
Preston E Loth 70 C4
Preston ER Yorks 53 F7
Preston Glos 17 A7
Preston Glos 26 E4
Preston Herts 29 F8
Preston Kent 21 E7
Preston Kent 21 E9
Preston Lancs 49 G5
Preston Northum 71 H10
Preston Rutl'd 36 E4
Preston Wilts 17 D10
Preston Wilts 17 D8
Preston Bagot Warwick 27 B8
Preston Bissett Bucks 28 F3
Preston Bowyer Som'set 7 D10
Preston Brockhurst Shrops 33 C11
Preston Brook Halton 43 D8
Preston Candover Hants 18 G3
Preston Capes Northants 28 C2

Preston Crowmarsh Oxon 18 B3
Preston Gubbals Shrops 33 D10
Preston on Stour Warwick 27 D9
Preston on the Hill Halton 43 D8
Preston on Wye Heref'd 25 D10
Preston Plucknett Som'set 8 C4
Preston Wynne Heref'd 26 D2
Prestonmill Dumf/Gal 60 H5
Prestonpans E Loth 70 C2
Prestwich Gtr Man 44 B2
Prestwick Northum 63 F7
Prestwick S Ayrs 67 D7
Prestwood Bucks 18 A5
Price Town Bridg 14 B5
Prickwillow Cambs 38 G1
Priddy Som'set 15 F11
Priest Hutton Lancs 49 B5
Priest Weston Shrops 33 F8
Priestcliffe Derby 44 E5
Priesthaugh Scot Borders 61 C10
Primethorpe Leics 35 F11
Primrose Green Norfolk 39 D6
Primrose Valley N Yorks 53 B7
Primrosehill Herts 19 A7
Princes Gate Pembs 22 E6
Princes Risborough Bucks 18 A5
Princethorpe Warwick 27 A11
Princetown Caerph 25 G8
Princetown Devon 5 D6
Prion Denbs 42 F3
Prior Muir Fife 77 F8
Prior Park Northum 71 E8
Priors Frome Heref'd 26 E2
Priors Hardwick Warwick 27 C11
Priors Marston Warwick 27 C11
Priorslee Telford 34 D3
Priory Wood Heref'd 25 D9
Priston Bath/NE Som'set 16 E3
Pristow Green Norfolk 39 G7
Prittlewell Southend 20 C5
Privett Hants 10 B5
Prixford Devon 6 C4
Probus Cornw'l 3 E7
Proncy H'land 87 B10
Prospect Cumb 56 B3
Prudhoe Northum 62 G6
Ptarmigan Lodge Stirl 74 G6
Pubil Perth/Kinr 75 C7
Puckeridge Herts 29 F10
Puckington Som'set 8 C2
Pucklechurch S Gloucs 16 D3
Pucknall Hants 10 B2
Puckrup Glos 26 E5
Puddinglake Ches 43 F10
Puddington Ches 42 E6
Puddington Devon 7 E7
Puddledock Norfolk 39 F6
Puddletown Dorset 8 E6
Pudleston Heref'd 26 C2
Pudsey W Yorks 51 F8
Pulborough W Sussex 11 C9
Puleston Telford 34 C3
Pulford Ches 43 G6
Pulham Dorset 8 D6
Pulham Market Norfolk 39 G7
Pulham St Mary Norfolk 39 G8
Pulloxhill Beds 29 E7
Pumpherston W Loth 69 D9
Pumsaint Carms 24 D3
Puncheston Pembs 22 D5
Puncknowle Dorset 8 F4
Punnett's Town E Sussex 12 D5
Purbrook Hants 10 D5
Purewell Dorset 9 E10
Purfleet Thurr'k 20 D2
Puriton Som'set 15 G9
Purleigh Essex 20 A5
Purley London 19 E10
Purley W Berks 18 D3
Purlogue Shrops 33 H8
Purls Bridge Cambs 37 G10
Purse Caundle Dorset 8 C5
Purslow Shrops 33 G9
Purston Jaglin W Yorks 51 H10
Purton Glos 16 A3
Purton Glos 16 A3
Purton Wilts 17 C7
Purton Stoke Wilts 17 B7
Pury End Northants 28 D4
Pusey Oxon 17 B10
Putley Heref'd 26 E3
Putney London 19 D9
Putsborough Devon 6 B3
Puttenham Herts 28 G5
Puttenham Surrey 18 G6
Puxton N Som'set 15 E10
Pwll Carms 23 F9
Pwll-glas Denbs 42 G4
Pwll-Meyric Monmouths 15 B11
Pwll-trap Carms 23 E7
Pwll-y-glaw Neath P Talb 14 B3
Pwllcrochan Pembs 22 F4
Pwllgloyw Powys 25 E7
Pwllheli Gwyn 40 G5
Pwllmeyric Monmouths 15 B11
Pye Corner Newp 15 C9
Pye Green Staffs 34 D5
Pyewipe NE Lincs 46 A6
Pyle I/Wight 10 G3
Pyle = Y Pîl Bridg 14 C4
Pylle Som'set 16 H3
Pymoor Cambs 37 G10
Pyrford Surrey 19 F7
Pyrton Oxon 18 B3
Pytchley Northants 28 A5
Pyworthy Devon 6 F2

Q

Quabbs Shrops 33 G8
Quadring Lincs 37 B8
Quainton Bucks 28 F4
Quarley Hants 17 G9
Quarndon Derby 35 A9
Quarrier's Homes Inverc 68 D2
Quarrington Lincs 37 A6
Quarrington Hill Durham 58 C4
Quarry Bank W Midlands 34 G5
Quarryford E Loth 70 D4
Quarryhill H'land 87 C10
Quarrywood Moray 88 B1
Quarter S Lanarks 68 E6
Quatford Shrops 34 F3
Quatt Shrops 34 G3
Quebec Durham 58 B2
Quedgeley Glos 26 G5
Queen Adelaide Cambs 38 G1
Queen Camel Som'set 8 B4
Queen Charlton Bath/NE Som'set 16 E3
Queen Dart Devon 7 E7
Queen Oak Dorset 8 A6
Queen Street Kent 20 G3
Queen Street Wilts 17 C7
Queenborough Kent 20 D6
Queenhill Worcs 26 E5
Queen's Head Shrops 33 C9
Queen's Park Beds 29 D7
Queen's Park Northants 28 B4
Queensbury W Yorks 51 F7
Queensferry C/Edinb 69 C10
Queensferry Flints 42 F6
Queenstown Blackp'l 49 F3
Queenzieburn N Lanarks 68 C5
Quemerford Wilts 17 E7
Quendale Shetl'd 96 M5
Quendon Essex 30 E2
Queniborough Leics 36 D2
Quenington Glos 17 A8
Quernmore Lancs 49 D5
Quethiock Cornw'l 4 E4
Quholm Orkney 95 G3
Quicks Green W Berks 18 D2
Quidenham Norfolk 38 G6
Quidhampton Hants 18 F2
Quidhampton Wilts 9 A10

Quilquox Aberds 89 E9
Quina Brook Shrops 33 B11
Quindry Orkney 95 J5
Quinton Northants 28 C4
Quinton W Midlands 34 G5
Quintrell Downs Cornw'l 3 C7
Quixhill Staffs 35 A7
Quoditch Devon 6 G3
Quoig Perth/Kinr 75 E11
Quorndon Leics 36 D1
Quothquan S Lanarks 69 G8
Quoyloo Orkney 95 F3
Quoyness Orkney 95 H3
Quoys Shetl'd 96 B8
Quoys Shetl'd 96 G6

R

Raasay Ho. H'land 85 F10
Rabbit's Cross Kent 20 G4
Raby Mersey 42 E6
Rachan Mill Scot Borders 69 G10
Rachub Gwyn 41 D8
Rackenford Devon 7 E7
Rackham W Sussex 11 C9
Rackheath Norfolk 39 D8
Racks Dumf/Gal 60 F6
Rackwick Orkney 95 J3
Rackwick Orkney 95 D5
Radbourne Derby 35 B8
Radcliffe Gtr Man 43 B10
Radcliffe Northum 63 C8
Radcliffe on Trent Notts 36 B2
Radclive Bucks 28 E3
Radcot Oxon 17 B9
Raddery H'land 87 F10
Radernie Fife 77 G7
Radford Semele Warwick 27 B10
Radipole Dorset 8 F5
Radlett Herts 19 B8
Radley Oxon 18 B2
Radmanthwaite Notts 45 F9
Radmoor Shrops 34 C2
Radmore Green Ches 43 G8
Radnage Bucks 18 B4
Radstock Bath/NE Som'set 16 F3
Radstone Northants 28 D2
Radway Warwick 27 D10
Radway Green Ches 43 G10
Radwell Beds 29 C7
Radwell Herts 29 E9
Radwinter Essex 30 E3
Radyr Card 15 C7
Rafford Moray 87 F13
Ragdale Leics 36 D2
Raglan Monmouths 25 H11
Ragnall Notts 46 E2
Rahane Arg/Bute 73 E11
Rainford Mersey 43 B7
Rainford Junction Mersey 43 B7
Rainham London 20 C2
Rainham Medway 20 E5
Rainhill Mersey 43 C7
Rainhill Stoops Mersey 43 C8
Rainow Ches 44 E3
Rainton N Yorks 51 B9
Rainworth Notts 45 G9
Raisbeck Cumb 57 F8
Raise Cumb 57 B9
Rait Perth/Kinr 76 E5
Raithby Lincs 47 D7
Raithby Lincs 47 F7
Rakewood Gtr Man 44 A3
Ram Carms 23 B10
Ram Lane Kent 20 G6
Ramasaig H'land 84 D6
Rame Cornw'l 3 G6
Rame Cornw'l 4 G5
Ramnageo Shetl'd 96 C8
Rampisham Dorset 8 D4
Rampside Cumb 49 C2
Rampton Cambs 29 B11
Rampton Notts 45 E11
Ramsburn Moray 88 C5
Ramsbury Wilts 17 D9
Ramscraigs H'land 94 H3
Ramsdean Hants 10 B6
Ramsdell Hants 18 F2
Ramsden Oxon 27 G10
Ramsden Bellhouse Essex 20 B4
Ramsden Heath Essex 20 B4
Ramsey Cambs 37 G8
Ramsey Essex 31 E8
Ramsey I/Man 48 C4
Ramsey Forty Foot Cambs 37 G9
Ramsey Heights Cambs 37 G8
Ramsey Island Essex 20 A6
Ramsey Mereside Cambs 37 G8
Ramsey St Mary's Cambs 37 G8
Ramseycleuch Scot Borders 61 B8
Ramsgate Kent 21 E10
Ramsgill N Yorks 51 B7
Ramshorn Staffs 44 H4
Ramsnest Common Surrey 11 A8
Ranby Lincs 46 E6
Ranby Notts 45 D10
Rand Lincs 46 E5
Randwick Glos 26 H5
Ranfurly Renf 68 D2
Rangag H'land 94 F3
Rangemore Staffs 35 C7
Rangeworthy S Gloucs 16 C3
Rankinston E Ayrs 67 E7
Ranmoor S Yorks 45 D7
Ranmore Common Surrey 19 F8
Rannerdale Cumb 56 E3
Rannoch School Perth/Kinr 75 B8
Rannoch Station Perth/Kinr 75 B7
Ranochan H'land 79 C11
Ranskill Notts 45 D10
Ranton Staffs 34 C4
Ranworth Norfolk 39 D9
Raploch Stirl 68 A6
Rapness Orkney 95 D6
Rascal Moor ER Yorks 52 F4
Rascarrel Dumf/Gal 55 E10
Rashiereive Aberds 89 F9
Raskelf N Yorks 51 B10
Rassau Bl Gwent 25 G8
Rastrick W Yorks 51 G7
Ratagan H'land 85 G14
Ratby Leics 35 E11
Ratcliffe Culey Leics 35 F9
Ratcliffe on Soar Leics 35 C10
Ratcliffe on the Wreake Leics 36 D2
Rathen Aberds 89 B10
Rathillet Fife 76 E6
Rathmell N Yorks 50 C4
Ratho C/Edinb 69 D10
Ratho Station C/Edinb 69 C10
Ratley Warwick 27 D10
Ratlinghope Shrops 33 F10
Rattar H'land 94 C4
Ratten Row Lancs 49 E4
Rattery Devon 5 E8
Rattlesden Suffolk 30 C6
Rattray Perth/Kinr 76 C4
Raughton Head Cumb 56 B5
Raunds Northants 28 A6
Ravenfield S Yorks 45 C8
Ravenglass Cumb 56 G2
Raveningham Norfolk 39 F9
Ravenscar N Yorks 59 F10
Ravenscraig Inverc 73 F11
Ravensdale I/Man 48 C3
Ravensden Beds 29 C7
Ravenshead Notts 45 G9
Ravensmoor Ches 43 G9
Ravensthorpe Northants 28 A3

Ravenstown Cumb 49 B3
Ravensworth N Yorks 58 F2
Raw N Yorks 59 F10
Rawcliffe ER Yorks 52 G2
Rawcliffe C/York 52 D1
Rawcliffe Bridge ER Yorks 52 G2
Rawdon W Yorks 51 F8
Rawmarsh S Yorks 45 C8
Rawreth Essex 20 B4
Rawridge Devon 7 F11
Rawtenstall Lancs 50 G4
Raxton Aberds 89 E8
Raydon Suffolk 31 E7
Raylees Northum 62 D5
Rayleigh Essex 20 B5
Rayne Essex 30 F4
Raynes Lane London 19 C8
Raynes Park London 19 E9
Reach Cambs 30 B2
Read Lancs 50 F3
Reading Reading 18 D4
Reading Street Kent 13 C8
Reagill Cumb 57 E8
Rearquhar H'land 87 B10
Rearsby Leics 36 D2
Reaster H'land 94 D4
Reawick Shetl'd 96 J5
Reay H'land 93 C12
Rechullin H'land 85 C13
Reculver Kent 21 E9
Red Dial Cumb 56 B4
Red Hill Worcs 26 C5
Red Houses Jersey 11 A7
Red Lodge Suffolk 30 A3
Red Rail Heref'd 26 F2
Red Rock Gtr Man 43 B8
Red Roses Carms 23 E7
Red Row Northum 63 D8
Red Street Staffs 44 G2
Red Wharf Bay Angl 41 B7
Redberth Pembs 22 F5
Redbourn Herts 29 G8
Redbourne N Lincs 46 C3
Redbrook Wrex 33 A11
Redbrook Monmouths 26 G2
Redburn H'land 87 G12
Redburn H'land 87 D11
Redburn Northum 62 G3
Redcar Redcar/Clevel'd 59 D7
Redcastle Angus 77 B9
Redcastle H'land 87 G8
Redcliff Bay N Som'set 15 D10
Redding Falk 69 C8
Reddingmuirhead Falk 69 C8
Reddish Gtr Man 44 C2
Redditch Worcs 27 B7
Rede Suffolk 30 C5
Redenhall Norfolk 39 G8
Redesdale Camp Northum 62 D4
Redesmouth Northum 62 E4
Redford Aberds 83 F9
Redford Angus 77 C8
Redford Durham 58 C1
Redfordgreen Scot Borders 61 B9
Redgorton Perth/Kinr 76 E3
Redgrave Suffolk 38 H6
Redhill Aberds 83 C9
Redhill Aberds 89 E6
Redhill N Som'set 15 E11
Redhill Surrey 19 F9
Redhouse Arg/Bute 73 G7
Redhouses Arg/Bute 64 B4
Redisham Suffolk 39 G10
Redland Bristol 16 D2
Redland Orkney 95 F4
Redlingfield Suffolk 39 H7
Redlynch Som'set 8 A6
Redlynch Wilts 9 B11
Redmarley D'Abitot Glos 26 E4
Redmarshall Stockton 58 D4
Redmile Leics 36 B3
Redmire N Yorks 58 G1
Rednal Shrops 33 C9
Redpath Scot Borders 70 G4
Redpoint H'land 85 B12
Redruth Cornw'l 2 E5
Redvales Gtr Man 44 B2
Redwick Newp 15 C10
Redwick S Gloucs 15 C11
Redworth D'lington 58 D3
Reed Herts 29 E10
Reedham Norfolk 39 E10
Reedness ER Yorks 52 G3
Reeds Beck Lincs 46 F6
Reepham Lincs 46 E4
Reepham Norfolk 39 C6
Reeth N Yorks 58 G1
Regaby I/Man 48 C4
Regil N Som'set 15 E11
Regoul H'land 87 F11
Reiff H'land 92 H2
Reigate Surrey 19 F9
Reighton N Yorks 53 B7
Reighton Gap N Yorks 53 B7
Reinigeadal W Isles 90 G7
Reiss H'land 94 E5
Rejerrah Cornw'l 3 D6
Releath Cornw'l 2 F5
Relubbus Cornw'l 2 F4
Relugas Moray 87 G12
Remenham Wokingham 18 C4
Remenham Hill Wokingham 18 C4
Remony Perth/Kinr 75 C10
Rempstone Notts 36 C1
Rendcomb Glos 27 H7
Rendham Suffolk 31 B10
Rendlesham Suffolk 31 C10
Renfrew Renf 68 D4
Renhold Beds 29 C7
Renishaw Derby 45 E8
Rennington Northum 63 B8
Renton W Dunb 68 C2
Renwick Cumb 57 B8
Repps Norfolk 39 D10
Repton Derby 35 C9
Reraig H'land 85 F13
Rescobie Angus 77 B8
Resipole H'land 79 E10
Resolis H'land 87 E9
Resolven Neath P Talb 14 A4
Reston Scot Borders 71 D7
Reswallie Angus 77 B8
Retew Cornw'l 3 D8
Retford Notts 45 D11
Rettendon Essex 20 B4
Rettendon Place Essex 20 B4
Revesby Lincs 46 F6
Revesby Bridge Lincs 47 F7
Rew Devon 5 F8
Rewe Devon 7 G8
Rexon Devon 4 C5
Reydon Suffolk 39 H11
Reydon Smear Suffolk 39 H11
Reymerston Norfolk 38 E6
Reynalton Pembs 22 F5
Reynoldston Swan 23 G9
Rezare Cornw'l 4 D4
Rhaeadr Gwy = Rhayader Powys 24 B6
Rhandirmwyn Carms 24 D4
Rhayader = Rhaeadr Gwy Powys 24 B6
Rhedyn Gwyn 40 G4
Rhemore H'land 79 G8
Rhencullen I/Man 48 C3
Rhes-y-cae Flints 42 E4
Rhewl Denbs 42 F4
Rhewl Denbs 33 A7
Rhian H'land 93 H8
Rhicarn H'land 92 G4
Rhiconich H'land 92 D5
Rhicullen H'land 87 D9
Rhidorroch Ho. H'land 86 B4
Rhifail H'land 93 E10
Rhigos Rh Cyn Taff 24 H6
Rhilochan H'land 93 J10
Rhiroy H'land 86 C4
Rhisga = Risca Caerph 15 B8
Rhiw Gwyn 40 H4
Rhiwabon = Ruabon Wrex 33 A8
Rhiwbina Card 15 C7
Rhiwbryfdir Gwyn 41 F8
Rhiwderin Newp 15 C8

Rhiwlas Gwyn 41 D7
Rhiwlas Gwyn 32 B5
Rhiwlas Powys 33 B7
Rhodes Gtr Man 44 B2
Rhodes Minnis Kent 21 G8
Rhodesia Notts 45 E9
Rhodiad Pembs 22 D2
Rhondda Rh Cyn Taff 14 B5
Rhonehouse or Kelton Hill Dumf/Gal 55 D10
Rhoose = Y Rhws V/Glam 14 E6
Rhôs Carms 23 C8
Rhôs Neath P Talb 14 A3
Rhos-fawr Gwyn 40 G5
Rhos-goch Angl 40 A6
Rhôs-hill Pembs 22 B6
Rhos-on-Sea Conwy 41 B10
Rhôs-y-brithdir Powys 33 C7
Rhôs-y-garth Ceredig'n 24 A3
Rhôs-y-gwaliau Gwyn 32 B5
Rhôs-y-llan Gwyn 40 G4
Rhôs-y-Madoc Wrex 33 A9
Rhôs-y-meirch Powys 25 B9
Rhosaman Carms 24 G4
Rhosbeirio Angl 40 A5
Rhoscefnhir Angl 41 C7
Rhoscolyn Angl 40 C4
Rhoscrowther Pembs 22 F4
Rhosesmor Flints 42 F4
Rhosgadfan Gwyn 41 E7
Rhosgoch Powys 25 D8
Rhoshirwaun Gwyn 40 H3
Rhoslan Gwyn 40 F6
Rhoslefain Gwyn 32 E1
Rhosllanerchrugog Wrex 42 H5
Rhosmaen Carms 24 F3
Rhosmeirch Angl 40 C6
Rhosneigr Angl 40 C5
Rhosnesni Wrex 42 G6
Rhosrobin Wrex 42 G6
Rhossili Swan 23 H8
Rhosson Pembs 22 D2
Rhostryfan Gwyn 40 E6
Rhostyllen Wrex 42 H6
Rhosybol Angl 40 B6
Rhu Arg/Bute 73 E11
Rhuallt Denbs 42 E3
Rhuddall Heath Ches 43 F8
Rhuddlan Ceredig'n 23 B9
Rhuddlan Denbs 42 E3
Rhue H'land 86 B3
Rhulen Powys 25 D8
Rhunahaorine Arg/Bute 65 D8
Rhuthun = Ruthin Denbs 42 G4
Rhyd Gwyn 41 F8
Rhyd Powys 32 E5
Rhyd-Ddu Gwyn 41 E7
Rhyd-moel-ddu Powys 33 H6
Rhyd-Rosser Ceredig'n 24 B2
Rhyd-uchaf Gwyn 32 B5
Rhyd-wen Gwyn 32 D3
Rhyd-y-clafdy Gwyn 40 G5
Rhyd-y-foel Conwy 42 E2
Rhyd-y-fro Neath P Talb 14 A3
Rhyd-y-gwin Swan 14 A2
Rhyd-y-meirch Monmouths 25 H10
Rhyd-y-meudwy Denbs 42 G4
Rhyd-y-pandy Swan 14 A2
Rhyd-y-sarn Gwyn 41 F8
Rhyd-yr-onen Gwyn 32 E2
Rhydaman = Ammanford Carms 24 G3
Rhydargaeau Carms 23 D9
Rhydcymerau Carms 23 C10
Rhydd Worcs 26 D5
Rhydding Neath P Talb 14 B3
Rhydfudr Ceredig'n 24 B2
Rhydlewis Ceredig'n 23 B8
Rhydlios Gwyn 40 G3
Rhydlydan Conwy 41 E10
Rhydness Powys 25 D8
Rhydowen Ceredig'n 23 B9
Rhydspence Heref'd 25 D9
Rhydtalog Flints 42 G5
Rhydwyn Angl 40 B5
Rhydycroesau Shrops 33 B8
Rhydyfelin Ceredig'n 32 H1
Rhydyfelin Rh Cyn Taff 14 C6
Rhydymain Gwyn 32 C4
Rhydymwyn Flints 42 F4
Rhyl = Y Rhyl Denbs 42 D3
Rhymney = Rhymni Caerph 25 H8
Rhymni = Rhymney Caerph 25 H8
Rhynd Fife 77 E7
Rhynd Perth/Kinr 76 E4
Rhynie Aberds 82 A6
Rhynie H'land 87 D11
Ribbesford Worcs 26 A4
Ribblehead N Yorks 50 B3
Ribbleton Lancs 50 F1
Ribchester Lancs 50 F2
Ribigill H'land 93 D8
Riby Lincs 46 B5
Riby Cross Roads Lincs 46 B5
Riccall N Yorks 52 F2
Riccarton E Ayrs 67 C7
Richards Castle Heref'd 25 B11
Richmond London 19 D8
Richmond N Yorks 58 F2
Rickarton Aberds 83 E10
Rickinghall Suffolk 38 H6
Rickleton Tyne/Wear 58 A3
Rickling Essex 29 E11
Rickling Green Essex 30 F2
Rickmansworth Herts 19 B7
Riddings Cumb 61 F10
Riddings Derby 45 G8
Riddlecombe Devon 6 E5
Riddlesden W Yorks 51 E6
Riddrie C/Glasg 68 D5
Ridge Dorset 9 F8
Ridge Hants 10 C2
Ridge Wilts 9 A8
Ridge Green Surrey 19 G10
Ridge Lane Warwick 35 F8
Ridgebourne Powys 25 B7
Ridgeway Cross Heref'd 26 D4
Ridgewell Essex 30 D4
Ridgewood E Sussex 12 D3
Ridgmont Beds 28 E6
Riding Mill Northum 62 G6
Ridleywood Wrex 43 G6
Ridlington Norfolk 39 B9
Ridlington Rutl'd 36 E4
Ridsdale Northum 62 E5
Riechip Perth/Kinr 76 C3
Riemore Perth/Kinr 76 C3
Rienachait H'land 92 F3
Rievaulx N Yorks 59 H6
Rift House Hartlep'l 58 C5
Rigg Dumf/Gal 61 G8
Riggend N Lanarks 68 C6
Rigsby Lincs 47 E8
Rigside S Lanarks 69 G7
Riley Green Lancs 50 G2
Rileyhill Staffs 35 D7
Rilla Mill Cornw'l 4 D3
Rillington N Yorks 52 B4
Rimington Lancs 50 E4
Rimpton Som'set 8 B5
Rimswell ER Yorks 53 G9
Rinaston Pembs 22 D4
Ringasta Shetl'd 96 M5
Ringford Dumf/Gal 55 D9
Ringinglow S Yorks 44 D6
Ringland Norfolk 39 D7
Ringles Cross E Sussex 12 D3
Ringmer E Sussex 12 E3
Ringmore Devon 5 G7
Ringorm Moray 88 D2
Ring's End Cambs 37 E9
Ringsfield Suffolk 39 G10
Ringsfield Corner Suffolk 39 G10
Ringshall Herts 28 G6
Ringshall Suffolk 31 C7
Ringshall Stocks Suffolk 31 C7
Ringstead Norfolk 38 A3
Ringstead Northants 36 H5
Ringwood Hants 9 D10
Ringwould Kent 21 G10
Rinmore Aberds 82 B6

Rinnigill Orkney 95 J4
Rinsey Cornw'l 2 G4
Riof W Isles 90 D6
Ripe E Sussex 12 E4
Ripley Derby 45 G7
Ripley Hants 9 E10
Ripley N Yorks 51 C8
Ripley Surrey 19 F7
Riplingham ER Yorks 52 F5
Ripon N Yorks 51 B9
Rippingale Lincs 37 C6
Ripple Kent 21 G10
Ripple Worcs 26 E5
Ripponden W Yorks 50 H6
Rireavach H'land 86 B3
Risabus Arg/Bute 64 D4
Risbury Heref'd 26 C2
Risby Suffolk 30 B4
Risca = Rhisga Caerph 15 B8
Rise ER Yorks 53 E7
Riseden E Sussex 12 C5
Risegate Lincs 37 C8
Riseholme Lincs 46 E3
Riseley Beds 29 B7
Riseley Wokingham 18 E4
Rishangles Suffolk 31 B8
Rishton Lancs 50 F3
Rishworth W Yorks 50 H6
Rising Bridge Lancs 50 G3
Risley Derby 35 B10
Risley Warrington 43 C9
Risplith N Yorks 51 C8
Rispond H'land 92 C7
Rivar Wilts 17 E10
Rivenhall End Essex 30 G5
River Bank Cambs 30 B2
Riverhead Kent 20 F2
Rivington Lancs 43 A9
Roa Island Cumb 49 C2
Roachill Devon 7 D7
Road Green Norfolk 39 F8
Roade Northants 28 C4
Roadhead Cumb 61 F11
Roadmeetings S Lanarks 69 F7
Roadside H'land 94 D3
Roadside of Catterline Aberds 83 F10
Roadside of Kinneff Aberds 83 F10
Roadwater Som'set 7 C9
Roag H'land 85 D7
Roath Card 15 D7
Roberton Scot Borders 61 B10
Roberton S Lanarks 69 H8
Robertsbridge E Sussex 12 D6
Roberttown W Yorks 51 G7
Robeston Cross Pembs 22 F3
Robeston Wathen Pembs 22 E5
Robin Hood W Yorks 51 G9
Robin Hood's Bay N Yorks 59 F10
Roborough Devon 6 E4
Roborough Devon 4 E6
Roby Mersey 43 C7
Roby Mill Lancs 43 B8
Rocester Staffs 35 B7
Roch Pembs 22 D3
Roch Gate Pembs 22 D3
Rochdale Gtr Man 44 A2
Roche Cornw'l 3 C8
Rochester Medway 20 E4
Rochester Northum 62 D4
Rochford Essex 20 B5
Rock Cornw'l 3 B8
Rock Northum 63 A8
Rock Worcs 26 A4
Rock W Sussex 11 C10
Rock Ferry Mersey 42 D6
Rockbeare Devon 7 G9
Rockbourne Hants 9 C10
Rockcliffe Cumb 61 G9
Rockcliffe Dumf/Gal 55 D11
Rockfield H'land 87 C12
Rockfield Monmouths 25 G11
Rockford Hants 9 D10
Rockhampton S Gloucs 16 B3
Rockingham Northants 36 F4
Rockland All Saints Norfolk 38 F5
Rockland St Mary Norfolk 39 E9
Rockland St Peter Norfolk 38 F5
Rockley Wilts 17 D8
Rockwell End Bucks 18 C4
Rockwell Green Som'set 7 D10
Rodborough Glos 16 A5
Rodbourne Swindon 17 C8
Rodbourne Wilts 16 C6
Rodbourne Cheney Swindon 17 C8
Rodd Heref'd 25 B10
Roddam Northum 62 A6
Rodden Dorset 8 F5
Rode Som'set 16 F5
Rode Heath Ches 44 G2
Rodeheath Ches 44 F2
Roden Telford 34 D1
Rodhuish Som'set 7 C9
Rodington Telford 34 D1
Rodley Glos 26 G4
Rodley W Yorks 51 F8
Rodmarton Glos 16 B6
Rodmell E Sussex 12 F3
Rodmersham Kent 20 E6
Rodney Stoke Som'set 15 F10
Rodsley Derby 35 A8
Rodway Som'set 15 H8
Rodwell Dorset 8 G5
Roe Green Herts 29 E10
Roecliffe N Yorks 51 C9
Roehampton London 19 D9
Roesound Shetl'd 96 G5
Roffey W Sussex 11 A10
Rogart H'land 93 J10
Rogart Station H'land 93 J10
Rogate W Sussex 11 B7
Rogerstone Newp 15 C8
Roghadal W Isles 90 J5
Rogiet Monmouths 15 C10
Rogue's Alley Cambs 37 E9
Roke Oxon 18 B3
Roker Tyne/Wear 63 H10
Rollesby Norfolk 39 D10
Rolleston Leics 36 E3
Rolleston Notts 45 G11
Rolleston-on-Dove Staffs 35 C8
Rolston ER Yorks 53 E8
Rolvenden Kent 13 C7
Rolvenden Layne Kent 13 C7
Romaldkirk Durham 57 D11
Romanby N Yorks 58 G4
Romannobridge Scot Borders 69 F10
Romansleigh Devon 7 D6
Romford London 20 C2
Romiley Gtr Man 44 C3
Romsey Hants 10 B2
Romsey Town Cambs 29 C11
Romsley Shrops 34 G3
Romsley Worcs 34 H5
Ronague I/Man 48 E2
Rookhope Durham 57 B11
Rookley I/Wight 10 F4
Rooks Bridge Som'set 15 F9
Roos ER Yorks 53 F8
Roosebeck Cumb 49 C2
Rootham's Green Beds 29 C8
Rootpark S Lanarks 69 E8
Ropley Hants 10 A5
Ropley Dean Hants 10 A5
Ropsley Lincs 36 B5
Rora Aberds 89 C10
Rorandle Aberds 83 B8
Rorrington Shrops 33 E9
Roscroggan Cornw'l 2 E5
Rose Cornw'l 3 D6
Rose Ash Devon 7 D6
Rose Green W Sussex 11 E8
Rose Grove Lancs 50 F4
Rose Hill E Sussex 12 E3
Rose Hill Lancs 50 F4
Rose Hill Suffolk 31 D8
Roseacre Kent 20 F4
Roseacre Lancs 49 F4
Rosebank S Lanarks 69 F7
Rosebrough Northum 71 H10
Rosebush Pembs 22 D5
Rosecare Cornw'l 4 B2
Rosedale Abbey N Yorks 59 G8
Roseden Northum 62 A6
Rosefield H'land 87 F11
Rosehall H'land 92 J7
Rosehaugh Mains H'land 87 F9
Rosehearty Aberds 89 B9
Rosehill Shrops 34 B2
Roseisle Moray 88 B1
Roselands E Sussex 12 F5
Rosemarket Pembs 22 F4
Rosemarkie H'land 87 F10
Rosemary Lane Devon 7 E10
Rosemount Perth/Kinr 76 C4
Rosenannon Cornw'l 3 C8
Rosewell Midloth 69 D11
Roseworth Stockton 58 D5
Roseworthy Cornw'l 2 F5
Rosgill Cumb 57 E7
Roshven H'land 79 D10
Roskhill H'land 85 D7
Roskill House H'land 87 F9
Rosley Cumb 56 B5
Roslin Midloth 69 D11
Rosliston Derby 35 D8
Rosneath Arg/Bute 73 E11
Ross Dumf/Gal 55 E9
Ross Northum 71 G10
Ross Perth/Kinr 75 E10
Ross-on-Wye Heref'd 26 F3
Rossett Wrex 42 G6
Rossett Green N Yorks 51 D9
Rossie Ochill Perth/Kinr 76 F3
Rossie Priory Perth/Kinr 76 D5
Rossington S Yorks 45 C10
Rosskeen H'land 87 E9
Rossland Renf 68 C3
Roster H'land 94 G4
Rostherne Ches 43 D10
Rosthwaite Cumb 56 E4
Roston Derby 35 A7
Rosyth Fife 69 B10
Rothbury Northum 62 C6
Rotherby Leics 36 D2
Rotherfield E Sussex 12 D4
Rotherfield Greys Oxon 18 C4
Rotherfield Peppard Oxon 18 C4
Rotherham S Yorks 45 C8
Rothersthorpe Northants 28 C4
Rotherwick Hants 18 F4
Rothes Moray 88 D2
Rothesay Arg/Bute 73 G9
Rothiebrisbane Aberds 89 E7
Rothienorman Aberds 89 E7
Rothiesholm Orkney 95 F7
Rothley Leics 36 D1
Rothley Northum 62 E6
Rothley Shield East Northum 62 D6
Rothmaise Aberds 89 E6
Rothwell Lincs 46 C5
Rothwell Northants 36 G4
Rothwell W Yorks 51 G9
Rothwell Haigh W Yorks 51 G9
Rotsea ER Yorks 53 D6
Rottal Angus 82 G5
Rotten End Suffolk 31 B10
Rottingdean Brighton/Hove 12 F2
Rottington Cumb 56 E1
Roud I/Wight 10 F4
Rough Close Staffs 34 B5
Rough Common Kent 21 F8
Rougham Norfolk 38 C4
Rougham Suffolk 30 B6
Rougham Green Suffolk 30 B6
Roughburn H'land 80 E5
Roughlee Lancs 50 E4
Roughley W Midlands 35 F7
Roughsike Cumb 61 F11
Roughton Lincs 46 F6
Roughton Norfolk 39 B8
Roughton Shrops 34 F3
Roughton Moor Lincs 46 F6
Roundhay W Yorks 51 F9
Roundstonefoot Dumf/Gal 61 C7
Roundstreet Common W Sussex 11 B9
Roundway Wilts 17 E7
Rous Lench Worcs 27 C7
Rousdon Devon 8 E1
Routenburn N Ayrs 73 G10
Routh ER Yorks 53 E6
Row Cornw'l 4 D1
Row Cumb 56 H6
Row Heath Essex 31 G8
Rowanburn Dumf/Gal 61 F10
Rowardennan Stirl 74 H6
Rowde Wilts 16 E6
Rowen Conwy 41 C9
Rowfoot Northum 62 G2
Rowhedge Essex 31 F7
Rowhook W Sussex 11 A10
Rowington Warwick 27 B9
Rowland Derby 44 E6
Rowland's Castle Hants 10 C6
Rowlands Gill Tyne/Wear 63 H7
Rowledge Surrey 18 G5
Rowley ER Yorks 52 F5
Rowley Shrops 33 E9
Rowley Hill W Yorks 44 A5
Rowley Regis W Midlands 34 G5
Rowlstone Heref'd 25 F10
Rowly Surrey 19 G7
Rowney Green Worcs 27 A7
Rownhams Hants 10 C2
Rowrah Cumb 56 E2
Rowsham Bucks 28 G5
Rowsley Derby 44 F6
Rowstock Oxon 17 C11
Rowston Lincs 46 G4
Rowton Ches 43 F7
Rowton Shrops 33 D9
Rowton Telford 34 D2
Roxburgh Scot Borders 70 G6
Roxby N Lincs 52 H5
Roxby N Yorks 59 E8
Roxton Beds 29 C8
Roxwell Essex 30 H3
Royal Leamington Spa Warwick 27 B10
Royal Oak D'lington 58 D3
Royal Oak Lancs 43 B7
Royal Tunbridge Wells Kent 12 C4
Roybridge H'land 80 E4
Roydhouse W Yorks 44 A6
Roydon Essex 29 H11
Roydon Norfolk 38 C3
Roydon Norfolk 39 G7
Roydon Hamlet Essex 29 H11
Royston Herts 29 D10
Royston S Yorks 45 A7
Royton Gtr Man 44 B3
Rozel Jersey 11
Ruabon = Rhiwabon Wrex 33 A9
Ruaig Arg/Bute 78 G3
Ruan Lanihorne Cornw'l 3 E7
Ruan Minor Cornw'l 2 H6
Ruarach H'land 80 A1
Ruardean Glos 26 G3
Ruardean Woodside Glos 26 G3
Rubery Worcs 34 H5
Ruckcroft Cumb 57 B7
Ruckhall Common Heref'd 25 E11
Ruckinge Kent 13 C9
Ruckland Lincs 47 E7
Ruckley Shrops 33 E11
Rudbaxton Pembs 22 D4
Rudby N Yorks 58 F5
Ruddington Notts 36 B1
Rudford Glos 26 F4
Rudge Shrops 34 F4
Rudge Som'set 16 F5
Rudgeway S Gloucs 16 C3
Rudgwick W Sussex 11 A9
Rudhall Heref'd 26 F3
Rudheath Ches 43 E9
Rudley Green Essex 20 A5
Rudry Caerph 15 C7
Rudston ER Yorks 53 C6
Rudyard Staffs 44 G3
Rufford Lancs 49 H4
Rufforth C/York 51 D11
Rugby Warwick 35 H11
Rugeley Staffs 34 D6
Ruglen S Ayrs 66 F5
Ruilick H'land 87 G8
Ruishton Som'set 8 B1
Ruisigearraidh W Isles 90 J4
Ruislip London 19 C7
Ruislip Common London 19 C7
Rumbling Bridge Perth/Kinr 76 H3
Rumburgh Suffolk 39 G9
Rumford Cornw'l 3 B7
Rumney Card 15 D8
Runcorn Halton 43 D8
Runcton W Sussex 11 D7
Runcton Holme Norfolk 38 E2
Rundlestone Devon 5 D6
Runfold Surrey 18 G5
Runhall Norfolk 39 E6
Runham Norfolk 39 E11
Runham Norfolk 39 D10
Runnington Som'set 7 D10
Runsell Green Essex 30 H4
Runswick Bay N Yorks 59 E9
Runwell Essex 20 B4
Ruscombe Wokingham 18 D4
Rush Green London 20 C2
Rush-head Aberds 89 D8
Rushall Heref'd 26 E3
Rushall Norfolk 39 G7
Rushall Wilts 17 F8
Rushall W Midlands 34 E6
Rushbrooke Suffolk 30 B5
Rushbury Shrops 33 F11
Rushden Herts 29 E10
Rushden Northants 28 B6
Rushenden Kent 20 D6
Rushford Norfolk 38 G5
Rushlake Green E Sussex 12 E5
Rushmere Suffolk 39 G10
Rushmere St Andrew Suffolk 31 D9
Rushmoor Surrey 18 G5
Rushmoor Wilts 9 C8
Rushock Worcs 26 A5
Rusholme Gtr Man 44 C2
Rushton Ches 43 F8
Rushton Northants 36 G4
Rushton Shrops 34 E2
Rushton Spencer Staffs 44 F3
Rushwick Worcs 26 C5
Rushyford Durham 58 D3
Ruskie Stirl 75 G9
Ruskington Lincs 46 G4
Rusland Cumb 56 H5
Rusper W Sussex 19 H9
Ruspidge Glos 26 G3
Russell's Water Oxon 18 C4
Russel's Green Suffolk 31 A9
Rusthall Kent 12 C4
Rustington W Sussex 11 D9
Ruston N Yorks 52 A5
Ruston Parva ER Yorks 53 C6
Ruswarp N Yorks 59 F9
Rutherford Scot Borders 70 G5
Rutherglen S Lanarks 68 D5
Ruthernbridge Cornw'l 3 C9
Ruthin = Rhuthun Denb 42 G4
Ruthrieston Aberd C 83 C11
Ruthven Aberds 88 D5
Ruthven Angus 76 C5
Ruthven H'land 87 H11
Ruthven H'land 81 D9
Ruthven House Angus 76 C6
Ruthvoes Cornw'l 3 C8
Ruthwell Dumf/Gal 60 G6
Ruyton-XI-Towns Shrops 33 C9
Ryal Northum 62 F6
Ryal Fold Blackb'n 50 G2
Ryall Dorset 8 E3
Ryarsh Kent 20 F3
Rydal Cumb 56 F5
Ryde I/Wight 10 E4
Rye E Sussex 13 D8
Rye Foreign E Sussex 13 D7
Rye Harbour E Sussex 13 E8
Rye Park Herts 29 G10
Rye Street Worcs 26 E4
Ryecroft Gate Staffs 44 F3
Ryehill ER Yorks 53 G8
Ryhall Rutl'd 36 D6
Ryhill W Yorks 45 A7
Ryhope Tyne/Wear 58 A5
Rylstone N Yorks 50 D5
Ryme Intrinseca Dorset 8 C4
Ryther N Yorks 52 F1
Ryton Glos 26 E4
Ryton N Yorks 52 B3
Ryton Shrops 34 E3
Ryton Tyne/Wear 63 G7
Ryton-on-Dunsmore Warwick 27 A10

S

Sabden Lancs 50 F3
Sacombe Herts 29 G10
Sacriston Durham 58 B3
Sadberge D'lington 58 E4
Saddell Arg/Bute 65 E8
Saddington Leics 36 F2
Saddle Bow Norfolk 38 D2
Saddlescombe W Sussex 12 E1
Sadgill Cumb 57 F6
Saffron Walden Essex 30 E2
Sageston Pembs 22 F5
Saham Hills Norfolk 38 E5
Saham Toney Norfolk 38 E5
Saighdinis W Isles 84 B3
Saighton Ches 43 F7
St Abb's Scot Borders 71 D8
St Abb's Haven Scot Borders 71 D8
St Agnes Cornw'l 2 D6
St Agnes I/Scilly 2 D2
St Albans Herts 29 H8
St Allen Cornw'l 3 D7
St Andrews Fife 77 F8
St Andrew's Major V/Glam 15 D7
St Anne Alderney 11
St Annes Lancs 49 G3
St Ann's Dumf/Gal 60 D6
St Ann's Chapel Cornw'l 4 D5
St Ann's Chapel Devon 5 G7
St Anthony Cornw'l 3 G6
St Anthony's Hill E Sussex 12 F5
St Arvans Monmouths 15 B11
St Asaph = Llanelwy Denbs 42 E3
St Athan V/Glam 14 E6
St Aubin Jersey 11
St Austell Cornw'l 3 D9
St Bees Cumb 56 E1
St Blazey Cornw'l 4 F1
St Boswells Scot Borders 70 G4
St Brelade Jersey 11
St Breock Cornw'l 3 B8
St Breward Cornw'l 4 D1
St Briavels Glos 16 A2
St Bride's Pembs 22 E3
St Brides Major V/Glam 14 D4
St Bride's Netherwent Monmouths 15 C10
St Brides super Ely V/Glam 14 D6
St Brides Wentlooge Newp 15 C8
St Budeaux Plym'th 4 F5
St Buryan Cornw'l 2 G3
St Catherine Bath/NE Som'set 16 D4
St Catherine's Arg/Bute 73 C10
St Clears = Sanclêr Carms 23 E7
St Cleer Cornw'l 4 E3
St Clement Cornw'l 3 E7
St Clements Jersey 11
St Clether Cornw'l 4 C3
St Colmac Arg/Bute 73 G9
St Columb Major Cornw'l 3 C8
St Columb Minor Cornw'l 3 C7
St Columb Road Cornw'l 3 D8
St Combs Aberds 89 B10
St Cross South Elmham Suffolk 39 G8
St Cyrus Aberds 77 A10
St David's Perth/Kinr 76 E2
St David's = Tyddewi Pembs 22 D2
St Day Cornw'l 2 E6
St Dennis Cornw'l 3 D8
St Devereux Heref'd 25 E11
St Dogmaels Pembs 22 B6
St Dogwells Pembs 22 D4
St Dominick Cornw'l 4 E5
St Donat's V/Glam 14 E5
St Edith's Wilts 16 E6
St Endellion Cornw'l 3 B8
St Enoder Cornw'l 3 D7
St Erme Cornw'l 3 D7
St Erney Cornw'l 4 F4
St Erth Cornw'l 2 F4
St Ervan Cornw'l 3 B7
St Eval Cornw'l 3 C7
St Ewe Cornw'l 3 E8
St Fagans Card 15 D7
St Fergus Aberds 89 C10
St Fillans Perth/Kinr 75 E9
St Florence Pembs 22 F5
St Genny's Cornw'l 4 B2
St George Conwy 42 E2
St George's V/Glam 14 D6
St Germans Cornw'l 4 F4
St Giles Lincs 46 E3
St Giles in the Wood Devon 6 E4
St Giles on the Heath Devon 6 G2
St Harmon Powys 24 A6
St Helen Auckland Durham 58 D2
St Helena Warwick 35 E8
St Helen's E Sussex 13 E7
St Helens I/Wight 10 F5
St Helens Mersey 43 C8
St Helier London 19 E9
St Helier Jersey 11
St Hilary Cornw'l 2 F4
St Hilary V/Glam 14 D6
Saint Hill W Sussex 12 C2
St Illtyd Bl Gwent 15 A8
St Ippollitts Herts 29 F8
St Ishmael's Pembs 22 F3
St Issey Cornw'l 3 B8
St Ive Cornw'l 4 E4
St Ives Cambs 29 A10
St Ives Cornw'l 2 E4
St Ives Dorset 9 D10
St James South Elmham Suffolk 39 G9
St Jidgey Cornw'l 3 C8
St John Cornw'l 4 F5
St John's I/Man 48 D2
St John's Jersey 11
St John's Surrey 18 F6
St John's Worcs 26 C5
St John's Chapel Durham 57 C10
St John's Fen End Norfolk 37 D11
St John's Highway Norfolk 37 D11
St John's Town of Dalry Dumf/Gal 55 A9
St Judes I/Man 48 C3
St Just Cornw'l 2 F2
St Just in Roseland Cornw'l 3 F7
St Katherine's Aberds 89 E7
St Keverne Cornw'l 3 G6
St Kew Cornw'l 3 B9
St Kew Highway Cornw'l 3 B9
St Keyne Cornw'l 4 E3
St Lawrence Cornw'l 3 C9
St Lawrence Essex 20 A6
St Lawrence I/Wight 10 G4
St Leonard's Bucks 28 H6
St Leonards Dorset 9 D10
St Leonards E Sussex 13 F6
Saint Leonards S Lanarks 68 E5
St Levan Cornw'l 2 G2
St Lythans V/Glam 15 D7
St Mabyn Cornw'l 3 B9
St Madoes Perth/Kinr 76 E4
St Margaret South Elmham Suffolk 39 G9
St Margaret's Heref'd 25 E10
St Margarets Herts 29 G10
St Margaret's at Cliffe Kent 21 G10
St Margaret's Hope Orkney 95 J5
St Mark's I/Man 48 E2
St Martin Cornw'l 4 F3
St Martins Cornw'l 2 G6
St Martin's Jersey 11
St Martins Perth/Kinr 76 D4
St Martin's Shrops 33 B9
St Mary Bourne Hants 17 F11
St Mary Church V/Glam 14 D6
St Mary Cray London 19 E11
St Mary Hill V/Glam 14 D5
St Mary Hoo Medway 20 D5
St Mary in the Marsh Kent 13 D9
St Mary's Jersey 11
St Mary's Orkney 95 H5
St Mary's Bay Kent 13 D9
St Maughans Monmouths 25 G11
St Mawes Cornw'l 3 F7
St Mawgan Cornw'l 3 C7
St Mellion Cornw'l 4 E4
St Mellons Card 15 C8
St Merryn Cornw'l 3 B7
St Mewan Cornw'l 3 D8
St Michael Caerhays Cornw'l 3 E8
St Michael Penkevil Cornw'l 3 E7
St Michael South Elmham Suffolk 39 G9
St Michael's Kent 13 C7
St Michaels Worcs 26 B2
St Michael's on Wyre Lancs 49 E4
St Minver Cornw'l 3 B8
St Monans Fife 77 G8
St Neot Cornw'l 4 E2
St Neots Cambs 29 B8
St Newlyn East Cornw'l 3 D7
St Nicholas Pembs 22 C3
St Nicholas V/Glam 14 D6
St Nicholas at Wade Kent 21 E9
St Ninians Stirl 68 A6
St Osyth Essex 31 G8
St Osyth Heath Essex 31 G8
St Ouens Jersey 11
St Owens Cross Heref'd 26 F2
St Paul's Cray London 19 E11
St Paul's Walden Herts 29 F8
St Peter Port Guernsey 11
St Peter's Jersey 11
St Peter's Kent 21 E10
St Petrox Pembs 22 G4
St Pinnock Cornw'l 4 E3
St Quivox S Ayrs 67 D6
St Ruan Cornw'l 2 H6
St Sampson Guernsey 11
St Stephen Cornw'l 3 D8
St Stephen's Cornw'l 4 C4
St Stephens Cornw'l 4 F5
St Stephens Herts 29 H8
St Teath Cornw'l 4 C1
St Thomas Devon 7 G8
St Tudy Cornw'l 4 D1
St Twynnells Pembs 22 G4
St Veep Cornw'l 4 F2
St Vigeans Angus 77 C9
St Wenn Cornw'l 3 C8
St Weonards Heref'd 25 F11
Saintbury Glos 27 E8
Salcombe Devon 5 H8
Salcombe Regis Devon 7 H10
Salcott Essex 30 G6
Sale Gtr Man 43 C10
Sale Green Worcs 26 C6
Saleby Lincs 47 E8
Salehurst E Sussex 12 D6
Salem Ceredig'n 32 G2
Salem Carms 24 F3
Salen Arg/Bute 79 G8
Salen H'land 79 E9
Salesbury Lancs 50 F2
Salford Beds 28 E6
Salford Gtr Man 44 C2
Salford Oxon 27 F9
Salford Priors Warwick 27 C7
Salfords Surrey 19 G9
Salhouse Norfolk 39 D9
Saline Fife 69 A9
Salisbury Wilts 9 B10
Sallachan H'land 74 A2
Sallachy H'land 86 H2
Sallachy H'land 93 J8
Salle Norfolk 39 C7
Salmonby Lincs 47 E7
Salmond's Muir Angus 77 D8
Salperton Glos 27 F7
Salph End Beds 29 C7
Salsburgh N Lanarks 69 D7
Salt Staffs 34 C5
Salt End ER Yorks 53 G7
Saltaire W Yorks 51 F7
Saltash Cornw'l 4 F5
Saltburn H'land 87 E10
Saltburn-by-the-Sea Redcar/Clevel'd 59 D7
Saltby Leics 36 C4
Saltcoats Cumb 56 G2
Saltcoats N Ayrs 66 B5
Saltdean Brighton/Hove 12 F2
Salter Lancs 50 C2
Salterforth Lancs 50 E4
Salterswall Ches 43 F9
Saltfleet Lincs 47 C8
Saltfleetby All Saints Lincs 47 C8
Saltfleetby St Clements Lincs 47 C8
Saltfleetby St Peter Lincs 47 D8
Saltford Bath/NE Som'set 16 E3
Salthouse Norfolk 39 A6
Saltmarshe ER Yorks 52 G3
Saltney Flints 43 F6
Salton N Yorks 52 B3
Saltwick Northum 63 F7
Saltwood Kent 21 H8
Salum Arg/Bute 78 G3
Salvington W Sussex 11 D10
Salwarpe Worcs 26 B5
Salway Ash Dorset 8 E3
Sambourne Warwick 27 B7
Sambrook Telford 34 C3
Samhla W Isles 84 B2
Samlesbury Lancs 50 F1
Samlesbury Bottoms Lancs 50 G2
Sampford Arundel Som'set 7 E10
Sampford Brett Som'set 7 B9
Sampford Courtenay Devon 6 F5
Sampford Peverell Devon 7 E9
Sampford Spiney Devon 4 D6
Sampool Bridge Cumb 56 H6
Samuelston E Loth 70 C3
Sanachan H'land 85 D13
Sanaigmore Arg/Bute 64 A3
Sanclêr = St Clears Carms 23 E7
Sancreed Cornw'l 2 G3
Sancton ER Yorks 52 F5
Sand H'land 86 B2
Sand Shetl'd 96 J5
Sand Hole ER Yorks 52 F4
Sand Hutton N Yorks 52 D2
Sandaig H'land 85 H12
Sandal Magna W Yorks 51 H9
Sandale Cumb 56 B4
Sandbach Ches 43 F10
Sandbank Arg/Bute 73 E10
Sandbanks Poole 9 F9
Sandend Aberds 88 B5
Sanderstead London 19 E10
Sandfields Glos 26 F6
Sandford Cumb 57 E9
Sandford Devon 7 F7
Sandford Dorset 9 F8
Sandford I/Wight 10 F4
Sandford N Som'set 15 F10
Sandford Shrops 34 B1
Sandford S Lanarks 68 F6
Sandford on Thames Oxon 18 A2
Sandford Orcas Dorset 8 B5
Sandford St Martin Oxon 27 F11
Sandfordhill Aberds 89 D11
Sandgate Kent 21 H8
Sandgreen Dumf/Gal 55 D8
Sandhaven Aberds 89 B9
Sandhead Dumf/Gal 54 E3
Sandhills Surrey 18 H6
Sandhoe Northum 62 G5
Sandholme ER Yorks 52 F4
Sandholme Lincs 37 B9
Sandhurst Bracknl'l 18 E5
Sandhurst Glos 26 F5
Sandhurst Kent 13 D6
Sandhurst Cross Kent 13 D6
Sandhutton N Yorks 51 A9
Sandiacre Derby 35 B10
Sandilands Lincs 47 D9
Sandilands S Lanarks 69 G7
Sandiway Ches 43 E9
Sandleheath Hants 9 C10
Sandling Kent 20 F4
Sandlow Green Ches 43 F10
Sandness Shetl'd 96 H3
Sandon Essex 20 A4
Sandon Herts 29 E10
Sandon Staffs 34 B5
Sandown I/Wight 10 F4
Sandplace Cornw'l 4 F3
Sandridge Herts 29 G8
Sandridge Wilts 16 E6
Sandringham Norfolk 38 C2
Sandsend N Yorks 59 E9
Sandside Ho. H'land 93 C12
Sandsound Shetl'd 96 J5
Sandtoft N Lincs 45 B11
Sandway Kent 20 F5
Sandwell W Midlands 34 G6
Sandwich Kent 21 F10
Sandwick Cumb 56 E6
Sandwick Orkney 95 K5
Sandwick Shetl'd 96 L6
Sandwith Cumb 56 E1
Sandy Beds 29 D8
Sandy Carms 23 F9
Sandy Bank Lincs 46 G6
Sandy Haven Pembs 22 F3
Sandy Lane Wilts 16 E6
Sandy Lane Wrex 33 A9
Sandycroft Flints 42 F6
Sandyford Dumf/Gal 61 D8
Sandyford Stoke 44 G2
Sandygate I/Man 48 C3
Sandyhills Dumf/Gal 55 D11
Sandylands Lancs 49 C4
Sandypark Devon 5 C8
Sandysike Cumb 61 G9
Sangobeg H'land 92 C7
Sangomore H'land 92 C7
Sanna H'land 78 E7
Sanndabhaig W Isles 91 D9
Sanndabhaig W Isles 84 D3
Sannox N Ayrs 66 B3
Sanquhar Dumf/Gal 60 C3
Santon N Lincs 46 A3
Santon Bridge Cumb 56 F3
Santon Downham Suffolk 38 G4
Sapcote Leics 35 F10
Sapey Common Heref'd 26 B4
Sapiston Suffolk 38 H5
Sapley Cambs 29 A9
Sapperton Glos 16 A6
Sapperton Lincs 36 B6
Saracen's Head Lincs 37 C9
Sarclet H'land 94 F5
Sardis Carms 23 F10
Sarn Bridg 14 C5
Sarn Powys 33 F8
Sarn Bach Gwyn 40 H5
Sarn Meyllteyrn Gwyn 40 G4
Sarnau Ceredig'n 23 A8
Sarnau Carms 23 E8
Sarnau Gwyn 32 B5
Sarnau Powys 25 E7
Sarnau Powys 33 D8
Sarnesfield Heref'd 25 C10
Saron Carms 23 E8
Saron Carms 24 G3
Saron Denbs 42 F3
Saron Gwyn 41 D7
Saron Gwyn 40 E6
Sarratt Herts 19 B7
Sarre Kent 21 E9
Sarsden Oxon 27 F9
Sarsgrum H'land 92 C6
Satley Durham 58 B2
Satron N Yorks 57 G11
Satterleigh Devon 6 D5
Satterthwaite Cumb 56 G5
Satwell Oxon 18 C4
Sauchen Aberds 83 B8
Saucher Perth/Kinr 76 D4
Sauchie Clack 69 A7
Sauchieburn Aberds 83 G8
Saughall Ches 42 E6
Saughtree Scot Borders 61 D11
Saul Glos 26 H4
Saundby Notts 45 D11
Saundersfoot Pembs 22 F6
Saunderton Bucks 18 A4
Saunton Devon 6 C3
Sausthorpe Lincs 47 F7
Saval H'land 93 J8
Savary H'land 79 G9
Savile Park W Yorks 51 G6
Sawbridge Warwick 28 B2
Sawbridgeworth Herts 29 G11
Sawdon N Yorks 59 H10
Sawley Derby 35 B10
Sawley Lancs 50 E3
Sawley N Yorks 51 C8
Sawston Cambs 29 D11
Sawtry Cambs 37 G7
Saxby Leics 36 D4
Saxby Lincs 46 D4
Saxby All Saints N Lincs 52 H5
Saxelbye Leics 36 C3
Saxham Street Suffolk 31 B7
Saxilby Lincs 46 E2
Saxlingham Norfolk 38 B6
Saxlingham Green Norfolk 39 F8
Saxlingham Nethergate Norfolk 39 F8
Saxlingham Thorpe Norfolk 39 F8
Saxmundham Suffolk 31 B10
Saxon Street Cambs 30 C3
Saxondale Notts 36 B2
Saxtead Suffolk 31 B9
Saxtead Green Suffolk 31 B9
Saxthorpe Norfolk 39 B7
Saxton N Yorks 51 F10
Sayers Common W Sussex 12 E1
Scackleton N Yorks 52 B2
Scadabhagh W Isles 90 H6
Scaftworth Notts 45 C10
Scagglethorpe N Yorks 52 B4
Scaitcliffe Lancs 50 G3
Scalasaig Arg/Bute 72 D2
Scalby ER Yorks 52 G4
Scalby N Yorks 59 G11
Scaldwell Northants 28 A4
Scale Houses Cumb 57 B7
Scaleby Cumb 61 G10
Scaleby Hill Cumb 61 G10
Scales Cumb 49 B2
Scales Cumb 56 D5
Scales Lancs 49 F4
Scalford Leics 36 C3
Scaling N Yorks 59 E8
Scaling Dam Redcar/Clevel'd 59 E8
Scallastle Arg/Bute 79 H9
Scalloway Shetl'd 96 K6
Scalpay W Isles 90 H7
Scalpay Ho. H'land 85 F11
Scalpsie Arg/Bute 73 H9
Scamadale H'land 79 B10
Scamblesby Lincs 46 E6
Scamodale H'land 79 D11
Scampston N Yorks 52 B4
Scampton Lincs 46 E3
Scapa Orkney 95 H5
Scapegoat Hill W Yorks 51 H6
Scar Orkney 95 D7
Scarborough N Yorks 59 H11
Scarcliffe Derby 45 F8
Scarcroft W Yorks 51 E9
Scarcroft Hill W Yorks 51 E9
Scardroy H'land 86 F5
Scarff Shetl'd 96 E4
Scarfskerry H'land 94 C4
Scargill Durham 58 E1
Scarinish Arg/Bute 78 G3
Scarisbrick Lancs 43 A6
Scarning Norfolk 38 D5
Scarrington Notts 36 A3
Scartho NE Lincs 46 B6
Scarwell Orkney 95 F3
Scatness Shetl'd 96 M5
Scatraig H'land 87 H10
Scawby N Lincs 46 B3
Scawsby S Yorks 45 B9
Scawton N Yorks 51 A11
Scayne's Hill W Sussex 12 D2
Scethrog Powys 25 F8
Scholar Green Ches 44 G2
Scholes W Yorks 44 B5
Scholes W Yorks 51 G7
Scholes W Yorks 51 F9
School Green Ches 43 F9
Scleddau Pembs 22 C4
Sco Ruston Norfolk 39 C8
Scofton Notts 45 D10
Scole Norfolk 39 H7
Scolpaig W Isles 84 A2
Scone Perth/Kinr 76 E4
Sconser H'land 85 E10
Scoonie Fife 76 G6
Scoor Arg/Bute 78 K7
Scopwick Lincs 46 G4
Scoraig H'land 86 B3
Scorborough ER Yorks 52 E6
Scorrier Cornw'l 2 E6
Scorton Lancs 49 E5
Scorton N Yorks 58 F3
Scotbheinn W Isles 84 C3
Scotby Cumb 61 H10
Scotch Corner N Yorks 58 F3
Scotforth Lancs 49 D4
Scothern Lincs 46 E4
Scotland Gate Northum 63 E8
Scotlandwell Perth/Kinr 76 G4
Scotsburn H'land 87 D10
Scotscalder Station H'land 94 E2
Scotscraig Fife 77 E7
Scots' Gap Northum 62 E6
Scotston Aberds 83 F9
Scotston Perth/Kinr 76 C2
Scotstoun C/Glasg 68 D4
Scotstown H'land 79 E11
Scotswood Tyne/Wear 63 G7
Scottas H'land 85 H12
Scotter Lincs 46 B2
Scotterthorpe Lincs 46 B2
Scottlethorpe Lincs 37 C6
Scotton Lincs 46 C2
Scotton N Yorks 58 G2
Scotton N Yorks 51 D9
Scottow Norfolk 39 C8
Scoughall E Loth 70 B5
Scoulag Arg/Bute 73 H10
Scoulton Norfolk 38 E5
Scourie H'land 92 E4
Scourie More H'land 92 E4
Scousburgh Shetl'd 96 M5
Scrabster H'land 94 C2
Scrafield Lincs 47 F7
Scrainwood Northum 62 C5
Scrane End Lincs 37 A9
Scraptoft Leics 36 E2
Scratby Norfolk 39 D11
Scrayingham N Yorks 52 C3
Scredington Lincs 37 A6
Scremby Lincs 47 F8
Scremerston Northum 71 F9
Screveton Notts 36 A3
Scrivelsby Lincs 46 F6
Scriven N Yorks 51 D9
Scrooby Notts 45 C10
Scropton Derby 35 B7
Scrub Hill Lincs 46 G6
Scruton N Yorks 58 G3
Sculcoates Kingston/Hull 53 F6
Sculthorpe Norfolk 38 B4
Scunthorpe N Lincs 46 A2
Scurlage Swan 23 H9
Sea Palling Norfolk 39 C10
Seaborough Dorset 8 D3
Seacombe Mersey 42 C6
Seacroft Lincs 47 F9
Seacroft W Yorks 51 F9
Seadyke Lincs 37 B9
Seafield S Ayrs 66 D6
Seafield W Loth 69 D9
Seaford E Sussex 12 G3
Seaforth Mersey 42 C6
Seagrave Leics 36 D2
Seaham Durham 58 B5
Seahouses Northum 71 G11
Seal Kent 20 F2
Sealand Flints 42 F6
Seale Surrey 18 G5
Seamer N Yorks 58 E5
Seamer N Yorks 52 A6
Seamill N Ayrs 66 B5
Searby Lincs 46 B4
Seasalter Kent 21 E7
Seascale Cumb 56 F2
Seathorne Lincs 47 F9
Seathwaite Cumb 56 G4
Seathwaite Cumb 56 E4
Seatoller Cumb 56 E4
Seaton Cornw'l 4 F4
Seaton Cumb 56 C2
Seaton Devon 8 F1
Seaton Durham 58 A4
Seaton ER Yorks 53 E7
Seaton Northum 63 F9
Seaton Rutl'd 36 F5
Seaton Burn Tyne/Wear 63 F8
Seaton Carew Hartlep'l 58 D6
Seaton Delaval Northum 63 F9
Seaton Ross ER Yorks 52 E3
Seaton Sluice Northum 63 F9
Seatown Aberds 88 B5
Seatown Dorset 8 E3
Seave Green N Yorks 59 F6
Seaview I/Wight 10 E5
Seaville Cumb 56 A3
Seavington St Mary Som'set 8 C3
Seavington St Michael Som'set 8 C3
Sebergham Cumb 56 B5
Seckington Warwick 35 E8
Second Coast H'land 86 B2
Sedbergh Cumb 57 G8
Sedbury Glos 15 B11
Sedbusk N Yorks 57 G10
Sedgeberrow Worcs 27 E7
Sedgebrook Lincs 36 B4
Sedgefield Durham 58 D4
Sedgeford Norfolk 38 B3
Sedgehill Wilts 9 B7
Sedgley W Midlands 34 F5
Sedgwick Cumb 57 H7
Sedlescombe E Sussex 13 E6
Sedlescombe Street E Sussex 13 E6
Seend Wilts 16 E6
Seend Cleeve Wilts 16 E6
Seer Green Bucks 18 B6
Seething Norfolk 39 F9
Sefton Mersey 42 B6
Seghill Northum 63 F8
Seifton Shrops 33 G10
Seighford Staffs 34 C4
Seilebost W Isles 90 H5
Seion Gwyn 41 D7
Seisdon Staffs 34 F4
Seisiadar W Isles 91 D10
Selattyn Shrops 33 B8
Selborne Hants 10 A6
Selby N Yorks 52 F2
Selham W Sussex 11 B8
Selhurst London 19 E10
Selkirk Scot Borders 70 H3
Sellack Heref'd 26 F2
Sellafield Station Cumb 56 F2
Sellafirth Shetl'd 96 D7
Sellibister Orkney 95 D8
Sellindge Kent 13 C9
Sellindge Lees Kent 13 C10
Selling Kent 21 F7
Sells Green Wilts 16 E6
Selly Oak W Midlands 34 G6
Selmeston E Sussex 12 F4
Selsdon London 19 E10
Selsey W Sussex 11 E7
Selsfield Common W Sussex 12 C2
Selsted Kent 21 G9
Selston Notts 45 G8
Selworthy Som'set 7 B8
Semblister Shetl'd 96 H5
Semer Suffolk 30 D6
Semington Wilts 16 E5
Semley Wilts 9 B7
Send Surrey 19 F7
Send Marsh Surrey 19 F7
Senghenydd Caerph 15 B7
Sennen Cornw'l 2 G2
Sennen Cove Cornw'l 2 G2
Sennybridge = Pont Senni Powys 24 F6
Serlby Notts 45 D10
Sessay N Yorks 51 B10
Setchey Norfolk 38 D2
Setley Hants 10 D2
Setter Shetl'd 96 E6
Setter Shetl'd 96 H5
Setter Shetl'd 96 J7
Settiscarth Orkney 95 G4
Settle N Yorks 50 C4
Settrington N Yorks 52 B4
Seven Kings London 19 C11
Seven Sisters Neath P Talb 24 H5
Sevenhampton Glos 27 F7
Sevenoaks Kent 20 F2
Sevenoaks Weald Kent 20 F2
Severn Beach S Gloucs 15 C11
Severn Stoke Worcs 26 D5
Severnhampton Swindon 17 B9
Sevington Kent 13 B9
Sewards End Essex 30 E2
Sewardstone Essex 19 B10
Sewardstonebury Essex 19 B10
Sewerby ER Yorks 53 C7
Seworgan Cornw'l 2 F6
Sewstern Leics 36 C4
Sezincote Glos 27 E8
Sgarasta Mhor W Isles 90 H5
Sgiogarstaigh W Isles 91 A10
Shabbington Bucks 28 H3
Shackerstone Leics 35 E9
Shackleford Surrey 18 G6
Shade W Yorks 50 G5
Shadforth Durham 58 B4
Shadingfield Suffolk 39 G10
Shadoxhurst Kent 13 C8
Shadsworth Blackb'n 50 G3
Shadwell Norfolk 38 G5
Shadwell W Yorks 51 F9
Shaftesbury Dorset 9 B7
Shafton S Yorks 45 A7
Shalbourne Wilts 17 E10
Shalcombe I/Wight 10 F2
Shalden Hants 18 G3
Shaldon Devon 5 D10
Shalfleet I/Wight 10 F3
Shalford Essex 30 F4
Shalford Surrey 19 G7
Shalford Green Essex 30 F4
Shallowford Devon 6 B6
Shalmsford Street Kent 21 F7
Shalstone Bucks 28 E3
Shamley Green Surrey 19 G7
Shandon Arg/Bute 73 E11
Shandwick H'land 87 D11
Shangton Leics 36 F3
Shankhouse Northum 63 F8
Shanklin I/Wight 10 F4
Shanquhar Aberds 88 E5
Shanzie Perth/Kinr 76 B5
Shap Cumb 57 E7
Shapwick Dorset 9 D8
Shapwick Som'set 15 H10
Shardlow Derby 35 B10

Starlings Green *Essex* 29 E11
Starston *Norfolk* 39 G8
Startforth *Durham* 58 E1
Startley *Wilts* 16 C6
Stathe *Som'set* 8 B2
Stathern *Leics* 36 B3
Station Town *Durham* 58 C5
Staughton Green *Cambs* 29 B8
Staughton Highway *Cambs* 29 B8
Staunton *Glos* [illegible]
Staunton *Glos* 26 F4
Staunton in the Vale *Notts* 36 A4
Staunton on Arrow *Heref'd* 25 B10
Staunton on Wye *Heref'd* 25 D10
Staveley *Cumb* 56 H5
Staveley *Cumb* 56 G6
Staveley *Derby* 45 E8
Staveley *N Yorks* 51 C9
Staverton *Devon* 5 E8
Staverton *Glos* 26 F5
Staverton *Northants* 28 B2
Staverton *Wilts* 16 E5
Staverton Bridge *Glos* 26 F5
Stawell *Som'set* 15 H9
Staxigoe *H'land* 94 E5
Staxton *N Yorks* 52 B6
Staylittle *Powys* 32 F4
Staynall *Lancs* 49 E3
Staythorpe *Notts* 45 G11
Stean *N Yorks* 51 B6
Stearsby *N Yorks* 52 B2
Steart *Som'set* 15 G8
Stebbing *Essex* 30 F3
Stebbing Green *Essex* 30 F3
Stedham *W Sussex* 11 B7
Steele Road *Scot Borders* 61 D11
Steen's Bridge *Heref'd* 26 C2
Steep *Hants* 10 B6
Steep Marsh *Hants* 11 B6
Steeple *Dorset* 9 F8
Steeple *Essex* 20 A6
Steeple Ashton *Wilts* 16 F6
Steeple Aston *Oxon* 27 F11
Steeple Barton *Oxon* 27 F11
Steeple Bumpstead *Essex* 30 D3
Steeple Claydon *Bucks* 28 F3
Steeple Gidding *Cambs* 37 G7
Steeple Langford *Wilts* 17 H7
Steeple Morden *Cambs* 29 D9
Steeton *W Yorks* 50 E6
Stein *H'land* 84 C7
Steinmanhill *Aberds* 89 D7
Stelling Minnis *Kent* 21 G8
Stemster *H'land* 94 D3
Stemster Ho. *H'land* 94 D3
Stenalees *Cornw'l* 3 D9
Stenhousemuir *Falk* 69 B7
Stenigot *Lincs* 46 D6
Stenness *Shetl'd* 96 F4
Stenscholl *H'land* 85 B9
Stenso *Orkney* 95 F4
Stenson *Derby* 35 C9
Stenton *E Loth* 70 C5
Stenton *Fife* 76 H5
Stenwith *Lincs* 36 B4
Stepaside *Pembs* 22 F6
Stepping Hill *Gtr Man* 44 D3
Steppingley *Beds* 29 E7
Stepps *N Lanarks* 68 D5
Sterndale Moor *Derby* 44 F5
Sternfield *Suffolk* 31 B10
Sterridge *Devon* 6 B4
Stert *Wilts* 17 F7
Stetchworth *Cambs* 30 C3
Stevenage *Herts* 29 F9
Stevenston *N Ayrs* 66 B5
Steventon *Hants* 18 G2
Steventon *Oxon* 17 B11
Stevington *Beds* 28 C6
Stewartby *Beds* 29 D7
Stewarton *Arg/Bute* 65 G7
Stewarton *E Ayrs* 67 B7
Stewkley *Bucks* 28 F5
Stewton *Lincs* 47 D7
Steyne Cross *I/Wight* 10 F5
Steyning *W Sussex* 11 C10
Steynton *Pembs* 22 F4
Stibb *Cornw'l* 6 E1
Stibb Cross *Devon* 6 E3
Stibb Green *Wilts* 17 E9
Stibbard *Norfolk* 38 C5
Stibbington *Cambs* 37 F6
Stichill *Scot Borders* 70 G6
Sticker *Cornw'l* 3 D8
Stickford *Lincs* 47 G7
Sticklepath *Devon* 6 G5
Stickney *Lincs* 47 G7
Stiffkey *Norfolk* 38 A5
Stifford's Bridge *Heref'd* 26 D4
Stillingfleet *N Yorks* 52 E1
Stillington *N Yorks* 52 C1
Stillington *Stockton* 58 D4
Stilton *Cambs* 37 G7
Stinchcombe *Glos* 16 B4
Stinsford *Dorset* 8 E6
Stirchley *Telford* 34 E3
Stirkoke Ho. *H'land* 94 E5
Stirling *Aberds* 89 D11
Stirling *Stirl* 68 A6
Stisted *Essex* 30 F4
Stithians *Cornw'l* 2 F6
Stittenham *H'land* 87 D9
Stivichall *W Midlands* 35 H9
Stixwould *Lincs* 46 F5
Stoak *Ches* 43 E7
Stobieside *S Lanarks* 68 G5
Stobo *Scot Borders* 69 G10
Stoborough *Dorset* 9 F8
Stoborough Green *Dorset* 9 F8
Stobshiel *E Loth* 70 D3
Stobswood *Northum* 63 D8
Stock *Essex* 20 B3
Stock Green *Worcs* 26 C6
Stock Wood *Worcs* 27 C7
Stockbridge *Hants* 10 A2
Stockbury *Kent* 20 E5
Stockcross *W Berks* 17 E11
Stockdalewath *Cumb* 56 B5
Stockerston *Leics* 36 F4
Stockheath *Hants* 10 D6
Stockiemuir *Stirl* 68 B4
Stocking Pelham *Herts* 29 F11
Stockingford *Warwick* 35 F9
Stockland *Devon* 8 D1
Stockland Bristol *Som'set* 15 G8
Stockleigh English *Devon* 7 F7
Stockleigh Pomeroy *Devon* 7 F7
Stockley *Wilts* 17 E7
Stocklinch *Som'set* 8 C2
Stockport *Gtr Man* 44 C2
Stocksbridge *S Yorks* 44 C6
Stocksfield *Northum* 62 G6
Stockton *Heref'd* 26 B2
Stockton *Norfolk* 39 F9
Stockton *Shrops* 33 E8
Stockton *Shrops* 34 F3
Stockton *Warwick* 27 B11
Stockton *Wilts* 16 H6
Stockton Heath *Warrington* 43 D9
Stockton-on-Tees *Stockton* 58 E5
Stockton on Teme *Worcs* 26 B4
Stockton on the Forest *C/York* 52 D2
Stodmarsh *Kent* 21 E9
Stody *Norfolk* 39 B6
Stoer *H'land* 92 G3
Stoford *Som'set* 8 C4
Stoford *Wilts* 17 H7
Stogumber *Som'set* 7 C9
Stogursey *Som'set* 7 B11
Stoke *Devon* 6 D1
Stoke *Hants* 17 F11
Stoke *Hants* 10 D6
Stoke *Medway* 20 D5
Stoke *Suffolk* 31 D8
Stoke Abbott *Dorset* 8 D3
Stoke Albany *Northants* 36 G4
Stoke Ash *Suffolk* 31 A8
Stoke Bardolph *Notts* 36 A2
Stoke Bliss *Worcs* 26 B3
Stoke Bruerne *Northants* 28 D4
Stoke by Clare *Suffolk* 30 D4
Stoke-by-Nayland *Suffolk* 30 E6
Stoke Canon *Devon* 7 G8
Stoke Charity *Hants* 17 H11
Stoke Climsland *Cornw'l* 4 D4
Stoke D'Abernon *Surrey* 19 F8
Stoke Doyle *Northants* 36 G6
Stoke Dry *Rutl'd* 36 F4
Stoke Farthing *Wilts* 9 B9
Stoke Ferry *Norfolk* 38 F3
Stoke Fleming *Devon* 5 G9
Stoke Gabriel *Devon* 5 F9
Stoke Gifford *S Gloucs* 16 D3
Stoke Golding *Leics* 35 F9
Stoke Goldington *M/Keynes* 28 D5
Stoke Green *Bucks* 18 C6
Stoke Hammond *Bucks* 28 F5
Stoke Heath *Shrops* 34 C2
Stoke Holy Cross *Norfolk* 39 E8
Stoke Lacy *Heref'd* 26 D3
Stoke Lyne *Oxon* 28 F2
Stoke Mandeville *Bucks* 28 G5
Stoke Newington *London* 19 C10
Stoke on Tern *Shrops* 34 C2
Stoke-on-Trent *Stoke* 44 H2
Stoke Orchard *Glos* 26 F6
Stoke Poges *Bucks* 18 C6
Stoke Prior *Heref'd* 26 C2
Stoke Prior *Worcs* 26 B6
Stoke Rivers *Devon* 6 C5
Stoke Rochford *Lincs* 36 C5
Stoke Row *Oxon* 18 C3
Stoke St Gregory *Som'set* 8 B2
Stoke St Mary *Som'set* 8 B1
Stoke St Michael *Som'set* 16 G3
Stoke St Milborough *Shrops* 34 G1
Stoke sub Hamdon *Som'set* 8 C3
Stoke Talmage *Oxon* 18 B3
Stoke Trister *Som'set* 8 B6
Stoke Wake *Dorset* 9 D6
Stokeford *Dorset* 9 F7
Stokeham *Notts* 45 E11
Stokeinteignhead *Devon* 5 D10
Stokenchurch *Bucks* 18 B4
Stokenham *Devon* 5 G9
Stokesay *Shrops* 33 G10
Stokesby *Norfolk* 39 D10
Stokesley *N Yorks* 59 F6
Stolford *Som'set* 7 B11
Ston Easton *Som'set* 16 F3
Stondon Massey *Essex* 20 A2
Stone *Bucks* 28 G4
Stone *Glos* 16 B3
Stone *Kent* 13 D8
Stone *Kent* 20 D2
Stone *Staffs* 34 B5
Stone *S Yorks* 45 D9
Stone *Worcs* 34 H4
Stone Allerton *Som'set* 15 F10
Stone Bridge Corner *Peterbro* 37 E8
Stone Chair *W Yorks* 51 G7
Stone Cross *E Sussex* 12 F5
Stone Cross *Kent* 21 F10
Stone-edge Batch *N Som'set* 15 D10
Stone House *Cumb* 57 H9
Stone Street *Kent* 20 F2
Stone Street *Suffolk* 30 E6
Stone Street *Suffolk* 39 G9
Stonebroom *Derby* 45 G8
Stoneferry *Kingston/Hull* 53 F7
Stonefield *S Lanarks* 68 E5
Stonegate *E Sussex* 12 D5
Stonegate *N Yorks* 59 F8
Stonegrave *N Yorks* 52 B2
Stonehaugh *Northum* 62 F3
Stonehaven *Aberds* 83 E10
Stonehouse *Glos* 26 H5
Stonehouse *Northum* 62 H2
Stonehouse *S Lanarks* 68 F6
Stoneleigh *Warwick* 27 A10
Stonely *Cambs* 29 B8
Stoner Hill *Hants* 10 B6
Stone's Green *Essex* 31 F8
Stonesby *Leics* 36 C4
Stonesfield *Oxon* 27 G10
Stonethwaite *Cumb* 56 E4
Stoney Cross *Hants* 10 C1
Stoney Middleton *Derby* 44 E6
Stoney Stanton *Leics* 35 F10
Stoney Stoke *Som'set* 8 A6
Stoney Stratton *Som'set* 16 H3
Stoney Stretton *Shrops* 33 E9
Stoneybreck *Shetl'd* 96 N8
Stoneyburn *W Loth* 69 D8
Stoneygate *Aberds* 89 E10
Stoneygate *Leics C* 36 E2
Stoneyhills *Essex* 20 B6
Stoneykirk *Dumf/Gal* 54 D3
Stoneywood *Aberd C* 83 B10
Stoneywood *Falk* 68 B6
Stonganess *Shetl'd* 96 C7
Stonham Aspal *Suffolk* 31 C8
Stonnall *Staffs* 35 E6
Stonor *Oxon* 18 C4
Stonton Wyville *Leics* 36 F3
Stony Cross *Heref'd* 26 D4
Stony Stratford *M/Keynes* 28 D4
Stonyfield *H'land* 87 D9
Stoodleigh *Devon* 7 E8
Stopes *S Yorks* 44 D6
Stopham *W Sussex* 11 C9
Stopsley *Luton* 29 F8
Stores Corner *Suffolk* 31 D10
Storeton *Mersey* 42 D6
Stornoway *W Isles* 91 D9
Storridge *Heref'd* 26 D4
Storrington *W Sussex* 11 C9
Storrs *Cumb* 56 G5
Storth *Cumb* 49 A4
Storwood *ER Yorks* 52 E3
Stotfield *Moray* 88 A2
Stotfold *Beds* 29 E9
Stottesdon *Shrops* 34 G2
Stoughton *Leics* 36 E2
Stoughton *Surrey* 18 F6
Stoughton *W Sussex* 11 C7
Stoul *H'land* 79 B10
Stoulton *Worcs* 26 D6
Stour Provost *Dorset* 9 B6
Stour Row *Dorset* 9 B7
Stourbridge *W Midlands* 34 G5
Stourpaine *Dorset* 9 D7
Stourport on Severn *Worcs* 26 A5
Stourton *Staffs* 34 G4
Stourton *Warwick* 27 E9
Stourton *Wilts* 9 A6
Stourton Caundle *Dorset* 8 C6
Stove *Orkney* 95 E7
Stove *Shetl'd* 96 L6
Stoven *Suffolk* 39 G10
Stow *Scot Borders* 70 F3
Stow *Lincs* 46 D2
Stow *Lincs* 37 B6
Stow Bardolph *Norfolk* 38 E2
Stow Bedon *Norfolk* 38 F5
Stow cum Quy *Cambs* 30 B2
Stow Longa *Cambs* 29 A8
Stow Maries *Essex* 20 B5
Stow-on-the-Wold *Glos* 27 F8
Stowbridge *Norfolk* 38 E2
Stowe *Shrops* 25 A10
Stowe-by-Chartley *Staffs* 34 C6
Stowe Green *Glos* 26 H2
Stowell *Som'set* 8 B5
Stowford *Devon* 4 C5
Stowlangtoft *Suffolk* 30 B6
Stowmarket *Suffolk* 31 C7
Stowting *Kent* 13 B10
Stowupland *Suffolk* 31 C7
Straad *Arg/Bute* 73 G9
Strachan *Aberds* 83 D8
Stradbroke *Suffolk* 31 A9
Stradishall *Suffolk* 30 C4
Stradsett *Norfolk* 38 E2
Stragglethorpe *Lincs* 46 G3
Straid *S Ayrs* 66 G4
Straith *Dumf/Gal* 60 E4
Straiton *C/Edinb* 69 D11
Straiton *S Ayrs* 67 F6
Straloch *Aberds* 89 F8
Straloch *Perth/Kinr* 76 A3
Stramshall *Staffs* 35 B6
Strang *I/Man* 48 E3
Stranraer *Dumf/Gal* 54 C3
Stratfield Mortimer *W Berks* 18 E3
Stratfield Saye *Hants* 18 E3
Stratfield Turgis *Hants* 18 F3
Stratford *London* 19 C10
Stratford St Andrew *Suffolk* 31 B10
Stratford St Mary *Suffolk* 31 E7
Stratford Sub Castle *Wilts* 9 A10
Stratford Tony *Wilts* 9 B9
Stratford-upon-Avon *Warwick* 27 C8
Strath *H'land* 94 E4
Strath *H'land* 85 A12
Strathan *H'land* 80 D1
Strathan *H'land* 93 C8
Strathan *H'land* 92 G3
Strathaven *S Lanarks* 68 F6
Strathblane *Stirl* 68 C4
Strathcanaird *H'land* 92 J4
Strathcarron *H'land* 86 G2
Strathcoil *Arg/Bute* 79 H9
Strathdon *Aberds* 82 B5
Strathellie *Aberds* 89 B10
Strathkinness *Fife* 77 F7
Strathmashie House *H'land* 81 D7
Strathmiglo *Fife* 76 F5
Strathmore Lodge *H'land* 94 F3
Strathpeffer *H'land* 86 F7
Strathrannoch *H'land* 86 D6
Strathtay *Perth/Kinr* 76 B2
Strathvaich Lodge *H'land* 86 D6
Strathwhillan *N Ayrs* 66 C3
Strathy *H'land* 93 C11
Strathyre *Stirl* 75 F8
Stratton *Cornw'l* 6 F1
Stratton *Dorset* 8 E5
Stratton *Glos* 17 A7
Stratton Audley *Oxon* 28 F3
Stratton on the Fosse *Som'set* 16 F3
Stratton St Margaret *Swindon* 17 C8
Stratton St Michael *Norfolk* 39 F8
Stratton Strawless *Norfolk* 39 C8
Stravithie *Fife* 77 F8
Streat *E Sussex* 12 E2
Streatham *London* 19 D10
Streatley *Beds* 29 F7
Streatley *W Berks* 18 C2
Street *Lancs* 49 D5
Street *N Yorks* 59 F8
Street *Som'set* 15 H10
Street Dinas *Shrops* 33 B9
Street End *Kent* 21 F8
Street End *W Sussex* 11 E7
Street Gate *Tyne/Wear* 63 H8
Street Lydan *Wrex* 33 B10
Streethay *Staffs* 35 D7
Streetlam *N Yorks* 58 G4
Streetly *W Midlands* 35 F6
Streetly End *Cambs* 30 D3
Strefford *Shrops* 33 G10
Strelley *Notts* 35 A11
Strensall *C/York* 52 C2
Stretcholt *Som'set* 15 G8
Strete *Devon* 5 G9
Stretford *Gtr Man* 44 C2
Strethall *Essex* 29 E11
Stretham *Cambs* 30 A2
Strettington *W Sussex* 11 D7
Stretton *Ches* 43 G7
Stretton *Derby* 45 F7
Stretton *Rutl'd* 36 D5
Stretton *Staffs* 34 D4
Stretton *Staffs* 35 C8
Stretton *Warrington* 43 D9
Stretton Grandison *Heref'd* 26 D3
Stretton-on-Dunsmore *Warwick* 27 A11
Stretton-on-Fosse *Warwick* 27 E9
Stretton Sugwas *Heref'd* 25 D11
Stretton under Fosse *Warwick* 35 G10
Stretton Westwood *Shrops* 34 F1
Strichen *Aberds* 89 C9
Strines *Gtr Man* 44 D3
Stringston *Som'set* 7 B10
Strixton *Northants* 28 B6
Stroat *Glos* 16 B2
Stromeferry *H'land* 85 E13
Stromemore *H'land* 85 E13
Stromness *Orkney* 95 H3
Stronaba *H'land* 80 E4
Stronachlachar *Stirl* 75 F7
Stronchreggan *H'land* 80 F2
Stronchrubie *H'land* 92 H5
Strone *Arg/Bute* 73 E10
Strone *H'land* 81 A7
Strone *H'land* 80 E3
Strone *Invercl* 73 F11
Stronmilchan *Arg/Bute* 74 E4
Strontian *H'land* 79 E11
Strood *Medway* 20 E4
Strood Green *Surrey* 19 G9
Strood Green *W Sussex* 11 B9
Strood Green *W Sussex* 11 A10
Stroud *Glos* 26 H5
Stroud *Hants* 10 B6
Stroud Green *Essex* 20 B5
Stroxton *Lincs* 36 B5
Struan *H'land* 85 E8
Struan *Perth/Kinr* 81 G10
Strubby *Lincs* 47 D8
Strumpshaw *Norfolk* 39 E9
Strutherhill *S Lanarks* 68 F6
Struy *H'land* 86 H6
Stryt-issa *Wrex* 42 H5
Stuartfield *Aberds* 89 D9
Stub Place *Cumb* 56 G2
Stubbington *Hants* 10 D4
Stubbins *Lancs* 50 H3
Stubbs Cross *Kent* 13 C8
Stubb's Green *Norfolk* 39 F8
Stubbs Green *Norfolk* 39 F9
Stubhampton *Dorset* 9 C8
Stubton *Lincs* 46 H2
Stuckgowan *Arg/Bute* 74 G6
Stuckton *Hants* 9 C10
Stud Green *Windsor* 18 D5
Studham *Beds* 29 G7
Studland *Dorset* 9 F9
Studley *Warwick* 27 B7
Studley *Wilts* 16 D6
Studley Roger *N Yorks* 51 B8
Stump Cross *Essex* 30 D2
Stuntney *Cambs* 38 H1
Sturbridge *Staffs* 34 B4
Sturmer *Essex* 30 D3
Sturminster Marshall *Dorset* 9 D8
Sturminster Newton *Dorset* 9 C6
Sturry *Kent* 21 E8
Sturton *N Lincs* 46 B3
Sturton by Stow *Lincs* 46 D2
Sturton le Steeple *Notts* 45 D11
Stuston *Suffolk* 39 H7
Stutton *N Yorks* 51 E10
Stutton *Suffolk* 31 E8
Styal *Ches* 44 D2
Styrrup *Notts* 45 C10
Suainebost *W Isles* 91 A10
Suardail *W Isles* 91 D9
Succoth *Aberds* 88 E4
Succoth *Arg/Bute* 74 G5
Suckley *Worcs* 26 C4
Suckquoy *Orkney* 95 K5
Sudborough *Northants* 36 G5
Sudbourne *Suffolk* 31 C11
Sudbrook *Lincs* 36 A5
Sudbrook *Monmouths* 15 C11
Sudbrooke *Lincs* 46 E4
Sudbury *Derby* 35 B7
Sudbury *London* 19 C8
Sudbury *Suffolk* 30 D5
Suddie *H'land* 87 F9
Sudgrove *Glos* 26 H6
Suffield *Norfolk* 39 B8
Suffield *N Yorks* 59 G10
Sugnall *Staffs* 34 B3
Suladale *H'land* 85 C8
Sulaisiadar *W Isles* 91 D10
Sulby *I/Man* 48 C3
Sulgrave *Northants* 28 D2
Sulham *W Berks* 18 D3
Sulhamstead *W Berks* 18 E3
Sulland *Orkney* 95 D6
Sullington *W Sussex* 11 C9
Sullom *Shetl'd* 96 F5
Sullom Voe Oil Terminal *Shetl'd* 96 F5
Sully *V/Glam* 15 E7
Sumburgh *Shetl'd* 96 N6
Summer Bridge *N Yorks* 51 C8
Summer-house *D'lington* 58 E3
Summercourt *Cornw'l* 3 D7
Summerfield *Norfolk* 38 B3
Summergangs *Kingston/Hull* 53 F7
Summerleaze *Monmouths* 15 C10
Summersdale *W Sussex* 11 D7
Summerseat *Gtr Man* 43 A10
Summertown *Oxon* 28 H2
Summit *Gtr Man* 44 B3
Sunbury-on-Thames *Surrey* 19 E8
Sundaywell *Dumf/Gal* 60 E4
Sunderland *Arg/Bute* 64 B3
Sunderland *Cumb* 56 C3
Sunderland *Tyne/Wear* 63 H9
Sunderland Bridge *Durham* 58 C3
Sundhope *Scot Borders* 70 H2
Sundon Park *Luton* 29 F7
Sundridge *Kent* 19 F11
Sunipol *Arg/Bute* 78 F6
Sunk Island *ER Yorks* 53 H8
Sunningdale *Windsor* 18 E6
Sunninghill *Windsor* 18 E6
Sunningwell *Oxon* 17 A11
Sunniside *Durham* 58 C2
Sunniside *Tyne/Wear* 63 H8
Sunnyhurst *Blackb'n* 50 G2
Sunnylaw *Stirl* 75 H10
Sunnyside *W Sussex* 12 C2
Sunton *Wilts* 17 F9
Surbiton *London* 19 E8
Surby *I/Man* 48 E2
Surfleet *Lincs* 37 C8
Surfleet Seas End *Lincs* 37 C8
Surlingham *Norfolk* 39 E9
Sustead *Norfolk* 39 B7
Susworth *Lincs* 46 B2
Sutcombe *Devon* 6 E2
Suton *Norfolk* 39 F6
Sutors of Cromarty *H'land* 87 E11
Sutterby *Lincs* 47 E7
Sutterton *Lincs* 37 B8
Sutton *Beds* 29 D9
Sutton *Cambs* 37 H10
Sutton *London* 19 E9
Sutton *Kent* 21 G10
Sutton *Mersey* 43 C8
Sutton *Norfolk* 39 C9
Sutton *Notts* 36 B3
Sutton *Notts* 45 D10
Sutton *N Yorks* 51 G10
Sutton *Oxon* 27 H11
Sutton *Peterbro* 37 F6
Sutton *Shrops* 34 G3
Sutton *Shrops* 34 B2
Sutton *Som'set* 8 A5
Sutton *Staffs* 34 C3
Sutton *Suffolk* 31 D10
Sutton *Surrey* 19 G7
Sutton *S Yorks* 45 A9
Sutton *W Sussex* 11 C8
Sutton at Hone *Kent* 20 D2
Sutton Bassett *Northants* 36 F3
Sutton Benger *Wilts* 16 D6
Sutton Bonington *Notts* 35 C11
Sutton Bridge *Lincs* 37 C10
Sutton Cheney *Leics* 35 E10
Sutton Coldfield *W Midlands* 35 F7
Sutton Courtenay *Oxon* 18 B2
Sutton Crosses *Lincs* 37 C10
Sutton Grange *N Yorks* 51 B8
Sutton Green *Surrey* 19 F7
Sutton Howgrave *N Yorks* 51 B9
Sutton In Ashfield *Notts* 45 G8
Sutton-in-Craven *N Yorks* 50 E6
Sutton in the Elms *Leics* 35 F11
Sutton Ings *Kingston/Hull* 53 F7
Sutton Lane Ends *Ches* 44 E3
Sutton Leach *Mersey* 43 C8
Sutton Maddock *Shrops* 34 E3
Sutton Mallet *Som'set* 15 H9
Sutton Mandeville *Wilts* 9 B8
Sutton Manor *Mersey* 43 C8
Sutton Montis *Som'set* 8 B5
Sutton on Hull *Kingston/Hull* 53 F7
Sutton on Sea *Lincs* 47 D9
Sutton-on-the-Forest *N Yorks* 52 C1
Sutton on the Hill *Derby* 35 B8
Sutton on Trent *Notts* 45 F11
Sutton St Edmund *Lincs* 37 D9
Sutton St James *Lincs* 37 D9
Sutton St Nicholas *Heref'd* 26 D2
Sutton Scarsdale *Derby* 45 F8
Sutton Scotney *Hants* 17 H11
Sutton under Brailes *Warwick* 27 E10
Sutton-under-Whitestonecliffe *N Yorks* 51 A10
Sutton upon Derwent *ER Yorks* 52 E3
Sutton Valence *Kent* 20 G5
Sutton Veny *Wilts* 16 G5
Sutton Waldron *Dorset* 9 C7
Sutton Weaver *Ches* 43 E8
Sutton Wick *Bath/NE Som'set* 16 F2
Swaby *Lincs* 47 E7
Swadlincote *Derby* 35 D9
Swaffham *Norfolk* 38 E4
Swaffham Bulbeck *Cambs* 30 B2
Swaffham Prior *Cambs* 30 B2
Swafield *Norfolk* 39 B8
Swainby *N Yorks* 58 F5
Swainshill *Heref'd* 25 D11
Swainsthorpe *Norfolk* 39 E8
Swainswick *Bath/NE Som'set* 16 E4
Swalcliffe *Oxon* 27 E10
Swalecliffe *Kent* 21 E8
Swallow *Lincs* 46 B5
Swallowcliffe *Wilts* 9 B8
Swallowfield *Wokingham* 18 E4
Swallownest *S Yorks* 45 D8
Swallows Cross *Essex* 20 B3
Swan Green *Ches* 43 E10
Swan Green *Suffolk* 31 A9
Swanage *Dorset* 9 G9
Swanbister *Orkney* 95 H4
Swanbourne *Bucks* 28 F5
Swanland *ER Yorks* 52 G5
Swanley *Kent* 20 E2
Swanley Village *Kent* 20 E2
Swanmore *Hants* 10 C4
Swannington *Leics* 35 D10
Swannington *Norfolk* 39 D7
Swanscombe *Kent* 20 D3
Swansea = Abertawe *Swan* 14 B2
Swanton Abbot *Norfolk* 39 C8
Swanton Morley *Norfolk* 38 D6
Swanton Novers *Norfolk* 38 B6
Swanton Street *Kent* 20 F5
Swanwick *Derby* 45 G8
Swanwick *Hants* 10 D4
Swarby *Lincs* 36 A6
Swardeston *Norfolk* 39 E8
Swarister *Shetl'd* 96 E7
Swarkestone *Derby* 35 C9
Swarland *Northum* 63 C7
Swarland Estate *Northum* 63 C7
Swarthmoor *Cumb* 49 B2
Swathwick *Derby* 45 F7
Swaton *Lincs* 37 B7
Swavesey *Cambs* 29 B10
Sway *Hants* 10 E1
Swayfield *Lincs* 36 C5
Swaythling *S'thampton* 10 C3
Sweet Green *Worcs* 26 B3
Sweetham *Devon* 7 G7
Sweethouse *Cornw'l* 4 E1
Sweffling *Suffolk* 31 B10
Swepstone *Leics* 35 D9
Swerford *Oxon* 27 E10
Swettenham *Ches* 44 F2
Swetton *N Yorks* 51 B7
Swffryd *Bl Gwent* 15 B8
Swiftsden *E Sussex* 12 D6
Swilland *Suffolk* 31 C8
Swillington *W Yorks* 51 F9
Swimbridge *Devon* 6 D5
Swimbridge Newland *Devon* 6 C5
Swinbrook *Oxon* 27 G9
Swinderby *Lincs* 46 F2
Swindon *Glos* 26 F6
Swindon *Staffs* 34 F4
Swindon *Swindon* 17 C8
Swine *ER Yorks* 53 F7
Swinefleet *ER Yorks* 52 G3
Swineshead *Beds* 29 B7
Swineshead *Lincs* 37 A8
Swineshead Bridge *Lincs* 37 A8
Swiney *H'land* 94 G4
Swinford *Leics* 36 H1
Swinford *Oxon* 27 H11
Swingate *Notts* 35 A11
Swingfield Minnis *Kent* 21 G9
Swingfield St *Kent* 21 G9
Swinhoe *Northum* 71 H11
Swinhope *Lincs* 46 C6
Swining *Shetl'd* 96 G6
Swinithwaite *N Yorks* 58 H1
Swinnow Moor *W Yorks* 51 F8
Swinscoe *Staffs* 44 H5
Swinside Hall *Scot Borders* 62 B3
Swinstead *Lincs* 36 C6
Swinton *Scot Borders* 71 F7
Swinton *Gtr Man* 43 B10
Swinton *N Yorks* 51 B8
Swinton *N Yorks* 52 B3
Swinton *S Yorks* 45 C8
Swintonmill *Scot Borders* 71 F7
Swithland *Leics* 35 D11
Swordale *H'land* 87 E8
Swordland *H'land* 79 B10
Swordly *H'land* 93 C10
Sworton Heath *Ches* 43 D9
Swydd-ffynnon *Ceredig'n* 24 B3
Swynnerton *Staffs* 34 B4
Swyre *Dorset* 8 F4
Sychtyn *Powys* 32 E5
Syde *Glos* 26 G6
Sydenham *London* 19 D10
Sydenham *Oxon* 18 A4
Sydenham Damerel *Devon* 4 D5
Syderstone *Norfolk* 38 B4
Sydling St Nicholas *Dorset* 8 E5
Sydmonton *Hants* 17 F11
Syerston *Notts* 45 H11
Syke *Gtr Man* 50 H4
Sykehouse *S Yorks* 52 H2
Sykes *Lancs* 50 D2
Syleham *Suffolk* 39 H8
Sylen *Carms* 23 F10
Symbister *Shetl'd* 96 G7
Symington *S Ayrs* 67 C6
Symington *S Lanarks* 69 G8
Symonds Yat *Heref'd* 26 G2
Symondsbury *Dorset* 8 E3
Synod Inn *Ceredig'n* 23 A9
Syre *H'land* 93 E9
Syreford *Glos* 27 F7
Syresham *Northants* 28 D3
Syston *Leics* 36 D2
Syston *Lincs* 36 A5
Sytchampton *Worcs* 26 B5
Sywell *Northants* 28 B5

T

Taagan *H'land* 86 E3
Tàbost *W Isles* 91 A10
Tabost *W Isles* 91 F8
Tackley *Oxon* 27 F11
Tacleit *W Isles* 90 D6
Tacolneston *Norfolk* 39 F7
Tadcaster *N Yorks* 51 E10
Taddington *Derby* 44 E5
Taddiport *Devon* 6 E3
Tadley *Hants* 18 E3
Tadlow *Beds* 29 D9
Tadmarton *Oxon* 27 E10
Tadworth *Surrey* 19 F9
Tafarn-y-gelyn *Denbs* 42 F4
Tafarnau-bach *Bl Gwent* 25 G8
Taff's Well *Rh Cyn Taff* 15 C7
Tafolwern *Powys* 32 E4
Tai *Conwy* 41 D9
Tai-bach *Powys* 33 C7
Tai-mawr *Conwy* 32 A5
Tai-Ucha *Denbs* 42 G3
Taibach *Neath P Talb* 14 C3
Taigh a Ghearraidh *W Isles* 84 A2
Tain *H'land* 87 C10
Tain *H'land* 94 D4
Tainant *Wrex* 42 H5
Tainlon *Gwyn* 40 E6
Tai'r-Bull *Powys* 24 F6
Tairbeart = Tarbert *W Isles* 90 G6
Tairgwaith *Neath P Talb* 24 G4
Takeley *Essex* 30 F2
Takeley Street *Essex* 30 F2
Tal-sarn *Ceredig'n* 23 A10
Tal-y-bont *Ceredig'n* 32 G2
Tal-y-Bont *Conwy* 41 D9
Tal-y-bont *Gwyn* 41 C8
Tal-y-bont *Gwyn* 32 C1
Tal-y-cafn *Conwy* 41 C9
Tal-y-llyn *Gwyn* 32 E3
Tal-y-wern *Powys* 32 E4
Talachddu *Powys* 25 E7
Talacre *Flints* 42 D4
Talardd *Gwyn* 32 C4
Talaton *Devon* 7 G9
Talbenny *Pembs* 22 E3
Talbot Green *Rh Cyn Taff* 14 C6
Talbot Village *Poole* 9 E9
Tale *Devon* 7 F9
Talerddig *Powys* 32 E5
Talgarreg *Ceredig'n* 23 A9
Talgarth *Powys* 25 E8
Talisker *H'land* 85 E8
Talke *Staffs* 44 G2
Talkin *Cumb* 61 H11
Talla Linnfoots *Scot Borders* 61 A7
Talladale *H'land* 86 D2
Tallarn Green *Wrex* 33 A10
Tallentire *Cumb* 56 C3
Talley *Carms* 24 E3
Tallington *Lincs* 37 E6
Talmine *H'land* 93 C8
Talog *Carms* 23 D8
Talsarn *Carms* 24 F4
Talsarnau *Gwyn* 41 G8
Talskiddy *Cornw'l* 3 C8
Talwrn *Angl* 40 C6
Talwrn *Wrex* 42 H5
Talybont-on-Usk *Powys* 25 F8
Talygarn *Rh Cyn Taff* 14 C6
Talyllyn *Powys* 25 F8
Talysarn *Gwyn* 40 E6
Talywain *Torf* 15 A8
Tame Bridge *N Yorks* 58 F6
Tamerton Foliot *Plym'th* 4 E5
Tamworth *Staffs* 35 E8
Tan Hinon *Powys* 32 G4
Tan-lan *Conwy* 41 D9
Tan-lan *Gwyn* 41 F8
Tan-y-bwlch *Gwyn* 41 F8
Tan-y-fron *Conwy* 42 F2
Tan-y-graig *Angl* 41 C7
Tan-y-graig *Gwyn* 40 G5
Tan-y-groes *Ceredig'n* 23 B7
Tan-y-pistyll *Powys* 33 C6
Tan-yr-allt *Gwyn* 40 E6
Tandem *W Yorks* 51 H7
Tanden *Kent* 13 C8
Tandridge *Surrey* 19 F10
Tanerdy *Carms* 23 D9
Tanfield *Durham* 63 H7
Tanfield Lea *Durham* 58 A2
Tangasdal *W Isles* 84 J1
Tangiers *Pembs* 22 E4
Tangley *Hants* 17 F10
Tanglwst *Carms* 23 C8
Tangmere *W Sussex* 11 D8
Tangwick *Shetl'd* 96 F4
Tankersley *S Yorks* 45 B7
Tankerton *Kent* 21 E8
Tannach *H'land* 94 F5
Tannachie *Aberds* 83 E9
Tannadice *Angus* 77 B7
Tannington *Suffolk* 31 B9
Tansley *Derby* 45 G7
Tansley Knoll *Derby* 45 F7
Tansor *Northants* 37 F6
Tantobie *Durham* 58 A2
Tanton *N Yorks* 58 E6
Tanworth-in-Arden *Warwick* 27 A8
Tanygrisiau *Gwyn* 41 F8
Tanyrhydiau *Ceredig'n* 24 B4
Taobh a Chaolais *W Isles* 84 G2
Taobh a Thuath Loch Aineort *W Isles* 84 F2
Taobh a Tuath Loch Baghasdail *W Isles* 84 F2
Taobh a'Ghlinne *W Isles* 91 F8
Taobh Tuath *W Isles* 90 J4
Taplow *Bucks* 18 C6
Tapton *Derby* 45 E7
Tarbat Ho. *H'land* 87 D10
Tarbert *Arg/Bute* 72 E5
Tarbert *Arg/Bute* 73 G7
Tarbert *Arg/Bute* 65 C7
Tarbert = Tairbeart *W Isles* 90 G6
Tarbet *Arg/Bute* 74 G6
Tarbet *H'land* 92 E4
Tarbet *H'land* 79 B10
Tarbock Green *Mersey* 43 D7
Tarbolton *S Ayrs* 67 D7
Tarbrax *S Lanarks* 69 E9
Tardebigge *Worcs* 27 B7
Tarfside *Angus* 82 F6
Tarland *Aberds* 82 C6
Tarleton *Lancs* 49 G4
Tarlogie *H'land* 87 C10
Tarlscough *Lancs* 43 A7
Tarlton *Glos* 16 B6
Tarnbrook *Lancs* 50 D1
Tarporley *Ches* 43 F8
Tarr *Som'set* 7 C10
Tarrant Crawford *Dorset* 9 D8
Tarrant Gunville *Dorset* 9 C8
Tarrant Hinton *Dorset* 9 C8
Tarrant Keyneston *Dorset* 9 D8
Tarrant Launceston *Dorset* 9 D8
Tarrant Monkton *Dorset* 9 D8
Tarrant Rawston *Dorset* 9 D8
Tarrant Rushton *Dorset* 9 D8
Tarrel *H'land* 87 C11
Tarring Neville *E Sussex* 12 F3
Tarrington *Heref'd* 26 D3
Tarsappie *Perth/Kinr* 76 E4
Tarskavaig *H'land* 85 H10
Tarves *Aberds* 89 E8
Tarvie *H'land* 86 F7
Tarvie *Perth/Kinr* 76 A3
Tarvin *Ches* 43 F7
Tasburgh *Norfolk* 39 F8
Tasley *Shrops* 34 F2
Taston *Oxon* 27 F10
Tatenhill *Staffs* 35 C8
Tathall End *M/Keynes* 28 D5
Tatham *Lancs* 50 C2
Tathwell *Lincs* 47 D7
Tatling End *Bucks* 19 C7
Tatsfield *Surrey* 19 F11
Tattenhall *Ches* 43 G7
Tatterford *Norfolk* 38 C4
Tattersett *Norfolk* 38 B4
Tattershall *Lincs* 46 G6
Tattershall Bridge *Lincs* 46 G5
Tattershall Thorpe *Lincs* 46 G6
Tattingstone *Suffolk* 31 E8
Tatworth *Som'set* 8 D2
Taunton *Som'set* 7 D11
Taverham *Norfolk* 39 D7
Tavernspite *Pembs* 22 E6
Tavistock *Devon* 4 D5
Taw Green *Devon* 6 G5
Tawstock *Devon* 6 D4
Taxal *Derby* 44 E4
Tay Bridge *Dundee C* 77 E7
Tayinloan *Arg/Bute* 65 D7
Taymouth Castle *Perth/Kinr* 75 C10
Taynish *Arg/Bute* 72 E6
Taynton *Glos* 26 F4
Taynton *Oxon* 27 G9
Taynuilt *Arg/Bute* 74 D3
Tayport *Fife* 77 E7
Tayvallich *Arg/Bute* 72 E6
Tealby *Lincs* 46 C5
Tealing *Angus* 77 D7
Teangue *H'land* 85 H11
Teanna Mhachair *W Isles* 84 B2
Tebay *Cumb* 57 F8
Tebworth *Beds* 28 F6
Tedburn St Mary *Devon* 7 G7
Teddington *Glos* 26 E6
Teddington *London* 19 D8
Tedstone Delamere *Heref'd* 26 C3
Tedstone Wafre *Heref'd* 26 C3
Teeton *Northants* 28 A3
Teffont Evias *Wilts* 9 A8
Teffont Magna *Wilts* 9 A8
Tegryn *Pembs* 23 C7
Teigh *Rutl'd* 36 D4
Teigncombe *Devon* 5 C7
Teigngrace *Devon* 5 D9
Teignmouth *Devon* 5 D10
Telford *Telford* 34 E2
Telham *E Sussex* 13 E6
Tellisford *Som'set* 16 F5
Telscombe *E Sussex* 12 F3
Telscombe Cliffs *E Sussex* 12 F2
Templand *Dumf/Gal* 60 E6
Temple *Cornw'l* 4 D2
Temple *C/Glasg* 68 D4
Temple *Midloth* 70 E2
Temple Balsall *W Midlands* 35 H8
Temple Bar *Ceredig'n* 23 A10
Temple Bar *Carms* 23 E10
Temple Cloud *Bath/NE Som'set* 16 F3
Temple Combe *Som'set* 8 B6
Temple Ewell *Kent* 21 G9
Temple Grafton *Warwick* 27 C8
Temple Guiting *Glos* 27 F7
Temple Herdewyke *Warwick* 27 C10
Temple Hirst *N Yorks* 52 G2
Temple Normanton *Derby* 45 F8
Temple Sowerby *Cumb* 57 D8
Templehall *Fife* 69 A11
Templeton *Devon* 7 E7
Templeton *Pembs* 22 E6
Templeton Bridge *Devon* 7 E7
Templetown *Durham* 58 A2
Tempsford *Beds* 29 C8
Ten Mile Bank *Norfolk* 38 F2
Tenbury Wells *Worcs* 26 B2
Tenby = Dinbych-y-Pysgod *Pembs* 22 F6
Tendring *Essex* 31 F8
Tendring Green *Essex* 31 F8
Tenston *Orkney* 95 G3
Tenterden *Kent* 13 C7
Terling *Essex* 30 G4
Ternhill *Shrops* 34 B2
Terregles Banks *Dumf/Gal* 60 F5
Terrick *Bucks* 28 H5
Terrington *N Yorks* 52 B2
Terrington St Clement *Norfolk* 37 D11
Terrington St John *Norfolk* 37 D11
Teston *Kent* 20 F4
Testwood *Hants* 10 C2
Tetbury *Glos* 16 B5
Tetbury Upton *Glos* 16 B5
Tetchill *Shrops* 33 B9
Tetcott *Devon* 6 G2
Tetford *Lincs* 47 E7
Tetney *Lincs* 47 B7
Tetney Lock *Lincs* 47 B7
Tetsworth *Oxon* 18 A3
Tettenhall *W Midlands* 34 F4
Teuchan *Aberds* 89 E10
Teversal *Notts* 45 F8
Teversham *Cambs* 29 C11
Teviothead *Scot Borders* 61 C10
Tewel *Aberds* 83 E10
Tewin *Herts* 29 G9
Tewkesbury *Glos* 26 E5
Teynham *Kent* 20 E6
Thackthwaite *Cumb* 56 D3
Thainston *Aberds* 83 F8
Thakeham *W Sussex* 11 C10
Thame *Oxon* 28 H4
Thames Ditton *Surrey* 19 E8
Thames Haven *Thurr'k* 20 C4
Thamesmead *London* 19 C11
Thanington *Kent* 21 F8
Thankerton *S Lanarks* 69 G8
Tharston *Norfolk* 39 F7
Thatcham *W Berks* 18 E2
Thatto Heath *Mersey* 43 C8
Thaxted *Essex* 30 E3
The Aird *H'land* 85 C9
The Arms *Norfolk* 38 F4
The Bage *Heref'd* 25 D9
The Balloch *Perth/Kinr* 75 F11
The Barony *Orkney* 95 F3
The Bog *Shrops* 33 F9
The Bourne *Surrey* 18 G5
The Braes *H'land* 85 E10
The Broad *Heref'd* 25 B11
The Butts *Som'set* 16 G4
The Camp *Glos* 26 H6
The Camp *Herts* 29 H8
The Chequer *Wrex* 33 A10
The City *Bucks* 18 B4
The Common *Wilts* 9 A11
The Craigs *H'land* 86 B7
The Cronk *I/Man* 48 C3
The Dell *Suffolk* 39 F10
The Den *N Ayrs* 66 A6
The Eals *Northum* 62 E3
The Eaves *Glos* 26 H3
The Flatt *Cumb* 61 F11
The Four Alls *Shrops* 34 B2
The Garths *Shetl'd* 96 B8
The Green *Cumb* 49 A1
The Green *Wilts* 9 A7
The Grove *Dumf/Gal* 60 F5
The Hall *Shetl'd* 96 D8
The Haven *W Sussex* 11 A9
The Heath *Norfolk* 39 C7
The Heath *Suffolk* 31 E8
The Hill *Cumb* 49 A1
The Howe *Cumb* 56 H6
The Howe *I/Man* 48 F1
The Hundred *Heref'd* 26 B2
The Lee *Bucks* 18 A6
The Lhen *I/Man* 48 B3
The Marsh *Powys* 33 F9
The Marsh *Wilts* 17 C7
The Middles *Durham* 58 A3
The Moor *Kent* 13 D6
The Mumbles = Y Mwmbwls *Swan* 14 C2
The Murray *S Lanarks* 68 E5
The Neuk *Aberds* 83 D9
The Oval *Bath/NE Som'set* 16 E4
The Pole of Itlaw *Aberds* 89 C6
The Quarry *Glos* 16 B4
The Rhos *Pembs* 22 E5
The Rock *Telford* 34 E2
The Ryde *Herts* 29 H9
The Sands *Surrey* 18 G5
The Stocks *Kent* 13 D8
The Throat *Wokingham* 18 E5
The Vauld *Heref'd* 26 D2
The Wyke *Shrops* 34 E3
Theakston *N Yorks* 58 H4
Thealby *N Lincs* 52 H4
Theale *Som'set* 15 G10
Theale *W Berks* 18 D3
Thearne *ER Yorks* 53 F6
Theberton *Suffolk* 31 B11
Theddingworth *Leics* 36 G2
Theddlethorpe All Saints *Lincs* 47 D8
Theddlethorpe St Helen *Lincs* 47 D8
Thelbridge Barton *Devon* 7 E6
Thelnetham *Suffolk* 38 H6
Thelveton *Norfolk* 39 G7
Thelwall *Warrington* 43 D9
Themelthorpe *Norfolk* 39 C6
Thenford *Northants* 28 D2
Therfield *Herts* 29 E10
Thetford *Lincs* 37 D7
Thetford *Norfolk* 38 G4
Theydon Bois *Essex* 19 B11
Thickwood *Wilts* 16 D5
Thimbleby *Lincs* 46 F6
Thimbleby *N Yorks* 58 G5
Thingwall *Mersey* 42 D5
Thirdpart *N Ayrs* 66 B4
Thirlby *N Yorks* 51 A10
Thirlestane *Scot Borders* 70 F4
Thirn *N Yorks* 58 H3
Thirsk *N Yorks* 51 A10
Thirtleby *ER Yorks* 53 F7
Thistleton *Lancs* 49 F4
Thistleton *Rutl'd* 36 D5
Thistley Green *Suffolk* 38 H2
Thixendale *N Yorks* 52 C4
Thockrington *Northum* 62 F5
Tholomas Drove *Cambs* 37 E9
Tholthorpe *N Yorks* 51 C10
Thomas Chapel *Pembs* 22 F6
Thomas Close *Cumb* 56 B6
Thomastown *Aberds* 88 E5
Thompson *Norfolk* 38 F5
Thomshill *Moray* 88 C2
Thong *Kent* 20 D3
Thongsbridge *W Yorks* 44 B5
Thoralby *N Yorks* 58 H1
Thoresway *Lincs* 46 C5
Thorganby *Lincs* 46 C6
Thorganby *N Yorks* 52 E2
Thorgill *N Yorks* 59 G8
Thorington *Suffolk* 31 A11
Thorington Street *Suffolk* 31 E7
Thorlby *N Yorks* 50 D5
Thorley *Herts* 29 G11
Thorley Street *Herts* 29 G11
Thorley Street *I/Wight* 10 F2
Thormanby *N Yorks* 51 B10
Thornaby on Tees *Stockton* 58 E5
Thornage *Norfolk* 38 B6
Thornborough *Bucks* 28 E4
Thornborough *N Yorks* 51 B8
Thornbury *Devon* 6 F3
Thornbury *Heref'd* 26 C3
Thornbury *S Gloucs* 16 B3
Thornbury *W Yorks* 51 F7
Thornby *Northants* 36 H2
Thorncliffe *Staffs* 44 G4
Thorncombe *Dorset* 8 D2
Thorncombe *Dorset* 9 D7
Thorncombe Street *Surrey* 19 G7
Thorncote Green *Beds* 29 D8
Thorncross *I/Wight* 10 F3
Thorndon *Suffolk* 31 B8
Thorndon Cross *Devon* 6 G4
Thorne *S Yorks* 45 A10
Thorne St Margaret *Som'set* 7 D9
Thorner *W Yorks* 51 E9
Thorney *Notts* 46 E2
Thorney *Peterbro* 37 E8
Thorney Crofts *ER Yorks* 53 G8
Thorney Green *Suffolk* 31 B7
Thorney Hill *Hants* 9 E10
Thorney Toll *Cambs* 37 E9
Thornfalcon *Som'set* 8 B1

Thornford *Dorset* 8 C5
Thorngumbald *ER Yorks* 53 G8
Thornham *Norfolk* 38 A3
Thornham Magna *Suffolk* 31 A8
Thornham Parva *Suffolk* 31 A8
Thornhaugh *Peterbro* 37 E6
Thornhill *Caerph* 15 C7
Thornhill *Cumb* 56 F2
Thornhill *Derby* 44 D5
Thornhill *Dumf/Gal* 60 D4
Thornhill *S'thampton* 10 C3
Thornhill *Stirl* 75 H9
Thornhill *W Yorks* 51 H8
Thornhill Edge *W Yorks* 51 H8
Thornhill Lees *W Yorks* 51 H8
Thornholme *ER Yorks* 53 C7
Thornley *Durham* 58 C2
Thornley *Durham* 58 C4
Thornliebank *E Renf* 68 E4
Thorns *Suffolk* 30 C4
Thorns Green *Ches* 43 D10
Thornsett *Derby* 44 D4
Thornthwaite *Cumb* 56 D4
Thornthwaite *N Yorks* 51 D7
Thornton *Angus* 76 C6
Thornton *Bucks* 28 E4
Thornton *ER Yorks* 52 E3
Thornton *Fife* 76 H5
Thornton *Lancs* 49 E3
Thornton *Leics* 35 E10
Thornton *Lincs* 46 F6
Thornton *Mersey* 42 B6
Thornton *Middlesbro'* 58 E5
Thornton *Northum* 71 F8
Thornton *Pembs* 22 F4
Thornton *W Yorks* 51 F7
Thornton Curtis *N Lincs* 53 H6
Thornton Heath *London* 19 E10
Thornton Hough *Mersey* 42 D6
Thornton in Craven *N Yorks* 50 E5
Thornton-le-Beans *N Yorks* 58 G4
Thornton-le-Clay *N Yorks* 52 C2
Thornton-le-Dale *N Yorks* 52 A4
Thornton le Moor *Lincs* 46 C4
Thornton-le-Moor *N Yorks* 58 H4
Thornton-le-Moors *Ches* 43 E7
Thornton-le-Street *N Yorks* 58 H5
Thornton Rust *N Yorks* 57 H11
Thornton Steward *N Yorks* 58 H2
Thornton Watlass *N Yorks* 58 H3
Thorntonhall *S Lanarks* 68 E4
Thorntonloch *E Loth* 70 C6
Thorntonpark *Northum* 71 F8
Thornwood Common *Essex* 19 A11
Thornydykes *Scot Borders* 70 F5
Thoroton *Notts* 36 A3
Thorp Arch *W Yorks* 51 E10
Thorpe *Derby* 44 G5
Thorpe *ER Yorks* 52 E5
Thorpe *Lincs* 47 D8
Thorpe *Norfolk* 39 F10
Thorpe *Notts* 45 H11
Thorpe *N Yorks* 50 C6
Thorpe *Surrey* 19 E7
Thorpe Abbotts *Norfolk* 39 H7
Thorpe Acre *Leics* 35 C11
Thorpe Arnold *Leics* 36 C3
Thorpe Audlin *W Yorks* 51 H10
Thorpe Bassett *N Yorks* 52 B4
Thorpe Bay *Southend* 20 C6
Thorpe by Water *Rutl'd* 36 F4
Thorpe Common *Suffolk* 31 E9
Thorpe Constantine *Staffs* 35 E8
Thorpe Culvert *Lincs* 47 F8
Thorpe End *Norfolk* 39 D8
Thorpe Fendykes *Lincs* 47 F8
Thorpe Green *Essex* 31 F8
Thorpe Green *Suffolk* 30 C6
Thorpe Hesley *S Yorks* 45 C7
Thorpe in Balne *S Yorks* 45 A9
Thorpe in the Fallows *Lincs* 46 D3
Thorpe Langton *Leics* 36 F3
Thorpe Larches *Durham* 58 D4
Thorpe-le-Soken *Essex* 31 F8
Thorpe le Street *ER Yorks* 52 E4
Thorpe Malsor *Northants* 36 H4
Thorpe Mandeville *Northants* 28 D2
Thorpe Market *Norfolk* 39 B8
Thorpe Marriot *Norfolk* 39 D7
Thorpe Morieux *Suffolk* 30 C6
Thorpe on the Hill *Lincs* 46 F3
Thorpe St Andrew *Norfolk* 39 E8
Thorpe St Peter *Lincs* 47 F8
Thorpe Salvin *S Yorks* 45 D9
Thorpe Satchville *Leics* 36 D3
Thorpe Thewles *Stockton* 58 D5
Thorpe Tilney *Lincs* 46 G5
Thorpe Underwood *N Yorks* 51 D10
Thorpe Waterville *Northants* 36 G6
Thorpe Willoughby *N Yorks* 52 F1
Thorpeness *Suffolk* 31 C11
Thorrington *Essex* 31 G7
Thorverton *Devon* 7 F8
Thrandeston *Suffolk* 39 H7
Thrapston *Northants* 36 H5
Thrashbush *N Lanarks* 68 D6
Threapland *Cumb* 56 C3
Threapland *N Yorks* 50 C5
Threapwood *Ches* 43 H7
Threapwood *Staffs* 34 A6
Three Ashes *Heref'd* 26 F2
Three Bridges *W Sussex* 12 C1
Three Burrows *Cornw'l* 2 E6
Three Chimneys *Kent* 13 C7
Three Cocks *Powys* 25 E8
Three Crosses *Swan* 23 G10
Three Cups Corner *E Sussex* 12 D5
Three Holes *Norfolk* 37 E11
Three Leg Cross *E Sussex* 12 C5
Three Legged Cross *Dorset* 9 D9
Three Oaks *E Sussex* 13 E7
Threehammer Common *Norfolk* 39 D9
Threekingham *Lincs* 37 B6
Threemile Cross *Wokingham* 18 E4
Threemilestone *Cornw'l* 3 E6
Threemiletown *W Loth* 69 C9
Threlkeld *Cumb* 56 D5
Threshfield *N Yorks* 50 C5
Thrigby *Norfolk* 39 D10
Thringarth *Durham* 57 D11
Thringstone *Leics* 35 D10
Thrintoft *N Yorks* 58 G4
Thriplow *Cambs* 29 D11
Throckenholt *Lincs* 37 E9
Throcking *Herts* 29 E10
Throckley *Tyne/Wear* 63 G7
Throckmorton *Worcs* 26 D6
Throphill *Northum* 63 E7
Thropton *Northum* 62 C6
Throsk *Stirl* 69 A7
Throwleigh *Devon* 6 G5
Throwley *Kent* 20 F6
Thrumpton *Notts* 35 B11
Thrumster *H'land* 94 F5
Thrunton *Northum* 62 B6
Thrupp *Glos* 16 A5
Thrupp *Oxon* 27 G11
Thrushelton *Devon* 4 C5
Thrussington *Leics* 36 D2
Thruxton *Hants* 17 G9
Thruxton *Heref'd* 25 E11
Thrybergh *S Yorks* 45 C8
Thulston *Derby* 35 B10
Thundergay *N Ayrs* 66 B1
Thundersley *Essex* 20 C4
Thundridge *Herts* 29 G10
Thurcaston *Leics* 36 D1
Thurcroft *S Yorks* 45 D8
Thurgarton *Norfolk* 39 B7
Thurgarton *Notts* 45 H10
Thurgoland *S Yorks* 44 B6
Thurlaston *Leics* 35 F11
Thurlaston *Warwick* 27 A11
Thurlbear *Som'set* 8 B1
Thurlby *Lincs* 37 D7
Thurlby *Lincs* 46 F3
Thurleigh *Beds* 29 C7
Thurlestone *Devon* 5 G7
Thurloxton *Som'set* 8 A1
Thurlstone *S Yorks* 44 B6
Thurlton *Norfolk* 39 F10
Thurlwood *Ches* 44 G2
Thurmaston *Leics* 36 E2
Thurnby *Leics* 36 E2
Thurne *Norfolk* 39 D10
Thurnham *Kent* 20 F5
Thurnham *Lancs* 49 D4
Thurning *Norfolk* 39 C6
Thurning *Northants* 37 G6
Thurnscoe *S Yorks* 45 B8
Thurnscoe East *S Yorks* 45 B8
Thursby *Cumb* 56 A5
Thursford *Norfolk* 38 B5
Thursley *Surrey* 18 H6
Thurso *H'land* 94 D3
Thurso East *H'land* 94 D3
Thurstaston *Mersey* 42 D5
Thurston *Suffolk* 30 B6
Thurstonfield *Cumb* 61 H9
Thurstonland *W Yorks* 44 A5
Thurton *Norfolk* 39 E9
Thurvaston *Derby* 35 B8
Thuxton *Norfolk* 38 E6
Thwaite *N Yorks* 57 G10
Thwaite *Suffolk* 31 B8
Thwaite St Mary *Norfolk* 39 F9
Thwaites *W Yorks* 51 E6
Thwaites Brow *W Yorks* 51 E6
Thwing *ER Yorks* 53 B6
Tibbermore *Perth/Kinr* 76 E3
Tibberton *Glos* 26 F4
Tibberton *Telford* 34 C2
Tibberton *Worcs* 26 C6
Tibenham *Norfolk* 39 G7
Tibshelf *Derby* 45 F8
Tibthorpe *ER Yorks* 52 D5
Ticehurst *E Sussex* 12 C5
Tichborne *Hants* 10 A4
Tickencote *Rutl'd* 36 E5
Tickenham *N Som'set* 15 D10
Tickhill *S Yorks* 45 C9
Ticklerton *Shrops* 33 F10
Ticknall *Derby* 35 C9
Tickton *ER Yorks* 53 E6
Tidcombe *Wilts* 17 F9
Tiddington *Oxon* 18 A3
Tiddington *Warwick* 27 C9
Tidebrook *E Sussex* 12 D5
Tideford *Cornw'l* 4 F4
Tideford Cross *Cornw'l* 4 E4
Tidenham *Glos* 16 B2
Tideswell *Derby* 44 E5
Tidmarsh *W Berks* 18 D3
Tidmington *Warwick* 27 E9
Tidpit *Hants* 9 C9
Tidworth *Wilts* 17 G9
Tiers Cross *Pembs* 22 E4
Tiffield *Northants* 28 C3
Tifty *Aberds* 89 D7
Tigerton *Angus* 77 A8
Tigh-na-Blair *Perth/Kinr* 75 F10
Tighnabruaich *Arg/Bute* 73 F8
Tighnafiline *H'land* 91 J13
Tigley *Devon* 5 E8
Tilbrook *Cambs* 29 B7
Tilbury *Thurr'k* 20 D3
Tilbury Juxta Clare *Essex* 30 D4
Tile Cross *W Midlands* 35 G7
Tile Hill *W Midlands* 35 H8
Tilehurst *Reading* 18 D3
Tilford *Surrey* 18 G5
Tilgate *W Sussex* 12 C1
Tilgate Forest Row *W Sussex* 12 C1
Tillathrowie *Aberds* 88 E4
Tilley *Shrops* 33 C11
Tillicoultry *Clack* 76 H2
Tillingham *Essex* 20 A6
Tillington *Heref'd* 25 D11
Tillington *W Sussex* 11 B8
Tillington Common *Heref'd* 25 D11
Tillyarblet *Angus* 83 G7
Tillybirloch *Aberds* 83 C8
Tillycorthie *Aberds* 89 F9
Tillydrine *Aberds* 83 D8
Tillyfour *Aberds* 83 B7
Tillyfourie *Aberds* 83 B8
Tillygarmond *Aberds* 83 D8
Tillygreig *Aberds* 89 F8
Tillykerrie *Aberds* 89 F8
Tilmanstone *Kent* 21 F10
Tilney All Saints *Norfolk* 38 D1
Tilney High End *Norfolk* 38 D1
Tilney St Lawrence *Norfolk* 37 D11
Tilshead *Wilts* 17 G7
Tilstock *Shrops* 33 B11
Tilston *Ches* 43 G7
Tilstone Fearnall *Ches* 43 F8
Tilsworth *Beds* 28 F6
Tilton on the Hill *Leics* 36 E3
Timberland *Lincs* 46 G5
Timbersbrook *Ches* 44 F2
Timberscombe *Som'set* 7 B8
Timble *N Yorks* 51 D7
Timperley *Gtr Man* 43 D10
Timsbury *Bath/NE Som'set* 16 F3
Timsbury *Hants* 10 B2
Timsgearraidh *W Isles* 90 D5
Timworth Green *Suffolk* 30 B5
Tincleton *Dorset* 9 E6
Tindale *Cumb* 62 H2
Tingewick *Bucks* 28 E3
Tingley *W Yorks* 51 G8
Tingrith *Beds* 29 E7
Tingwall *Orkney* 95 F4
Tinhay *Devon* 4 C4
Tinshill *W Yorks* 51 F8
Tinsley *S Yorks* 45 C8
Tintagel *Cornw'l* 4 C1
Tintern Parva *Monmouths* 15 A11
Tintinhull *Som'set* 8 C4
Tintwistle *Derby* 44 C4
Tinwald *Dumf/Gal* 60 E6
Tinwell *Rutl'd* 36 E6
Tipperty *Aberds* 89 F9
Tipsend *Norfolk* 37 F11
Tipton *W Midlands* 34 F5
Tipton St John *Devon* 7 G9
Tiptree *Essex* 30 G5
Tir-y-dail *Carms* 24 G3
Tirabad *Powys* 24 D5
Tiraghoil *Arg/Bute* 78 J6
Tirley *Glos* 26 F5
Tirphil *Caerph* 15 A7
Tirril *Cumb* 57 D7
Tisbury *Wilts* 9 B8
Tisman's Common *W Sussex* 11 A9
Tissington *Derby* 44 G5
Titchberry *Devon* 6 D1
Titchfield *Hants* 10 D4
Titchmarsh *Northants* 36 H6
Titchwell *Norfolk* 38 A3
Tithby *Notts* 36 B2
Titley *Heref'd* 25 B10
Titlington *Northum* 63 B7
Titsey *Surrey* 19 F11
Tittensor *Staffs* 34 B4
Tittleshall *Norfolk* 38 C4
Tiverton *Ches* 43 F8
Tiverton *Devon* 7 E8
Tivetshall St Margaret *Norfolk* 39 G7
Tivetshall St Mary *Norfolk* 39 G7
Tividale *W Midlands* 34 F5
Tivy Dale *S Yorks* 44 B6
Tixall *Staffs* 34 C5
Tixover *Rutl'd* 36 E5
Toab *Orkney* 95 H6
Toab *Shetl'd* 96 M5
Toadmoor *Derby* 45 G7
Tobermory *Arg/Bute* 79 F8
Toberonochy *Arg/Bute* 72 C6
Tobha Mor *W Isles* 84 E2
Tobhtarol *W Isles* 90 D6
Tobson *W Isles* 90 D6
Tocher *Aberds* 89 E6
Tockenham *Wilts* 17 D7
Tockenham Wick *Wilts* 17 C7
Tockholes *Blackb'n* 50 G2
Tockington *S Gloucs* 16 C3
Tockwith *N Yorks* 51 D10
Todber *Dorset* 9 B7
Todding *Heref'd* 33 H10
Toddington *Beds* 29 F7
Toddington *Glos* 27 E7
Todenham *Glos* 27 E9
Todhills *Cumb* 61 G9
Todlachie *Aberds* 83 B8
Todmorden *W Yorks* 50 G5
Todrig *Scot Borders* 61 B10
Todwick *S Yorks* 45 D8
Toft *Cambs* 29 C10
Toft *Lincs* 37 D6
Toft Hill *Durham* 58 D2
Toft Hill *Lincs* 46 F6
Toft Monks *Norfolk* 39 F10
Toft next Newton *Lincs* 46 D4
Toftrees *Norfolk* 38 C4
Tofts *H'land* 94 D5
Toftwood *Norfolk* 38 D5
Togston *Northum* 63 C8
Toravaig *H'land* 85 G11
Tokers Green *Oxon* 18 D4
Tolastadh a Chaolais *W Isles* 90 D6
Tolastadh bho Thuath *W Isles* 91 C10
Toll Bar *S Yorks* 45 B9
Toll End *W Midlands* 34 F5
Toll of Birness *Aberds* 89 E10
Tolland *Som'set* 7 C10
Tollard Royal *Wilts* 9 C8
Tollbar End *W Midlands* 35 H9
Toller Fratrum *Dorset* 8 E4
Toller Porcorum *Dorset* 8 E4
Tollerton *Notts* 36 B2
Tollerton *N Yorks* 51 C11
Tollesbury *Essex* 30 G6
Tolleshunt D'Arcy *Essex* 30 G6
Tolleshunt Major *Essex* 30 G6
Tolm *W Isles* 91 D9
Tolpuddle *Dorset* 9 E6
Tolvah *H'land* 81 D10
Tolworth *London* 19 E8
Tomatin *H'land* 81 A10
Tombreck *H'land* 87 H9
Tomchrasky *H'land* 80 B4
Tomdoun *H'land* 80 C3
Tomich *H'land* 80 A5
Tomich *H'land* 87 D9
Tomich House *H'land* 87 G8
Tomintoul *Aberds* 82 D3
Tomintoul *Moray* 82 B3
Tomnaven *Moray* 88 E4
Tomnavoulin *Moray* 82 A4
Ton-Pentre *Rh Cyn Taff* 14 B5
Tonbridge *Kent* 20 G2
Tondu *Bridg* 14 C4
Tonfanau *Gwyn* 32 E1
Tong *Shrops* 34 E3
Tong *W Yorks* 51 F8
Tong Norton *Shrops* 34 E3
Tonge *Leics* 35 C10
Tongham *Surrey* 18 G5
Tongland *Dumf/Gal* 55 D9
Tongue *H'land* 93 D8
Tongue End *Lincs* 37 D7
Tongwynlais *Card* 15 C7
Tonna *Neath P Talb* 14 B3
Tonwell *Herts* 29 G10
Tonypandy *Rh Cyn Taff* 14 B5
Tonyrefail *Rh Cyn Taff* 14 C6
Toot Baldon *Oxon* 18 A2
Toot Hill *Essex* 20 A2
Toothill *Hants* 10 C2
Top of Hebers *Gtr Man* 44 B2
Topcliffe *N Yorks* 51 B10
Topcroft *Norfolk* 39 F8
Topcroft Street *Norfolk* 39 F8
Toppesfield *Essex* 30 E4
Toppings *Gtr Man* 43 A10
Topsham *Devon* 5 C10
Torbay *Torbay* 5 F10
Torbeg *N Ayrs* 66 D2
Torboll Farm *H'land* 87 B10
Torbrex *Stirl* 68 A6
Torbryan *Devon* 5 E9
Torcross *Devon* 5 G9
Tore *H'land* 87 F9
Torinturk *Arg/Bute* 73 G7
Torksey *Lincs* 46 E2
Torlum *W Isles* 84 C2
Torlundy *H'land* 80 F3
Tormarton *S Gloucs* 16 D4
Tormisdale *Arg/Bute* 64 C2
Tormitchell *S Ayrs* 66 G5
Tormore *N Ayrs* 66 C1
Tornagrain *H'land* 87 G10
Tornahaish *Aberds* 82 C4
Tornaveen *Aberds* 83 C8
Torness *H'land* 81 A7
Toronto *Durham* 58 C2
Torpenhow *Cumb* 56 C4
Torphichen *W Loth* 69 C8
Torphins *Aberds* 83 C8
Torpoint *Cornw'l* 4 F5
Torquay *Torbay* 5 E10
Torquhan *Scot Borders* 70 F3
Torran *Arg/Bute* 73 C7
Torran *H'land* 85 D10
Torran *H'land* 87 D10
Torrance *E Dunb* 68 C5
Torrans *Arg/Bute* 78 J7
Torranyard *N Ayrs* 67 B6
Torre *Torbay* 5 E10
Torridon *H'land* 86 F2
Torridon Ho. *H'land* 85 C13
Torrin *H'land* 85 F10
Torrisdale *H'land* 93 C9
Torrisdale-Square *Arg/Bute* 65 E8
Torrish *H'land* 93 H12
Torrisholme *Lancs* 49 C4
Torroble *H'land* 93 J8
Torry *Aberd C* 83 C11
Torry *Aberds* 88 E4
Torryburn *Fife* 69 B9
Torterston *Aberds* 89 D10
Torthorwald *Dumf/Gal* 60 F6
Tortington *W Sussex* 11 D9
Tortworth *S Gloucs* 16 B4
Torvaig *H'land* 85 D9
Torver *Cumb* 56 G4
Torwood *Falk* 69 B7
Torworth *Notts* 45 D10
Tosberry *Devon* 6 D1
Toscaig *H'land* 85 E12
Toseland *Cambs* 29 B9
Tosside *N Yorks* 50 D3
Tostock *Suffolk* 30 B6
Totaig *H'land* 84 C7
Totaig *H'land* 85 F13
Tote *H'land* 85 D9
Totegan *H'land* 93 C11
Tothill *Lincs* 47 D8
Totland *I/Wight* 10 F2
Totnes *Devon* 5 E9
Toton *Notts* 35 B11
Totronald *Arg/Bute* 78 F4
Totscore *H'land* 85 B8
Tottenham *London* 19 B10
Tottenhill *Norfolk* 38 D2
Tottenhill Row *Norfolk* 38 D2
Totteridge *London* 19 B9
Totternhoe *Beds* 28 F6
Tottington *Gtr Man* 43 A10
Totton *Hants* 10 C2
Touchen End *Windsor* 18 D5
Tournaig *H'land* 91 J13
Toux *Aberds* 89 C9
Tovil *Kent* 20 F4
Tow Law *Durham* 58 C2
Toward *Arg/Bute* 73 G10
Towcester *Northants* 28 D3
Towednack *Cornw'l* 2 F3
Tower End *Norfolk* 38 D2
Towersey *Oxon* 28 H4
Towie *Aberds* 82 B6
Towie *Aberds* 89 B8
Towiemore *Moray* 88 D3
Town End *Cambs* 37 F10
Town End *Cumb* 49 A4
Town Row *E Sussex* 12 C4
Town Yetholm *Scot Borders* 71 H7
Townend *W Dunb* 68 C3
Towngate *Lincs* 37 D7
Townhead *Cumb* 57 C7
Townhead *Dumf/Gal* 55 E9
Townhead *S Ayrs* 66 F5
Townhead *S Yorks* 44 B5
Townhead of Greenlaw *Dumf/Gal* 55 C10
Townhill *Fife* 69 B10
Townsend *Bucks* 28 H4
Townsend *Herts* 29 H8
Townshend *Cornw'l* 2 F4
Towthorpe *C/York* 52 D2
Towton *N Yorks* 51 F10
Towyn *Conwy* 42 E2
Toxteth *Mersey* 42 D6
Toynton All Saints *Lincs* 47 F7
Toynton Fen Side *Lincs* 47 F7
Toynton St Peter *Lincs* 47 F8
Toy's Hill *Kent* 19 F11
Trabboch *E Ayrs* 67 D7
Traboe *Cornw'l* 2 G6
Tradespark *H'land* 87 F11
Tradespark *Orkney* 95 H5
Trafford Park *Gtr Man* 43 C10
Trallong *Powys* 24 F6
Tranent *E Loth* 70 C3
Tranmere *Mersey* 42 D6
Trantlebeg *H'land* 93 D11
Trantlemore *H'land* 93 D11
Tranwell *Northum* 63 E7
Trapp *Carms* 24 G3
Traprain *E Loth* 70 C4
Traquair *Scot Borders* 70 G2
Trawden *Lancs* 50 F5
Trawsfynydd *Gwyn* 41 G9
Tre-Gibbon *Rh Cyn Taff* 24 H6
Tre-Taliesin *Ceredig'n* 32 F2
Tre-vaughan *Carms* 23 D8
Tre-wyn *Monmouths* 25 F10
Trealaw *Rh Cyn Taff* 14 B6
Treales *Lancs* 49 F4
Trearddur *Angl* 40 C4
Treaslane *H'land* 85 C8
Trebanog *Rh Cyn Taff* 14 B6
Trebanos *Neath P Talb* 14 A3
Trebartha *Cornw'l* 4 D3
Trebarwith *Cornw'l* 4 C1
Trebetherick *Cornw'l* 3 B8
Treborough *Som'set* 7 C9
Trebudannon *Cornw'l* 3 C7
Trebullett *Cornw'l* 4 D4
Treburley *Cornw'l* 4 D4
Trebyan *Cornw'l* 4 E1
Trecastle *Powys* 24 F5
Trecenydd *Caerph* 15 C7
Trecwn *Pembs* 22 C4
Trecynon *Rh Cyn Taff* 14 A5
Tredavoe *Cornw'l* 2 G3
Treddiog *Pembs* 22 D3
Tredegar *Bl Gwent* 25 H8
Tredegar Newydd = New Tredegar *Caerph* 15 A7
Tredington *Glos* 26 F6
Tredington *Warwick* 27 D9
Tredinnick *Cornw'l* 3 B8
Tredomen *Powys* 25 E8
Tredunnock *Monmouths* 15 B9
Tredustan *Powys* 25 E8
Treen *Cornw'l* 2 G2
Treeton *S Yorks* 45 D8
Tref-y-Clawdd = Knighton *Powys* 25 A9
Trefaldwyn = Montgomery *Powys* 33 F8
Trefasser *Pembs* 22 C3
Trefdraeth *Angl* 40 C6
Trefdraeth = Newport *Pembs* 22 C5
Trefecca *Powys* 25 E8
Trefechan *Ceredig'n* 32 G1
Trefeglwys *Powys* 32 F5
Trefenter *Ceredig'n* 24 B3
Treffgarne *Pembs* 22 D4
Treffynnon *Pembs* 22 D3
Treffynnon = Holywell *Flints* 42 E4
Trefgarn Owen *Pembs* 22 D3
Trefil *Bl Gwent* 25 G8
Trefilan *Ceredig'n* 23 A10
Trefin *Pembs* 22 C3
Treflach *Shrops* 33 C8
Trefnanney *Powys* 33 D8
Trefnant *Denbs* 42 E3
Trefonen *Shrops* 33 C8
Trefor *Angl* 40 B5
Trefor *Gwyn* 40 F5
Treforest *Rh Cyn Taff* 14 C6
Trefriw *Conwy* 41 D9
Trefynwy = Monmouth *Monmouths* 26 G2
Tregadillett *Cornw'l* 4 C3
Tregaian *Angl* 40 C6
Tregare *Monmouths* 25 G11
Tregaron *Ceredig'n* 24 C3
Tregarth *Gwyn* 41 D8
Tregeare *Cornw'l* 4 C3
Tregeiriog *Wrex* 33 B7
Tregele *Angl* 40 A5
Tregidden *Cornw'l* 3 G6
Treglemais *Pembs* 22 D3
Tregole *Cornw'l* 4 B2
Tregonetha *Cornw'l* 3 C8
Tregony *Cornw'l* 3 E8
Tregoss *Cornw'l* 3 C8
Tregoyd *Powys* 25 E9
Tregroes *Ceredig'n* 23 B9
Tregurrian *Cornw'l* 3 C7
Tregynon *Powys* 33 F6
Trehafod *Rh Cyn Taff* 14 B6
Treharris *Merth Tyd* 14 B6
Treherbert *Rh Cyn Taff* 14 B5
Trekenner *Cornw'l* 4 D4
Treknow *Cornw'l* 4 C1
Trelan *Cornw'l* 2 H6
Trelash *Cornw'l* 4 B2
Trelassick *Cornw'l* 3 D7
Trelawnyd *Flints* 42 E3
Trelech *Carms* 23 C7
Treleddyd-fawr *Pembs* 22 D2
Trelewis *Merth Tyd* 15 B7
Treligga *Cornw'l* 4 C1
Trelights *Cornw'l* 3 B8
Trelill *Cornw'l* 3 B9
Trelissick *Cornw'l* 3 F7
Trellech *Monmouths* 26 H2
Trelleck Grange *Monmouths* 15 A10
Trelogan *Flints* 42 D4
Trelystan *Powys* 33 E8
Tremadog *Gwyn* 41 F7
Tremail *Cornw'l* 4 C2
Tremain *Ceredig'n* 23 B7
Tremaine *Cornw'l* 4 C3
Tremar *Cornw'l* 4 E3
Trematon *Cornw'l* 4 F4
Tremeirchion *Denbs* 42 E3
Trenance *Cornw'l* 3 C7
Trenarren *Cornw'l* 3 E9
Trench *Telford* 34 D2
Treneglos *Cornw'l* 4 C3
Trenewan *Cornw'l* 4 F2
Trent *Dorset* 8 C4
Trent Vale *Stoke* 34 A4
Trentham *Stoke* 34 A4
Trentishoe *Devon* 6 B5
Treoes *V/Glam* 14 D5
Treorchy = Treorci *Rh Cyn Taff* 14 B5
Treorci = Treorchy *Rh Cyn Taff* 14 B5
Tre'r-ddôl *Ceredig'n* 32 F2
Trerule Foot *Cornw'l* 4 F4
Tresaith *Ceredig'n* 23 A7
Tresawle *Cornw'l* 3 E7
Trescott *Staffs* 34 F4
Trescowe *Cornw'l* 2 F4
Tresham *Glos* 16 B4
Tresillian *Cornw'l* 3 E7
Tresinwen *Pembs* 22 B4
Treskinnick Cross *Cornw'l* 4 B3
Tresmeer *Cornw'l* 4 C3
Tresparrett *Cornw'l* 4 B2
Tresparrett Posts *Cornw'l* 4 B2
Tressait *Perth/Kinr* 75 A11
Tresta *Shetl'd* 96 H5
Tresta *Shetl'd* 96 D8
Treswell *Notts* 45 E11
Trethosa *Cornw'l* 3 D8
Trethurgy *Cornw'l* 3 D9
Tretio *Pembs* 22 D2
Tretire *Heref'd* 26 F2
Tretower *Powys* 25 F8
Treuddyn *Flints* 42 G5
Trevalga *Cornw'l* 4 C1
Trevalyn *Wrex* 43 G6
Trevanson *Cornw'l* 3 B8
Trevarren *Cornw'l* 3 C8
Trevarrian *Cornw'l* 3 C7
Trevarrick *Cornw'l* 3 E8
Trevaughan *Carms* 22 E6
Treveighan *Cornw'l* 4 D1
Trevellas *Cornw'l* 2 D6
Treverva *Cornw'l* 3 F6
Trevethin *Torf* 15 A8
Trevigro *Cornw'l* 4 E4
Treviscoe *Cornw'l* 3 D8
Trevone *Cornw'l* 3 B7
Trewarmett *Cornw'l* 4 C1
Trewassa *Cornw'l* 4 C2
Trewellard *Cornw'l* 2 F2
Trewen *Cornw'l* 4 C3
Trewennack *Cornw'l* 2 G5
Trewern *Powys* 33 D8
Trewethern *Cornw'l* 3 B9
Trewidland *Cornw'l* 4 F3
Trewint *Cornw'l* 4 C3
Trewint *Cornw'l* 4 B2
Trewithian *Cornw'l* 3 F7
Trewoofe *Cornw'l* 2 G3
Trewoon *Cornw'l* 3 D8
Treworga *Cornw'l* 3 E7
Treworlas *Cornw'l* 3 F7
Treyarnon *Cornw'l* 3 B7
Treyford *W Sussex* 11 C7
Trezaise *Cornw'l* 3 D8
Triangle *W Yorks* 50 G6
Trickett's Cross *Dorset* 9 D9
Triffleton *Pembs* 22 D4
Trimdon *Durham* 58 C4
Trimdon Colliery *Durham* 58 C4
Trimdon Grange *Durham* 58 C4
Trimingham *Norfolk* 39 B8
Trimley Lower Street *Suffolk* 31 E9
Trimley St Martin *Suffolk* 31 E9
Trimley St Mary *Suffolk* 31 E9
Trimpley *Worcs* 34 H3
Trimsaran *Carms* 23 F9
Trimstone *Devon* 6 B3
Trinafour *Perth/Kinr* 75 A10
Trinant *Caerph* 15 A8
Tring *Herts* 28 G6
Tring Wharf *Herts* 28 G6
Trinity *Angus* 77 A9
Trinity *Jersey* 11
Trisant *Ceredig'n* 32 H3
Trislaig *H'land* 80 F2
Trispen *Cornw'l* 3 D7
Tritlington *Northum* 63 D8
Trochry *Perth/Kinr* 76 C2
Trodigal *Arg/Bute* 65 F7
Troed rhiwdalar *Powys* 24 C6
Troedyraur *Ceredig'n* 23 B8
Troedyrhiw *Merth Tyd* 14 A6
Tromode *I/Man* 48 E3
Trondavoe *Shetl'd* 96 F5
Troon *Cornw'l* 2 F5
Troon *S Ayrs* 66 C6
Trosaraidh *W Isles* 84 G2
Trossachs Hotel *Stirl* 75 G8
Troston *Suffolk* 30 A5
Trottiscliffe *Kent* 20 E3
Trotton *W Sussex* 11 B7
Troutbeck *Cumb* 56 F6
Troutbeck *Cumb* 56 D5
Troutbeck Bridge *Cumb* 56 F6
Trow Green *Glos* 26 H2
Trowbridge *Wilts* 16 F5
Trowell *Notts* 35 B10
Trowle Common *Wilts* 16 F5
Trowley Bottom *Herts* 29 G7
Trows *Scot Borders* 70 G5
Trowse Newton *Norfolk* 39 E8
Trudoxhill *Som'set* 16 G4
Trull *Som'set* 7 D11
Trumaisgearraidh *W Isles* 84 A3
Trumpan *H'land* 84 B7
Trumpet *Heref'd* 26 E3
Trumpington *Cambs* 29 C11
Trunch *Norfolk* 39 B8
Trunnah *Lancs* 49 E3
Truro *Cornw'l* 3 E7
Trusham *Devon* 5 C9
Trusley *Derby* 35 B8
Trusthorpe *Lincs* 47 D9
Trysull *Staffs* 34 F4
Tubney *Oxon* 17 B11
Tuckenhay *Devon* 5 F9
Tuckhill *Shrops* 34 G3
Tuckingmill *Cornw'l* 2 E5
Tuddenham *Suffolk* 30 A4
Tuddenham St Martin *Suffolk* 31 D8
Tudeley *Kent* 20 G3
Tudhoe *Durham* 58 C3
Tudorville *Heref'd* 26 F2
Tudweiliog *Gwyn* 40 G4
Tuesley *Surrey* 18 G6
Tuffley *Glos* 26 G5
Tufton *Hants* 17 G11
Tufton *Pembs* 22 D5
Tugby *Leics* 36 E3
Tugford *Shrops* 34 G1
Tullibardine *Perth/Kinr* 76 F2
Tullibody *Clack* 75 H11
Tullich *Arg/Bute* 73 B9
Tullich *H'land* 81 A8
Tullich Muir *H'land* 87 D10
Tulliemet *Perth/Kinr* 76 B2
Tulloch *Aberds* 83 F9
Tulloch *Aberds* 89 E8
Tulloch *Perth/Kinr* 76 E3
Tulloch Castle *H'land* 87 E8
Tullochgorm *Arg/Bute* 73 D8
Tulloes *Angus* 77 C8
Tullybannocher *Perth/Kinr* 75 E10
Tullybelton *Perth/Kinr* 76 D3
Tullyfergus *Perth/Kinr* 76 C5
Tullymurdoch *Perth/Kinr* 76 B4
Tullynessle *Aberds* 83 B7
Tumble *Carms* 23 E10
Tumby Woodside *Lincs* 46 G6
Tummel Bridge *Perth/Kinr* 75 B10
Tunga *W Isles* 91 D9
Tunstall *ER Yorks* 53 F9
Tunstall *Kent* 20 E5
Tunstall *Lancs* 50 B2
Tunstall *Norfolk* 39 E10
Tunstall *N Yorks* 58 G3
Tunstall *Stoke* 44 G2
Tunstall *Suffolk* 31 C10
Tunstall *Tyne/Wear* 58 A4
Tunstead *Derby* 44 E5
Tunstead *Gtr Man* 44 B4
Tunstead *Norfolk* 39 C8
Tunworth *Hants* 18 G3
Tupsley *Heref'd* 26 D2
Tupton *Derby* 45 F7
Tur Langton *Leics* 36 F3
Turgis Green *Hants* 18 F3
Turin *Angus* 77 B8
Turkdean *Glos* 27 G8
Turleigh *Wilts* 16 E5
Turn *Lancs* 50 H4
Turnastone *Heref'd* 25 E10
Turnberry *S Ayrs* 66 F5
Turnditch *Derby* 44 H6
Turners Hill *W Sussex* 12 C2
Turners Puddle *Dorset* 9 E7
Turnford *Herts* 19 A10
Turnhouse *C/Edinb* 69 C10
Turnworth *Dorset* 9 D7
Turriff *Aberds* 89 C7
Turton Bottoms *Blackb'n* 50 H3
Turves *Cambs* 37 F9
Turvey *Beds* 28 C6
Turville *Bucks* 18 B4
Turville Heath *Bucks* 18 B4
Turweston *Bucks* 28 E3
Tushielaw *Scot Borders* 61 B9
Tutbury *Staffs* 35 C8
Tutnall *Worcs* 26 A6
Tutshill *Glos* 15 B11
Tuttington *Norfolk* 39 C8
Tutts Clump *W Berks* 18 D2
Tuxford *Notts* 45 E11
Twatt *Orkney* 95 F3
Twatt *Shetl'd* 96 H5
Twechar *E Dunb* 68 C6
Tweedmouth *Northum* 71 E8
Tweedsmuir *Scot Borders* 60 A6
Twelve Heads *Cornw'l* 3 E6
Twemlow Green *Ches* 43 F10
Twenty *Lincs* 37 C7
Twerton *Bath/NE Som'set* 16 E4
Twickenham *London* 19 D8
Twigworth *Glos* 26 F5
Twineham *W Sussex* 12 E1
Twinhoe *Bath/NE Som'set* 16 F4
Twinstead *Essex* 30 E5
Twinstead Green *Essex* 30 E5
Twiss Green *Warrington* 43 C9
Twiston *Lancs* 50 E4
Twitchen *Devon* 7 C6
Twitchen *Shrops* 33 H9
Two Bridges *Devon* 5 D7
Two Dales *Derby* 44 F6
Two Mills *Ches* 42 E6
Twycross *Leics* 35 E9
Twyford *Bucks* 28 F3
Twyford *Derby* 35 C9
Twyford *Hants* 10 B3
Twyford *Leics* 36 D3
Twyford *Lincs* 36 C5
Twyford *Norfolk* 38 C6
Twyford *Wokingham* 18 D4
Twyford Common *Heref'd* 26 E2
Twyn-y-Sheriff *Monmouths* 25 H11
Twynholm *Dumf/Gal* 55 D9
Twyning *Glos* 26 E5
Twyning Green *Glos* 26 E6
Twynllanan *Carms* 24 F4
Twynmynydd *Carms* 24 G3
Twywell *Northants* 36 H5
Ty-draw *Conwy* 41 E10
Ty-hen *Carms* 23 D8
Ty-hen *Gwyn* 40 G3
Ty-mawr *Angl* 40 B6
Ty Mawr *Carms* 23 B10
Ty Mawr Cwm *Conwy* 42 H2
Ty-nant *Conwy* 32 A5
Ty-nant *Gwyn* 32 C5
Ty-uchaf *Powys* 32 C6
Tyberton *Heref'd* 25 E10
Tyburn *W Midlands* 35 F7
Tycroes *Carms* 24 G3
Tycrwyn *Powys* 33 D7
Tydd Gote *Lincs* 37 D10
Tydd St Giles *Cambs* 37 D10
Tydd St Mary *Lincs* 37 D10
Tyddewi = St David's *Pembs* 22 D2
Tyddyn-mawr *Gwyn* 41 F7
Tye Green *Essex* 30 E2
Tye Green *Essex* 30 F4
Tye Green *Essex* 29 H11
Tyldesley *Gtr Man* 43 B9
Tyler Hill *Kent* 21 E8
Tylers Green *Bucks* 18 B6
Tylorstown *Rh Cyn Taff* 14 B6
Tylwch *Powys* 32 G5
Tyn-y-celyn *Wrex* 33 B7
Tyn-y-coed *Shrops* 33 C8
Tyn-y-fedwen *Powys* 33 B7
Tyn-y-ffridd *Powys* 33 B7
Tyn-y-graig *Powys* 25 C7
Ty'n-y-groes *Conwy* 41 C9
Ty'n-y-maes *Gwyn* 41 D8
Tyn-y-pwll *Angl* 40 B6
Ty'n-yr-eithin *Ceredig'n* 24 B3
Tyncelyn *Ceredig'n* 24 B3
Tyndrum *Stirl* 74 D6
Tyne Tunnel *Tyne/Wear* 63 G9
Tyneham *Dorset* 9 F7
Tynehead *Midloth* 70 E2
Tynemouth *Tyne/Wear* 63 G9
Tynewydd *Rh Cyn Taff* 14 B5
Tyninghame *E Loth* 70 C5
Tynron *Dumf/Gal* 60 D4
Tynygongl *Angl* 41 B7
Tynygraig *Ceredig'n* 24 B3
Tŷ'r-felin-isaf *Conwy* 41 D10
Tyrie *Aberds* 89 B9
Tyringham *M/Keynes* 28 D5
Tythecott *Devon* 6 E3
Tythegston *Bridg* 14 D4
Tytherington *Ches* 44 E3
Tytherington *S Gloucs* 16 C3
Tytherington *Som'set* 16 G4
Tytherington *Wilts* 16 G6
Tytherleigh *Devon* 8 D2
Tywardreath *Cornw'l* 4 F1
Tywyn *Conwy* 41 C9
Tywyn *Gwyn* 32 E1

U

Uachdar *W Isles* 84 C2
Uags *H'land* 85 E12
Ubbeston Green *Suffolk* 31 A10
Ubley *Bath/NE Som'set* 15 F11
Uckerby *N Yorks* 58 F3
Uckfield *E Sussex* 12 D3
Uckington *Glos* 26 F6
Uddingston *S Lanarks* 68 D5
Uddington *S Lanarks* 69 G7
Udimore *E Sussex* 13 E7
Udny Green *Aberds* 89 F8
Udny Station *Aberds* 89 F9
Udston *S Lanarks* 68 E5
Udstonhead *S Lanarks* 68 F6
Uffcott *Wilts* 17 D8
Uffculme *Devon* 7 E9
Uffington *Lincs* 37 E6
Uffington *Oxon* 17 C10
Uffington *Shrops* 33 D11
Ufford *Peterbro* 37 E6
Ufford *Suffolk* 31 C9
Ufton *Warwick* 27 B10
Ufton Nervet *W Berks* 18 E3
Ugadale *Arg/Bute* 65 F8
Ugborough *Devon* 5 F7
Uggeshall *Suffolk* 39 G10
Ugglebarnby *N Yorks* 59 F9
Ughill *S Yorks* 44 C6
Ugley *Essex* 30 F2
Ugley Green *Essex* 30 F2
Ugthorpe *N Yorks* 59 E8
Uidh *W Isles* 84 J1
Uig *Arg/Bute* 73 E10
Uig *H'land* 85 B8
Uig *H'land* 84 C6
Uigen *W Isles* 90 D5
Uigshader *H'land* 85 D9
Uisken *Arg/Bute* 78 K6
Ulbster *H'land* 94 F5
Ulceby *Lincs* 47 E8
Ulceby *N Lincs* 46 A5
Ulceby Skitter *N Lincs* 46 A5
Ulcombe *Kent* 20 G5
Uldale *Cumb* 56 C4
Uley *Glos* 16 B4
Ulgham *Northum* 63 D8
Ullapool *H'land* 86 B4
Ullenhall *Warwick* 27 B8
Ullenwood *Glos* 26 G6
Ulleskelf *N Yorks* 51 E11
Ullesthorpe *Leics* 35 G11
Ulley *S Yorks* 45 D8
Ullingswick *Heref'd* 26 D2
Ullinish *H'land* 85 E8
Ullock *Cumb* 56 D2
Ulnes Walton *Lancs* 49 H5
Ulpha *Cumb* 56 G3
Ulrome *ER Yorks* 53 D7
Ulsta *Shetl'd* 96 E6
Ulva House *Arg/Bute* 78 H7
Ulverston *Cumb* 49 B2
Ulwell *Dorset* 9 F9
Umberleigh *Devon* 6 D5
Unapool *H'land* 92 F5
Unasary *W Isles* 84 F2
Underbarrow *Cumb* 56 G6
Undercliffe *W Yorks* 51 F7
Underhoull *Shetl'd* 96 C7
Underriver *Kent* 20 F2
Underwood *Notts* 45 G8
Undy *Monmouths* 15 C10
Unifirth *Shetl'd* 96 H4
Union Cottage *Aberds* 83 D10
Union Mills *I/Man* 48 E3
Union Street *E Sussex* 12 C6
Unstone *Derby* 45 E7
Unstone Green *Derby* 45 E7
Unthank *Cumb* 56 C6
Unthank *Cumb* 57 B8
Unthank End *Cumb* 56 C6
Up Cerne *Dorset* 8 D5
Up Exe *Devon* 7 F8
Up Hatherley *Glos* 26 F6
Up Holland *Lancs* 43 B8
Up Marden *W Sussex* 11 C6
Up Nately *Hants* 18 F3
Up Somborne *Hants* 10 A2
Up Sydling *Dorset* 8 D5
Upavon *Wilts* 17 F8
Upchurch *Kent* 20 E5
Upcott *Heref'd* 25 C10
Upend *Cambs* 30 C3
Upgate *Norfolk* 39 D7
Uphall *W Loth* 69 C9
Uphall Station *W Loth* 69 C9
Upham *Devon* 7 F7
Upham *Hants* 10 B4
Uphampton *Worcs* 26 B5
Uphill *N Som'set* 15 F9
Uplawmoor *E Renf* 68 E3
Upleadon *Glos* 26 F4
Upleatham *Redcar/Clevel'd* 59 E7
Uplees *Kent* 20 E6
Uploders *Dorset* 8 E4
Uplowman *Devon* 7 E9
Uplyme *Devon* 8 E2
Upminster *London* 20 C2
Upnor *Medway* 20 D4
Upottery *Devon* 7 F11
Upper Affcot *Shrops* 33 G10
Upper Ardchronie *H'land* 87 C9
Upper Arley *Worcs* 34 G3
Upper Arncott *Oxon* 28 G3
Upper Astrop *Northants* 28 E2
Upper Badcall *H'land* 92 E4
Upper Basildon *W Berks* 18 D2
Upper Beeding *W Sussex* 11 C10
Upper Benefield *Northants* 36 G5
Upper Bighouse *H'land* 93 D11
Upper Boddington *Northants* 27 C11
Upper Borth *Ceredig'n* 32 G2
Upper Boyndlie *Aberds* 89 B9
Upper Brailes *Warwick* 27 E10
Upper Breakish *H'land* 85 F11
Upper Breinton *Heref'd* 25 D11
Upper Broadheath *Worcs* 26 C5
Upper Broughton *Notts* 36 C2
Upper Bucklebury *W Berks* 18 E2
Upper Burnhaugh *Aberds* 83 D10
Upper Caldecote *Beds* 29 D8
Upper Catesby *Northants* 28 C2
Upper Chapel *Powys* 25 D7
Upper Church Village *Rh Cyn Taff* 14 C6
Upper Chute *Wilts* 17 F9
Upper Clatford *Hants* 17 G10
Upper Clynnog *Gwyn* 40 F6
Upper Cumberworth *W Yorks* 44 B6
Upper Cwm-twrch *Powys* 24 G4
Upper Cwmbran *Torf* 15 B8
Upper Dallachy *Moray* 88 B3
Upper Dean *Beds* 29 B7
Upper Denby *W Yorks* 44 B6
Upper Denton *Cumb* 62 G2
Upper Derraid *H'land* 87 H13
Upper Dicker *E Sussex* 12 F4
Upper Dovercourt *Essex* 31 E9
Upper Druimfin *Arg/Bute* 79 F8
Upper Dunsforth *N Yorks* 51 C10
Upper Eathie *H'land* 87 E10
Upper Elkstone *Staffs* 44 G4
Upper End *Derby* 44 E4
Upper Farringdon *Hants* 18 H4
Upper Framilode *Glos* 26 G4
Upper Glenfintaig *H'land* 80 E4
Upper Gornal *W Midlands* 34 F5
Upper Gravenhurst *Beds* 29 E8
Upper Green *Monmouths* 25 G10
Upper Green *W Berks* 17 E10
Upper Grove Common *Heref'd* 26 F2
Upper Hackney *Derby* 44 F6
Upper Hale *Surrey* 18 G5
Upper Halistra *H'land* 84 C7
Upper Halling *Medway* 20 E3
Upper Hambleton *Rutl'd* 36 E5
Upper Hardres Court *Kent* 21 F8
Upper Hartfield *E Sussex* 12 C3
Upper Haugh *S Yorks* 45 C8
Upper Heath *Shrops* 34 G1
Upper Hellesdon *Norfolk* 39 D8
Upper Helmsley *N Yorks* 52 D2
Upper Hergest *Heref'd* 25 C9
Upper Heyford *Northants* 28 C3
Upper Heyford *Oxon* 27 F11
Upper Hill *Heref'd* 25 C11
Upper Hopton *W Yorks* 51 H7
Upper Horsebridge *E Sussex* 12 E4
Upper Hulme *Staffs* 44 F4
Upper Inglesham *Swindon* 17 B9
Upper Inverbrough *H'land* 87 H11
Upper Killay *Swan* 23 G10
Upper Knockando *Moray* 88 D1
Upper Lambourn *W Berks* 17 C10
Upper Leigh *Staffs* 34 B6
Upper Lenie *H'land* 81 A7
Upper Lochton *Aberds* 83 D8
Upper Longdon *Staffs* 35 D6
Upper Lybster *H'land* 94 G4
Upper Lydbrook *Glos* 26 G3
Upper Maes-coed *Heref'd* 25 E10
Upper Midway *Derby* 35 C8
Upper Milovaig *H'land* 84 D6
Upper Minety *Wilts* 17 B7
Upper Mitton *Worcs* 26 A5
Upper North Dean *Bucks* 18 B5
Upper Obney *Perth/Kinr* 76 D3
Upper Ollach *H'land* 85 E10
Upper Padley *Derby* 44 E6
Upper Pollicott *Bucks* 28 G4
Upper Poppleton *C/York* 52 D1
Upper Quinton *Warwick* 27 D8
Upper Ratley *Hants* 10 B2
Upper Rissington *Glos* 27 G9
Upper Rochford *Worcs* 26 B3
Upper Sandaig *H'land* 85 G12
Upper Sanday *Orkney* 95 H6
Upper Sapey *Heref'd* 26 B3
Upper Seagry *Wilts* 16 C6
Upper Shelton *Beds* 28 D6
Upper Sheringham *Norfolk* 39 A7
Upper Skelmorlie *N Ayrs* 73 G11
Upper Slaughter *Glos* 27 F8
Upper Soudley *Glos* 26 G3
Upper Stondon *Beds* 29 E8
Upper Stowe *Northants* 28 C3
Upper Stratton *Swindon* 17 C8
Upper Street *Hants* 9 C10
Upper Street *Norfolk* 39 D9
Upper Street *Norfolk* 39 D9
Upper Street *Suffolk* 31 E8
Upper Strensham *Worcs* 26 E6

Upper Sundon Beds 29 F7
Upper Swell Glos 27 F8
Upper Tean Staffs 34 B6
Upper Tillyrie Perth/Kinr 76 G4
Upper Tooting London 19 D9
Upper Tote H'land 85 C10
Upper Town N Som'set 15 E11
Upper Treverward Shrops 33 H8
Upper Tysoe Warwick 27 D10
Upper Upham Wilts 17 D9
Upper Wardington Oxon 27 D11
Upper Weald M/Keynes 28 E4
Upper Weedon Northants 28 C3
Upper Wield Hants 18 H3
Upper Winchendon Bucks 28 G4
Upper Witton W Midlands 35 F6
Upper Woodend Aberds 83 B8
Upper Woodford Wilts 17 H8
Upper Wootton Hants 18 F2
Upper Wyche Worcs 26 D4
Upperby Cumb 56 A6
Uppermill Gtr Man 44 B3
Uppersound Shetl'd 96 J6
Upperthong W Yorks 44 B5
Upperthorpe N Lincs 45 B11
Upperton W Sussex 11 B8
Uppertown Derby 45 F7
Uppertown H'land 94 C5
Uppertown Orkney 95 J5
Uppingham Rutl'd 36 F4
Uppington Shrops 34 E2
Upsall N Yorks 58 H5
Upshire Essex 19 A11
Upstreet Kent 21 E9
Upthorpe Suffolk 30 A6
Upton Cambs 37 H7
Upton Ches 43 F7
Upton Cornw'l 6 F1
Upton Dorset 8 F6
Upton Dorset 9 E8
Upton Hants 10 C2
Upton Hants 17 F10
Upton Leics 35 F9
Upton Lincs 46 D2
Upton Mersey 42 D5
Upton Norfolk 39 D9
Upton Notts 45 G11
Upton Notts 45 E11
Upton Northants 28 B4
Upton Oxon 18 C2
Upton Peterbro 37 E7
Upton Slough 18 D6
Upton Som'set 7 D8
Upton W Yorks 45 A8
Upton Bishop Heref'd 26 F3
Upton Cheyney S Gloucs 16 E3
Upton Cressett Shrops 34 F2
Upton Cross Cornw'l 4 D3
Upton Grey Hants 18 G3
Upton Hellions Devon 7 F7
Upton Lovell Wilts 16 G6
Upton Magna Shrops 34 D1
Upton Noble Som'set 16 H4
Upton Pyne Devon 7 G8
Upton St Leonard's Glos 26 G5
Upton Scudamore Wilts 16 G5
Upton Snodsbury Worcs 26 C6
Upton upon Severn Worcs 26 D5
Upton Warren Worcs 26 B6
Upwaltham W Sussex 11 C8
Upware Cambs 30 A2
Upwell Norfolk 37 E10
Upwey Dorset 8 F5
Upwood Cambs 37 G8
Uradale Shetl'd 96 K6
Urafirth Shetl'd 96 F5
Urchfont Wilts 17 F7
Urdimarsh Heref'd 26 D2
Ure Shetl'd 96 F4
Ure Bank N Yorks 51 B9
Urgha W Isles 90 H6
Urishay Common Heref'd 25 E10
Urlay Nook Stockton 58 E4
Urmston Gtr Man 43 C10
Urpeth Durham 58 A3
Urquhart H'land 87 F8
Urquhart Moray 88 B2
Urra N Yorks 59 F6
Urray H'land 87 F8
Ushaw Moor Durham 58 B3
Usk = Brynbuga Monmouths 15 A9
Usselby Lincs 46 C4
Usworth Tyne/Wear 63 H9
Utkinton Ches 43 F8
Utley W Yorks 50 E6
Uton Devon 7 G7
Utterby Lincs 47 C7
Uttoxeter Staffs 35 B6
Uwchmynydd Gwyn 40 H3
Uxbridge London 19 C7
Uyeasound Shetl'd 96 C7
Uzmaston Pembs 22 E4

V

Valley Angl 40 C4
Valley Truckle Cornw'l 4 C1
Valleyfield Dumf/Gal 55 D9
Valsgarth Shetl'd 96 B8
Valtos H'land 85 B10
Van Powys 32 G5
Vange Essex 20 C4
Varteg Torf 25 H9
Vatten H'land 85 D7
Vaul Arg/Bute 78 G3
Vaynor Merth Tyd 25 G7
Veensgarth Shetl'd 96 J6
Velindre Powys 25 E8
Vellow Som'set 7 C9
Veness Orkney 95 F6
Venn Green Devon 6 E2
Venn Ottery Devon 7 G9
Vennington Shrops 33 E9
Venny Tedburn Devon 7 G7
Ventnor I/Wight 10 G4
Vernham Dean Hants 17 F10
Vernham Street Hants 17 F10
Vernolds Common Shrops 33 G10
Verwood Dorset 9 D9
Veryan Cornw'l 3 F8
Vicarage Devon 7 H11
Vickerstown Cumb 49 C1
Victoria Cornw'l 3 C8
Victoria S Yorks 44 B5
Vidlin Shetl'd 96 G6
Viewpark N Lanarks 68 D6
Vigo Village Kent 20 E3
Vinehall Street E Sussex 13 D6
Vine's Cross E Sussex 12 E4
Viney Hill Glos 26 H3
Virginia Water Surrey 18 E6
Virginstow Devon 6 G2
Vobster Som'set 16 G4
Voe Shetl'd 96 G6
Voe Shetl'd 96 E5
Vowchurch Heref'd 25 E10
Voxter Shetl'd 96 F5
Voy Orkney 95 G3

W

Wackerfield Durham 58 D2
Wacton Norfolk 39 F7
Wadbister Shetl'd 96 J6
Wadborough Worcs 26 D6
Waddesdon Bucks 28 G4
Waddingham Lincs 46 C3
Waddington Lancs 50 E3
Waddington Lincs 46 F3
Wadebridge Cornw'l 3 B8
Wadeford Som'set 8 C2
Wadenhoe Northants 36 G6
Wadesmill Herts 29 G10
Wadhurst E Sussex 12 C5
Wadshelf Derby 45 E7
Wadsley S Yorks 45 C7
Wadsley Bridge S Yorks 45 C7
Wadworth S Yorks 45 C9
Waen Denbs 42 F4
Waen Denbs 42 F2
Waen Fach Powys 33 D8
Waen Goleugoed Denbs 42 E3
Wag H'land 93 G13
Wainfleet All Saints Lincs 47 G8
Wainfleet Bank Lincs 47 G8
Wainfleet St Mary Lincs 47 G9
Wainfleet Tofts Lincs 47 G8
Wainhouse Corner Cornw'l 4 B2
Wainscott Medway 20 D4
Wainstalls W Yorks 50 G6
Waitby Cumb 57 F9
Waithe Lincs 46 B6
Wake Lady Green N Yorks 59 G7
Wakefield W Yorks 51 G9
Wakerley Northants 36 F5
Wakes Colne Essex 30 F5
Walberswick Suffolk 31 A11
Walberton W Sussex 11 D8
Walbottle Tyne/Wear 63 G7
Walcot Lincs 37 B6
Walcot N Lincs 52 G4
Walcot Shrops 33 G9
Walcot Telford 34 D1
Walcot Swindon 17 C8
Walcot Green Norfolk 39 G7
Walcote Leics 36 G1
Walcote Warwick 27 C8
Walcott Lincs 46 G5
Walcott Norfolk 39 B9
Walden N Yorks 50 A6
Walden Head N Yorks 50 A5
Walden Stubbs N Yorks 52 H1
Waldersey Cambs 37 E10
Walderslade Medway 20 E4
Walderton W Sussex 11 C6
Walditch Dorset 8 E3
Waldley Derby 35 B7
Waldridge Durham 58 A3
Waldringfield Suffolk 31 D9
Waldringfield Heath Suffolk 31 D9
Waldron E Sussex 12 E4
Wales S Yorks 45 D8
Walesby Lincs 46 C5
Walesby Notts 45 E10
Walford Heref'd 25 A10
Walford Heref'd 26 F2
Walford Shrops 33 C10
Walford Heath Shrops 33 D10
Walgherton Ches 43 H9
Walgrave Northants 28 A5
Walhampton Hants 10 E2
Walk Mill Lancs 50 F4
Walkden Gtr Man 43 B10
Walker Tyne/Wear 63 G8
Walker Barn Ches 44 E3
Walker Fold Lancs 50 E2
Walkerburn Scot Borders 70 G2
Walkeringham Notts 45 C11
Walkerith Lincs 45 C11
Walkern Herts 29 F9
Walker's Green Heref'd 26 D2
Walkerville N Yorks 58 G3
Walkford Dorset 9 E11
Walkhampton Devon 4 E6
Walkington ER Yorks 52 F5
Walkley S Yorks 45 D7
Wall Northum 62 G5
Wall Staffs 35 E7
Wall Bank Shrops 33 F11
Wall Heath W Midlands 34 G4
Wall under Heywood Shrops 33 F11
Wallaceton Dumf/Gal 60 E4
Wallacetown S Ayrs 66 F5
Wallacetown S Ayrs 66 D6
Wallands Park E Sussex 12 E3
Wallasey Mersey 42 C6
Wallcrouch E Sussex 12 C5
Wallingford Oxon 18 C3
Wallington London 19 E9
Wallington Hants 10 D4
Wallington Herts 29 E9
Wallis Pembs 22 D5
Walliswood Surrey 19 H8
Walls Shetl'd 96 J4
Wallsend Tyne/Wear 63 G8
Wallston V/Glam 15 D7
Wallyford E Loth 70 C2
Walmer Kent 21 F10
Walmer Bridge Lancs 49 G4
Walmersley Gtr Man 44 A2
Walmley W Midlands 35 F7
Walpole Suffolk 31 A10
Walpole Cross Keys Norfolk 37 D11
Walpole Highway Norfolk 37 D11
Walpole Marsh Norfolk 37 D10
Walpole St Andrew Norfolk 37 D11
Walpole St Peter Norfolk 37 D11
Walsall W Midlands 34 F6
Walsall Wood W Midlands 34 E6
Walsden W Yorks 50 G5
Walsgrave on Sowe W Midlands 35 G9
Walsham le Willows Suffolk 30 A6
Walshaw Gtr Man 43 A10
Walshford N Yorks 51 D10
Walsoken Cambs 37 D10
Walston S Lanarks 69 F9
Walsworth Herts 29 E9
Walters Ash Bucks 18 B5
Walterston V/Glam 14 D6
Walterstone Heref'd 25 F10
Waltham Kent 21 G8
Waltham NE Lincs 46 B6
Waltham Abbey Essex 19 A10
Waltham Chase Hants 10 C4
Waltham Cross Herts 19 A10
Waltham on the Wolds Leics 36 C4
Waltham St Lawrence Windsor 18 D5
Walthamstow London 19 C10
Walton Cumb 61 G11
Walton Derby 45 F7
Walton Leics 36 G1
Walton Mersey 42 C6
Walton M/Keynes 28 E5
Walton Peterbro 37 E7
Walton Powys 25 C9
Walton Som'set 15 H10
Walton Staffs 34 B4
Walton Suffolk 31 E9
Walton Telford 34 D1
Walton Warwick 27 C9
Walton W Yorks 51 H9
Walton W Yorks 51 E10
Walton Cardiff Glos 26 E6
Walton East Pembs 22 D5
Walton-in-Gordano N Som'set 15 D10
Walton-le-Dale Lancs 50 G1
Walton on Thames Surrey 19 E8
Walton on the Hill Staffs 34 C5
Walton on the Hill Surrey 19 F9
Walton-on-the-Naze Essex 31 F9
Walton on the Wolds Leics 36 D1
Walton-on-Trent Derby 35 D8
Walton West Pembs 22 E3
Walwen Flints 42 E5
Walwick Northum 62 F5
Walworth D'lington 58 E3
Walworth Gate D'lington 58 D3
Walwyn's Castle Pembs 22 E3
Wambrook Som'set 8 D1
Wanborough Surrey 18 G6
Wanborough Swindon 17 C9
Wandsworth London 19 D9
Wangford Suffolk 39 H10
Wanlockhead Dumf/Gal 60 B4
Wansford ER Yorks 53 D6
Wansford Peterbro 37 F6
Wanstead London 19 C11
Wanstrow Som'set 16 G4
Wanswell Glos 16 A3
Wantage Oxon 17 C10
Wapley S Gloucs 16 D4
Wappenbury Warwick 27 B10
Wappenham Northants 28 D3
Warbleton E Sussex 12 E5
Warblington Hants 10 D6
Warborough Oxon 18 B2
Warboys Cambs 37 G9
Warbreck Blackp'l 49 F3
Warbstow Cornw'l 4 B3
Warburton Gtr Man 43 D10
Warcop Cumb 57 E9
Ward End W Midlands 35 G7
Ward Green Suffolk 31 B7
Warden Kent 21 D7
Warden Northum 62 G5
Wardhill Orkney 95 F7
Wardington Oxon 27 D11
Wardlaw Scot Borders 61 B8
Wardle Ches 43 G9
Wardle Gtr Man 50 H5
Wardley Rutl'd 36 E4
Wardlow Derby 44 E5
Wardy Hill Cambs 37 G10
Ware Herts 29 G10
Ware Kent 21 E9
Wareham Dorset 9 F8
Warehorne Kent 13 C8
Waren Mill Northum 71 G10
Warenford Northum 71 H10
Warenton Northum 71 G10
Wareside Herts 29 G10
Waresley Cambs 29 C9
Waresley Worcs 26 A5
Warfield Brackn'l 18 D5
Warfleet Devon 5 F9
Wargrave Wokingham 18 D4
Warham Norfolk 38 A5
Warhill Gtr Man 44 C3
Wark Northum 62 F4
Wark Northum 71 G7
Warkleigh Devon 6 D5
Warkton Northants 36 H4
Warkworth Northants 27 D11
Warkworth Northum 63 C8
Warlaby N Yorks 58 G4
Warland W Yorks 50 G5
Warleggan Cornw'l 4 E2
Warlingham Surrey 19 F10
Warmfield W Yorks 51 G9
Warmingham Ches 43 F10
Warmington Northants 37 F6
Warmington Warwick 27 D11
Warminster Wilts 16 G5
Warmlake Kent 20 F5
Warmley S Glouc 16 D3
Warmley Tower S Gloucs 16 D3
Warmonds Hill Northants 28 B6
Warmsworth S Yorks 45 B9
Warmwell Dorset 9 F6
Warndon Worcs 26 C5
Warnford Hants 10 B5
Warnham W Sussex 11 A10
Warninglid W Sussex 11 B11
Warren Ches 44 E2
Warren Pembs 22 G4
Warren Heath Suffolk 31 D9
Warren Row Windsor 18 C5
Warren Street Kent 20 F6
Warrington M/Keynes 28 C5
Warrington Warrington 43 D9
Warsash Hants 10 D3
Warslow Staffs 44 G4
Warter ER Yorks 52 D4
Warthermarske N Yorks 51 B8
Warthill N Yorks 52 D2
Wartling E Sussex 12 F5
Wartnaby Leics 36 C3
Warton Lancs 49 G4
Warton Lancs 49 B4
Warton Northum 62 C6
Warton Warwick 35 E8
Warwick Warwick 27 B9
Warwick Bridge Cumb 61 H10
Warwick on Eden Cumb 61 H10
Wasbister Orkney 95 E4
Wasdale Head Cumb 56 F3
Wash Common W Berks 17 E11
Washaway Cornw'l 3 C9
Washbourne Devon 5 F8
Washfield Devon 7 E8
Washfold N Yorks 58 F1
Washford Som'set 7 B9
Washford Pyne Devon 7 E7
Washingborough Lincs 46 E4
Washington Tyne/Wear 63 H9
Washington W Sussex 11 C10
Wasing W Berks 18 E2
Waskerley Durham 58 B1
Wasperton Warwick 27 C9
Wasps Nest Lincs 46 F4
Wass N Yorks 52 B1
Watchet Som'set 7 B9
Watchfield Oxon 17 B9
Watchfield Som'set 15 G9
Watchgate Cumb 57 G7
Watchhill Cumb 56 B3
Watcombe Torbay 5 E10
Watendlath Cumb 56 E4
Water Devon 5 C8
Water Lancs 50 G4
Water End ER Yorks 52 F3
Water End Herts 29 G7
Water End Herts 19 A9
Water Newton Cambs 37 F7
Water Orton Warwick 35 F7
Water Stratford Bucks 28 E3
Water Yeat Cumb 56 H4
Waterbeach Cambs 29 B11
Waterbeck Dumf/Gal 61 F8
Waterden Norfolk 38 B4
Waterfall Staffs 44 G4
Waterfoot E Renf 68 E4
Waterfoot Lancs 50 G4
Waterford Hants 10 E2
Waterford Herts 29 G10
Waterhead Cumb 56 F5
Waterhead Dumf/Gal 61 D7
Waterheads Scot Borders 69 E11
Waterhouses Durham 58 B2
Waterhouses Staffs 44 G4
Wateringbury Kent 20 F3
Waterloo Gtr Man 44 B3
Waterloo H'land 85 F11
Waterloo Mersey 42 C6
Waterloo N Lanarks 69 E7
Waterloo Norfolk 39 D8
Waterloo Perth/Kinr 76 D3
Waterloo Poole 9 E9
Waterloo Shrops 33 B11
Waterloo Port Gwyn 40 D6
Waterlooville Hants 10 D5
Watermeetings S Lanarks 60 B5
Watermillock Cumb 56 D6
Waterperry Oxon 28 H3
Waterrow Som'set 7 D9
Water's Nook Gtr Man 43 B9
Waters Upton Telford 34 D2
Watersfield W Sussex 11 C9
Waterside Aberds 89 F10
Waterside Blackb'n 50 G3
Waterside Cumb 56 B4
Waterside E Ayrs 67 G7
Waterside E Ayrs 67 B7
Waterside E Dunb 68 C5
Waterside E Renf 68 E4
Waterstock Oxon 28 H3
Waterston Pembs 22 F4
Watford Herts 19 B8
Watford Northants 28 B3
Watford Gap W Midlands 35 E7
Wath N Yorks 51 C7
Wath N Yorks 51 B9
Wath N Yorks 52 B2
Wath Brow Cumb 56 E2
Wath upon Dearne S Yorks 45 B8
Watley's End S Gloucs 16 C3
Watlington Norfolk 38 D2
Watlington Oxon 18 B3
Watnall Notts 45 H9
Watten H'land 94 E4
Wattisfield Suffolk 31 A7
Wattisham Suffolk 31 C7
Wattlesborough Heath Shrops 33 D9
Watton ER Yorks 52 D6
Watton Norfolk 38 E5
Watton at Stone Herts 29 G10
Wattston N Lanarks 68 C6
Wattstown Rh Cyn Taff 14 B6
Wauchan H'land 80 E1
Waulkmill Lodge Orkney 95 H4
Waun Powys 32 E4
Waun-y-clyn Carms 23 F9
Waunarlwydd Swan 14 B2
Waunclunda Carms 24 E3
Waunfawr Gwyn 41 E7
Waungron Swan 23 F10
Waunlwyd Bl Gwent 25 H8
Wavendon M/Keynes 28 E6
Waverbridge Cumb 56 B4
Waverton Ches 43 F7
Waverton Cumb 56 B4
Wavertree Mersey 43 D6
Wawne ER Yorks 53 F6
Waxham Norfolk 39 C10
Waxholme ER Yorks 53 G9
Way Kent 21 E10
Way Village Devon 7 E7
Wayfield Medway 20 E4
Wayford Som'set 8 D3
Waymills Shrops 34 A1
Wayne Green Monmouths 25 G11
Wdig = Goodwick Pembs 22 C4
Weachyburn Aberds 89 C6
Weald Oxon 17 A10
Wealdstone London 19 C8
Weardley W Yorks 51 E8
Weare Som'set 15 F10
Weare Giffard Devon 6 D3
Wearhead Durham 57 C10
Weasdale Cumb 57 F8
Weasenham All Saints Norfolk 38 C4
Weasenham St Peter Norfolk 38 C4
Weatherhill Surrey 12 B2
Weaverham Ches 43 E9
Weaverthorpe N Yorks 52 B5
Webheath Worcs 27 B7
Wedderlairs Aberds 89 E8
Wedderlie Scot Borders 70 E5
Weddington Warwick 35 F9
Wedhampton Wilts 17 F7
Wedmore Som'set 15 G10
Wednesbury W Midlands 34 F5
Wednesfield W Midlands 34 E5
Weedon Bucks 28 G5
Weedon Bec Northants 28 C3
Weedon Lois Northants 28 D3
Weeford Staffs 35 E7
Week Devon 7 E6
Week St Mary Cornw'l 4 B3
Weeke Hants 10 A3
Weekley Northants 36 G4
Weel ER Yorks 53 F6
Weeley Essex 31 F8
Weeley Heath Essex 31 F8
Weem Perth/Kinr 75 C11
Weeping Cross Staffs 34 C5
Weethley Gate Warwick 27 C7
Weeting Norfolk 38 G3
Weeton ER Yorks 53 G9
Weeton Lancs 49 F3
Weeton N Yorks 51 E8
Weetwood Hall Northum 71 H9
Weir Lancs 50 G4
Weir Quay Devon 4 E5
Welborne Norfolk 39 E6
Welbourn Lincs 46 G3
Welburn N Yorks 52 C3
Welburn N Yorks 52 A2
Welbury N Yorks 58 F4
Welby Lincs 36 B5
Welches Dam Cambs 37 G10
Welcombe Devon 6 E1
Weld Bank Lancs 50 H1
Weldon Northum 63 D7
Welford Northants 36 G2
Welford W Berks 17 D11
Welford-on-Avon Warwick 27 C8
Welham Leics 36 F3
Welham Notts 45 D11
Welham Green Herts 29 H9
Well Hants 18 G4
Well Lincs 47 E8
Well N Yorks 51 A8
Well End Bucks 18 C5
Well Heads W Yorks 51 F6
Well Hill Kent 19 E11
Well Town Devon 7 F8
Welland Worcs 26 D4
Wellbank Angus 77 D7
Welldale Dumf/Gal 61 G7
Wellesbourne Warwick 27 C9
Welling London 19 D11
Wellingborough Northants 28 B5
Wellingham Norfolk 38 C4
Wellingore Lincs 46 G3
Wellington Cumb 56 F2
Wellington Heref'd 25 D11
Wellington Som'set 7 D10
Wellington Telford 34 D2
Wellington Heath Heref'd 26 D4
Wellington Hill W Yorks 51 F9
Wellow Bath/NE Som'set 16 F4
Wellow I/Wight 10 F2
Wellow Notts 45 F10
Wellpond Green Herts 29 F11
Wells Som'set 15 G11
Wells Green Ches 43 G9
Wells-next-the-Sea Norfolk 38 A5
Wellsborough Leics 35 E9
Wellswood Torbay 5 E10
Wellwood Fife 69 B9
Welney Norfolk 37 F11
Welsh Bicknor Heref'd 26 G2
Welsh End Shrops 33 B11
Welsh Frankton Shrops 33 B9
Welsh Hook Pembs 22 D4
Welsh Newton Heref'd 25 G11
Welsh St Donats V/Glam 14 D6
Welshampton Shrops 33 B10
Welshpool = Y Trallwng Powys 33 E8
Welton Cumb 56 B5
Welton ER Yorks 52 G5
Welton Lincs 46 E4
Welton Northants 28 B2
Welton Hill Lincs 46 D4
Welton le Marsh Lincs 47 F8
Welton le Wold Lincs 46 D6
Welwick ER Yorks 53 G9
Welwyn Herts 29 G9
Welwyn Garden City Herts 29 G9
Wem Shrops 33 C11
Wembdon Som'set 15 H8
Wembley London 19 C8
Wembury Devon 4 G6
Wembworthy Devon 6 F5
Wemyss Bay Inverc'l 73 G10
Wenallt Ceredig'n 24 A3
Wenallt Gwyn 32 A5
Wendens Ambo Essex 30 E2
Wendlebury Oxon 28 G2
Wendling Norfolk 38 D5
Wendover Bucks 28 H5
Wendron Cornw'l 2 F5
Wendy Cambs 29 D10
Wenfordbridge Cornw'l 4 D1
Wenhaston Suffolk 39 H10
Wennington Cambs 37 H8
Wennington London 20 C2
Wennington Lancs 50 B2
Wensley Derby 44 F6
Wensley N Yorks 58 H1
Wentbridge W Yorks 51 H10
Wentnor Shrops 33 F9
Wentworth Cambs 37 H10
Wentworth S Yorks 45 C7
Wenvoe V/Glam 15 D7
Weobley Heref'd 25 C11
Weobley Marsh Heref'd 25 C11
Wereham Norfolk 38 E2
Wergs W Midlands 34 E4
Wern Powys 32 D5
Wern Powys 33 D8
Wernffrwd Swan 23 G10
Wernyrheolydd Monmouths 25 G10
Werrington Cornw'l 4 C4
Werrington Peterbro 37 E7
Werrington Staffs 44 H3
Wervin Ches 43 E7
Wesham Lancs 49 F4
Wessington Derby 45 G7
West Acre Norfolk 38 D3
West Adderbury Oxon 27 E11
West Allerdean Northum 71 F8
West Alvington Devon 5 G8
West Amesbury Wilts 17 G8
West Anstey Devon 7 D7
West Ashby Lincs 46 E6
West Ashling W Sussex 11 D7
West Ashton Wilts 16 F5
West Auckland Durham 58 D2
West Ayton N Yorks 52 A5
West Bagborough Som'set 7 C10
West Barkwith Lincs 46 D5
West Barnby N Yorks 59 E9
West Barns E Loth 70 C5
West Barsham Norfolk 38 B5
West Bay Dorset 8 E3
West Beckham Norfolk 39 B7
West Bedfont Surrey 19 D7
West Benhar N Lanarks 69 D7
West Bergholt Essex 30 F6
West Bexington Dorset 8 F4
West Bilney Norfolk 38 D3
West Blatchington Brighton/Hove 12 F1
West Bowling W Yorks 51 F7
West Bradford Lancs 50 E3
West Bradley Som'set 16 H2
West Bretton W Yorks 44 A6
West Bridgford Notts 36 B1
West Bromwich W Midlands 34 F6
West Buckland Devon 6 C5
West Buckland Som'set 7 D10
West Burrafirth Shetl'd 96 H4
West Burton N Yorks 58 H1
West Burton W Sussex 11 C8
West Butterwick N Lincs 46 B2
West Byfleet Surrey 19 E7
West Caister Norfolk 39 D11
West Calder W Loth 69 D9
West Camel Som'set 8 B4
West Challow Oxon 17 C10
West Chelborough Dorset 8 D4
West Chevington Northum 63 D8
West Chiltington W Sussex 11 C9
West Chinnock Som'set 8 C3
West Chisenbury Wilts 17 F8
West Clandon Surrey 19 F7
West Cliffe Kent 21 G10
West Clyne H'land 93 J11
West Clyth H'land 94 G4
West Coker Som'set 8 C4
West Compton Dorset 8 E4
West Compton Som'set 16 G2
West Cowick ER Yorks 52 G2
West Cranmore Som'set 16 G3
West Cross Swan 14 C2
West Cullery Aberds 83 C9
West Curry Cornw'l 6 G1
West Curthwaite Cumb 56 B5
West Darlochan Arg/Bute 65 F7
West Dean Wilts 10 B1
West Dean W Sussex 11 C7
West Deeping Lincs 37 E7
West Derby Mersey 43 C6
West Dereham Norfolk 38 E2
West Didsbury Gtr Man 44 C2
West Ditchburn Northum 63 A7
West Down Devon 6 B4
West Drayton London 19 D7
West Drayton Notts 45 E11
West Ella ER Yorks 52 G6
West End Beds 28 C6
West End ER Yorks 52 F5
West End ER Yorks 53 F7
West End Hants 10 C3
West End Lancs 50 G3
West End Norfolk 38 E5
West End Norfolk 39 D11
West End N Som'set 15 E10
West End N Yorks 51 D7
West End Oxon 17 A11
West End S Lanarks 69 F8
West End Suffolk 39 G10
West End Surrey 18 E6
West End S Yorks 45 B10
West End Wilts 9 B8
West End Wilts 16 D6
West End W Sussex 11 C11
West End Green Hants 18 E3
West Farleigh Kent 20 F4
West Felton Shrops 33 C9
West Fenton E Loth 70 B3
West Ferry Dundee C 77 D7
West Firle E Sussex 12 F3
West Ginge Oxon 17 C11
West Grafton Wilts 17 E9
West Green Hants 18 F4
West Greenskares Aberds 89 B7
West Grimstead Wilts 9 B11
West Grinstead W Sussex 11 B10
West Haddlesey N Yorks 52 G1
West Haddon Northants 28 A3
West Hagbourne Oxon 18 C2
West Hagley Worcs 34 G5
West Hall Cumb 61 G11
West Hallam Derby 35 A10
West Halton N Lincs 52 G5
West Ham London 19 C11
West Handley Derby 45 E7
West Hanney Oxon 17 B11
West Hanningfield Essex 20 B4
West Hardwick W Yorks 51 H10
West Harnham Wilts 9 B10
West Harptree Bath/NE Som'set 16 F2
West Hatch Som'set 8 B1
West Head Norfolk 38 E1
West Heath Ches 44 F2
West Heath Hants 18 F5
West Heath Hants 18 F2
West Helmsdale H'land 93 H13
West Hendred Oxon 17 C11
West Heslerton N Yorks 52 B5
West Hill Devon 7 G9
West Hill ER Yorks 53 C7
West Hill N Som'set 15 D10
West Hoathly W Sussex 12 C2
West Holme Dorset 9 F7
West Horndon Essex 20 C3
West Horrington Som'set 16 G2
West Horsley Surrey 19 F7
West Horton Northum 71 G9
West Hougham Kent 21 G9
West Houlland Shetl'd 96 H4
West-houses Derby 45 G8
West Huntington C/York 52 D2
West Hythe Kent 13 C10
West Ilsley W Berks 17 C11
West Itchenor W Sussex 11 D6
West Keal Lincs 47 F7
West Kennett Wilts 17 E8
West Kilbride N Ayrs 66 B5
West Kingsdown Kent 20 E2
West Kington Wilts 16 D5
West Kinharrachie Aberds 89 E9
West Kirby Mersey 42 D5
West Knapton N Yorks 52 B4
West Knighton Dorset 8 F6
West Knoyle Wilts 9 A7
West Kyloe Northum 71 F9
West Lambrook Som'set 8 C3
West Langdon Kent 21 G10
West Langwell H'land 93 J9
West Lavington Wilts 17 F7
West Lavington W Sussex 11 B7
West Layton N Yorks 58 F2
West Lea Durham 58 B5
West Leake Notts 35 C11
West Learmouth Northum 71 G7
West Leigh Devon 6 F5
West Lexham Norfolk 38 D4
West Lilling N Yorks 52 C2
West Linton Scot Borders 69 E10
West Liss Hants 11 B6
West Littleton S Gloucs 16 D4
West Looe Cornw'l 4 F3
West Luccombe Som'set 7 B7
West Lulworth Dorset 9 F7
West Lutton N Yorks 52 C5
West Lydford Som'set 8 A4
West Lyng Som'set 8 B2
West Lynn Norfolk 38 C2
West Malling Kent 20 F3
West Malvern Worcs 26 D4
West Marden W Sussex 11 C6
West Marina E Sussex 13 F6
West Markham Notts 45 E11
West Marsh NE Lincs 46 A6
West Marton N Yorks 50 D4
West Meon Hants 10 B5
West Mersea Essex 31 G7
West Milton Dorset 8 E4
West Minster Kent 20 D6
West Molesey Surrey 19 E8
West Monkton Som'set 8 B1
West Moors Dorset 9 D9
West Morriston Scot Borders 70 F5
West Muir Angus 77 A8
West Ness N Yorks 52 B2
West Newham Northum 62 F6
West Newton ER Yorks 53 F7
West Newton Norfolk 38 C2
West Norwood London 19 D10
West Ogwell Devon 5 D9
West Orchard Dorset 9 C7
West Overton Wilts 17 E8
West Park Hartlep'l 58 C5
West Parley Dorset 9 E9
West Peckham Kent 20 F3
West Pelton Durham 58 A3
West Pennard Som'set 15 H11
West Pentire Cornw'l 3 C6
West Perry Cambs 29 B8
West Putford Devon 6 E2
West Quantoxhead Som'set 7 B10
West Rainton Durham 58 B4
West Rasen Lincs 46 D4
West Raynham Norfolk 38 C4
West Retford Notts 45 D10
West Rounton N Yorks 58 F5
West Row Suffolk 38 H2
West Rudham Norfolk 38 C4
West Runton Norfolk 39 A7
West Saltoun E Loth 70 D3
West Sandwick Shetl'd 96 E6
West Scrafton N Yorks 51 A6
West Sleekburn Northum 63 E8
West Somerton Norfolk 39 D10
West Stafford Dorset 8 F6
West Stockwith Notts 45 C11
West Stoke W Sussex 11 D7
West Stonesdale N Yorks 57 F10
West Stoughton Som'set 15 G10
West Stour Dorset 9 B6
West Stourmouth Kent 21 E9
West Stow Suffolk 30 A5
West Stowell Wilts 17 E8
West Strathan H'land 93 C8
West Stratton Hants 18 G2
West Street Kent 20 F6
West Tanfield N Yorks 51 B8
West Taphouse Cornw'l 4 E2
West Tarbert Arg/Bute 73 G7
West Thirston Northum 63 D7
West Thorney W Sussex 11 D6
West Thurrock Thurr'k 20 D2
West Tilbury Thurr'k 20 D3
West Tisted Hants 10 B5
West Tofts Norfolk 38 F4
West Tofts Perth/Kinr 76 D4
West Torrington Lincs 46 D5
West Town Hants 10 E6
West Town N Som'set 15 E10
West Tytherley Hants 10 B1
West Tytherton Wilts 16 D6
West Walton Norfolk 37 D10
West Walton Highway Norfolk 37 D10
West Wellow Hants 10 C1
West Wemyss Fife 70 A2
West Wick N Som'set 15 E9
West Wickham Cambs 30 D3
West Wickham London 19 E10
West Williamston Pembs 22 F5
West Willoughby Lincs 36 A5
West Winch Norfolk 38 D2
West Winterslow Wilts 9 A11
West Wittering W Sussex 11 E6
West Witton N Yorks 58 H1
West Woodburn Northum 62 E4
West Woodhay W Berks 17 E10
West Woodlands Som'set 16 G4
West Worldham Hants 18 H4
West Worlington Devon 7 E6
West Worthing W Sussex 11 D10
West Wratting Cambs 30 C3
West Wycombe Bucks 18 B5
West Wylam Northum 63 G7
West Yell Shetl'd 96 E6
Westacott Devon 6 C4
Westbere Kent 21 E8
Westborough Lincs 36 A4
Westbourne Bournem'th 9 E9
Westbourne Suffolk 31 D8
Westbourne W Sussex 11 D6
Westbrook W Berks 17 D11
Westbury Bucks 28 E3
Westbury Shrops 33 E9
Westbury Wilts 16 F5
Westbury Leigh Wilts 16 F5
Westbury-on-Severn Glos 26 G4
Westbury on Trym Bristol 16 D2
Westbury-sub-Mendip Som'set 15 G11
Westby Lancs 49 F3
Westcliff-on-Sea Southend 20 C5
Westcombe Som'set 16 H3
Westcote Glos 27 F9
Westcott Bucks 28 G4
Westcott Devon 7 F9
Westcott Surrey 19 G8
Westcott Barton Oxon 27 F11
Westdean E Sussex 12 G4
Westdene Brighton/Hove 12 F1
Wester Aberchalder H'land 81 A7
Wester Balgedie Perth/Kinr 76 G4
Wester Culbeuchly Aberds 89 B6
Wester Dechmont W Loth 69 D9
Wester Denoon Angus 76 C6
Wester Fintray Aberds 83 B10
Wester Gruinards H'land 87 B8
Wester Lealty H'land 87 D9
Wester Milton H'land 87 F12
Wester Newburn Fife 77 G7
Wester Quarff Shetl'd 96 K6
Wester Skeld Shetl'd 96 J4
Westerdale H'land 94 E3
Westerdale N Yorks 59 F7
Westerfield Shetl'd 96 H5
Westerfield Suffolk 31 D8
Westergate W Sussex 11 D8
Westerham Kent 19 F11
Westerhope Tyne/Wear 63 G7
Westerleigh S Gloucs 16 D4
Westerton Angus 77 B9
Westerton Durham 58 C3
Westerton W Sussex 11 D7
Westerwick Shetl'd 96 J4
Westfield Cumb 56 D1
Westfield E Sussex 13 E7
Westfield H'land 94 D2
Westfield N Lanarks 68 C6
Westfield Norfolk 38 E5
Westfield W Loth 69 C8
Westfields Dorset 8 D6
Westfields of Rattray Perth/Kinr 76 C4
Westgate Durham 57 C11
Westgate N Lincs 45 B11
Westgate Norfolk 38 A5
Westgate on Sea Kent 21 D10
Westhall Aberds 83 A8
Westhall Suffolk 39 G10
Westham Dorset 8 G5
Westham E Sussex 12 F5
Westham Som'set 15 G10
Westhampnett W Sussex 11 D7
Westhay Som'set 15 G10
Westhead Lancs 43 B7
Westhide Heref'd 26 D2
Westhill Aberds 83 C10
Westhill H'land 87 G10
Westhope Heref'd 25 C11
Westhope Shrops 33 G10
Westhorpe Lincs 37 B8
Westhorpe Suffolk 31 B7
Westhoughton Gtr Man 43 B9
Westhouse N Yorks 50 B2
Westhumble Surrey 19 F8
Westing Shetl'd 96 C7
Westlake Devon 5 F7
Westleigh Devon 6 D3
Westleigh Devon 7 E9
Westleigh Gtr Man 43 B9
Westleton Suffolk 31 B11
Westley Shrops 33 E9
Westley Suffolk 30 B5
Westley Waterless Cambs 30 C3
Westlington Bucks 28 G4
Westlinton Cumb 61 G9
Westmarsh Kent 21 E9
Westmeston E Sussex 12 E2
Westmill Herts 29 F10
Westminster London 19 D10
Westmuir Angus 76 B6
Westness Orkney 95 F4
Westnewton Cumb 56 B3
Westnewton Northum 71 G8
Westoe Tyne/Wear 63 G9
Weston Bath/NE Som'set 16 E4
Weston Ches 43 G10
Weston Devon 7 H10
Weston Dorset 8 G5
Weston Halton 43 D8
Weston Hants 10 B6
Weston Herts 29 E9
Weston Lincs 37 C8
Weston Notts 45 F11
Weston Northants 28 D2
Weston N Yorks 51 E7
Weston Shrops 34 F1
Weston Shrops 34 C1
Weston Staffs 34 C5
Weston W Berks 17 D10
Weston Beggard Heref'd 26 D2
Weston by Welland Northants 36 F3
Weston Colville Cambs 30 C3
Weston Coyney Stoke 34 A5
Weston Favell Northants 28 B4
Weston Green Cambs 30 C3
Weston Green Norfolk 39 D7
Weston Heath Shrops 34 D3
Weston Hills Lincs 37 C8
Weston-in-Gordano N Som'set 15 D10
Weston Jones Staffs 34 C3
Weston Longville Norfolk 39 D7
Weston Lullingfields Shrops 33 C10
Weston-on-the-Green Oxon 28 G2
Weston-on-Trent Derby 35 C10
Weston Patrick Hants 18 G3
Weston Rhyn Shrops 33 B8
Weston-Sub-Edge Glos 27 D8
Weston-super-Mare N Som'set 15 E9
Weston Turville Bucks 28 G5
Weston under Lizard Staffs 34 D4
Weston under Penyard Heref'd 26 F3
Weston under Wetherley Warwick 27 B10
Weston Underwood Derby 35 A8
Weston Underwood M/Keynes 28 C5
Westonbirt Glos 16 C5
Westoncommon Shrops 33 C10
Westoning Beds 29 E7
Westonzoyland Som'set 8 A2
Westow N Yorks 52 C3
Westport Arg/Bute 65 F7
Westport Som'set 8 C2
Westrigg W Loth 69 D8
Westruther Scot Borders 70 F5
Westry Cambs 37 F9
Westville Notts 45 H9
Westward Cumb 56 B4
Westward Ho! Devon 6 D3
Westwell Kent 20 G6
Westwell Oxon 27 H9
Westwell Leacon Kent 20 G6
Westwick Cambs 29 B11
Westwick Durham 58 E1
Westwick Norfolk 39 C8
Westwood Devon 7 G9
Westwood Wilts 16 F5
Westwoodside N Lincs 45 C11
Wetheral Cumb 56 A6
Wetherby W Yorks 51 E10
Wetherden Suffolk 31 B7
Wetheringsett Suffolk 31 B8
Wethersfield Essex 30 E4
Wethersta Shetl'd 96 G5
Wetherup Street Suffolk 31 B8
Wetley Rocks Staffs 44 H3
Wettenhall Ches 43 F9
Wetton Staffs 44 G5
Wetwang ER Yorks 52 D5
Wetwood Staffs 34 B3
Wexcombe Wilts 17 F9
Wexham Street Bucks 18 C6
Weybourne Norfolk 39 A7
Weybread Suffolk 39 G8
Weybridge Surrey 19 E7
Weycroft Devon 8 E2
Weydale H'land 94 D3
Weyhill Hants 17 G10
Weymouth Dorset 8 G5
Whaddon Bucks 28 E5
Whaddon Cambs 29 D10
Whaddon Glos 26 G5
Whaddon Wilts 9 B10
Whale Cumb 57 D7
Whaley Derby 45 E9
Whaley Bridge Derby 44 D4
Whaley Thorns Derby 45 E9
Whaligoe H'land 94 F5
Whalley Lancs 50 F3
Whalton Northum 63 E7
Wham N Yorks 50 C3
Whaplode Lincs 37 C9
Whaplode Drove Lincs 37 D9
Whaplode St Catherine Lincs 37 C9
Wharfe N Yorks 50 C3
Wharles Lancs 49 F4
Wharncliffe Side S Yorks 44 C6
Wharram-le-Street N Yorks 52 C4
Wharton Ches 43 F9
Wharton Green Ches 43 F9
Whashton N Yorks 58 F2
Whatcombe Dorset 9 D7
Whatcote Warwick 27 D10
Whatfield Suffolk 31 D7
Whatley Som'set 8 D2
Whatley Som'set 16 G4
Whatlington E Sussex 13 E6
Whatstandwell Derby 45 G7
Whatton Notts 36 B3
Whauphill Dumf/Gal 55 E7
Whaw N Yorks 57 F11
Wheatacre Norfolk 39 F10
Wheatcroft Derby 45 G7
Wheathampstead Herts 29 G8
Wheathill Shrops 34 G2
Wheatley Devon 7 G8
Wheatley Hants 18 G4
Wheatley Oxon 28 H2
Wheatley S Yorks 45 B9
Wheatley W Yorks 51 G6

Place	County	Page	Grid
Wheatley Hill	Durham	58	C4
Wheaton Aston	Staffs	34	D4
Wheddon Cross	Som'set	7	C8
Wheedlemont	Aberds	82	A6
Wheelerstreet	Surrey	18	G6
Wheelock	Ches	43	G10
Wheelock Heath	Ches	43	G10
Wheelton	Lancs	50	G2
Wheen	Angus	81	A7
Wheldrake	C/York	52	E2
Whelford	Glos	17	B8
Whelpley Hill	Bucks	18	A6
Whempstead	Herts	29	F10
Whenby	N Yorks	52	C2
Whepstead	Suffolk	30	C5
Wherstead	Suffolk	31	D8
Wherwell	Hants	17	G10
Wheston	Derby	44	E5
Whetsted	Kent	20	G3
Whetstone	Leics	36	F1
Whicham	Cumb	49	A1
Whichford	Warwick	27	E10
Whickham	Tyne/Wear	63	G8
Whiddon	Devon	6	G4
Whiddon Down	Devon	77	C7
Whilton	Northants	28	B3
Whim Farm	Scot Borders	69	E11
Whimble	Devon	6	F2
Whimple	Devon	7	G9
Whimpwell Green	Norfolk	39	C9
Whinburgh	Norfolk	38	E6
Whinnieliggate	Dumf/Gal	55	D10
Whinnyfold	Aberds	89	E10
Whippingham	I/Wight	10	E4
Whipsnade	Beds	29	G7
Whipton	Devon	7	G8
Whirlow	S Yorks	45	D7
Whisby	Lincs	46	F3
Whissendine	Rutl'd	36	D4
Whissonsett	Norfolk	38	C5
Whistlefield	Arg/Bute	73	D10
Whistlefield	Arg/Bute	73	D11
Whistley Green	Wokingham	18	D4
Whiston	Mersey	43	C7
Whiston	Northants	28	B5
Whiston	Staffs	34	D4
Whiston	Staffs	44	H4
Whiston	S Yorks	45	D8
Whitbeck	Cumb	49	A1
Whitbourne	Heref'd	26	C4
Whitburn	Tyne/Wear	63	G10
Whitburn	W Loth	69	D8
Whitburn Colliery	Tyne/Wear	63	G10
Whitby	Ches	43	E6
Whitby	N Yorks	59	E9
Whitbyheath	Ches	43	E6
Whitchurch	Bath/NE Som'set	16	E3
Whitchurch	Bucks	28	F4
Whitchurch	Card	15	C7
Whitchurch	Devon	4	D5
Whitchurch	Hants	17	G11
Whitchurch	Heref'd	26	G2
Whitchurch	Oxon	18	D3
Whitchurch	Pembs	22	D2
Whitchurch	Shrops	33	A11
Whitchurch Canonicorum	Dorset	8	E2
Whitcombe	Dorset	8	F6
Whitcott Keysett	Shrops	33	G8
White Coppice	Lancs	50	H2
White Lackington	Dorset	8	E5
White Ladies Aston	Worcs	26	C6
White Lund	Lancs	49	C4
White Mill	Carms	23	D9
White Ness	Shetl'd	96	J5
White Notley	Essex	30	G4
White Pit	Lincs	47	E7
White Post	Notts	45	G10
White Rocks	Heref'd	25	F11
White Roding	Essex	30	G2
White Waltham	Windsor	18	D5
Whiteacen	Moray	88	D2
Whiteacre Heath	Warwick	35	F8
Whitebridge	H'land	81	B6
Whitebrook	Monmouths	26	H2
Whiteburn	Scot Borders	70	F4
Whitecairn	Dumf/Gal	54	D5
Whitecairns	Aberds	83	B11
Whitecastle	S Lanarks	69	F9
Whitechapel	Lancs	50	E1
Whitecleat	Orkney	95	H6
Whitecraig	E Loth	70	C2
Whitecroft	Glos	26	H3
Whitecross	Corn'l	3	C8
Whitecross	Falk	69	C8
Whitecross	Staffs	34	C4
Whiteface	H'land	87	C10
Whitefarland	N Ayrs	66	B1
Whitefaulds	S Ayrs	66	F5
Whitefield	Gtr Man	44	B2
Whitefield	Perth/Kinr	76	D4
Whiteford	Aberds	83	A9
Whitegate	Ches	43	F9
Whitehall	Blackb'n	50	G2
Whitehall	W Sussex	11	B10
Whitehall Village	Orkney	95	F7
Whitehaven	Cumb	56	E1
Whitehill	Hants	11	A6
Whitehills	Aberds	89	B6
Whitehills	S Lanarks	68	E5
Whitehough	Derby	44	D4
Whitehouse	Aberds	83	B8
Whitehouse	Arg/Bute	73	G7
Whitekirk	E Loth	70	B4
Whitelaw	S Lanarks	68	F5
Whiteleas	Tyne/Wear	63	G9
Whiteley Bank	I/Wight	10	F4
Whiteley Green	Ches	44	E3
Whiteley Village	Surrey	19	E7
Whitemans Green	W Sussex	12	D2
Whitemire	Moray	87	F12
Whitemoor	Corn'l	3	D8
Whitemore	Staffs	44	F2
Whitenap	Hants	10	B2
Whiteoak Green	Oxon	27	G10
Whiteparish	Wilts	9	B11
Whiterashes	Aberds	89	F8
Whiteshill	Glos	26	H5
Whiteside	Northum	62	G3
Whiteside	W Loth	69	D8
Whitesmith	E Sussex	12	E4
Whitestaunton	Som'set	7	E10
Whitestone	Devon	7	G7
Whitestone	Devon	6	B3
Whitestone	Warwick	35	G9
Whitestones	Aberds	89	C8
Whitestreet Green	Suffolk	30	E6
Whitewall Corner	N Yorks	52	B3
Whiteway	Glos	16	B5
Whiteway	Glos	16	A6
Whitewell	Aberds	89	B9
Whitewell	Lancs	50	E2
Whitewell Bottom	Lancs	50	G4
Whiteworks	Devon	5	D7
Whitfield	Kent	21	G10
Whitfield	Northants	28	D3
Whitfield	Northum	62	A3
Whitfield	S Gloucs	16	B3
Whitford	Devon	8	E1
Whitford	Flints	42	E4
Whitgift	ER Yorks	52	G4
Whitgreave	Staffs	34	C4
Whithorn	Dumf/Gal	55	E7
Whiting Bay	N Ayrs	66	D3
Whitkirk	W Yorks	51	F9
Whitland	Carms	22	E6
Whitletts	S Ayrs	66	D6
Whitley	N Yorks	52	G1
Whitley	Reading	18	D4
Whitley	Wilts	16	E5
Whitley Bay	Tyne/Wear	63	F9
Whitley Chapel	Northum	62	A5
Whitley Lower	W Yorks	51	H8
Whitley Row	Kent	19	F11
Whitlock's End	W Midlands	35	H7
Whitminster	Glos	26	H4
Whitmore	Staffs	34	A4
Whitnage	Devon	7	E9
Whitnash	Warwick	27	B10
Whitrigg	Cumb	56	C4
Whitrigg	Cumb	61	H8
Whitsbury	Hants	9	C10
Whitstable	Kent	21	E8
Whitstone	Corn'l	6	G1
Whittingham	Northum	62	B6
Whittingslow	Shrops	33	G10
Whittington	Glos	27	F7
Whittington	Lancs	50	B2
Whittington	Shrops	33	B9
Whittington	Staffs	34	G4
Whittington	Staffs	35	E7
Whittington	Worcs	26	C5
Whittle-le-Woods	Lancs	50	G1
Whittlebury	Northants	28	D3
Whittlesey	Cambs	37	F8
Whittlesford	Cambs	29	D11
Whittlestone Head	Blackb'n	50	H3
Whitton	Scot Borders	62	A3
Whitton	N Lincs	52	G5
Whitton	Northum	62	C6
Whitton	Powys	25	B9
Whitton	Shrops	26	A2
Whitton	Stockton	58	D3
Whitton	Suffolk	31	D8
Whittonditch	Wilts	17	D9
Whittonstall	Northum	62	H6
Whitway	Hants	17	F11
Whitwell	Derby	45	E9
Whitwell	Herts	29	F8
Whitwell	I/Wight	10	G4
Whitwell	N Yorks	58	G3
Whitwell	Rutl'd	36	E5
Whitwell-on-the-Hill	N Yorks	52	C3
Whitwell Street	Norfolk	39	C7
Whitwick	Leics	35	D10
Whitwood	W Yorks	51	G10
Whitworth	Lancs	50	H4
Whixall	Shrops	33	B11
Whixley	N Yorks	51	D10
Whoberley	W Midlands	35	H9
Whorlton	Durham	58	E1
Whorlton	N Yorks	58	F5
Whygate	Northum	62	F3
Whyle	Heref'd	26	B2
Whyteleafe	Surrey	19	F10
Wibdon	Glos	16	B2
Wibsey	W Yorks	51	F7
Wibtoft	Leics	35	G10
Wichenford	Worcs	26	B4
Wichling	Kent	20	F6
Wick	Bourn'm'th	9	E10
Wick	Devon	7	E10
Wick	H'land	94	E5
Wick	S Gloucs	16	D4
Wick	Shetl'd	96	K6
Wick	V/Glam	14	D5
Wick	W Sussex	11	D9
Wick Hill	Wokingham	18	E4
Wick St Lawrence	N Som'set	15	E9
Wicken	Cambs	30	A2
Wicken	Northants	28	E4
Wicken Bonhunt	Essex	29	E11
Wickenby	Lincs	46	D4
Wickersley	S Yorks	45	C8
Wickford	Essex	20	B4
Wickham	Hants	10	C4
Wickham	W Berks	17	D10
Wickham Bishops	Essex	30	G5
Wickham Market	Suffolk	31	C10
Wickham St Paul	Essex	30	E5
Wickham Skeith	Suffolk	31	B7
Wickham Street	Suffolk	30	C4
Wickham Street	Suffolk	31	B7
Wickhambreaux	Kent	21	F9
Wickhambrook	Suffolk	30	C4
Wickhamford	Worcs	27	D7
Wickhampton	Norfolk	39	E10
Wicklewood	Norfolk	39	E6
Wickmere	Norfolk	39	B7
Wickwar	S Gloucs	16	C4
Widdington	Essex	30	E2
Widdrington	Northum	63	D8
Widdrington Station	Northum	63	D8
Wide Open	Tyne/Wear	63	F8
Widecombe in the Moor	Devon	5	D8
Widegates	Corn'l	4	F3
Widemouth Bay	Corn'l	4	A3
Widewall	Orkney	95	J5
Widford	Essex	30	H3
Widford	Herts	29	G11
Widham	Wilts	17	C7
Widmer End	Bucks	18	B5
Widmerpool	Notts	36	C2
Widnes	Halton	43	D8
Wigan	Gtr Man	43	B8
Wiggaton	Devon	7	G10
Wiggenhall St Germans	Norfolk	38	D1
Wiggenhall St Mary Magdalen	Norfolk	38	D1
Wiggenhall St Mary the Virgin	Norfolk	38	D1
Wigginton	Herts	28	G6
Wigginton	Oxon	27	E10
Wigginton	Staffs	35	E8
Wigginton	C/York	52	D1
Wigglesworth	N Yorks	50	D4
Wiggonby	Cumb	56	A4
Wiggonholt	W Sussex	11	C9
Wighill	N Yorks	51	E10
Wighton	Norfolk	38	B5
Wigley	Hants	10	C2
Wigmore	Heref'd	25	B11
Wigmore	Medway	20	E5
Wigsley	Notts	46	E2
Wigsthorpe	Northants	36	G6
Wigston	Leics	36	F2
Wigthorpe	Notts	45	D10
Wigtoft	Lincs	37	B8
Wigton	Cumb	56	B4
Wigtown	Dumf/Gal	55	D7
Wigtwizzle	S Yorks	44	C6
Wike	W Yorks	51	E9
Wike Well End	S Yorks	45	A11
Wilbarston	Northants	36	G4
Wilberfoss	ER Yorks	52	D3
Wilberlee	W Yorks	44	A4
Wilburton	Cambs	29	A11
Wilby	Norfolk	38	F5
Wilby	Northants	28	B5
Wilby	Suffolk	31	B9
Wilcot	Wilts	17	E8
Wilcott	Shrops	33	D9
Wilcrick	Newp	15	C10
Wilday Green	Derby	45	E7
Wildboarclough	Ches	44	F3
Wilden	Beds	29	C7
Wilden	Worcs	34	H4
Wildhill	Herts	29	H9
Wildmoor	Worcs	34	H5
Wildsworth	Lincs	46	C2
Wilford	Notts	36	B1
Wilkesley	Ches	34	A2
Wilkhaven	H'land	87	C12
Wilkieston	W Loth	69	D10
Willand	Devon	7	E9
Willaston	Ches	42	E6
Willaston	Ches	43	G9
Willen	M/Keynes	28	D5
Willenhall	W Midlands	35	H9
Willenhall	W Midlands	34	F5
Willerby	ER Yorks	52	F6
Willerby	N Yorks	52	B6
Willersey	Glos	27	D8
Willersley	Heref'd	25	D10
Willesborough	Kent	13	B9
Willesborough Lees	Kent	13	B9
Willesden	London	19	C9
Willett	Som'set	7	C10
Willey	Shrops	34	F2
Willey	Warwick	35	G10
Willey Green	Surrey	18	F6
Williamscott	Oxon	27	D11
Willian	Herts	29	E9
Willingale	Essex	30	H2
Willingdon	E Sussex	12	F4
Willingham	Cambs	29	A11
Willingham by Stow	Lincs	46	D2
Willington	Beds	29	D8
Willington	Derby	35	C8
Willington	Durham	58	C2
Willington	Tyne/Wear	63	G9
Willington	Warwick	27	E9
Willington Corner	Ches	43	F8
Willisham Tye	Suffolk	31	C7
Willitoft	ER Yorks	52	F3
Williton	Som'set	7	B9
Willoughbridge	Staffs	34	A3
Willoughby	Lincs	47	E8
Willoughby	Warwick	27	B11
Willoughby-on-the-Wolds	Notts	36	C2
Willoughby Waterleys	Leics	36	F1
Willoughton	Lincs	46	C3
Willows Green	Essex	30	G4
Willsbridge	S Gloucs	16	D3
Willsworthy	Devon	4	C6
Wilmcote	Warwick	27	C8
Wilmington	Devon	7	G11
Wilmington	E Sussex	12	F4
Wilmington	Kent	20	D2
Wilminstone	Devon	4	D5
Wilmslow	Ches	44	D2
Wilnecote	Staffs	35	E8
Wilpshire	Lancs	50	F2
Wilsden	W Yorks	51	F6
Wilsford	Lincs	36	A6
Wilsford	Wilts	17	F8
Wilsford	Wilts	17	H8
Wilsill	N Yorks	51	C7
Wilsley Pound	Kent	13	C6
Wilsom	Hants	18	H4
Wilson	Leics	35	C10
Wilsontown	S Lanarks	69	E8
Wilstead	Beds	29	D7
Wilsthorpe	Lincs	37	D6
Wilstone	Herts	28	G6
Wilton	Cumb	56	E2
Wilton	N Yorks	59	H7
Wilton	Redcar/Clevel'd	59	E6
Wilton	Wilts	9	A9
Wilton	Wilts	17	E9
Wimbish	Essex	30	E2
Wimbish Green	Essex	30	E3
Wimblebury	Staffs	34	D6
Wimbledon	London	19	D9
Wimblington	Cambs	37	F10
Wimborne Minster	Dorset	9	D9
Wimborne St Giles	Dorset	9	C9
Wimbotsham	Norfolk	38	E2
Wimpson	S'thampton	10	C2
Wimpstone	Warwick	27	D9
Wincanton	Som'set	8	B6
Wincham	Ches	43	E9
Winchburgh	W Loth	69	C9
Winchcombe	Glos	27	F7
Winchelsea	E Sussex	13	E8
Winchelsea Beach	E Sussex	13	E8
Winchester	Hants	10	B3
Winchet Hill	Kent	12	B6
Winchfield	Hants	18	F4
Winchmore Hill	Bucks	18	B6
Winchmore Hill	London	19	B10
Wincle	Ches	44	F3
Wincobank	S Yorks	45	C7
Windermere	Cumb	56	G6
Winderton	Warwick	27	D10
Windhill	H'land	87	G8
Windhouse	Shetl'd	96	D6
Windlehurst	Gtr Man	44	D3
Windlesham	Surrey	18	E6
Windley	Derby	45	H7
Windmill Hill	E Sussex	12	E5
Windmill Hill	Som'set	8	C2
Windrush	Glos	27	G8
Windsor	N Lincs	45	A11
Windsor	Windsor	18	D6
Windsoredge	Glos	16	A5
Windygates	Fife	76	G6
Windyknowe	W Loth	69	D8
Windywalls	Scot Borders	70	G6
Wineham	W Sussex	11	B11
Winestead	ER Yorks	53	G8
Winewall	Lancs	50	E5
Winfarthing	Norfolk	39	G7
Winford	I/Wight	10	F4
Winford	N Som'set	15	E11
Winforton	Heref'd	25	D9
Winfrith Newburgh	Dorset	9	F7
Wing	Bucks	28	F5
Wing	Rutl'd	36	E4
Wingate	Durham	58	C4
Wingates	Gtr Man	43	B9
Wingates	Northum	63	D7
Wingerworth	Derby	45	F7
Wingfield	Beds	29	F7
Wingfield	Suffolk	39	H8
Wingfield	Wilts	16	F5
Wingham	Kent	21	F9
Wingmore	Kent	21	G8
Wingrave	Bucks	28	G5
Winkburn	Notts	45	G11
Winkfield	Brack'l	18	D5
Winkfield Row	Brack'l	18	D5
Winkhill	Staffs	44	G4
Winklebury	Hants	18	F3
Winkleigh	Devon	6	F5
Winksley	N Yorks	51	B8
Winkton	Dorset	9	E10
Winlaton	Tyne/Wear	63	G7
Winless	H'land	94	E5
Winmarleigh	Lancs	49	E4
Winnal	Hants	26	E2
Winnersh	Wokingham	18	D4
Winscales	Cumb	56	D2
Winscombe	N Som'set	15	F10
Winsford	Ches	43	F9
Winsford	Som'set	7	C8
Winsham	Som'set	8	D2
Winshill	Staffs	35	C8
Winskill	Cumb	57	C7
Winslade	Hants	18	G3
Winsley	Wilts	16	E5
Winslow	Bucks	28	F4
Winson	Glos	27	H7
Winson Green	W Midlands	34	G6
Winsor	Hants	10	C2
Winster	Cumb	56	G6
Winster	Derby	44	F6
Winston	Durham	58	E2
Winston	Suffolk	31	B8
Winston Green	Suffolk	31	B8
Winstone	Glos	26	H6
Winswell	Devon	6	E3
Winter Gardens	Essex	20	C4
Winterborne Bassett	Wilts	17	D7
Winterborne Clenston	Dorset	9	D7
Winterborne Herringston	Dorset	8	F5
Winterborne Houghton	Dorset	9	D7
Winterborne Kingston	Dorset	9	E7
Winterborne Monkton	Dorset	8	F5
Winterborne Stickland	Dorset	9	D7
Winterborne Whitechurch	Dorset	9	D7
Winterborne Zelston	Dorset	9	E7
Winterbourne	S Gloucs	16	C3
Winterbourne	W Berks	17	D11
Winterbourne Abbas	Dorset	8	E5
Winterbourne Dauntsey	Wilts	9	A10
Winterbourne Down	S Gloucs	16	D3
Winterbourne Earls	Wilts	9	A10
Winterbourne Gunner	Wilts	17	H8
Winterbourne Steepleton	Dorset	8	F5
Winterbourne Stoke	Wilts	17	G7
Winterburn	N Yorks	50	D5
Winteringham	N Lincs	52	G5
Wintersett	W Yorks	51	H9
Wintershill	Hants	10	C4
Winterton	N Lincs	52	H5
Winterton-on-Sea	Norfolk	39	D10
Winthorpe	Lincs	47	F9
Winthorpe	Notts	46	G2
Winton	Bourn'm'th	9	E9
Winton	Cumb	57	E9
Winton	N Yorks	58	G5
Wintringham	N Yorks	52	B4
Winwick	Cambs	37	G7
Winwick	Northants	28	A3
Winwick	Warrington	43	C9
Wirksworth	Derby	44	G6
Wirksworth Moor	Derby	45	G7
Wirswall	Ches	33	A11
Wisbech	Cambs	37	E10
Wisbech St Mary	Cambs	37	E10
Wisborough Green	W Sussex	11	B9
Wiseton	Notts	45	D11
Wishaw	N Lanarks	68	E6
Wishaw	Warwick	35	F7
Wisley	Surrey	19	F7
Wispington	Lincs	46	E6
Wissenden	Kent	13	B8
Wissett	Suffolk	39	H9
Wistanstow	Shrops	33	G10
Wistanswick	Shrops	34	C2
Wistaston	Ches	43	G9
Wistaston Green	Ches	43	G9
Wiston	Pembs	22	E5
Wiston	S Lanarks	69	G8
Wiston	W Sussex	11	C10
Wistow	Cambs	37	G8
Wistow	Leics	36	F2
Wistow	N Yorks	52	F1
Wiswell	Lancs	50	F3
Witcham	Cambs	37	G10
Witchampton	Dorset	9	D8
Witchford	Cambs	37	H11
Witham	Essex	30	G5
Witham Friary	Som'set	16	G4
Witham on the Hill	Lincs	37	D6
Withcall	Lincs	46	D6
Withdean	Brighton/Hove	12	F2
Witherenden Hill	E Sussex	12	D5
Witheridge	Devon	7	E7
Witherley	Leics	35	F9
Withern	Lincs	47	D8
Withernsea	ER Yorks	53	G9
Withernwick	ER Yorks	53	E7
Withersdale Street	Suffolk	39	G8
Withersfield	Suffolk	30	D3
Witherslack	Cumb	49	A4
Withiel	Corn'l	3	C8
Withiel Florey	Som'set	7	C8
Withington	Glos	27	G7
Withington	Gtr Man	44	C2
Withington	Heref'd	26	D2
Withington	Shrops	34	D1
Withington	Staffs	34	B6
Withington Green	Ches	44	E2
Withleigh	Devon	7	E8
Withnell	Lancs	50	G2
Withybrook	Warwick	35	G10
Withycombe	Som'set	7	B9
Withycombe Raleigh	Devon	5	C11
Witham	E Sussex	12	C3
Withypool	Som'set	7	C7
Witley	Surrey	18	H6
Witnesham	Suffolk	31	C8
Witney	Oxon	27	G10
Wittering	Peterbro	37	E6
Wittersham	Kent	13	D7
Witton	Angus	83	F7
Witton	Worcs	26	B5
Witton Bridge	Norfolk	39	B9
Witton Gilbert	Durham	58	B3
Witton-le-Wear	Durham	58	C2
Witton Park	Durham	58	C2
Wiveliscombe	Som'set	7	D9
Wivelrod	Hants	18	H3
Wivelsfield	E Sussex	12	D2
Wivelsfield Green	E Sussex	12	D2
Wivenhoe	Essex	31	F7
Wivenhoe Cross	Essex	31	F7
Wiveton	Norfolk	38	A6
Wix	Essex	31	F8
Wixford	Warwick	27	C7
Wixhill	Shrops	34	C1
Wixoe	Suffolk	30	D4
Woburn	Beds	28	E6
Woburn Sands	M/Keynes	28	E6
Wokefield Park	W Berks	18	E3
Woking	Surrey	19	F7
Wokingham	Wokingham	18	E5
Wolborough	Devon	5	D9
Wold Newton	ER Yorks	52	B6
Wold Newton	NE Lincs	46	C6
Woldingham	Surrey	19	F10
Wolfclyde	S Lanarks	69	G9
Wolferton	Norfolk	38	C2
Wolfhill	Perth/Kinr	76	D4
Wolf's Castle	Pembs	22	D4
Wolfsdale	Pembs	22	D4
Woll	Scot Borders	61	A10
Wollaston	Northants	28	B6
Wollaston	Shrops	33	D9
Wollaton	Nott'ham	35	B11
Wollerton	Shrops	34	B2
Wollescote	W Midlands	34	G5
Wolsingham	Durham	58	C1
Wolstanton	Staffs	44	H2
Wolston	Warwick	35	H10
Wolvercote	Oxon	27	H11
Wolverhampton	W Midlands	34	F5
Wolverley	Shrops	33	B10
Wolverley	Worcs	34	H4
Wolverton	Hants	18	F2
Wolverton	M/Keynes	28	D5
Wolverton	Warwick	27	B9
Wolverton Common	Hants	18	F2
Wolvesnewton	Monmouths	15	B10
Wolvey	Warwick	35	G10
Wolviston	Stockton	58	D5
Wombleton	N Yorks	59	H6
Wombourne	Staffs	34	F4
Wombwell	S Yorks	45	B7
Womenswold	Kent	21	F9
Womersley	N Yorks	51	H11
Wonastow	Monmouths	25	G11
Wonersh	Surrey	19	G7
Wonson	Devon	5	C7
Wonston	Hants	17	H11
Wooburn	Bucks	18	C6
Wooburn Green	Bucks	18	C6
Wood Dalling	Norfolk	39	C6
Wood End	Herts	29	F10
Wood End	Warwick	27	A8
Wood End	Warwick	35	F8
Wood Enderby	Lincs	46	F6
Wood Field	Surrey	19	F8
Wood Green	London	19	B10
Wood Hayes	W Midlands	34	E5
Wood Lanes	Ches	44	D3
Wood Norton	Norfolk	38	C6
Wood Street	Norfolk	39	C9
Wood Street	Surrey	18	F6
Wood Walton	Cambs	37	G8
Woodacott	Devon	6	F2
Woodale	N Yorks	51	B6
Woodbank	Arg/Bute	65	G7
Woodbastwick	Norfolk	39	D9
Woodbeck	Notts	45	E11
Woodborough	Notts	45	H10
Woodborough	Wilts	17	F8
Woodbridge	Dorset	8	C6
Woodbridge	Suffolk	31	D9
Woodbury	Devon	5	C11
Woodbury Salterton	Devon	5	C11
Woodchester	Glos	16	A5
Woodchurch	Kent	13	C8
Woodchurch	Mersey	42	D5
Woodcombe	Som'set	7	B8
Woodcote	Oxon	18	C3
Woodcott	Hants	17	F11
Woodcroft	Glos	15	B11
Woodcutts	Dorset	9	C8
Woodditton	Cambs	30	C3
Woodeaton	Oxon	28	G2
Woodend	Cumb	56	G3
Woodend	Northants	28	D3
Woodend	W Sussex	11	D7
Woodend Green	Northants	28	D3
Woodfield	Oxon	28	F2
Woodfield	S Ayrs	66	D6
Woodford	Corn'l	6	E1
Woodford	Devon	5	F8
Woodford	Glos	16	B3
Woodford	London	19	B11
Woodford	Gtr Man	44	D2
Woodford	Northants	36	H5
Woodford Bridge	London	19	B11
Woodford Halse	Northants	28	C2
Woodgate	Norfolk	38	D6
Woodgate	W Midlands	34	G5
Woodgate	Worcs	26	B6
Woodgate	W Sussex	11	D8
Woodgreen	Hants	9	C10
Woodhall	Herts	29	G9
Woodhall	Invercl	68	C2
Woodhall	N Yorks	57	G11
Woodhall Spa	Lincs	46	F5
Woodham	Surrey	19	E7
Woodham Ferrers	Essex	20	A4
Woodham Mortimer	Essex	20	A5
Woodham Walter	Essex	30	H5
Woodhaven	Fife	77	E7
Woodhead	Aberds	89	E7
Woodhey	Gtr Man	50	H3
Woodhill	Shrops	34	G3
Woodhorn	Northum	63	E8
Woodhouse	Leics	35	D11
Woodhouse	N Yorks	51	G9
Woodhouse	S Yorks	45	D8
Woodhouse	W Yorks	51	F8
Woodhouse	W Yorks	51	G9
Woodhouse Eaves	Leics	35	D11
Woodhouse Park	Gtr Man	44	D2
Woodhouselee	Midloth	69	D11
Woodhouselees	Dumf/Gal	61	F9
Woodhouses	Staffs	35	D7
Woodhurst	Cambs	37	H9
Woodingdean	Brighton/Hove	12	F2
Woodkirk	W Yorks	51	G8
Woodland	Devon	5	E8
Woodland	Durham	58	D1
Woodlands	Aberds	83	D9
Woodlands	Dorset	9	D9
Woodlands	Hants	10	C2
Woodlands	H'land	87	E8
Woodlands	N Yorks	51	D9
Woodlands	S Yorks	45	B9
Woodlands Park	Windsor	18	D5
Woodlands St Mary	W Berks	17	D10
Woodlane	Staffs	35	C7
Woodleigh	Devon	5	G8
Woodlesford	W Yorks	51	G9
Woodley	Gtr Man	44	C3
Woodley	Wokingham	18	D4
Woodmancote	Glos	16	A4
Woodmancote	Glos	26	E6
Woodmancote	Glos	27	F7
Woodmancote	W Sussex	11	D6
Woodmancote	W Sussex	12	E1
Woodmancott	Hants	18	G2
Woodmansey	ER Yorks	53	F6
Woodmansterne	Surrey	19	F9
Woodminton	Wilts	9	B9
Woodnesborough	Kent	21	F10
Woodnewton	Northants	37	F6
Woodplumpton	Lancs	49	F5
Woodrising	Norfolk	38	E5
Wood's Green	E Sussex	12	C5
Woodseaves	Shrops	34	B2
Woodseaves	Staffs	34	C3
Woodsend	Wilts	17	D9
Woodsetts	S Yorks	45	D9
Woodsford	Dorset	9	E6
Woodside	Aberd'n	83	C11
Woodside	Aberds	89	D10
Woodside	Brack'l	18	D5
Woodside	Fife	77	G7
Woodside	Hants	10	E2
Woodside	Herts	29	H9
Woodside	Perth/Kinr	76	D5
Woodside of Arbeadie	Aberds	83	D9
Woodstock	Oxon	27	G11
Woodstock	Pembs	22	D5
Woodthorpe	Derby	45	E8
Woodthorpe	Leics	35	D11
Woodthorpe	Lincs	47	D8
Woodthorpe	C/York	52	E1
Woodton	Norfolk	39	F8
Woodtown	Devon	6	D3
Woodtown	Devon	6	D3
Woodvale	Mersey	42	A6
Woodville	Derby	35	D9
Woodyates	Dorset	9	C9
Woofferton	Shrops	26	B2
Wookey	Som'set	15	G11
Wookey Hole	Som'set	15	G11
Wool	Dorset	9	F7
Woolacombe	Devon	6	B3
Woolage Green	Kent	21	G9
Woolaston	Glos	16	B2
Woolavington	Som'set	15	G9
Woolbeding	W Sussex	11	B7
Wooldale	W Yorks	44	B5
Wooler	Northum	71	H8
Woolfardisworthy	Devon	7	F7
Woolfardisworthy	Devon	6	D2
Woolfords Cottages	S Lanarks	69	E9
Woolhampton	W Berks	18	E2
Woolhope	Heref'd	26	E3
Woolhope Cockshoot	Heref'd	26	E3
Woolland	Dorset	9	D6
Woollaton	Devon	6	E3
Woolley	Bath/NE Som'set	16	E4
Woolley	Cambs	37	H7
Woolley	Corn'l	6	E1
Woolley	Derby	45	F7
Woolley	W Yorks	45	A7
Woolmer Green	Herts	29	G9
Woolmere Green	Worcs	26	B6
Woolpit	Suffolk	30	B6
Woolscott	Warwick	27	B11
Woolsington	Tyne/Wear	63	G7
Woolstanwood	Ches	43	G9
Woolstaston	Shrops	33	F10
Woolsthorpe	Lincs	36	C4
Woolsthorpe	Lincs	36	C5
Woolston	Devon	5	G8
Woolston	Shrops	33	C9
Woolston	Shrops	33	G10
Woolston	S'thampton	10	C3
Woolston	Warrington	43	D9
Woolstone	M/Keynes	28	E5
Woolstone	Oxon	17	C9
Woolton	Mersey	43	D7
Woolton Hill	Hants	17	E11
Woolverstone	Suffolk	31	E8
Woolverton	Som'set	16	F4
Woolwich	London	19	D11
Woolwich Ferry	London	19	D11
Woonton	Heref'd	25	C10
Wooperton	Northum	62	A6
Woore	Shrops	34	A3
Wootten Green	Suffolk	31	A9
Wootton	Bedford	29	D7
Wootton	Hants	9	E11
Wootton	Kent	21	G9
Wootton	N Lincs	52	H6
Wootton	Northants	28	C4
Wootton	Oxon	27	G11
Wootton	Oxon	27	H11
Wootton	Shrops	33	H10
Wootton	Shrops	33	C9
Wootton	Staffs	34	C4
Wootton	Staffs	44	H5
Wootton Bassett	Wilts	17	C7
Wootton Bridge	I/Wight	10	E4
Wootton Common	I/Wight	10	E4
Wootton Courtenay	Som'set	7	B8
Wootton Fitzpaine	Dorset	8	E2
Wootton Green	Suffolk	31	A9
Wootton Rivers	Wilts	17	E8
Wootton St Lawrence	Hants	18	F2
Wootton Wawen	Warwick	27	B8
Worcester	Worcs	26	C5
Worcester Park	London	19	E9
Wordsley	W Midlands	34	G4
Worfield	Shrops	34	F3
Work	Orkney	95	G5
Workington	Cumb	56	D1
Worksop	Notts	45	E9
Worlaby	N Lincs	46	A4
World's End	W Berks	17	D11
Worle	N Som'set	15	E9
Worleston	Ches	43	G9
Worlingham	Suffolk	39	G10
Worlington	Suffolk	30	A3
Worlingworth	Suffolk	31	B9
Wormald Green	N Yorks	51	C9
Wormbridge	Heref'd	25	E11
Wormegay	Norfolk	38	D2
Wormelow Tump	Heref'd	25	E11
Wormhill	Derby	44	E5
Wormingford	Essex	30	E6
Wormleighton	Warwick	27	C11
Wormley	Herts	29	H10
Wormley	Surrey	18	H6
Wormley West End	Herts	29	H10
Wormshill	Kent	20	F5
Wormsley	Heref'd	25	D11
Worplesdon	Surrey	18	F6
Worrall	S Yorks	45	C7
Worsbrough	S Yorks	45	B7
Worsbrough Common	S Yorks	45	B7
Worsley	Gtr Man	43	B10
Worstead	Norfolk	39	C9
Worsthorne	Lancs	50	F4
Worston	Lancs	50	E3
Worswell	Devon	4	G6
Worth	Kent	21	F10
Worth	W Sussex	12	C1
Worth Matravers	Dorset	9	G8
Wortham	Suffolk	39	H6
Worthen	Shrops	33	E9
Worthenbury	Wrex	43	H7
Worthing	Norfolk	38	D5
Worthing	W Sussex	11	D10
Worthington	Leics	35	C10
Worting	Hants	18	F3
Wortley	S Yorks	45	C7
Wortley	W Yorks	51	F8
Worton	N Yorks	57	G11
Worton	Wilts	16	F6
Wortwell	Norfolk	39	G8
Wotherton	Shrops	33	E8
Wotter	Devon	5	E6
Wotton	Surrey	19	G8
Wotton-under-Edge	Glos	16	B4
Wotton Underwood	Bucks	28	G3
Woughton on the Green	M/Keynes	28	E5
Wouldham	Kent	20	E4
Wrabness	Essex	31	E8
Wrafton	Devon	6	C3
Wragby	Lincs	46	E5
Wragby	W Yorks	51	H10
Wragholme	Lincs	47	C7
Wramplingham	Norfolk	39	E7
Wrangbrook	W Yorks	45	A8
Wrangham	Aberds	89	E6
Wrangle	Lincs	47	G8
Wrangle Bank	Lincs	47	G8
Wrangle Lowgate	Lincs	47	G8
Wrangway	Som'set	7	E10
Wrantage	Som'set	8	B2
Wrawby	N Lincs	46	B4
Wraxall	Dorset	8	D4
Wraxall	N Som'set	15	D10
Wraxall	Som'set	16	H3
Wray	Lancs	50	C2
Wraysbury	Windsor	19	D7
Wrayton	Lancs	50	B2
Wrea Green	Lancs	49	F4
Wreay	Cumb	56	C6
Wreay	Cumb	56	D6
Wrecclesham	Surrey	18	G5
Wrecsam = Wrexham	Wrex	42	G6
Wrekenton	Tyne/Wear	63	H8
Wrelton	N Yorks	59	H7
Wrenbury	Ches	43	H9
Wreningham	Norfolk	39	F7
Wrentham	Suffolk	39	G10
Wrenthorpe	W Yorks	51	G9
Wrentnall	Shrops	33	E10
Wressle	ER Yorks	52	F3
Wressle	N Lincs	46	B3
Wrestlingworth	Beds	29	D9
Wretham	Norfolk	38	F5
Wretton	Norfolk	38	F2
Wrexham = Wrecsam	Wrex	42	G6
Wrexham Industrial Estate	Wrex	43	H6
Wribbenhall	Worcs	34	H3
Wrightington Bar	Lancs	43	A8
Wrinehill	Staffs	43	H10
Wrington	N Som'set	15	E10
Writhlington	Bath/NE Som'set	16	F4
Writtle	Essex	30	H3
Wrockwardine	Telford	34	D2
Wroot	N Lincs	45	B11
Wrotham	Kent	20	F3
Wrotham Heath	Kent	20	F3
Wroughton	Swindon	17	C8
Wroxall	I/Wight	10	G4
Wroxall	Warwick	27	A9
Wroxeter	Shrops	34	E1
Wroxham	Norfolk	39	D9
Wroxton	Oxon	27	D11
Wyaston	Derby	35	A7
Wyberton	Lincs	37	A9
Wyboston	Beds	29	C8
Wybunbury	Ches	43	H10
Wych Cross	E Sussex	12	C3
Wychbold	Worcs	26	B6
Wyck	Hants	18	H4
Wyck Rissington	Glos	27	F8
Wycombe Marsh	Bucks	18	B5
Wyddial	Herts	29	E10
Wye	Kent	21	G7
Wyesham	Monmouths	25	G11
Wyfordby	Leics	36	D3
Wyke	Dorset	8	B6
Wyke	Shrops	34	E2
Wyke	Surrey	18	F6
Wyke	W Yorks	51	G7
Wyke Regis	Dorset	8	G5
Wykeham	N Yorks	52	A5
Wykeham	N Yorks	52	B4
Wyken	W Midlands	35	G9
Wykey	Shrops	33	C9
Wylam	Northum	63	G7
Wylde Green	W Midlands	35	F7
Wyllie	Caerph	15	B7
Wylye	Wilts	17	H7
Wymering	Portsm'th	10	D5
Wymeswold	Leics	36	C2
Wymington	Beds	28	B6
Wymondham	Leics	36	D4
Wymondham	Norfolk	39	E6
Wyndham	Bridg	14	B5
Wynford Eagle	Dorset	8	E4
Wyng	Orkney	95	J4
Wynyard Village	Stockton	58	D5
Wyre Piddle	Worcs	26	D6
Wysall	Notts	36	C2
Wythall	Worcs	35	H6
Wytham	Oxon	27	H11
Wythburn	Cumb	56	E5
Wythenshawe	Gtr Man	44	D2
Wythop Mill	Cumb	56	D3
Wyton	Cambs	37	H8
Wyverstone	Suffolk	31	B7
Wyverstone Street	Suffolk	31	B7
Wyville	Lincs	36	C4
Wyvis Lodge	H'land	86	D7

Y

Place	County	Page	Grid
Y Bala = Bala	Gwyn	32	B5
Y Barri = Barry	V/Glam	15	E7
Y Bont-Faen = Cowbridge	V/Glam	14	D5
Y Drenewydd = Newtown	Powys	33	F7
Y Felinheli	Gwyn	41	D7
Y Fenni = Abergavenny	Monmouths	25	G9
Y Fflint = Flint	Flints	42	E5
Y Ffôr	Gwyn	40	G5
Y-Ffrith	Denbs	42	D3
Y Gelli Gandryll = Hay-on-Wye	Powys	25	D9
Y Mwmbwls = The Mumbles	Swan	14	C2
Y Pîl = Pyle	Bridg	14	C4
Y Rhws = Rhoose	V/Glam	14	E6
Y Rhyl = Rhyl	Denbs	42	D3
Y Trallwng = Welshpool	Powys	33	E8
Y Waun = Chirk	Wrex	33	B8
Yaddlethorpe	N Lincs	46	B2
Yafford	I/Wight	10	F3
Yafforth	N Yorks	58	G4
Yalding	Kent	20	G3
Yanworth	Glos	27	G7
Yapham	ER Yorks	52	D3
Yapton	W Sussex	11	D8
Yarburgh	Lincs	47	C7
Yarcombe	Devon	7	F10
Yard	Som'set	7	C9
Yardley	W Midlands	35	G7
Yardley Gobion	Northants	28	D4
Yardley Hastings	Northants	28	C5
Yardro	Powys	25	C9
Yarkhill	Heref'd	26	D3
Yarlet	Staffs	34	C5
Yarlington	Som'set	8	B5
Yarlside	Cumb	49	C2
Yarm	Stockton	58	E5
Yarmouth	I/Wight	10	F2
Yarnbrook	Wilts	16	F5
Yarnfield	Staffs	34	B4
Yarnscombe	Devon	6	D4
Yarnton	Oxon	27	G11
Yarpole	Heref'd	25	B11
Yarrow	Scot Borders	70	H2
Yarrow Feus	Scot Borders	70	H2
Yarsop	Heref'd	25	D11
Yarwell	Northants	37	F6
Yate	S Gloucs	16	C4
Yateley	Hants	18	E5
Yatesbury	Wilts	17	D7
Yattendon	W Berks	18	D2
Yatton	Heref'd	26	B2
Yatton	N Som'set	15	E10
Yatton Keynell	Wilts	16	D5
Yaverland	I/Wight	10	F5
Yaxham	Norfolk	38	D6
Yaxley	Cambs	37	F7
Yaxley	Suffolk	31	A8
Yazor	Heref'd	25	D11
Yeading	London	19	C8
Yeadon	W Yorks	51	E8
Yealand Conyers	Lancs	49	B5
Yealand Redmayne	Lancs	49	B5
Yealmpton	Devon	5	F6
Yearby	Redcar/Clevel'd	59	D7
Yearsley	N Yorks	52	B1
Yeaton	Shrops	33	D10
Yeaveley	Derby	35	A7
Yedingham	N Yorks	52	B4
Yeldon	Beds	28	B6
Yelford	Oxon	17	A10
Yelland	Devon	6	C3
Yelling	Cambs	29	B9
Yelvertoft	Northants	36	H1
Yelverton	Devon	4	E6
Yelverton	Norfolk	39	E8
Yenston	Som'set	8	B6
Yeo Mill	Devon	7	D7
Yeoford	Devon	7	G6
Yeolmbridge	Corn'l	4	C4
Yeovil	Som'set	8	C4
Yeovil Marsh	Som'set	8	C4
Yeovilton	Som'set	8	B4
Yerbeston	Pembs	22	F5
Yesnaby	Orkney	95	G3
Yetlington	Northum	62	C6
Yetminster	Dorset	8	C4
Yettington	Devon	7	H9
Yetts o'Muckhart	Clack	76	G3
Yieldshields	S Lanarks	69	E7
Yiewsley	London	19	C7
Ynys-meudwy	Neath P Talb	24	H4
Ynysboeth	Rh Cyn Taff	14	B6
Ynysddu	Caerph	15	B7
Ynysgyfflog	Gwyn	32	D2
Ynyshir	Rh Cyn Taff	14	B6
Ynyslas	Ceredig'n	32	F2
Ynystawe	Swan	14	A2
Ynysybwl	Rh Cyn Taff	14	B6
Yockenthwaite	N Yorks	50	B5
Yockleton	Shrops	33	D9
Yokefleet	ER Yorks	52	G4
Yoker	C/Glasg	68	D4
Yonder Bognie	Aberds	88	D5
York	C/York	52	D1
York Town	Surrey	18	E5
Yorkletts	Kent	21	E7
Yorkley	Glos	26	H3
Yorton	Shrops	33	C11
Youlgreave	Derby	44	F6
Youlstone	Devon	6	E1
Youlthorpe	ER Yorks	52	D3
Youlton	N Yorks	51	C10
Young Wood	Lincs	46	E5
Young's End	Essex	30	G4
Yoxall	Staffs	35	D7
Yoxford	Suffolk	31	B10
Yr Hôb = Hope	Flints	42	G6
Yr Wyddgrug = Mold	Flints	42	F5
Ysbyty Cynfyn	Ceredig'n	32	H3
Ysbyty Ifan	Conwy	41	E10
Ysbyty Ystwyth	Ceredig'n	32	H3
Ysceifiog	Flints	42	E4
Yspitty	Carms	23	G10
Ystalyfera	Neath P Talb	24	H4
Ystrad	Rh Cyn Taff	14	B5
Ystrad Aeron	Ceredig'n	23	A10
Ystrad-mynach	Caerph	15	B7
Ystradfellte	Powys	24	G6
Ystradgynlais	Powys	24	G4
Ystradmeurig	Ceredig'n	24	C4
Ystradowen	Carms	24	G4
Ystradowen	V/Glam	14	D6
Ystumtuen	Ceredig'n	32	H3
Ythanbank	Aberds	89	E9
Ythanwells	Aberds	89	E6
Ythsie	Aberds	89	E8

Z

Place	County	Page	Grid
Zeal Monachorum	Devon	6	F6
Zeals	Wilts	9	A6
Zelah	Corn'l	3	D7
Zennor	Corn'l	2	F3